CRIME AND THE JUSTICE SYSTEM IN AMERICA

CRIME AND THE JUSTICE SYSTEM IN AMERICA

—— *An Encyclopedia* ——

Edited by
FRANK SCHMALLEGER
with Gordon M. Armstrong

GREENWOOD PRESS
Westport, Connecticut • London

Library of Congress Cataloging-in-Publication Data

Crime and the justice system in America : an encyclopedia / edited by
  Frank Schmalleger, with Gordon M. Armstrong.
    p. cm.
  Includes bibliographical references and index.
  ISBN 0–313–29409–7 (alk. paper)
    1. Crime—United States—Encyclopedias. 2. Criminology—United
States—Encyclopedias. 3. Criminal justice, Administration of—
United States—Encyclopedias. I. Schmalleger, Frank.
II. Armstrong, Gordon M.
HV6789.C6884 1997
364′.0973—dc20   96–10748

British Library Cataloguing in Publication Data is available.

Library of Congress Catalog Card Number: 96–10748
ISBN: 0–313–29409–7

First published in 1997

Greenwood Press, 88 Post Road West, Westport, CT 06881
An imprint of Greenwood Publishing Group, Inc.

Printed in the United States of America

The paper used in this book complies with the
Permanent Paper Standard issued by the National
Information Standards Organization (Z39.48–1984).

10 9 8 7 6 5 4 3 2 1

For

Linda Ann Armstrong

(March 24, 1997–August 26, 1997)

CONTENTS

PREFACE

The field of criminal justice is as exciting today as at any time in the past. Growing public concern with crime is seen in an emerging attitude that criminal offenders should be held fully responsible for their lawlessness. Policy initiatives seeking to restrain the "rights" of criminal offenders and suspects while enhancing the investigatory and enforcement powers of police agencies and correctional organizations are being introduced almost daily—and are quickly challenged in courts across the land.

Today, more offenders are arrested than ever before, a larger number of prisoners languish in our nation's prisons and jails than at any time in our history, and court dockets are filled to overflowing with record numbers of defendants, many of whom simply cycle repeatedly through an over-burdened justice system. Add to this the burgeoning number of young people now wending their way through the juvenile justice system, and the magnitude of our nation's criminal justice undertaking appears massive indeed.

As a consequence of heightened social and political concern over law-violating behavior, the criminal justice system has experienced dynamic growth. The last few years have seen tremendous increases in the body of official and unofficial criminal justice terminology, precedent-setting case law, innovative correctional and crime prevention programs, and crime-related legislation. Similarly, evolving theoretical and legal conceptualizations related to the justice field have increased massively.

Hence, while this one-volume encyclopedia strives to include significant terminology, precedent-setting cases, key historical and contemporary figures, notable policy initiatives, and significant findings, studies, agencies, and programs, it cannot hope to cover every conceivable term, idea, or concept within the purview of the criminal justice field. What we have tried to do in this encyclopedia is to capture and distill the essence of a vital field—one that is changing constantly, and one which we hope holds much promise for the future of American society.

We are grateful to the many contributors and colleagues who rendered invaluable assistance in the production of this work. In particular, the research efforts of James P. Harshaw, a top-notch Georgia Southern University student, and the advice of many members of the research staff at Georgia Southern's Henderson Library are greatly appreciated. Thanks, too, to Shelia C. Armstrong for her outstanding work in producing the manuscript. Lastly, special thanks to Nita Romer, Liz Leiba, and the crew at Greenwood. Your patience (!) and guidance are truly appreciated.

Frank Schmalleger
Hilton Head Island, SC

Gordon M. Armstrong
Statesboro, GA

THE ENCYCLOPEDIA

A

ABEL v. U.S., **362 U.S. 217 (1960).** An important case involving a spy for the Soviet Union, which raised a number of important issues regarding searches. These included the limits of permissible cooperation between federal investigative agencies, the appropriate scope of a search incident to an administrative arrest, and the application of the "abandonment" doctrine.

The Federal Bureau of Investigation (FBI) had been investigating Rudolf Abel for espionage (spying), but had not unearthed sufficient evidence to prove its case. However, it did find evidence that Abel was an alien illegally residing in the United States. That information was given to the Immigration and Naturalization Service (INS), the federal agency that handles such cases.

Agents from both organizations went to the hotel where Abel was staying. INS agents entered the room, arrested him on an administrative warrant, and searched parts of the room. They found a number of items that were subsequently used as evidence against him in criminal proceedings. While the INS agents were searching, FBI agents watched from nearby. Abel then agreed to check out of the hotel. After he had checked out, a FBI agent obtained consent from the hotel clerk to search Abel's room. Other items were found that were also used as evidence in Abel's conviction.

The Supreme Court, in a 5–4 decision, held that the level of cooperation between the two agencies was neither inappropriate nor undertaken in bad faith. The majority also held that the evidence found after the arrest was admissible because the extent of a search incident to an administrative arrest should be no less than that incident to a criminal arrest. Moreover, the items seized in the FBI search undertaken subsequent to Abel's checking out of his room were admissible under the "abandonment" doctrine—Abel had left them, and could not assert an interest in them under the Fourth Amendment after he had thrown them away. Abel's conviction was thus affirmed.

David Jones

ADJUDICATION HEARING (JUVENILE). In juvenile court there is a hearing that is similar to the trial in the adult system. The hearing is called the *adjudication hearing* and is designed to determine if a child did in fact commit the delinquent act that is alleged in the juvenile petition. Although the adjudication hearing is equivalent to the trial in adult court, there are significant differences.

Early Juvenile Court and the Adjudication Process. When the juvenile court was first created in 1899, the court was designed to be an informal process, with the judge acting as a surrogate father to the troubled child and offering the child a rehabilitative plan to curb troublesome tendencies. The main focus of the court was what plan was suitable for the child, not what the child had done to come to the attention of the juvenile court. The actor, and not the act itself, was most important. Hence a formal process, attorneys, rules of evidence, and a strict courtroom ritual were not necessary. In fact, it was thought that the more informal the process, the more likely that the child would open up to the kindly parent-judge, and the more the child revealed, the greater the likelihood that the rehabilitative plan would address the needs of the child. Not only was there no formal court process, juveniles enjoyed no constitutional rights, because constitutional rights were not necessary in a process that operated "in the best interests of the child." Therefore, the adjudication hearing was simply a process to get to the disposition of the case and the treatment plan, with no rules, regulations, or rights to define the hearing.

The Adjudication Hearing and the Due Process for Juveniles Era. In the 1960s the growing national concern for juvenile offenders and the juvenile court process was brought to the attention of the U.S. Supreme Court. Many constitutional rights that juveniles are accorded in the adjudication hearing were handed down in cases heard in the 1960s and the 1970s. The 1967 landmark juvenile justice case *In re Gault* gave juveniles the right to notice of the charges pending, the right to an attorney, the right to confront and cross-examine witnesses, and the right to remain silent. This case redefined the adjudication hearing and redefined the focus of that hearing from a rehabilitative process into a legal process. In 1970 *In re Winship* raised the burden of proof in a juvenile hearing to "beyond a reasonable doubt" as the Supreme Court likened juvenile sanctions to adult sanctions and offered juveniles the higher burden of proof. Surprisingly, in 1971 the Supreme Court seemingly backed off from the trend it had been setting when in *McKeiver v. Pennsylvania* the Court held that juveniles did not enjoy a constitutional right to a trial by jury. The Court did not forbid states to experiment with their own trial-by-jury statutes. Presently, whether or not juveniles have the right to be heard by a jury in the adjudication hearing is a state-by-state decision.

The Adjudication Hearing and the Changing Issues. There are several issues today about juvenile justice processes, specifically the adjudication hearing, that are being addressed state by state and that continue to address the rights and special treatment received historically by juveniles. Many due-process rights have redefined the juvenile adjudication hearing, but there are other issues that could further change the almost one-hundred-year-old face of juvenile court. Issues that are being examined include the confidentiality and privacy of the juvenile court. Historically, juvenile hearings, including the adjudication, have been closed to the public, and the results of those hearings, including adjudication as a juvenile delinquent, have usually been wiped from juvenile records upon the age of maturity. Today, several states are considering changing or have changed their statutes to open juvenile court to the public and to let a juvenile record follow the juvenile into adulthood. Although seemingly procedural in nature, the changes that the juvenile court hearings, including the adjudication hearing, are facing are really philosophical in nature. Changes are narrowing the gap between the juvenile and adult courts, and are questioning the philosophy, goals, process, fairness, and effectiveness of the juvenile court.

RECOMMENDED READING: Samuel M. Davis, *Rights of Juveniles: The Juvenile Justice System*, 2nd ed. (New York: Clark Boardman Company, 1980).

Frances P. Reddington

ADMINISTRATIVE LAW. This rapidly expanding area of law governs the various processes involving administrative agencies in their dealings with the public. Due to the rapid proliferation of technology and the complexity of modern society, the United States has witnessed a virtual explosion in administrative law.

In 1946 the U.S. Congress passed the Administrative Procedure Act (APA) to govern federal administrative proceedings. Likewise, many states have passed administrative procedure acts that govern state administrative proceedings.

The administrative process is an interesting one. Administrative agencies, which are created by legislative bodies, are delegated the power to regulate certain areas, such as welfare or environmental policy, where legislative oversight is difficult or impractical. Such oversight may be difficult to provide for any number of reasons including a lack of expertise regarding certain regulatory matters. Administrative agencies develop standards that govern regulatory processes. This power is termed rule making. An administrative agency may also be empowered to hold hearings to determine if violations of its rules have occurred. This quasi-judicial power is termed adjudication. For example, the U.S. Congress created the Nuclear Regulatory Commission (NRC) to regulate atomic energy. The NRC employs nuclear physicists and other individuals who have substantial expertise in nuclear-energy issues. These agency employees develop regulatory standards or rules for the nuclear-energy industry. The NRC is also empowered to determine if its rules have been violated. For example, in the event of a nuclear power plant accident, the NRC could be expected to conduct extensive hearings to determine if the operators of that nuclear facility violated NRC rules.

Administrative law is procedural law. It is directly concerned with the manner in which an administrative agency's power is exercised. Although legislatures have delegated certain powers to administrative agencies, these agencies are not granted unlimited power. Agencies must exercise their power in a fair and unbiased manner and may not make arbitrary decisions. They must also develop procedures to ensure that those who are subjected to official agency action receive fair treatment.

In general, the U.S. courts hesitate to overrule administrative-agency decisions unless it is clear that the agency has abused its authority. The U.S. Supreme Court's most important administrative law precedent is *Goldberg v. Kelly* (1970). In that case New York State and New York City administrative officials sought to terminate the welfare benefits of several persons receiving aid to families with dependent children (AFDC) without prior notice and without giving them a pre-termination hearing. The recipients challenged the constitutional adequacy of the procedures used to terminate their benefits. The U.S. Supreme Court held that the administrative agency's interest in conserving scarce resources did not outweigh the recipients' interest in continuing to receive their welfare benefits. Therefore, the agency's actions violated due process of law. The Supreme Court further held that a pretermination hearing, which provided recipients with procedural safeguards, was required prior to terminating a person's welfare benefits. These safeguards included notice of the impending hearing; opportunities to confront and cross-examine adverse witnesses and present oral evidence, and to retain counsel for the proceeding; a decision based solely on the evidence presented at the hearing; an impartial decision maker; and a statement on the record of the evidence that the decision maker relied upon in reaching his or her decision.

Goldberg v. Kelly represents the high-water mark of due-process rights in administrative law cases. Part of the basis for that decision involved the Court's belief those welfare benefits were crucial to the recipients and could determine their continued ability to survive. The Supreme Court has held that in cases involving less crucial entitlements, such as the right to receive veteran benefits, such stringent due-process safeguards are not required.

RECOMMENDED READING: Kenneth Davis, *Administrative Law Text*, 3rd ed. (St. Paul: West Publishing Co., 1972); Peter Strauss, *An Introduction to Administrative Justice in the United States* (Durham, NC: Carolina Academic Press, 1989).

Thomas J. Hickey

ADMINISTRATIVE OFFICE OF THE UNITED STATES COURTS (AOC). A body established by law in 1939 to aid the administration of the federal judiciary. A director, who is appointed by the chief justice of the U.S. Supreme Court after consultation with the Judicial Conference, heads it. The agency deals with many of the mundane (or housekeeping) administrative duties associated with the operation of the federal courts, excluding the U.S. Supreme Court. Administrative responsibilities of the Office include preparation and submission of court budgets; general supervision of the accounts and practices of federal probation offices, subject to primary control by the respective district courts they serve; establishment of pretrial services in the district courts; recommending to the Judicial Conference the official duty stations and places of holding courts of bankruptcy judges; general supervision over administrative matters in offices of U.S. magistrate judges, including compilation and evaluation of statistical data relating to such offices; and submission of required and requested reports to the Judicial Conference. It also oversees the budget of federal defenders appointed to work with indigent defendants.

In addition, the AOC also serves a liaison function between the federal court system and Congress. While it has many duties, the AOC has few formal enforcement powers beyond the power to suggest activities.

RECOMMENDED READING: Peter G. Fish, *The Politics of Federal Judicial Administration* (Princeton: Princeton University Press, 1973); *The United States Government Manual* (Washington, DC: U.S. Government Printing Office, 1996).

David Jones

ADMISSION. As distinguished in law from a confession and narrower in scope, an admission takes place when the accused admits facts that may be used to infer guilt. For instance, the accused may acknowledge that s/he was at the scene of the crime at a particular time and date while not confessing to the crime. However, the trier of fact may infer from this that the defendant did indeed commit the crime. Admissions might thus become part of a chain of evidence used to convict an individual. Admissions may be used to corroborate or confirm other evidence.

The legal rules governing the admissibility of admissions and confessions are essentially the same. Although technically they may be considered "hearsay," admissions are often admissible in court.

RECOMMENDED READING: Joseph D. Grano, *Confessions, Truth, and the Law* (Ann Arbor: University of Michigan Press, 1996); Jon R. Waltz, *Introduction to Criminal Evidence*, 4th ed. (Chicago: Nelson Hall, 1997).

David Jones

AGGRAVATED ASSAULT. Aggravated assault is an assault with a deadly weapon without intent to kill or with intent to commit a felony. In some states it may also include an assault while disguised in any manner designed to conceal identity. In states where the elements of assault and battery are combined into one crime, this crime becomes aggravated when great bodily injury is inflicted upon the person assaulted or when committed by a person of robust health or strength upon one who is aged, decrepit, or incapacitated.

RECOMMENDED READING: 46 Fla. Stat. Ann. Sec. 784.021 (West 1992); Kan. Stat. Ann. Sec. 21-3410(b) (1993); 21 Okla. Stat. Ann. Sec. 646 (West 1994).

Lee E. Parker

AGGRAVATING CIRCUMSTANCES. Circumstances surrounding a crime that make the crime even worse than it would have been. These might include such things as extreme injury to the victim, the existence of multiple victims, premeditation, the use of torture in committing the offense, or (in death-penalty cases) committing a killing while perpetrating of a felony.

If the defendant is pronounced guilty, and the existence of aggravating circumstances is found, s/he may receive a harsher sentence than is typical. For instance, in some states that utilize sentencing guidelines, a judge may mete out a harsher sentence than suggested by the guidelines if s/he finds aggravating circumstances to be present.

The existence of aggravating circumstances is also very important in death-penalty cases. Under the laws of states using the death penalty, if a jury finds a defendant guilty, it must then consider whether aggravating circumstances were present. The jury must, at a minimum, find the existence of at least one aggravating circumstance before it can recommend the death penalty. In most jurisdictions a verdict of death may be applied only if aggravating circumstances outweigh mitigating circumstances.

RECOMMENDED READING: Welsh S. White, *The Death Penalty in the Nineties: An Examination of the Modern System of Capital Punishment* (Ann Arbor: University of Michigan Press, 1991).

David Jones

AIDS IN PRISON. AIDS (acquired immune deficiency syndrome) is one of the nation's and the world's most serious public health problems. The human immunodeficiency virus (HIV) causes AIDS by infecting and destroying the body's immune system (i.e., its defenses). AIDS is the often-fatal last stage of a wide spectrum of opportunistic infections and diseases that result from HIV infection. At the end of 1996 no cure or vaccine for HIV was yet available.

The HIV epidemic poses daunting challenges for prison systems. The incidence of HIV in the offender population is deemed to be five or six times greater than that in the general population. For example, in 1993 HIV-related diseases were the leading cause of death among Illinois prison inmates, accounting for one of every four deaths. In Illinois correctional facilities, from 1992 to 1993, the number of AIDS cases increased 555 percent, from 27 to 177. Nationwide, the total number of correctional inmates with AIDS increased 600 percent between 1985 and 1990. The HIV epidemic has had its greatest impact on state and local correctional facilities in New York, New Jersey, Florida, Texas, and California.

Because of the absence of a cure or a vaccine, prevention is crucial in stemming the HIV epidemic, a goal that is best achieved through education. The Institutes of Medicine (1988) underscored the importance of educating various target populations at high risk for HIV because of their drug use and sexual behavior. Several states have implemented educational programs for inmates, including New York, Mississippi, Florida, and Vermont. According to the AIDS Foundation of Chicago

(1995), inmates have a right to HIV/AIDS prevention education. Prevention education is the least costly and most effective strategy to stem the spread of HIV. Prevention education should address activities actually occurring in prisons that put people at risk of HIV infection, including consensual and coercive sex, tattooing, and razor and needle sharing.

AIDS education is also important for correctional staff. Education can prepare criminal justice personnel to respond properly to situations that may require precautions (e.g., cleaning blood spills and avoiding needlesticks). Furthermore, correctional facilities and agencies can avoid any liability associated with occupational exposure to HIV if they are able to demonstrate that their staffs have been properly educated about HIV.

In 1989, sixteen state prisons segregated all prisoners with AIDS, five segregated those with HIV-related symptoms, and four those who had merely tested positive for HIV. Some inmates have filed suits against prisons demanding that HIV-infected prisoners be segregated from the general population for its own protection. Conversely, inmates who have been isolated because of positive HIV test results have alleged that they have been unfairly denied access to work programs, religious services, and educational and recreational facilities. Segregation is also regarded as cruel and unusual punishment, which may subject HIV-infected inmates to assaults and discrimination.

Research and prison medical records indicate that few, if any, cases of HIV infection have been transmitted within penal institutions. Hence segregation may have little public health merit, either in society at large or in isolated groups such as those in correctional institutions. Indeed, heated argument swirls that segregation measures are inherently unfair and violative of individual rights. In general, courts have upheld the discretion of correctional administrators whose decisions to segregate were found to be based on health, safety, and security considerations.

RECOMMENDED READING: Theodore M Hammett and Saira Moini, *Update on AIDS in Prisons and Jails* (Washington, DC: National Institute of Justice, 1990); National Commission on Acquired Immune Deficiency Syndrome, *HIV Disease in Correctional Facilities* (Washington, DC: The Commission, 1991).

Arthur J. Lurigio

AKE V. OKLAHOMA, **470 U. S. 68 (1985).** This is a case involving the right of an indigent defendant to receive access to psychiatric services. In an opinion written by Justice Thurgood Marshall, the U.S. Supreme Court held that when a defendant has made a preliminary showing that his sanity at the time of the offense is likely to be a significant factor at trial, the Constitution requires that a state provide access to a psychiatrist's assistance on this issue if the defendant cannot otherwise afford one. The Court held that such a position was a logical extension of its reasoning in the famous case *Gideon v. Wainwright* 372 U.S. 335 (1963).

In this case petitioner Glen B. Ake was charged with first-degree murder and shooting with intent to kill. At his arraignment Ake was acting in such a bizarre manner that the presiding judge asked that a psychiatrist examine him. The psychiatrist who examined him testified that the defendant was mentally incompetent to stand trial. Later, after having been confined to a mental hospital, the defendant was found to be competent to stand trial on the condition that he continue to be sedated with an antipsychotic drug.

At pretrial conference Ake's lawyer said that he would raise an insanity defense and requested a psychiatric evaluation at state expense to determine the defendant's mental state at the time of the offense. The trial court refused the request.

After the guilt phase of the trial, examining psychiatrists testified that Ake was a danger to society, but there was no testimony concerning his sanity at the time of the offense. The jury rejected the insanity defense and found him guilty. At sentencing the state asked for the death penalty, relying on the examining psychiatrists' testimony to establish the likelihood of petitioner's future dangerous behavior. The petitioner had no expert testimony to rebut these allegations or to give evidence in mitigation of his punishment, and he was sentenced to death. The U.S. Supreme Court overturned the sentence because Ake had received no access to psychiatric assistance, even though such had been requested.

David Jones

ALCOHOL ABUSE. Alcohol abuse is a common form of drug abuse. The use of alcohol in a manner that causes individual or societal harm is considered abusive. Alcohol abuse can be distinguished from alcoholism in that it is not necessarily progressive in nature. The abuse of alcohol has historically been more acceptable by society than abuse of other drugs. This has recently begun to change with special-interest groups, such as Mothers Against Drunk Driving (MADD), pushing for a stronger societal response against alcohol abuse.

RECOMMENDED READING: Howard Abadinsky, *Drug Abuse: An Introduction* (Chicago: Nelson-Hall Publishers, 1989); Steven Olson and Dean R. Gerstein, *Alcohol in America: Taking Action to Prevent Abuse* (Washington, DC: National Academy Press, 1985).

Glenn Zuern

AMERICAN JAIL ASSOCIATION. The American Jail Association (AJA) got its start from a merger of the National Jail Association and the National Jail Managers' Association. The National Institute of Corrections Jail Center informed these two associations that unless they merged into one association, it would cease to deal with the two associations in matters of training and technical assistance. AJA began on June 1, 1981, with a small membership of several hundred. The president, the chairman of the board, and the secretary-treasurer did the needed chores, including the publication of a quarterly newsletter. In 1986, an executive director was hired to run daily operations. Membership totaled around 700, and the staff included the executive director, a managing editor for a proposed magazine, and a part-time typist.

Today, AJA membership exceeds 5,000, and its headquarters occupies a two-story office building with eleven full-time staff members. *American Jails*, an award-winning magazine, evolved from a quarterly to a bimonthly magazine in 1990 and is read by government personnel at the local, state, and national levels in addition to numerous academics and people in the private sector. *American Jails* is the only criminal justice publication geared solely to jail issues, with articles covering both the American and foreign jail scenes.

The major purposes of AJA are to improve conditions of confinement, advance jail staff professionalism, provide leadership in regard to professional standards, legislation, management practices, programs, and services, and advance the interests of those who work in U.S. jails. AJA focuses heavily on jail staff training, which has often been overlooked or downgraded by the fifty states, which have the principal responsibility for jail standards and training. As a result, AJA publishes a monthly *Jail Operations Bulletin (JOB)*, the *Jail Managers Bulletin (JMB)*, and various video training tapes, including one specifically produced to coincide with the JOB program. AJA does monthly contract training seminars throughout the nation and hosts an annual Jail Expo and Training Conference at different cities throughout the country.

AJA also publishes a national jail directory, *Who's Who in Jail Management*, which lists all of the country's jails, jail administrators, rated capacities, jail inspection programs, medically accredited jails, accredited jails, direct-supervision jails, and a jail yellow pages. Each year a product/service directory is produced, listing hundreds of companies and the particular products and services they offer.

Membership in AJA is open to any individual in agreement with AJA goals and objectives. AJA makes a special effort to cooperate with other government, private, and academic institutions to further the interests of professionalism in jails. Its headquarters staff fields thousands of annual inquiries by mail and phone to keep interested citizens apprised of what is happening on the American jail scene.

Ken Kerle

AMNESTY. One of several forms of the clemency power. Although "amnesty" is not mentioned in the Constitution, the Supreme Court has ruled it part of the pardoning power of Article II, Section 2. Sometimes described as a "general pardon," an amnesty suggests the crime committed by a group of individuals has been overlooked because that course of action benefits the public welfare more than punishment would. Amnesties may be the result of either legislative or executive action, may be full or "conditional" in character, and are typically granted in cases involving offenses against the sovereignty of the state, or "political offenses" (e.g., rebellion or civil disorder). To date, the administrations of George Washington, James Madison, Abraham Lincoln, Andrew Johnson, and Harry Truman account for about 70 percent of the formal proclamations or executive orders involving amnesty. While pardons are typically granted to individuals after conviction, amnesties are typically granted to groups of individuals subject to trial, but not yet convicted.

RECOMMENDED READING: Joseph R. Nolan and Jacqueline M. Nolan-Haley, *Black's Law Dictionary*, 6th ed. (St. Paul: West Publishing Co., 1991).

Peter S. Ruckman, Jr.

ANTI-DRUG ABUSE ACT. The act was passed as a result of the presidential election campaign of 1988. The issue of drugs was an important campaign issue and led to the enactment of the Anti-Drug Abuse Act in the final days of the 100th Congress. It increased funding for drug interdiction and prevention programs by over 50 percent. It mandated a wide array of measures to reduce drug use and abuse. It was one of the key pieces of legislation that resulted from the war on drugs.

Glenn Zuern

APPEALS. After imposition of sentence a defendant has the right to appeal the conviction to the appellate division of the appropriate state or federal court. Appeals are generally directed at the legal rulings of the judges made prior to or during the trial. If the appellate court finds a legal error in the proceedings that it considers substantial (i.e., the appellate judges believe that the error may have affected the outcome of the trial), the court will reverse the conviction and remand the case to the trial court for further necessary action. This may result in a new trial being conducted without the legal error that gave rise to the reversal or, if a new trial is not possible, dismissal of the charge against the defendant. The highest court in a state, generally referred to as the state supreme court, may be requested by the losing party on the first appeal, as a matter of right, to review the findings of the lower appellate court. The state supreme court has discretion under the law as to whether or not to review the case. This is the court of last appeal in the state. Depending upon the sentence, the defendant may be subject to the supervision of other government officials such as probation officers, prison officials, or parole officers until such time as the sentence is completed.

RECOMMENDED READING: Peter F. Nardulli, "The Societal Costs of the Exclusionary Rule Revisited," *University of Illinois Law Review* Vol. 1987, no. 2: 223–239; U.S. Court of Appeals (DC Circuit), *Appellate Mediation Program* (Washington, DC: Administrative Office of the U.S. Courts, 1993).

Christopher J. Morse

ARCHITECTURE, CORRECTIONAL. Criminal justice and correctional architecture encompasses a wide variety of facilities that include federal and state prisons, county and local detention centers, juvenile detention and correctional facilities, police facilities, and federal, state, and county court facilities. The dynamic field of criminal justice and correctional architecture is based on a thorough understanding not only of architectural principles, but also of law enforcement, judicial, and correctional philosophy and operations. The design of criminal justice facilities starts with the understanding of function and is often referred to as a design that starts from the inside out. When a complete understanding of the function and operations of a proposed facility has been attained, a space-utilization analysis is developed that becomes the basis for the design of that facility.

Current design of correctional facilities revolves around the housing unit and is based on the inmate-management system chosen by a particular institution's administration. Today, the design of housing units has evolved into stacked podular design permitting ease of surveillance and compactness. The underlying philosophy and goals for correctional design are economy, security, and normalcy.

A tendency toward larger units has evolved as a means of meeting the demand of growing populations within the correctional system. Larger facilities have produced economies of scale and staff minimization. Earlier restrictions of size advanced by various state and national standards have been relaxed in order to accommodate escalating inmate populations. The basic thrust of traditional American correctional standards relied heavily upon single cell occupancy. This has also given way to double bunking and multiple cell occupancy. This trend will probably continue as inmate populations continue to grow due to increases in criminal activity and developments in political and government philosophy.

A recent trend in the operation of correctional facilities has been direct supervision, which is an inmate-management system where the correctional officer deals with the inmate directly on a one-to-one basis and is not separated from the inmate by a secured control room. Another trend is the growing use of boot camps (frequently called shock incarceration) that utilize a quasi-military program similar to military basic training. These are being offered to youthful first-time offenders with the hope that such programs will limit their future criminal conduct and keep them out of further serious penalties and expensive incarceration.

RECOMMENDED READING: Craig M. Zimring, *Accountable Public Architecture* (Atlanta: Georgia Institute of Technology, 1994-1995).

Harvey Siegel

ARMED ROBBERY. Many states have replaced the crime of armed robbery with a sentence enhancement on the crime of robbery when the perpetrator uses a firearm, whether loaded or not, a blank or imitation firearm capable of raising a fear that it is a real firearm, or any other dangerous or deadly weapon. Other states have incorporated armed robbery into the broader crime of aggravated robbery, which has been defined as committing a robbery while causing serious bodily injury to another, using or exhibiting a dangerous or deadly weapon, or threatening or placing in fear of imminent bodily injury or death an individual over sixty-five years of age or with a mental, physical, or developmental disability who is substantially unable to protect himself or herself from harm.

RECOMMENDED READING: 46 Fla. Stat. Ann. Sec. 812.13(2)(a) (West 1992); Kan. Stat. Ann. Sec. 21–3427 (1993); 21 Okla. Stat. Ann. Sec. 801 (West 1994); Texas Penal Code Ann. Sec. 29.03 (Vernon's 1994); Burt Rapp, *The 211 Book: Armed Robbery Investigation*, (Port Townsend, WA: Loompanics Unlimited, 1989).

Lee E. Parker

ARRAIGNMENT. Following the arrest and charging process, a defendant is brought before the court and arraigned on an accusatory instrument setting forth the charge against the defendant. The judge advises defendant of his/her constitutional rights; informs him/her of the charge; initially resolves the issue of representation by an attorney; and determines whether defendant should be released on bail or his/her own recognizance. Also, an adjourned date is set for the next appearance, which may be a preliminary hearing to decide if probable cause exists for the charge in the accusatory instrument. From this point the process diverges depending upon the seriousness of the charge against the defendant. If the charge constitutes a felony (a crime punishable by more than a year in prison), the matter will be referred to a grand jury to ascertain if probable cause exists to try the defendant. If the accusatory instrument sets forth a lesser charge (misdemeanor), the grand-jury process will not occur. Generally speaking, the case could be disposed of at this point by the judge or resolved at the adjourned date.

RECOMMENDED READING: J. Scott Harr, *Constitutional Law for Criminal Justice Professionals* (Belmont, CA: Wadsworth Publishing Co., 1997); Irving J. Klein, *Constitutional Law for Criminal Justice Professionals*, 3rd ed. (South Miami, FL: Coral Gables Publishing Co., 1992).

Christopher J. Morse

ARREST. An arrest is the taking of a person into custody to be held to answer for a criminal offense. Once probable cause exists, police activity centers upon finding and arresting the suspect. The procedures to be followed in making an arrest are set forth in the criminal procedure law. Since an arrest constitutes the seizure of a person, these procedures must comply with the requirements of both the federal and state constitutions. Arrests may be made without a warrant of arrest (the vast majority are) or with a warrant of arrest. Under certain circumstances a warrant of arrest is required in order to accomplish a lawful arrest. Police, without a warrant, may also stop a person on less than probable cause and make a superficial search of the person for weapons (stop and frisk procedures), which may result in an arrest. Contemporaneous with the arrest, the police will undertake a search of the arrestee and the surrounding area. The person in custody may be advised of his/her constitutional rights and interrogated. The arrestee will then be taken to the police station for required administrative purposes permitted by the law and, in some instances, for continuing investigative activities.

RECOMMENDED READING: Irving J. Klein, *Principles of the Law of Arrest, Search, Seizure, and Liability Issues* (South Miami, FL: Coral Gables Publishing Co., 1994); Lloyd L. Weinreb and James D. Whaley, *The Field Guide to Law Enforcement* (Westbury, NY: Foundation Press, 1996).

Christopher J. Morse

ARSON. Arson is defined by the Uniform Crime Reporting Program as any willful or malicious burning or attempt to burn, with or without intent to defraud, a dwelling house, public building, motor vehicle or aircraft, personal property of another (such as a barn or storage shed), or other property. Only fires determined through investigation to have been willfully or maliciously set are classified as arsons. Fires of suspicious or unknown origins are excluded.

The 1995 figures represent only 8,940 agencies covering 72 percent of the U.S. population reporting for all twelve months of the year. The data user should be aware that while the figures are conservative indicators, they do not represent the nation's total arson experience. The reported number of offenses in 1995 nationwide was 94,926 with a rate per 100,000 inhabitants of 44.8.

RECOMMENDED READING: Federal Bureau of Investigation, *Uniform Crime Reports for the United States, 1995* (Washington, DC: U.S. Government Printing Office, 1996).

Ransom A. Whittle

***ASHCRAFT V. TENNESSEE*, 322 U.S. 143 (1944).** One of the earliest cases before the U.S Supreme Court involving the rights of defendants in state criminal proceedings. In this case the Court held that some types of interrogation tactics are so "inherently coercive" that their use is forbidden under the Fourteenth Amendment of the U.S. Constitution.

Petitioner Ashcraft's wife had been found murdered a few miles outside of her home community of Nashville. Some time after the crime was discovered, on a Saturday evening, Ashcraft was picked up by the police and taken into custody. At the police station he was interrogated almost without respite (and without access to an attorney) by relays of police officers for approximately thirty-six hours. Eventually a confession was extracted and used to convict him. The Supreme Court overturned the conviction because, it held, the confession had been coerced and could not be admitted into evidence at trial.

David Jones

ASSAULT. An unlawful attempt, coupled with a present ability, to commit a violent injury on the person of another. In some states this must result in reasonable apprehension of immediate bodily harm, although no bodily contact is necessary. In other states the elements of assault and battery are combined into one crime and may also include intentionally, knowingly, or recklessly causing bodily injury to another or intentionally or knowingly causing physical contact with another when the person knows or should reasonably believe the other will regard the contact as offensive or provocative.

RECOMMENDED READING: Joseph R. Nolan and Jacqueline M. Nolan-Haley, *Black's Law Dictionary: Definitions of the Terms and Phrases of American and English Jurisprudence, Ancient and Modern*, 6th ed. (St. Paul, MN: West Publishing Co., 1991).

Lee E. Parker

ATTEMPT. An attempt is any overt act toward the perpetration of a crime done by a person who intends to commit such crime but who fails in the perpetration thereof or is prevented or intercepted in executing such crime. An attempt to commit a crime consists of two elements: a specific intent to commit the crime and a direct but ineffectual act done toward its commission. The act must amount to more than mere preparation. In some states the offense of attempt includes the act of an adult who, with the intent to commit an offense prohibited by law, allures, seduces, coaxes, or induces a child under the age of twelve to engage in an offense prohibited by law. The punishment for attempting to commit a crime is usually less than the punishment for actually committing the crime.

RECOMMENDED READING: Cal. Penal Code Secs. 21a, 664 (West 1992); 46 Fla. Stat. Ann. Sec. 777.04(1) (West 1992); Kan. Stat. Ann. Sec. 21-3301 (1993); Texas Penal Code Ann. Sec. 15.1(a) (Vernon's 1994).

Lee E. Parker

ATTORNEY GENERAL. This is the highest legal officer in the United States. As such, the attorney general is the head of the Department of Justice and serves as the chief law enforcement officer of the federal government. In this capacity s/he represents the United States in legal matters generally and gives advice and opinions to the president and to the heads of the executive departments of the government when so requested. The U.S. attorney general may represent the government before the U.S. Supreme Court. This is a very rare event, however.

The position of attorney general is one of the oldest in the federal government, having been created in 1789. The Department of Justice (which s/he heads) was established in 1870. As head of the Department of Justice, the attorney general is responsible for many legal activities, both civil and criminal. It is his/her job to see that presidential policies in this area are carried out effectively by members of the department.

Presidential nomination and senatorial confirmation fill the position of attorney general of the United States. S/he serves at the pleasure of the president. In addition to rendering legal advice to the president, the attorney general may also serve as an important political or policy advisor to the chief executive. Many individuals who fill the position were close political allies of the president before his election. For instance, Edwin Meese, one of Ronald Reagan's attorneys general, was one of that president's closest political advisors. John Mitchell, Richard Nixon's attorney general, was similarly situated. Mitchell, because of his involvement in the Watergate scandal, was the only attorney general who has served prison time. The closest relationship between the president and his attorney general could be found in the Kennedy administration—the President appointed his brother Robert (who was also his closest political advisor) to serve in this position. Robert Kennedy was an important advisor to his brother in foreign as well as legal policy. Not all attorneys general serve as close political advisors to the president. The current incumbent, Janet Reno (the first woman appointed to this post) was not a strong political supporter of President Clinton before his election.

Most states also have a constitutional position of attorney general. In most states this is an elective position and a partisan one. It is possible in many states for the state attorney general to be a member of a political party different from that of the state's governor. A state attorney general is that state's legal officer and has, for that state, administrative and legal powers and responsibilities analogous to those of the U.S. attorney general.

RECOMMENDED READING: Nancy V. Baker, *Conflicting Loyalties* (Lawrence: University Press of Kansas, 1992); Cornell W. Clayton, *The Politics of Justice* (New York: M. E. Sharpe, 1992); Victor Navasky, *Kennedy Justice* (New York: Atheneum, 1971); *The United States Government Manual* (Washington, DC: U.S. Government Printing Office, 1996).

David Jones

AUBURN PENITENTIARY. Opened in New York State in 1817, Auburn Penitentiary was committed to testing the new pillars of the penitentiary movement: silence and work. Auburn differed from the model of the penitentiary developed at Pennsylvania's Eastern State Penitentiary. At Auburn inmates worked in congregate work areas during the day and returned to their individual cells when they were not at work. Cells at Auburn were small (3.5 by 7 by 7 feet) and did not have toilets. Also, because the daily walk to and from work provided exercise, no exercise area was required for each cell. This permitted multi-story cellblocks at Auburn, which were cheaper to build.

Although Auburn departed from the principle of solitary confinement, it adhered strongly to the belief that the reform of criminals could be accomplished by prohibiting communication. To circumvent this rule, inmates at Auburn developed secret means of communicating. If they were caught breaking the rule of silence, inmates were punished through severe whippings. As a consequence, Auburn Penitentiary became synonymous with physical punishment. America adopted the Auburn system, which became the model for correctional institutions in this country until nearly the end of the nineteenth century. The word *penitentiary* was eventually replaced by the more familiar term *prison*, but it is still used as a descriptive term for prisons in some states (e.g., Statesville Penitentiary in Illinois), and in the Federal Bureau of Prisons the term *penitentiary* is used to designate maximum-security institutions.

RECOMMENDED READING: Frederick A. Packard, *Memorandum of a Late Visit to the Auburn Penitentiary* (Philadelphia: J. Harding, Printer, 1842).

Magnus Seng and Arthur J. Lurigio

AUGUSTUS, JOHN (1784–1859). Of the numerous correctional reforms and innovations that emerged in the nineteenth century, few were as widely diffused or as readily adopted as probation. Although it is rooted in common-law practices such as suspension of sentence, credit for the first actual implementation of probation is generally attributed to the unofficial, voluntary efforts of an altruistic Boston bootmaker, John Augustus. Between 1841 and 1859 Augustus acted as advisor and surety for nearly 2,000 offenders.

Augustus was an early and vociferous proponent of rehabilitation. Declaring that "the object of the law is to reform criminals and to prevent crime and not to punish maliciously or from a spirit of revenge" (Augustus 1972, 23), he promptly rebuked police, judges, or others who did not share his views. Augustus' patently humanitarian and progressive treatment of offenders was designed to promote in them healthy changes and personal growth.

The father of probation, as Augustus is generally recognized to be, assisted lawbreakers by supplying them with bail and counseling and supervising them during release periods. He noted in his journal that of the first 1,100 probationers on whom he kept records, only 1 forfeited bond. If any of his charges were too poor to pay court costs, Augustus would advance them a loan and extend lodging and subsistence. Rudiments of case selectiveness appear in his subjective judgment of the accused's "firm resolve" to remain temperate, and in his evaluation of whether the offender was capable of being rehabilitated. Not everyone was pleased with Augustus' work, however: Prosecutors viewed him as an intruder who clogged up court calendars by preventing cases from being disposed of quickly, and policemen and court clerks opposed his work since they received a fee for each case committed to the House of Corrections.

During Augustus' time other concerned citizens mimicked his efforts by putting up bail and offering employment to persons brought before magistrates. Their success with a large number of cases greatly impressed the court and was instrumental in encouraging Massachusetts to become the forerunner in probation legislation. Almost twenty years after Augustus' death the Probation Act of 1878 called for the appointment of a paid probation officer to serve the courts of Boston.

RECOMMENDED READING: John Augustus, *John Augustus: First Probation Officer* (Montclair, NJ: Patterson Smith, 1972).

Arthur J. Lurigio

AUTOMATED FINGERPRINT IDENTIFICATION SYSTEMS (AFIS). Although a relatively new, computer-based fingerprint technology, by 1994 automated fingerprint identification systems were a $1-billion business worldwide. Using computers to accurately match fingerprints that have previously been filed in the database allows police departments to move away from ink prints to save turnaround time in identifications and to check for aliases and false identification materials more frequently than in the past. Some of the newer AFIS computers have live-scan networks that dispense with fingerprint cards altogether and read the suspect's prints while he/she places them on the machine. The largest of the live-scan networks is in Los Angeles, connecting that city's police department with the Los Angeles County Sheriff's Department and forty-six smaller departments in Los Angeles County. In an attempt to minimize "officer-created aliases" that occur when suspects' names are misspelled during the booking process, Los Angeles County hopes to add a magnetic-strip card reader to its system to permit information contained on state drivers' licenses to be immediately transferred to subjects' automated fingerprints and booking records. Some vendors of AFIS equipment are already test-marketing portable scanners that will permit police officers to take and transmit fingerprints in the field, allowing them to know almost instantly the identification and possible wanted status of the person they have stopped. (See **Fingerprinting**.)

RECOMMENDED READING: Bonnie Clay, "Los Angeles County's Live-Scan Fingerprinting Network Is World's Largest," *Law and Order*, November 1994: 24–25, 28–29; "Inkless Fingerprint Scanner: AFIS Now Available to the Mainstream," *Law and Order*, July 1994: 110–112; Malcolm K. Sparrow, "Measuring AFIS Matcher Accuracy," *Police Chief*, April 1994: 147–151; E. Roland Menzel, "Automatic Fingerprint Identification Systems," in *Advances in Fingerprint Technology*, ed. Henry C. Lee and Robert E. Gaensslen (Boca Raton, FL: CRC Press, Inc., 1994): 25–27.

Dorothy Moses Schulz

AUTOMATED TELLER MACHINES (ATMs). The first ATM was installed in 1969 by Chemical Bank at a Rockville Center, New York, branch. A number of state and local laws have since been created in response to highly publicized robberies at the now more than 87,000 ATM locations in the United States. Of the 7.2 billion ATM transactions completed in 1992, about 4,000 resulted in customer robberies, a number that it seems reasonable to expect to continue. In 1990 California became the first state to establish minimum ATM physical security standards, followed by Nevada, Georgia, Washington, and Oregon. New York City's rules are the most demanding and expensive (estimates for compliance by banks have run as high as $20,000 per ATM site); Chicago is another major city with its own set of rules. A number of other cities have passed or strengthened anti-panhandling laws due to the concentration of beggars in and around ATM locations. Studies indicate that the number of ATM specialist robbers (those who commit only or multiple ATM customer robberies) is increasing; that more than 60 percent of ATM robbers test positive for drugs at the time of their arrest; and that very young offenders are involved in these crimes. Attempting to address the fear many patrons express about using ATMs, particularly at night or in desolate areas, the city of Chicago in 1994 permitted installation of an ATM inside a police station. In addition to customer robberies, ATM sites have themselves become targets of such crimes as burglars attempting to remove the machine itself. In one highly publicized fraud case in Connecticut, a fake ATM was installed in a shopping mall to permit the conspirators to record the customers' ATM numbers and enough other information to withdraw money from victims' bank accounts. The two principals in this case received thirty-month sentences in federal prison for their scam. Edward Smith, America's first bank robber, who opened the door of the City Bank in New York's Wall Street with duplicate keys on October 19, 1831, was more severely penalized; although more than $185,000 of the $245,000 he stole was recovered, Smith spent five years in prison.

RECOMMENDED READING: Marion Davis, "Banking on NYC," *New York Daily News*, November 13, 1994, 2; Barry Schreiber, "The Future of ATM Security," *Security Management*, March 1994, 18A–21A; Don Terry, "Police Station Becomes a Cash Station," *New York Times*, April 1, 1994, A12.

Dorothy Moses Schulz

AUTO THEFT. Technically defined as the theft or attempted theft of an automobile. This, however, is not the way the word is commonly used in criminal justice circles. More commonly, the criminal justice system utilizes the Uniform Crime Reports (UCR) definition of motor-vehicle theft, which includes not only automobiles, but trucks, buses, motorcycles, motor scooters, and snowmobiles—in other words, any motorized vehicle that travels on land.

The definition excludes the taking of a motor vehicle for temporary use by a person having lawful access. An example of this might be a police officer commandeering an automobile to chase an escaping bank robber.

According to the Uniform Crime Reports, in 1995 there were 1,472,732 reported motor-vehicle thefts, for a rate per 100,000 inhabitants of 560.5. This comprised 13 percent of all property crimes. The UCR also noted that there was a variation in the regional distribution of these thieveries: 33 percent in the southern states, 30 percent in the western states, 19 percent in the midwestern states, and 18 percent in the northeastern states. During 1995 the estimated value of motor vehicles stolen nationwide was nearly $7.6 billion. In 1995, 58 percent of all persons arrested for this offense were under twenty-one years of age, and those under eighteen comprised 42 percent of the total.

RECOMMENDED READING: Federal Bureau of Investigation, *Uniform Crime Reports for the United States, 1995* (Washington, DC: U.S. Government Printing Office, 1996).

Ransom A. Whittle

B

BAIL. A monetary condition for pretrial release. Money is deposited with the court as a form of insurance that the defendant will meet subsequent court appearances. If bail is imposed, it is usually set at the defendant's arraignment or initial appearance. If the defendant meets conditions of bail, the money deposited with the court will be refunded; if s/he does not do so, the surety is forfeited to the court.

In many jurisdictions the inability of the defendant to "make bail" has meant that s/he will remain incarcerated until trial. The Eighth Amendment to the U.S. Constitution forbids "excessive bail," a concept that has not been closely defined by the U.S. Supreme Court. The Court has held that the only legitimate purpose of bail is to ensure the appearance of the defendant at trial and that bail set higher than a reasonable estimate of what is needed to meet that requirement is excessive under the Constitution. Bail cannot legitimately be used as a form of punishment.

Factors that judicial officers can legitimately consider when setting bail include the defendant's financial ability, the nature and gravity of the offense charged, the criminal background of the defendant (if any), and the character of the defendant. "Bail schedules" for some offenses have been established in some jurisdictions. In these situations a defendant charged with a particular offense automatically finds his/her bail set at a certain amount. In other jurisdictions and for other offenses judicial officers have greater discretion in the bail-setting process.

Bail may be set in terms of cash or property. In many jurisdictions individuals unable to raise the funds necessary for bail may turn to bail bondsmen, who, for a nonrefundable fee (usually 10 percent of the total bail set), will guarantee surety for the defendant. A number of states and localities have eliminated the need for the bail bondsman by instituting a "cash 10 percent system." In this system the defendant deposits 10 percent of the total amount with the court; if s/he appears at trial, most of that deposit is returned.

Because persons with fewer assets find it relatively more difficult to make bail, the system has been accused of being biased against the poor. In part because of such criticisms, bail systems have been replaced in many jurisdictions by practices such as release on recognizance (ROR) and supervised release. (See **Cash Bail Bond; Release on Recognizance**.)

RECOMMENDED READING: Jonathan D. Schiffman, *Fundamentals of the Criminal Justice Process*, 3rd ed. (Deerfield, IL: Clark Boardman Callaghan, 1994); *Wisconsin Court Rules and Procedure, State and Federal* (St. Paul: West Publishing Co., 1988).

David Jones

BAILIFF. The individual whose primary responsibility is that of assisting the judge in maintaining appropriate decorum and security in the courtroom. In fulfilling this duty s/he performs such jobs as keeping custody of defendants and providing various services for jurors. S/he also has the duty of seeing that "sequestered" jurors are appropriately housed, fed, and kept away from items that could taint their deliberations.

In some states judges appoint bailiffs, while in others they are employees of sheriff's departments. There is also variation in levels of professionalism among bailiffs. Some are patronage employees, while others are covered by state civil service regulations.

RECOMMENDED READING: James A. Gazell, *The Future of State Court Management* (Port Washington, NY: Kennikat Press, 1978); N. Gary Holten and Lawson L. Lamar, *The Criminal Courts: Structures, Personnel, and Processes* (New York: McGraw-Hill, 1991); Paul Wice, *Judges and Lawyers: The Human Side of Justice* (New York: Harper Collins, 1991).

David Jones

BALLISTICS. Ballistics is the science of projectiles: bullets, bombs, rockets and missiles. In criminal justice the term is applied to the identification of the weapon from which a bullet was fired. Microscopic imperfections in a gun barrel make characteristic scratches and grooves on bullets fired through it.

There are three types of ballistics. Exterior ballistics is the study of the motion of the projectile after it leaves the barrel of the fired weapon. Interior ballistics is the study of the motion of the projectile within the firearm from the moment of igniting of the primer until the projectile leaves the barrel. The third type of ballistics, terminal ballistics, is the study of the effect of a projectile's impact on the target.

There are many types of firearms. Among the different types are the semi-automatic pistols, rifles, and shotguns. Typically, the longer the barrel of a firearm, such as that of a rifle, the straighter the projectile's path over long distances. The type of projectile used in firearms also determines the speed, accuracy, and impact of the projectile. For example, in a shotgun small balls or pellets encased in a cartridge are used. When the pellets are released, these pellets are less accurate than bullets in hitting their targets, because pellets tend to disperse rather than travel together.

A barrel may have grooves and lands in the interior barrel. This allows the grooves in the barrel to grip a bullet tightly. These grooves in the interior barrel produce a higher fired-bullet rotational velocity. This produces greater gyroscopic precision and stability and a greater accuracy, range, and energy impact. However, in a smooth-bore barrel bullets travel in a tumbling fashion and in a less accurate direction with a lower velocity.

The degree of hardness of the lead in bullets varies with the alloy used. Because of the softness of lead bullets, they tend to display distinctive impressions of the surfaces of the barrel through which they are fired. When a lead bullet makes contact with a hard surface or object, distortion may result. On the other hand, jacketed bullets are more resistant to external distortion than lead bullets. Because of the hardness of the jacket surface, it is more difficult for the barrel to imprint its characteristics on this type of bullet.

RECOMMENDED READING: Tom A. Warlow, *Firearms, the Law, and Forensic Ballistics* (London: Taylor & Francis, 1996).

James R. Farris

BAZELON, DAVID (1920–1993). A federal judge of the U.S. Court of Appeals for the Washington, DC, Circuit, 1949–1985, chief judge, 1962–1978. In this capacity Judge Bazelon sat on a court seen by many to be the second most powerful judicial body in the United States. A liberal and activist judge, Bazelon sought to apply findings from social science and psychiatry to federal case law. For instance, in 1954 he fashioned the "Durham Rule" as a standard for legal insanity. He was also a supporter from the bench of the extension of defendants' rights and took the position that solving underlying social problems, not the imposition of tougher sentences, was the appropriate means of attacking the problem of crime in the United States.

RECOMMENDED READING: David Bazelon, "New Gods for Old: 'Efficient' Courts in a Democratic Society," 46 N.Y.U. L. REV. 653, 658 (1971); David Bazelon, *Questioning Authority: Justice and Criminal Law* (New York: New York University Press, 1990).

David Jones

BEAN, ROY (1825–1903). Roy Bean was born in Mason County, Kentucky, in 1825. In 1882 he set up a saloon near the Pecos River in Texas to serve working men who were building the Southern Pacific Railroad. At this small crossroads, which he renamed Langtry after the beautiful English actress, Lillie Langtry (the saloon he called the Jersey Lily in her honor), Bean ruled with the approval of the Texas Rangers as justice of the peace and coroner, calling himself the "law west of the Pecos." Part of the saloon was his courtroom. He often relied on his six-guns to keep order. Known for his informal but shrewd decisions, Bean once was unwilling to bury a corpse for the fee of $5. He searched the body, found a gun and $40, and fined the corpse $40 for possession of a concealed weapon. Bean died in 1903 in Langtry.

RECOMMENDED READING: Everett Lloyd, *Law West of the Pecos: The Story of Roy Bean* (Holmes Beach, FL: Gaunt, 1996); Charles L. Sonnichsen, *Roy Bean: Law West of the Pecos* (New York: MacMillan Company, 1943).

Martin Gruberg

BEARDEN v. GEORGIA, 461 U.S. 660 (1983). This case involved the rights of parolees unable to pay fines levied as a condition of probation. In this instance the U.S. Supreme Court held that a sentencing court cannot automatically revoke a defendant's probation and turn a fine into a prison sentence if the probationer fails to pay a fine and make restitution unless there are evidence and findings that s/he was responsible for the failure or that alternative forms of punishment were inadequate to meet the state's interest in punishment and deterrence. To do so would be contrary to the "fundamental fairness" required by the Fourteenth Amendment.

David Jones

BECARRIA, CESARE (1738–1794). Cesare Beccaria (whose Italian name was Cesare Bonesana, but who held the title Marchese di Beccaria) was born in Milan, Italy. The eldest of four children, he was trained at Catholic schools and earned a doctor of laws degree by the time he was 20.

In 1764 Beccaria published his *Essay on Crimes and Punishment.* Although the work appeared originally in Italian, it was translated in London into English in 1767. Beccaria's *Essay*, which established him as one of the founders of the Classical School of Criminology, consisted of forty-two short chapters covering only a few major themes.

Beccaria's purpose in penning the *Essay* was not to set forth a theory of crime, but to communicate his observations on the laws and justice system of his time. In the *Essay,* Beccaria distilled the notion of the social contract into the idea that "[l]aws are the conditions under which independent and isolated men united to form a society."

More than anything else, however, his writings consisted of a philosophy of punishment. Beccaria claimed, for example, that although most criminals are punished based upon an assessment of their criminal intent, they should be punished instead based upon the degree of injury they cause. The purpose of punishment, he said, should be deterrence rather than retribution, and punishment should be imposed to prevent offenders from committing additional crimes. Beccaria saw punishment as a tool to an end and not an end in itself, and crime prevention was more important to him than revenge.

Beccaria concluded that punishment should be only severe enough to outweigh the personal benefits to be derived from crime commission.

Beccaria's ideas were widely recognized as progressive by his contemporaries. His principles were incorporated into the French penal code of 1791, and significantly influenced the justice-related activities of European leaders such as Catherine the Great of Russia, Frederick the Great of Prussia, and the Austrian Emperor Joseph II. There is evidence that Beccaria's *Essay* influenced framers of the American Constitution. Some scholars claim that the first ten amendments to the Constitution, known as the Bill of Rights, might not have existed were it not for Beccaria's emphasis on the rights of individuals in the face of state power. Perhaps more than anyone else, Beccaria is responsible for the contemporary belief that criminals have control over their behavior, that they choose to commit crimes, and that they can be deterred by the threat of punishment.

RECOMMENDED READING: Cesare Beccaria, *On Crimes and Punishments*, translated by Henry Paolucci (New York: Bobbs-Merrill, 1963).

Frank Schmalleger

BELLI, MELVIN (1907–1996). Melvin M. Belli was born on July 29, 1907, in Sonora, California. He began practicing law in 1933. By 1954 *Life* magazine called him the "King of Torts." He was flamboyant, an American folk hero, good copy for the media. An example of his colorful style: In September 1964 he filed a suit to keep Barry Goldwater from running for president on the grounds that Goldwater was not a native-born U.S. citizen, having been born in Arizona ten years before it became a state. Belli had a large following of young lawyers who emulated his methods. He revolutionized the practice of negligence law. Belli brought to damage-suit trials demonstrative evidence (models, chalkboard) previously used in criminal cases. He authored a three-volume handbook for personal-injury lawyers. Starting in 1953, he conducted the annual one-day Belli Seminar in Law, honing the attorneys' evidence techniques and trial tactics. He was president of the National Association of Claimants Compensation Attorneys and cofounder of the International Academy of Trial Lawyers. Belli frequently lectures at law schools. His clients included Jack Ruby, Errol Flynn, Mae West, Lenny Bruce, Mickey Cohen, the Rolling Stones, the families of the Soledad Brothers, George Foreman, and the Berkeley Free Speech Movement. He was a foe of capital punishment and corporate crime.

RECOMMENDED READING: Melvin M. Belli, *The Belli Files: Reflections on the Wayward Law* (Englewood Cliffs, NJ: Prentice-Hall 1983); Bob Schildgen, "Melvin Belli's Fighting Spirit," *Bay Area Business Magazine*, Vol. 5, no. 5 (February 1987).

Martin Gruberg

BENNETT, WILLIAM J. (1943–   ). America's first "drug czar." Bennett was appointed to serve as director of the Office of National Control Policy by President George Bush in 1989. He served in that office for approximately two years. While serving in the position of drug czar, Bennett, an outspoken conservative, took a hard line in the war on drugs. He took a strong public stand against the legalization of drugs and publicly endorsed the concept of capital punishment for major drug dealers. He worked to develop an integrated attack on drug use, seeking to coordinate such disparate components as drug interdiction, education, prevention, law enforcement, and treatment. In his view his approach had positive effects since, by a number of measures, drug use, especially casual drug use, appeared to decline during his tenure in office. Others have disputed this assessment. (See **Drug Czar**.)

RECOMMENDED READING: William J. Bennett, *The De-Valuing of America* (New York: Summit Books, 1992).

David Jones

BENTHAM, JEREMY (1748–1832). Jeremy Bentham was an English philosopher who is, alongside Cesare Beccaria, an exemplar of classical criminological theory. Bentham's philosophy, known as utilitarianism, places criminological concerns within a framework for empirical inquiry into the motives of human action. Utilitarian psychology emphasizes the role of pain and pleasure as factors each individual will consider in deciding upon a course of action that is likely to maximize pleasure and/or minimize pain to himself or herself. Criminals, and all other persons for that matter, are assumed to be rational in a utilitarian sense of seeking pleasure over pain. The prevention and correction of criminal activity will then require sufficient disincentive to counter the benefit gained in commission of a crime. Yet Bentham also emphasized that unduly harsh punishment will not necessarily diminish crime; he once observed that there was a high incidence of pickpocketing within a crowd attending the hanging of a pickpocket. Effective punishment requires an economical balance of pleasure and pain.

In corrections Bentham devised a prison design known as the Panopticon that allows for constant surveillance of the inmates in concert with intensive rehabilitation efforts. Critical social theorists, such as Michel Foucault, have portrayed the Panopticon as emblematic of modern regimes of dominating power based in technology and knowledge. From a utilitarian perspective, Bentham's goal was to produce "the greatest happiness [i.e., pleasure] for the greatest number." Even the pain of the criminal perpetrator and of the prison inmate is included in the utilitarian's calculus of happiness. Bentham's goal was to minimize the human misery associated with crime and punishment through a rational combination of punishment and rehabilitation. Bentham's legacy informs behaviorism, the positivist school of criminology, and indeed all efforts to develop a rigorously scientific criminology and penology.

However, some of the later theories lose something of Bentham's emphasis on the close association between theory and research on the one hand and practical policy application on the other.

RECOMMENDED READING: Jeremy Bentham, *An Introduction to the Principles of Morals and Legislation* (London: Athlone Publishers, 1970); Michel Foucault, *Discipline and Punish* (New York: Vintage Books, 1979); John Stuart Mill, *Utilitarianism* (Indianapolis: Bobbs-Merrill, 1957).

Daniel Skidmore-Hess

BERGER v. NEW YORK, **388 U.S. 41 (1967).** One of the important decisions of the U.S. Supreme Court concerning electronic eavesdropping. In this case the Court held that the practice of "bugging" a suspect's telephones was governed by Fourth Amendment rules concerning search and seizure, because (following *Mapp v. Ohio, 1961*) provisions of the Fourth Amendment apply to state action under the U.S. Constitution. The Court held that the New York law of the time, which allowed phone taps to be authorized by a court on the basis of a law enforcement official's assertion that there were "reasonable grounds" to believe that evidence of a crime might be obtained was unconstitutional "on its face" because it did not meet the Fourth Amendment's criterion of "particularity," nor did it provide for "prompt execution" of the warrant as required by that provision of the Bill of Rights.

David Jones

BIOCHEMICAL SCHOOL OF CRIMINOLOGY. As the techniques of science have evolved and the sophistication of science's tools has been enhanced, more scientifically accurate and powerful explanations of human behavior from a biological or biochemical perspective have been generated. Such explanations do not exclude environment as a mitigating circumstance. However, there is a problem of misconception that the biological and biochemical criminologists claim that biology causes crime, while these theorists and researchers maintain that biology only causes or is a correlate of behaviors that are ex post facto socially defined as crime.

Scientific biological inquiry into the correlates and causes of crime originated in Italy with Cesare Lombroso, who related bodily characteristics (anomalies) of individuals to deviant behavior. He acknowledged social influences on behavior while developing the concept of the atavist or biological throwback. Lombroso's work was followed by the school of somatotyping in the work of Ernst Kretschmer, Sheldon and Eleanor Glueck, and William H. Sheldon where human physique was related to temperament and then to behaviors that can be identified as criminal or delinquent.

There has been a strong argument from Mednick, Jeffrey, and others in twin and adoptee studies that there are biological conditions, some of which may be hereditary, that create stresses or problems in people's lives and put them at risk of behaviors that may be defined as criminal. More modern biological approaches have moved from testing general body features to inquiry into complex chemical and microbiological features including effects of hormones, diet (orthomolecular biology), brain damage, chromosomal damage and aberrations, toxins, pollutants, climate, light levels, and seasonal effects on human behavior. The nature and function of the nervous system have attracted singular interest.

The more modern writers in the field general field of criminology, including Wilson and Herrnstein, have come to accept that biology matters. The Project on Human Development led by Albert Reiss and Felton Earls is seeking to factor out of the complex of variables that affect humans those biological, social and psychological factors that are most directly related to behaviors labeled as criminal.

RECOMMENDED READING: Arthur Fisher, "A New Synthesis Comes of Age," *Mosaic,* Vol. 22, no. 1 (Spring 1991): 2–9; Edward O. Wilson, *Sociobiology: The New Synthesis* (Cambridge, MA: The Belknap Press of Harvard University Press, 1975).

David R. Struckhoff

BLACK, HUGO L. (1886–1971). Hugo Black was born on February 27, 1886, in Clay County, Alabama. After obtaining his law degree at the University of Alabama, he engaged in private practice and served as a police-court judge and as a county prosecuting attorney. He was elected to the U.S. Senate in 1926. When Franklin Roosevelt became president, Black was a key legislative lieutenant. Roosevelt appointed Black to the Supreme Court in 1937 despite the revelation that he had been a member of the Ku Klux Klan.

Black, a consistent liberal, emerged as the intellectual leader of the Court. He clashed for many years with Felix Frankfurter, who espoused judicial restraint. Black denied that the courts should uphold restriction of rights guaranteed to individuals in the Constitution merely because good reasons could be shown for these restrictions under particular circumstances. Black was an absolutist regarding the First Amendment. He believed that the Fourteenth Amendment incorporated the Bill of Rights. Black was moved by the plight of the poor and oppressed and joined the judges who expressed a preferred-position doctrine, that the benefit of the doubt should be given by the judiciary to legislative restrictions on property rights, but claims to personal rights should have priority over efforts by the state to curb them.

Black advocated court-enforced legislative reapportionment, judicial enforcement of racial desegregation, separation of church and state, freedom of the press, and protection of U.S. citizenship against involuntary denaturalization. (However, he upheld the World War II incarceration of those of Japanese ancestry). He allied with Justice William O. Douglas in opposing laws against Communist activities. Black was a major participant in the Warren Court's equal-rights decisions as well as decisions enlarging the rights of criminal suspects (such as *Gideon v. Wainwright* [1963] and *Miranda v. Arizona* [1966]). However, he did not support the claims of civil rights protesters. His interpretation of the Fourth Amendment generally accepted law enforcement actions including warrantless searches and wiretapping. In his last years on the Court Black became less innovative and more rigid, even strident, in his reading of the Constitution.

Black was noted for his searching questions from the bench to lawyers who were arguing before the Court. He left the Court in 1971 and died shortly thereafter.

RECOMMENDED READING: Gerald T. Dunne, *Hugo Black and the Judicial Revolution* (New York: Simon and Schuster, 1977); Wallace Mendelson, *Justices Black and Frankfurter: Conflict in the Court*, 2nd ed. (Chicago: University of Chicago Press, 1966).

Martin Gruberg

BLACKMUN, HARRY A. (1908–   ). Harry A. Blackmun was born on November 12, 1908, in Nashville, Illinois, but he spent most of his life in Minnesota. He attended Harvard College and Harvard Law School and returned to Minnesota to practice. He was for sixteen years a member of a prestigious Minneapolis law firm. He also taught at William Mitchell College and the University of Minnesota Law School. Blackmun became an expert on medical law and served from 1950 to 1959 as counsel for the Mayo Clinic.

In 1959 President Eisenhower appointed him to the U.S. court of appeals, where he served until 1970. He was among the first federal judges to declare prison conditions violative of the Eighth Amendment. In 1970 President Nixon was unsuccessful in two attempts to name southern judges, Clement F. Haynsworth and G. Harrold Carswell, to the Supreme Court. Chief Justice Warren Burger recommended his lifelong friend, Blackmun. When Blackmun was first appointed, those following the Court thought that he would be a clone of Burger and called the two the "Minnesota Twins." However, Blackmun established his own path. He was a conservative in the criminal justice area, having little sympathy for lawbreakers, but was an independent, even a liberal, on civil rights and liberties. He had empathy for the powerless and voted with William Brennan and Thurgood Marshall.

His medical-law background (and his fathering three daughters) may have led to his being the voice for the Court in the *Roe v. Wade* (1973) decision. He dissented from Burger in *Regents of the University of California v. Bakke* (1978), contending that the effects of racial discrimination could not be overcome without first taking race into account. Blackmun was known for his scholarly and thorough opinions. He opposed the death penalty but did not think that judges should make such a policy decision. Blackmun left the Court in 1994.

RECOMMENDED READING: Mark Schneider, "Justice Blackmun: A Wise Man Walking the Corridors of Power, Gently," *Georgetown Law Journal*, Vol. 83, no. 1 (November 1994): 11-15; Stephen L. Wasby, "Justice Blackmun and Criminal Justice: A Modest Overview," *Akron Law Review*, Vol. 28, no. 2 (Fall/Winter 1995): 125-186.

Martin Gruberg

BLACKSTONE, SIR WILLIAM (1723–1780). William Blackstone was the author of a four-volume work, *Commentaries on the Laws of England*. This was an extremely influential systematic statement of the principles of the common law as they existed in the Britain of his day. By using historical examples and examples from the laws of other nations, Blackstone sought to show that the English law of his day conformed to principles of natural law as he understood that concept. In short, Blackstone sought to justify the English legal system as it had evolved to his time.

In his view the highest principle of law was the protection and expansion of private property. While there were logical inconsistencies in the *Commentaries*, the work was very influential because it captured the spirit of the age in Britain and the United States. It was also very significant in the United States during the first half of the nineteenth century because it served as the primary (and often sole) basis for the education of many American lawyers.

RECOMMENDED READING: Daniel J. Boorstin, *The Mysterious Science of the Law* (Boston: Beacon Press, 1958).

David Jones

BLOCK v. RUTHERFORD, 468 U.S. 576 (1984). A case involving the rights of pretrial detainees concerning their conditions of confinement. In this case, as in previous cases, the U.S. Supreme Court held that deference should be given to the judgment of the correctional institution's officers when deciding conditions of confinement cases.

In this case pretrial detainees in the Los Angeles County Jail challenged the right of jail officials to prohibit "contact" visits with loved ones and close relatives, as well as the jail's practice of conducting random searches of cells while the detainees were away. A federal district court sustained the challenges, and the federal court of appeals affirmed.

Chief Justice Burger, writing for the Court majority, held that where it is alleged (as here) that a pretrial detainee has been deprived of liberty without due process, the dispositive inquiry is whether the challenged practice constitutes punishment or is reasonably related to a legitimate government objective. The majority also held that when considering whether a specific practice or policy is reasonably related to security interests, the courts should generally defer to the expertise of the professional correctional officers.

In both cases, the Court held, the jail practices were reasonably related to legitimate security interests. Illegal material could be smuggled in during contact and could be hidden in jail cells. Therefore, the prohibitions and the random cell searches were held to be reasonable, and the lower-court decisions were overturned.

Victor J. Larragoite

BLOODS. The Bloods, a street gang, is a substitute family to numerous adolescents across the nation. Similar to other gangs, it has its own hierarchies, uniforms, and culture. The members of the gang view the gang as their family. The adolescents in the gang address each other as "homie," "homeboy," or "blood." The older members of the gang serve as father figures for the juveniles and young adults in the gang. The attraction for the juveniles and young adults to the gang is mostly for the needed attention. The older members congratulate the youth each time they shoot someone or recruit a new member, who is called a combat soldier.

A gang member's behavior, speech, dress, and car are all part of an elaborate set of rituals that convey status and respect. Respect is the highest honor worth dying for, according to members of the Bloods. Gang wars have been less about race than about power, revenge, and respect. According to the Bloods, "gang-banging" is no part-time thing, it is a full-time career. It means getting caught and not telling. It is being down when nobody else is down with you. It is killing and not caring, and dying without fear. It is love for your set (a geographic division of the gang), and hate for the enemy. Part of the respect comes from the ritual of initiation into the gang. The average age for initiation in the Bloods is between ten and twelve. The ritual usually consists of a barrage of tests, the first being a physical beating by all other members who wish to participate. An additional test may require the shooting of someone.

RECOMMENDED READING: Bureau of Alcohol, Tobacco, and Firearms, *Crips and Bloods Street Gangs* (Washington, DC: The Bureau, 1989); Yusuf Jah and Shah'Keyah Jah, *Uprising: Crips and Bloods Tell the Story of America's Youth in the Crossfire* (New York: Simon & Schuster, 1997).

James R. Farris

BLYSTONE v. PENNSYLVANIA, 494 U.S. 299 (1990). One of a number of cases following *Gregg v. Georgia* in which the U.S. Supreme Court clarified its basic ruling that the death penalty was not automatically or invariably an unconstitutional punishment. In this case (a 5-4 decision in which Chief Justice Rehnquist wrote the majority opinion) the Supreme Court held that a Pennsylvania statute providing for a mandatory death penalty if the jury found at least one aggravating circumstance and no mitigating circumstances was constitutional. The Supreme Court has generally held that to be constitutional, a death-penalty statute must give guidance to the jury while at the same time allowing it some discretion to interpret individual situations. Under this interpretation, "mandatory" death-penalty statutes, which gave juries no discretion, were declared unconstitutional. The Court held that the Pennsylvania law met these criteria because it did give guidance while at the same time allowing a capital sentencing jury to consider and give effect to all relevant mitigating evidence.

In this case petitioner Blystone picked up a hitchhiker, robbed him, and, for no apparent reason, killed him by shooting him in the back of the head six times. Blystone was caught and convicted of first-degree murder, robbery, criminal conspiracy to commit homicide, and criminal conspiracy to commit robbery. In the penalty phase of the trial the jury also found that as an "aggravating circumstance" the defendant had committed a killing while in the perpetration of a felony. It also found no mitigating circumstances, and Blystone was sentenced to death.

The question before the Court was: Does the mandatory aspect of the Pennsylvania death-penalty statute render the penalty imposed on petitioner unconstitutional because it improperly limited the discretion of the jury in deciding the appropriate penalty for his crime? The majority of the Court held that the law did not overly restrict the jury's ability to consider all relevant mitigating circumstances, and, hence, it was constitutionally applied in this case.

RECOMMENDED READING: Welsh S. White, *The Death Penalty in the Nineties: An Examination of the Modern System of Capital Punishment* (Ann Arbor: University of Michigan Press, 1991).

David Jones

BOESKY, IVAN (1937–   ). One of the first of the Wall Street stock-market manipulators convicted of "insider trading," the illegal practice of using privileged corporate information not yet available to the general public. Boesky's conviction, the product of plea bargaining, was for one count of filing a false share-ownership statement. For this offense he was fined $100,000,000, accepted a lifetime ban on securities dealing in the United States, and received a three-year prison sentence. His assets at the time of the verdict (1986) were estimated to be approximately $2 billion.

In return for what many regarded as a relatively light sentence, Boesky agreed to cooperate with the government in the pursuit of other stock-market manipulators.

RECOMMENDED READING: Peter De Trolio, III, "Ivan F. Boesky," in *Encyclopedia of American Business History and Biography*, Vol. 7 (New York: Facts On File, 1990): 31-33.

David Jones

BOOKING (THE PROCESS). At the police station a record of the arrest is made. The charge, evidence, and circumstances of the arrest are reviewed by a booking officer to assure that probable cause for the arrest exists. The prisoner is fully searched and any property s/he may have in his or her possession is taken away. A receipt is provided. The prisoner is afforded an opportunity to telephone a friend, relative, or attorney for assistance. In an appropriate case s/he is fingerprinted and photographed, and further investigative activities may take place, such as requiring the prisoner to stand in a lineup for identification purposes by the victim of the crime or witnesses to it. The prisoner may also be further interrogated. These steps constitute the booking process.

RECOMMENDED READING: J. Scott Harr and Karen M. Hess, *Constitutional Law for Criminal Justice Professionals* (Belmont, CA: Wadsworth Publishing, 1997); Irving J. Klein, *Constitutional Law for Criminal Justice Professionals*, 3rd ed. (South Miami, FL: Coral Gables Publishing Co., 1992).

Chistopher J. Morse

BOSTON POLICE STRIKE. When members of the Boston Police Department went on strike for higher wages in September 1919, they had no idea that they would gain national attention and all but crush the nascent police labor-union movement. Although other cities had previously been targets of strike actions by police, only in Boston did the absence of police on the street lead to widespread disorder and looting, as well as a number of robberies. Within twenty-four hours of the start of the strike, Calvin Coolidge, then governor of Massachusetts, ordered the state guard to patrol the streets. Coolidge replaced all police officers except the twenty-four who had remained on duty and set in motion the beginnings of numerous state and local laws forbidding police officers from unionizing.

Despite the development of local police benevolent associations that generally provided welfare benefits to police officers and members of their families, police unionism remained dormant in the United States until the 1960s, well after other government employees had won the right to join unions. Unionization battles remained pitched; in 1979 more than a dozen cities experienced police strikes or "blue flues" (officers calling in sick, following rule-book slowdowns, wearing sneakers while in uniform, refusing to shave, or engaging in disorderly street protests). Despite these sometimes contentious organizing activities, by 1979 more than 50 percent of police officers belonged to unions, and close to 70 percent of larger departments were unionized.

RECOMMENDED READING: Dorothy Guyot, *Policing As Though People Matter* (Philadelphia: Temple University Press, 1991); Richard N. Holden, *Modern Police Management*, 2nd ed. (Englewood Cliffs, NJ: Prentice-Hall, 1994); Edward A. Thibault, Lawrence M. Lynch, and R. Bruce McBride, *Proactive Police Management*, 3rd ed. (Englewood Cliffs, NJ: Prentice Hall, 1995).

Dorothy Moses Schulz

BOUNDS V. SMITH, **430 U.S. 817 (1977).** One of a number of cases involving the rights of prisoners. In this case the U.S. Supreme Court, speaking through Justice Thurgood Marshall, held that the states are constitutionally mandated to protect the rights of prisoners to access to the courts by providing them with law libraries or alternative sources of legal knowledge. The Court left some leeway to the states for them to determine how they would provide this right to inmates.

David Jones

BREED V. JONES, **421 U.S. 519 (1975).** In 1971 a seventeen-year-old juvenile in California, accused of committing armed robbery, was ordered detained pending juvenile court action. The child was adjudicated delinquent. During the child's disposition hearing the juvenile court found that the child was not "amenable to the care, treatment and training program available through the facilities of the juvenile court." The matter was continued, and one week later the court found that the juvenile was still not amenable to treatment through the juvenile court and should thus be prosecuted as an adult. A writ of *habeas corpus* was filed for the child claiming that the adult prosecution of the juvenile after the adjudication as a juvenile delinquent would violate the Fifth and Fourteenth Amendments. When the petition was denied, a writ of *habeas corpus* was presented to the California court of appeal, which denied the petition for hearing. An information charging that the child committed armed robbery was filed, and the child pled not guilty and also pled that his constitutional right against double jeopardy was being violated. The child was convicted of the crime and sent to the California Youth Authority.

The child's attorney filed a writ of *habeas corpus* in the U.S. district court. The court denied the petition, saying that the differences between the adult and juvenile courts were many and made the two courts distinct. The court of appeals reversed the decision, saying that the double-jeopardy clause did apply to juvenile proceedings. The court of appeals held that once a juvenile was adjudicated delinquent for a delinquent act, that juvenile could not be retried as a juvenile or adult for the same delinquent act. The Supreme Court granted *certiorari* because it felt that this was an issue faced by many states and at question in many cases.

Again, the issue for the Supreme Court was whether or not the child was put in double jeopardy in adult court after having been adjudicated delinquent on the same offense in juvenile court. The Court cited that previous court cases had leaned in favor of granting juveniles constitutional rights, as the Court "recognized that there is a gap between the original benign conception of the system and its realities." Because the consequences of both the adult and juvenile court hearings could be similar, namely, deprivation of freedom, the two courts were virtually indistinguishable in possible outcome. As such, the Court held that the respondent was indeed put in jeopardy at the adjudication hearing and faced double jeopardy at the adult trial. Thus the adult hearing violated the double-jeopardy clause of the Fifth Amendment, as applied to the states through the Fourteenth Amendment.

The Court noted that the process of transferring jurisdiction of the child to the adult court was a viable alternative in most states and would remain so. The decision to transfer, and thus the transfer hearing guaranteed in *Kent v. U.S.* (1966), would have to be decided upon and scheduled before the adjudication hearing. Then the child would not be placed in double jeopardy and his or her rights would not be violated.

Frances P. Roddington

BREYER, STEPHEN (1938–   ). Associate Justice of the U.S. Supreme Court, born August 15, 1938, in San Francisco, California, to Irving G. and Anne R. Breyer. Justice Breyer married Joanna Hare on September 4, 1967, by whom he has three children, Chloe, Nell, and Michael.

Justice Breyer attended public school in San Francisco, then graduated from Stanford University (A.B. 1959) with Great Distinction. He received a B.A. from Magdalen College of Oxford University with honors in 1961, and his law degree from Harvard Law School, *magna cum laude,* in 1964. While at Harvard, he served as an editor of the *Harvard Law Review*.

After graduation from law school, Justice Breyer clerked for the Honorable Arthur J. Goldberg, Associate Justice, Supreme Court of the United States, during the 1964–1965 term, then taught law at Harvard University, where he was an Assistant Professor (1967–1970) and Professor of Law (1970–1980). He was also a Professor in Harvard's Kennedy School of Government from 1977–1980. Justice Breyer has been a visiting professor at the College of Law, Sydney, Australia (1975) and the University of Rome (1993).

Justice Breyer served as a judge on the U.S. Court of Appeals for the First Circuit from 1980 until 1990, and was that court's chief judge from 1990 until 1994. During his service on the First District court, Justice Breyer concurrently served as a member of both the U.S. Sentencing Commission (1985–1989) and the Judicial Conference of the United States (1990–1994).

Following nomination by President Clinton, Justice Breyer assumed his current position as an Associate Justice on the Supreme Court of the United States on August 3, 1994.

Frank Schmalleger

BROWN v. MISSISSIPPI, 297 U.S. 278 (1936). One of the first cases in which the U.S. Supreme Court ruled on the issue of the voluntariness of confessions in state cases. It was one of the first cases in which provisions of the Fourteenth Amendment were applied in a state criminal case. In this case the Court held that there were limits to what law officers can do to extract confessions from defendants. The facts of the case also show the near-barbaric treatment of some defendants by some law enforcement officials in some parts of the United States at this point in American history.

The defendants, who were black, were convicted of murder. The only evidence admitted into court that was used to convict them was their confessions. These confessions were extracted by torture and were later denied by the defendants. Despite the defendants' retraction of their confessions, they were found guilty and sentenced to death.

The question before the Supreme Court, as framed by Chief Justice Charles Evans Hughes, was "whether convictions, which rest solely upon confessions shown to have been extorted by officers of the state by brutality and violence, are consistent with the due process of law required by the Fourteenth Amendment of the Constitution of the United States." After reviewing the means used to extract the confessions, which included hangings and severe whippings, Hughes concluded, "[I]t would be difficult to conceive of methods more revolting to the sense of justice than those taken to procure the confessions of these petitioners, and the use of the confessions thus obtained as the basis for conviction and sentence was clear denial of due process." The Court reversed the convictions.

David Jones

BUREAU OF ALCOHOL, TOBACCO, AND FIREARMS (ATF). Tracing its history back to 1791, when the U.S. Congress began taking cognizance of distilled spirits, ATF, part of the U.S. Treasury Department, is the primary agency responsible for enforcing federal laws relating to alcohol, tobacco, and firearms violations, although in the last decade enforcing laws pertaining to the manufacture, sale, and possession of firearms and explosives has overshadowed the other ATF areas of responsibility. The ATF also is responsible for investigating arson and bombings of federal buildings and institutions that receive federal funds. Its early history is one of the most colorful of the federal law enforcement agencies. In 1862 "revenue agents" were first hired to enforce tax laws on alcohol and tobacco. Responsibilities were increased during Prohibition (1919–1933), when such agents as Eliot Ness gained fame for their investigations of organized crime's efforts to circumvent laws pertaining to the manufacture and transport of alcohol. The agency received considerable negative publicity in 1993 when it raided the compound of David Koresh, a religious-cult leader. Numerous cult members, including young children, were killed in the ensuing fire. Four ATF agents also died during the siege.

RECOMMENDED READING: John S. Dempsey, *Policing: An Introduction to Law Enforcement* (Minneapolis/St. Paul: West Publishing Co., 1994); Thomas A. Reppetto, *The Blue Parade* (New York: Free Press, 1978).

Dorothy Moses Schulz

BURGLARY. Burglary is entering any house, room, apartment, tenement, shop, warehouse, store, mill, barn, stable, outhouse, building, tent, vessel, railroad car, locked or sealed cargo container, trailer coach, house car, mobile home, camper, vehicle, aircraft, watercraft, or mine or any underground portion thereof with the intent to commit a felony or theft therein. The term *entering* has been defined as intruding any part of the body or any physical object connected with the body, or remaining concealed within. One state also includes breaking into or forcibly opening any coin-operated or vending machine or device with the intent to steal any property therein.

RECOMMENDED READING: Joseph R. Nolan and Jacqueline M. Nolan-Haley, *Black's Law Dictionary: Definitions of the Terms and Phrases of American and English Jurisprudence, Ancient and Modern*, 6th ed. (St. Paul, MN: West Publishing Co., 1991).

Lee E. Parker

C

CALIFORNIA v. HODARI D., 499 U.S. 621 (1991). An important issue concerning search and seizure recently decided by the Supreme Court. In this case the Court addressed the issue of what constitutes "seizure" under the law. The Court gave the phrase a narrow definition, thus giving law enforcement officials fairly wide latitude in dealing with potential suspects.

In this case a group of young people, including Hodari D., fled at the approach of an unmarked police car. One of the officers gave chase and came upon Hodari. Hodari did not see the officer until the officer was almost upon him, whereupon Hodari tossed away a small rock. The officer tackled Hodari, and the police recovered the rock, which turned out to be crack cocaine. In the juvenile proceedings against Hodari the court denied his motion to suppress the evidence relating to the cocaine. The state court of appeals reversed, holding that Hodari had been "seized" when he saw the officer running toward him; that his "seizure" was unreasonable under the Fourth Amendment because the police did not have the "reasonable suspicion" (to say nothing of probable cause) required to justify stopping Hodari; and therefore that the evidence had to be suppressed as the fruit of the illegal seizure.

As defined by Justice Antonin Scalia, speaking for seven members of the Court, the only issue before the Court was whether at the time he dropped the drugs Hodari had been seized within the meaning of the Fourth Amendment. Based on common-law definitions of seizure, the answer to the question was no. In the majority's view, to constitute seizure of a person there must either be the application of physical force, however slight, or, where this is absent, submission to an officer's "show of authority" to restrain the subject's liberty. No physical force had been applied. Moreover, assuming that the officer's pursuit constituted a "show of authority" enjoining Hodari to halt, Hodari did not comply with that injunction, and, therefore, he was not seized until tackled. Therefore, the cocaine abandoned while he was running was not the fruit of a seizure, and his motion to exclude evidence of it was properly denied.

David Jones

CAMPUS POLICE. That agency or subunit within an institution of higher education responsible for regulation and control of nonacademic aspects of that institution, with special reference to maintaining and enforcing law and order, security of the campus, and overall public safety for the campus community.

Although the first recognized "campus police" department was established in 1894 with two commissioned police officers by Yale University, it was not until the 1920s that the campus watchman or guard came into prominence. In the 1950s the trend changed to a more formal model as retired police officers were hired as upper-level campus administrators who tended to develop campus guard forces along a more traditional public police model. The campus-bred upheavals of the late 1960s caused officials to take a closer look at the mission and professional development of campus police nationwide.

Today there is considerable diversity in college and university police forces. There are three main types of forces. At one extreme there still exist civilian guards (or contract guard forces) who are relatively untrained and whose main duties consist of fire watch, detecting vandalism, locking and unlocking doors, and other miscellaneous maintenance problems. The second type is a more modern security force in which the guard function has been expanded to encompass pseudopolice roles even including the internal regulation of student conduct. At the other extreme, the third type is a sophisticated police force whose officers are professionally trained in law enforcement academies, have full state- or local-level peace officer authority, project a strong police image in their uniforms, equipment, and organization, and are concerned with the straightforward application of criminal and traffic laws within their respective academic institution's jurisdictions. If one categorizes institutions of higher education into two main types, private and public, the tendency appears for smaller private colleges and universities to lean toward the first two "guard or security force" types, while institutions in the second category of public colleges and state universities (along with the larger private universities) tend toward professional campus police forces, although there are exceptions in both categories.

Philip R. Orawiec

CAMPUS SECURITY ACT. More properly cited as Title IV Amendments to the Higher Education Act of 1965 (HEA): The Student Right-to-Know and Campus Security Act (Public Law 101–542). This federal legislation enacted in November 1990 was the result, in part, of lobbying efforts by numerous victims' rights groups and parents of college students who were the victims of increasing violent crime on campuses nationwide. This legislation addressed charges that for public relations purposes and perceptions, some colleges and universities hid or covered up crime statistics under the guise of "educational record privacy;" failed to properly report serious violent crime to either campus or other police authorities; or handled such serious crime through confidential and often undisclosed "internal disciplinary procedures."

In general, this act requires all institutions of higher education to disseminate a broad range of information about campus security and crime-prevention policies, publish statistics on campus crime, and provide timely warnings to the campus community about certain crimes. Among its more specific requirements, institutions are required to publish and distribute an annual security report by September 1 of each year. This annual report must also contain the following specific issues and statistics as enumerated by the act: (1) a statement of current campus policies regarding procedures and facilities for reporting crimes and emergencies, and the institution's response to such reports; (2) a statement of current policies concerning security of and access to campus facilities; (3) a statement of the status of current campus law enforcement, including authority and composition of campus police personnel, and policies encouraging reporting of crime; (4) a description of the type and frequency of various campus crime-prevention programs and procedures; (5) actual statistics on the occurrence on campus of certain crimes; (6) a statement of policy on monitoring and recording, through local police agencies, off-campus crime affecting or involving campus-related personnel, or activities; (7) statistics on arrests for drug, alcohol, and weapons violations; (8) a statement of policy on the possession, use, and sale of alcohol and illegal drugs; (9) a description of alcohol and drug-abuse education programs; (10) a statement of policy regarding the institution's programs to prevent sex offenses, and procedures to follow when a sex offense occurs; and (11) a statement of policy on how the institution provides timely warnings to the campus community on crimes that are considered to be a threat to students and employees.

This report must be distributed annually to all current and prospective students and employees. Each annual report must include crime statistics for the three most recent calendar years. The act has been modified several times since its original November 1990 enactment via the rule-making and revision procedures of the U.S. Department of Education.

Philip R. Orawiec

CARDOZO, BENJAMIN N. (1870-1938). Benjamin N. Cardozo was born in New York City on May 14, 1870. His father was a Tammany judge. Horatio Alger tutored young Benjamin, who went on to graduate from Columbia College at nineteen, then received master's and law degrees from Columbia.

Cardozo served as judge on the Supreme Court of New York (actually a court of original jurisdiction) from 1914 to 1917. From 1917 to 1932 he was associate and then chief judge on the New York Court of Appeals (the highest court in New York). He was known for the quality of his opinions, displaying a mastery of the law. His ideas were found not only in his opinions but also in his four books on the nature of law. He was concerned with the reconciling of the conflicting demands of stability and change in law.

In 1932 he succeeded Oliver Wendell Holmes on the U.S. Supreme Court. Cardozo had a reputation resembling that of Holmes. President Hoover nominated him even though the Court already had a New Yorker and a Jewish member. Cardozo served for only six years, but he made his mark. He often sided in dissent with Louis Brandeis and Harlan F. Stone in supporting the constitutionality of New Deal social legislation and in giving deference to legislative judgments in economic matters.

Cardozo authored the Supreme Court's opinion in *Palko v. Connecticut* (1937), a case involving a claim of double jeopardy, applying the due-process clause of the Fourteenth Amendment to those portions of the Bill of Rights that were fundamental (that is, a doctrine of selective incorporation). He died July 9, 1938.

RECOMMENDED READING: Joseph P. Pollard, *Mr. Justice Cardozo: A Liberal Mind in Action* (Westport, CT: Greenwood Press, 1970), Richard A. Posner, *Cardozo: A Study in Reputation* (Chicago: University of Chicago Press, 1990).

Martin Gruberg

CARJACKING. Every nineteen seconds a car is stolen in the United States, and every day about seventy automobiles are carjacked. The term *carjacking* is a relatively new word even though the crime itself is not new. The crime is committed when an unsuspecting motorist is stopped at a traffic light or a stop sign while the vehicle's motor is running. The driver is then approached by one or more thieves most likely carrying some kind of weapon at the time of the crime. The driver is then forced out of the vehicle and oftentimes hurt or killed in the process of the vehicle being stolen.

The fear of being carjacked is growing in the United States and in the process is changing the way America drives. The FBI estimates that there were 25,000 carjackings in 1993, up an alarming 25 percent from the year before. Police officers urge victims to give up their cars without a fight. In Los Angeles County nine out of ten cars are recovered within two weeks of the theft. Drivers are encouraged to "fall in love with their lives, not their cars." Officers advise motorists to keep distances between cars and not to drive in unfamiliar neighborhoods, especially with windows down. These thieves do not discriminate toward the type of car that is driven, and they do not care who the driver is.

James R. Farris

CARROLL v. UNITED STATES, 267 U.S. 132 (1925). An important federal case in which the U.S. Supreme Court first announced the vehicle exception to the warrant clause of the Fourth Amendment. The Court held that because of the nature of the automobile, in particular its mobility, law enforcement officials need not obtain a search warrant before searching such a vehicle. If the officer can demonstrate that s/he has probable cause to do so, s/he can stop a vehicle and search it.

David Jones

CASH BAIL BOND. A form of bail in which the defendant deposits the full amount of the surety, in cash, with the court. It is most typically used in cases where the charge is less serious and the amount of bail set is relatively low.

RECOMMENDED READING: Joseph R. Nolan and Jacqueline M. Nolan-Haley, *Black's Law Dictionary: Definitions of the Terms and Phrases of American and English Jurisprudence, Ancient and Modern*, 6th ed. (St. Paul, MN: West Publishing Co., 1991).

David Jones

CHAPMAN v. CALIFORNIA, 386 U.S. 18 (1967). This case dealt with the issue of "harmless error" as it relates to violations of the exercise of federal constitutional rights. The facts in this case were as follows: Petitioner Chapman was convicted following a California state criminal trial during which the prosecutor, as then permitted under the California constitution, commented extensively on the refusal of the defendant to testify at trial. Defendant was convicted.

After the trial, but before appeals began, the U.S. Supreme Court ruled, in the case of *Griffin v. California (1965)*, that the relevant provision of the California constitution was an unconstitutional violation of defendant's Fifth Amendment rights. Though admitting that petitioner had been denied a federal constitutional right, the California Supreme Court, applying the state's "harmless error" doctrine, upheld the conviction.

The question before the Supreme Court was twofold: Where there is a violation of *Griffin v. California*, (1) can error be held to be harmless, and (2) if so, was the error harmless in this case? The Court held that since a federal constitutional right was in question, federal criteria concerning "harmless error" should be applied. The federal criterion is: Was there a reasonable possibility that the evidence complained of might have contributed to the petitioner's conviction? If the possibility was present, harmless error could not be invoked. The Court argued that while harmless error is possible, even when constitutional rights are violated, in this case the trial court's error was not "harmless." Consequently, the conviction was reversed.

Ransom A. Whittle

CHARGE TO JURY. Also known as jury instructions. This is the process by which the judge explains, or tries to explain, the law of the case to the jury before it begins its deliberations. Typically, this is done after the prosecution and the defense have concluded their presentations. It is usually the last thing the jury hears before it begins its deliberations. In many jurisdictions the lawyers for each side will submit proposed instructions to the judge before s/he prepares them and delivers them to the jury.

Jury instructions are appealable, and it has happened that verdicts have been overturned because an appeals court held that the trial judge's instructions were legally defective. Consequently, judges often craft instructions to meet legal requirements. Unfortunately, according to many critics, this has meant that instructions are not given in plain English and are thus difficult for the jury to understand. The fact that jurors may have misunderstood the instructions is not a basis for a successful appeal. Many legal reformers have advocated a change to the greater use of plain English in jury instructions, and in some jurisdictions this reform has made some progress.

RECOMMENDED READING: Jeffrey Abramson, *We, the Jury* (New York: Basic Books, 1994); Stephen J. Adler, *The Jury* (New York: Random House, 1994); Jerome Frank, *Courts on Trial* (New York: Atheneum, 1963);

David Jones

CHARGING (THE PROCESS). The charge is the criminal violation of which the arrestee is accused. Depending upon the seriousness of the charge that resulted in an arrest, a member of the prosecutor's office may be present at the police station and take part in the investigatory process by reviewing evidence, questioning victims, witnesses, and the police, interrogating prisoners, and taking statements. The law requires the prisoner to be brought before a court within thirty-six hours of arrest for the opportunity of a probable-cause hearing before a judge. This limits the time available for the booking process. So far, the police have been the principal criminal justice actors in the procedure involving receipt of the report of a crime, the preliminary investigation, and the arrest and booking process. From this point on the principal figure is the prosecutor of the county in which the criminal offense occurred or the judge. The prisoner is transported to the courthouse and detained there by custodial personnel. The victim (the complaining witness or complainant in the case) and/or the arresting or investigating officer in the case appear in the complaint room of the court and are interviewed by a complaint clerk. The complaint clerk, usually an assistant prosecutor, verifies existence of probable cause that the person arrested committed a criminal offense, then prepares an appropriate accusatory instrument that will be filed in the court at the initial appearance of the defendant (the prisoner is now referred to as the defendant). The filing of this charge commences the criminal action and may form the basis of prosecution.

RECOMMENDED READING: Patricia Mary Harris, *Offenders in Criminal and Juvenile Courts: A Comparison of Charging and Sentencing Practices*, Ph.D. thesis (Newark, NJ: Rutgers University Graduate School, 1985); Irving J. Klein, *Constitutional Law for Criminal Justice Professionals*, 3rd ed. (South Miami, FL: Coral Gables Publishing Co., 1992).

Christopher J. Morse

CHIMEL v. CALIFORNIA, 395 U.S. 752 (1969). The leading case dealing with the permissible scope under the Fourth Amendment of a search incident to a lawful arrest. The Court held that a search incident to a legal arrest is legal because the suspect may be armed, may have a means of escape, or may try to destroy evidence held on his person. However, the law enforcement officer is limited to a search of the person arrested and the area into which an arrestee might reach in order to grasp a weapon or evidentiary items. The officer cannot, generally, go beyond that without a search warrant.

In this case officers visited Mr. Chimel's house with an arrest warrant but not a search warrant. Chimel was not in, but his wife allowed the officers to enter the home and wait. When Chimel arrived at his home, he was arrested. The officers then asked if they could look around the house. Chimel demurred. Despite this, the officers proceeded to search every room in the house, and they found incriminating materials. These were entered as evidence in Chimel's trial, and Chimel was convicted. Although state courts held that the search was incident to a legal arrest (and hence valid), the U.S. Supreme Court reversed their decisions on the basis that the police had gone too far in their search after they had arrested Chimel.

David Jones

CIRCUMSTANIAL EVIDENCE. Evidence that indirectly proves a fact. It is a form of evidence that requires the trier of fact to make an inference or use a presumption to prove the existence of a fact. For example, proof that the defendant was in the vicinity of the victim during the period of time in which the victim was killed might be used as circumstantial evidence against the defendant in a murder trial.

Circumstantial evidence may be used to establish any element of a crime charged. For instance, evidence that the defendant hated the victim might be used to help establish intent to commit murder on the part of the accused. Circumstantial evidence can also be used to establish guilt; for example, possession of stolen property may lead to an inference that the possessor took the material in question illegally. Flight to avoid detention may be used as circumstantial evidence in the proof of guilt.

Circumstantial evidence may be admitted into trial by the trial judge, who must consider, among other things, the relevance of the material submitted. While circumstantial evidence may not always be as compelling as direct evidence (in part because other inferences besides guilt may be drawn from it), it is not considered to be inferior evidence. The Supreme Court has upheld convictions based solely on circumstantial evidence.

RECOMMENDED READING: John C. Klotter, *Criminal Evidence*, 6th ed. (Cincinnati: Anderson Publishing Co., 1996); Christopher B. Mueller and Laird C. Kirkpatrick, *Evidence Under the Rules*, 3rd ed. (Boston: Little, Brown, and Co., 1996).

David Jones

CLASSICAL SCHOOL OF CRIMINOLOGY. As thinking in Western European culture evolved, a number of ideas generated by thinkers of the Enlightenment such as Montesquieu, Voltaire, Hobbes, Locke, and Rousseau, especially social contract notions, were formulated into a set of principles both for dealing with crime and, by implication, for a theory of behavior. In his *Dei delitti e delle pene* of 1764, Cesare Bonesana, Marchese di Beccaria, crystallized a set of their ideas that offered a systematic approach to balancing punishments with crime in a humane, consistent, and rational way. Beccaria's intent was to forcefully reject the superstition and injustice that had typified the jurisprudence of his era. Classical criminology focused on the concepts of crime and punishment as opposed to a focus on the criminal or his intent, as has emerged in positivist criminology.

The assumptions that underlie this system include that society must strive for the greatest happiness for the greatest number (the social contract), that man can rationally choose his destiny through reason and knowledge, that man is hedonistic and will base behavior on reward and punishment, that punishment should be proportional to the harm done to society, and that punishments should be swift and certain to foster positive behavioral change in individuals who deviate from the laws.

The classical notions of behavior and the relationship of crime to punishment in affecting behavior have persisted in our culture. The current state of affairs is called neoclassicism and holds the same basic tenets while allowing some adjustments to the calculation of the relationship between crime and punishments for mitigating or aggravating circumstances such as insanity, biological conditions, patterns of conduct, and life traumas experienced by individuals accused of crime. Classical notions have removed much that was arbitrary from our jurisprudence, while neoclassicism now allows us to account for variations in human conditions. This current state of affairs remains exceptionally flexible and evolutionary as advancing knowledge and insights about the causes and correlates of behavior are developed.

RECOMMENDED READING: Cesare Beccaria, *On Crimes and Punishments*, translated by Henry Paolucci (New York: Bobbs-Merrill, 1963); Jeremy Bentham, *An Introduction to the Principles of Morals and Legislation* (London: Printed for T. Payne and Son, 1789); Eric Goode, *Deviant Behavior*, 5th ed. (Upper Saddle River, NJ: Prentice Hall, 1997).

David R. Struckhoff

CLEMENCY. A generic term covering legal processes that result in an act of leniency or determination to mitigate some consequence of a sentence. Although the word *clemency* does not appear in the U.S. Constitution, Article II provides that the President "shall have power to grant Reprieves and Pardons for Offenses against the United States, except in cases of impeachment." Looking to common-law origins of the constitutional provision, the U.S. Supreme Court has recognized—in addition to reprieves and pardons—the following forms of clemency: amnesty (*Ex parte Garland*, 1866; *United States v. Klein*, 1871; *Brown v. Walker*, 1896), commutation (*Ex parte Wells*, 1856; *Biddle v. Perovich*, 1927), and remission of fines and forfeitures (*Illinois Central Railroad v. Bosworth*, 1890).

The clemency process was the responsibility of the State Department from 1789 to 1854. From 1854 to 1891 the attorney general or an assistant controlled the process while under the supervision of the State Department. An 1891 act of Congress (26 Stat. 946) created the Office of the Pardon Attorney in the Department of Justice in order to prepare cases for the president to consider.

The president's ability to exercise the clemency power cannot be modified, abridged, or diminished by Congress (*Schick v. Reed*, 1974), and, in all like-lihood, clemency is exercised with much greater frequency than the average American might assume. The pardon of Richard Nixon was, in fact, one of over three hundred pardons issued during the Ford administration. Jimmy Carter's controversial commutation of the sentence of Patricia Hearst was one of thirty-two commutations issued during his administration. Carter also issued over five hundred pardons. In the period 1900 to 1993 presidents averaged over two hundred acts of clemency per year.

Clemency power rests with the governor alone in twenty-nine states. Most have established advisory bodies that make nonbinding recommendations. In sixteen states the governor shares the power to make clemency decisions with an administrative board or panel. In the five remaining states an administrative panel (usually appointed by the governor) has the principal authority to make clemency decisions. Only a handful of states have promulgated statutory or administrative standards for use of the power.

RECOMMENDED READING: Kellie Dworaczyk, *After the Death Sentence: Appeals, Clemency, and Representation* (Austin, TX: House Research Organization, 1994); David L. Sartori, *Executive Clemency: Threat, Challenge, or Perversion?* (Milwaukee: Wisconsin Law Enforcement Officers Association, 197?).

Peter S. Ruckman, Jr.

CLERK OF COURT. The custodian of all legal documents and records of judicial proceedings. At the appellate level in most states and throughout the entire federal system the person who fills this position is appointed by the court and serves at its pleasure. However, in most states the clerk of court for trial courts is an elected official, often selected in a partisan election for a fixed term. Because of this selection method and be-cause the clerk may be re-elected for several terms, the person holding this position may be relatively independent of the judge(s) s/he is supposed to serve.

The powers and duties of the clerk of court vary according to state law, but in general, s/he has the responsibility of scheduling cases, managing juror selection, collecting fees, and maintaining court records. Clerks are often locally oriented individuals who are not specifically trained for their positions. Because of these characteristics, clerks of court are seen by some as obstacles to the efficient and effective administration of local courts.

RECOMMENDED READING: N. Gary Holten and Lawson L. Lamar, *The Criminal Courts: Structures, Personnel, and Processes* (New York: McGraw-Hill, 1991); David W. Neubauer, *America's Courts and the Criminal Justice System*, 5th ed. (Belmont, CA: Wadsworth Publishing Company, 1996).

David Jones

CLOSING ARGUMENT. The last words given to the jury by each of the parties in a case. The order of presentation in criminal cases varies among jurisdictions. In some the prosecution presents the first part of its closing argument first. This is followed by the defense's closing argument, which is followed, in turn, by the prosecution's final closing argument. In others the defense presents its closing arguments, and these are followed by the prosecution's. In either instance, since the burden of proof is on the prosecution, it gets the last word.

The goal of each side is to present the elements of its case that counsel believes might be most persuasive to the jury. New evidence is not presented at this point. The arguments presented must be based on evidence already admitted; references to material that was suppressed are forbidden, as are inflammatory arguments and appeals to prejudice. Each side is given a time limit (of equal length) by the judge, and each is expected to stay within it. Since this is the "last shot" counsel gets before the jury, it is seen as being very important. Because of this, most trial attorneys work very hard at making their closing arguments as good as possible.

RECOMMENDED READING: Jonathan D. Schiffman, *Fundamentals of the Criminal Justice Process*, 3rd ed. (Deerfield, IL: Clark Boardman Callaghan, 1994); Jon R. Waltz, *Introduction to Criminal Evidence*, 4th ed. (Chicago: Nelson Hall Publishers, 1997).

David Jones

COCAINE. Cocaine is a drug made by processing the leaves of the coca plant, which is found in several South American countries. In particular, Colombia, Peru, and Bolivia have large numbers of coca plants. Originally, the native population as a method of using the drug chewed the leaves of the plant. Cocaine provides a sense of energy and euphoria to its users. When first purified from coca leaves by Albert Niemann, a German chemist, cocaine was viewed as a wonder drug. It was thought to have no detrimental physical addicting effect, and was touted as a cure for medical problems such as alcoholism and for use as a local anesthetic. Until 1914, when its use was restricted by law, cocaine was widely used by a large percentage of the American population. As the severe psychologically addicting effects of cocaine became apparent, the medical profession moved away from the use of cocaine as a prescription drug. Illegal use of cocaine began to rise in the late 1970s and early 1980s. The death of several famous people from the use of cocaine and its spread into middle-class suburbia led the Reagan administration to launch the war on drugs. Research has shown that the number of people using the drug has declined. However, after marijuana, it remains the most popular illicit drug. The distribution of cocaine has become a multibillion-dollar illegal industry in the United States.

RECOMMENDED READING: Drug Enforcement Administration, *Drugs of Abuse* (Washington, D.C.: U.S. Department of Justice, 1990); National Narcotics Intelligence Consumer's Committee, *The NNICC Report: The Supply of Illicit Drugs to the United States* (Washington, D.C.: NNICC, 1995).

Glenn Zuern

COKE, SIR EDWARD (1552-1634). An English lawyer and judge who was very influential in the development of the English common law. His writings (published posthumously in 1641) include the *Institutes* and thirteen volumes of *Reports*. These did much to enhance the importance and understanding of the common law.

Coke was also important for his exaltation of an independent judiciary by seeking through his decisions and practice to limit the power of the monarchy and that of the ecclesiastical (church-related) courts that were powerful in England of his time. One of Coke's most famous decisions was a dispute in 1610 between Dr. Thomas Bonham and the Royal College of Physicians. In this case Coke wrote that a law passed by Parliament was contrary to a basic principle of the common law. He held that the common law constituted the fundamental law of the land, to which the king and Parliament were subordinate. Thus the actions of both the legislature and the king were susceptible to review by judges and could be overruled by them if found to be in conflict with the higher law. Some authorities see in this ruling the origin of the doctrine of judicial review.

RECOMMENDED READING: Jesse Turner, *Concerning Divers Notable Stirs Between Sir Edward Coke and His Lady* (St. Louis: Nixon-Jones Printing Co., 1918).

David Jones

COKER v. GEORGIA, 433 U.S. 584 (1977). One of many death-penalty cases decided by the U.S. Supreme Court following its seminal decision in *Gregg v. Georgia*. In this case the Court held that Georgia's death penalty for rape was unconstitutional because it was forbidden by the Eighth Amendment to the Constitution as "cruel and unusual" punishment. Justice Byron White wrote the opinion of the Court, joined by three other members. Three other justices concurred in the result.

While serving various sentences for murder, rape, kidnapping, and aggravated assault, Lawrence Coker escaped from a Georgia prison. During his short period of freedom Coker raped an adult woman in the course of committing an armed robbery and other offenses. He was caught, tried, and convicted of rape and other offenses. Coker was sentenced to death on the rape charge when the jury found two of the aggravating circumstances present for invoking such a sentence, namely, that the rape was committed (1) by a person with prior capital felony convictions and (2) in the course of committing another capital felony, armed robbery.

The Court concluded that the sentence of death for the crime of rape was grossly disproportionate and excessive punishment and was therefore forbidden by the Eighth Amendment. In the view of Justice White, who wrote the Court's opinion, the Eighth Amendment bars not only those punishments that are "barbaric" but also those that are "excessive" in relation to the crime committed. A punishment is "excessive" and unconstitutional if it (1) makes no measurable contribution to acceptable goals of punishment and hence is nothing more than the purposeless and needless imposition of pain and suffering or (2) is grossly out of proportion to the severity of the crime.

Justice White reasoned that the fact that Georgia was, at the time, the only state imposing the death penalty for rape of an adult woman strongly indicated that the punishment was disproportionate. Moreover, although rape is serious and deserves serious punishment, the death penalty—unique because of its severity and its irrevocability—is an excessive penalty for the rapist who, as such (and as opposed to the murderer), does not unjustifiably take human life.

David Jones

COLLATERAL CHALLENGE. For a defendant whose appeal of a guilty verdict is unsuccessful, a collateral challenge may be the only other means available to attack the conviction. These include such measures as *habeas corpus* proceedings in the state or federal courts or a writ of *certiorari* to the U.S. Supreme Court.

RECOMMENDED READING: J. Scott Harr and Karen M. Hess, *Constitutional Law for Criminal Justice Professionals* (Belmont, CA: Wadsworth Publishing, 1997); Irving J. Klein, *Constitutional Law for Criminal Justice Professionals*, 3rd ed. (South Miami, FL: Coral Gables Publishing Co., 1992).

Christopher J. Morse

COLLATERAL ESTOPPEL. The doctrine that when an issue of ultimate fact has once been determined by a valid and final judgment, that issue cannot again be litigated by the same parties in any future lawsuit. It was developed in civil litigation in order to bring finality to an issue and (by barring relitigation of settled issues) to conserve judicial resources. It has also been applied to criminal litigation in the United States for most of the twentieth century. In the case of *Ashe v. Swenson* (1970) the U.S. Supreme Court held that the Fifth Amendment guarantee against double jeopardy, applicable to the states through the Fourteenth Amendment, embodies collateral estoppel as a constitutional requirement.

RECOMMENDED READING: Lester Brickman, "Collateral Estoppel as a Basis for Attorney Discipline: The Next Step," in *Georgetown Journal of Legal Ethics*, Vol. 5, no. 1 (Summer 1991): 1–33; Craig R. Callen, "Efficiency After All: A Reply to Professor Flanagan's Theory of Offensive Collateral Estoppel," in *Arizona State Law Journal*, Vol. 1983, no. 4: 799–834; Warren Freedman, *Res Judicata and Collateral Estoppel: Tools for Plaintiffs and Defendants* (New York: Quorum Books, 1988).

David Jones

COLORADO v. KELLY, **479 U.S. 157 (1986).** In this case the U.S. Supreme Court addressed the issue of whether, absent state coercion, a defendant's mental state should enter into the calculation of the voluntariness of his/her confession. The Court held that coercive police activity is a necessary predicate to finding that a confession is not "voluntary" within the meaning of the due-process clause. In this case, since law enforcement officers had acted properly, the defendant's confession should be considered voluntary even though a psychiatrist testified that the defendant was suffering from chronic schizophrenia.

David Jones

COMMUNITY POLICING.   Community policing has been adopted in various forms in over 300 agencies nationwide. While there is no formal definition of what is meant by the term, the philosophy of community policing indicates a change in the direction of policing in U.S. society. For some, it represents a fundamental shift from incident-driven and reactive policing to problem-oriented or proactive policing. Others however have criticized community policing as an effort to legitimate police actions and placate citizens' fears through the manipulation of symbols such as "community control" or "citizen participation."

While community policing appears in many forms, there are two core components in most initiatives. These are a commitment to community involvement and cooperation and a commitment to a problem-solving approach (Bureau of Justice Assistance 1994). Geographic decentralization and decentralization of decision making to the lowest level of the organization are common. Many other elements have been incorporated into some programs, including efforts to make environmental changes, and cooperation with neighborhood organizations and other social service agencies. Use of foot and/or bike patrols is also common.

Many community policing efforts attempt to involve citizens in solving neighborhood problems. Community policing seeks to increase the degree of responsibility citizens feel for their neighborhood's quality of life as well as increasing cooperation between the citizens and police. Involvement ranges from participation in neighborhood crime watches and patrols to calling police hot lines. The model calls upon the police to listen to the wants and desires of citizens and subsequently to act upon them.

One problem with this approach is in determining community norms and desires. This is often due to the lack of citizen participation in community groups and the fact that some neighborhoods appear to have a lack of shared norms (Mastrofski 1988). Critics have also noted that it is often the more powerful and wealthy citizens whose views dominate these groups (Mastrofski 1988).

Community policing also advocates problem-oriented policing, a process in which problems are systematically defined and researched, rather than simply responding to calls for service. Alternative solutions are then explored through an interactive process involving both the police and the community (Goldstein 1979), sometimes using a computerized problem-solving model. This perspective is intended to enhance a police officer's ability to look at the "big picture" instead of viewing problems as a series of isolated incidents (Reichers and Roberg 1990). Community policing allows officers to work on particular problems for extended time periods in attempts to solve them.

A common technique of many community policing efforts is to have officers work the same "beat" or area on a regular basis. This activity allows officers to establish ties with the community, while still enforcing the law. This activity also improves relations between the community and the police by increasing officers' opportunities for positive, nonconflictual relations with local residents and businesses. These interactions are intended to improve future cooperation as residents get to know and trust their community policing officer.

Community policing, while seen as a new concept by many, actually incorporates modern technology with some traditional practices. Officers in the "political" era of policing between the 1840s and the early 1900s performed a wide variety of services to citizens (Kelling and Moore 1988). In addition to crime prevention, control, and order maintenance, the police assisted with soup lines, provided brief lodging for immigrants, and helped immigrants in their search for work. Police officers during this period often resided in the neighborhood where they patrolled on foot.

Similarly, modern community policing programs attempt to broaden the officers' purpose from merely reacting to crimes to improving the quality of life in the community. For example, departments seek to eradicate drugs in the community through application of concentrated drug-law enforcement practices (see **Concentrated Drug-Law Enforcement**).

Community policing is a concept that has recently received a great deal of attention, as well as federal and state funding. This attention is likely to increase as more agencies incorporate elements of the community policing philosophy into their operations.

RECOMMENDED READING: Bureau of Justice Assistance, *Understanding Community Policing: A Framework for Action* (Washington, DC: The Bureau, 1994); H. Goldstein, "Improving Policing: A Problem Oriented Approach," *Crime and Delinquency* 25, (1979): 236–258; G. L. Kelling and M. H. Moore, "The Evolving Strategy of Policing," *Perspectives on Policing* 4 (Washington DC: National Institute of Justice and Harvard University, 1988); L. M. Reichers and R. R. Roberg, "Community Policing: A Critical Review of Underlying Assumptions," *Journal of Police Science and Administration* Vol. 1990, no. 17: 105–114; Robert Trojanowicz and B. Bucqueroux, *Community Policing: A Contemporary Perspective* (Cincinnati: Anderson Publishing, 1990).

C. Aaron McNeece

COMMUTATION. One of several forms of clemency in which a milder punishment is substituted for the punishment imposed by a court. A president or governor may, for example, "commute" a death sentence to life imprisonment or reduce the sentence for a given period to a shorter period. A commutation may even merely modify the conditions of imprisonment (e.g., transferring a prisoner from a pentientiary to a reformatory or transferring a prisoner to an asylum for the insane). In practice, commutations are typically granted in consequences of an offense.

Like the pardon, a commutation may also be conditional. In 1971, for example, Richard Nixon commuted the thirteen-year sentence of James R. Hoffa (convicted for mail fraud and jury tampering) to time served under the condition that Hoffa refrain from "direct or indirect management of any labor organization." If the condition was violated, Hoffa was to return to prison in order to serve the remainder of his sentence. The Supreme Court has ruled that conditions placed on commutations (1) must not "offend" the Constitution, (2) cannot "aggravate" the existing sentence, and (3) must be properly "accepted" (*Schick v. Reed*, 1974).

RECOMMENDED READING: Joseph R. Nolan and Jacqueline M. Nolan-Haley, *Black's Law Dictionary: Definitions of the Terms and Phrases of American and English Jurisprudence, Ancient and Modern*, 6th ed. (St. Paul, MN: West Publishing Co., 1991).

Peter S. Ruckman, Jr.

COMPREHENSIVE DRUG ABUSE PREVENTION AND CONTROL ACT. This 1984 act is a major revision of the Omnibus Crime Control Act of 1968 and other federal statutes and acts. Major impetus for the passage of this act, along with many of its provisions, was the war on drugs launched by the Reagan administration. The Controlled Substances Penalties, the Comprehensive Forfeiture Act, and the National Narcotic Act all came out of this act and were related to the war on drugs.

Troy D. Livingston

COMPUTER-AIDED DISPATCH (CAD). Computer-aided dispatch (CAD) is an automated system, composed of computer and radio communication hardware and software, that is designed to allow manually operated dispatch systems to become faster, more accurate, and more efficient through its functions. Some CAD functions include maintaining the status of forces, vehicle monitoring, recommending units for responses, providing histories of calls to addresses, assignment of case numbers, and prioritizing calls. CAD systems vary due to the needs of different agencies, the type of equipment being used, and the management style of those implementing such a system.

RECOMMENDED READING: Lee Ellis and Wilburt Reichert, *A Computer-Assisted Dispatch System for Small Police Departments* (Champaign, IL: Community Technology, 1975); Public Technology, Inc., *Uniform Design for a Computer Aided Dispatch System* (Washington, DC: The Corporation, 1979); Sachs/Freeman Associates and Chicago Fire Department, *CAD Center Dispatch Operations: Deficiencies and Corrections* (Lake Bluff, IL: Sachs/Freeman, 1985).

Troy D. Livingston

COMPUTER-AIDED INVESTIGATIONS (CAI). Computer-aided investigations (CAI) refers to an agency or investigator using computer technology as a tool for inquiry or crime fighting. The computer aids investigations by gathering information from volumes of known data about individuals and groups of criminals and their methods of operation. The knowledge gained in CAI allows for the correlation of information about other crimes. This helps indicate which crimes are likely to occur and who may be committing them. In other words, CAI assists in predictability, which allows law enforcement to engage in crime prevention and criminal apprehension.

RECOMMENDED READING: Joseph Theodore Jadick, *The Use of Computers in Crime Analysis*, M.B.A. thesis (San Diego State University, 1979).

Troy D. Livingston

CONCENTRATED DRUG-LAW ENFORCEMENT. Concentrated drug-law enforcement, often known as drug crackdowns, is a direct result of President Reagan's 1982 declaration of a war on drugs. Legislation in 1982 provided greater restrictions on both pretrial release and post-conviction bail for drug-law violators. Warrantless searches, an increase in court-authorized wiretaps, increased urine testing, and legal confiscation of drug offenders' property have all been used during the past decade in concentrated drug-law enforcement. Special federal funding was made available to communities under the Anti–Drug Abuse Act of 1988. There are some concerns that all of these measures may represent a serious departure from traditional due-process guarantees under the Constitution (Wisotsky 1987).

Some evidence indicates that street-level crackdowns on drug markets not only reduce drug crime, but reduce associated crimes (burglary and robbery), as well as drug use. Other evidence indicates that concentrated drug-law enforcement in a community simply shifts the geographic location of drug crimes and related activities to adjacent neighborhoods that do not employ such crackdowns (Kleiman et al. 1988). A later study (Reed, Graham, and Uchida 1993) found that concentrated drug-law enforcement is effective only as long as a high-profile police presence remains in the community. Some cities are now experimenting with crackdown follow-up efforts by opening ministations in the neighborhood, deploying foot patrols, using state or local building-code laws to evict occupants of "crack houses," or, in extreme cases, using eminent-domain and nuisance-abatement laws to condemn such property. Concentrated drug-law enforcement is an integral part of almost all community policing projects in the nation (see **Community Policing**), since a common objective of community policing is to reduce drug crimes.

RECOMMENDED READING: M. Kleiman, A. Barnett, A. Bouza, and K Burke, *Street-Level Drug Enforcement: Examining the Issues* (Washington, DC: Government Printing Office, 1988); W. Reed, M. Graham, and C. Uchida, *Searching for Answers: Annual Evaluation Report on Drugs and Crime* (Washington, DC: Government Printing Office, 1993); S. Wisotsky, "The Emerging 'Drug Exception' to the Bill of Rights," *Hastings Law Journal*, Vol. 1987, no. 38: 889-926.

C. Aaron McNeece

CONFESSION. A statement by the accused that s/he committed a particular crime. It is broader than an admission. To be admissible as evidence in court, a confession must be voluntary. At the very least, this means that the confession cannot be coerced. The issue of coercion has frequently been addressed by the U.S. Supreme Court in such renowned cases as *Ashcraft v. Tennessee (1944)* and *Miranda v. Arizona(1966)*. The Court has held that receipt in evidence of a coerced confession will result in the reversal of a conviction even if other evidence was presented that could support the finding of guilty. That is, the admission of a coerced confession cannot constitute "harmless error." It is important that other evidence corroborate confessions, because it is not unknown for individuals to "confess" to crimes they did not actually commit.

RECOMMENDED READING: Joseph D. Grano, *Confessions, Truth, and the Law* (Ann Arbor: University of Michigan Press, 1993); Joseph R. Nolan and Jacqueline M. Nolan-Haley, *Black's Law Dictionary: Definitions of the Terms and Phrases of American and English Jurisprudence, Ancient and Modern*, 6th ed. (St. Paul, MN: West Publishing Co., 1991); Jon R. Waltz, *Introduction to Criminal Evidence*, 4th ed. (Chicago: Nelson-Hall Publishers, 1997).

David Jones

CONFLICT THEORY. Conflict theorists in the social sciences emphasize the divisions and struggles between diverse social groups and interests. Conflict theory is frequently contrasted to consensus perspectives that stress underlying agreements and core values in society. Applied to criminal justice studies, a conflict approach will focus upon the relationship between crime and social interests. In this perspective the application of justice may be unequal across various social groups (e.g., studies that emphasize the differential treatment received by the poor or by racial minorities in the criminal justice system), the definition of crime may be biased by social interests, and criminal activity per se will be rooted ultimately in the social structure as an expression of conflict. George Vold, for example, argued that crime often reflects a challenge by subordinate groups to more powerful groups.

Radical, critical, and Marxist criminology are closely associated with conflict theory. In a Marxist perspective the state is portrayed as a means by which the power of the dominant social class is maintained and its interests (such as the protection of property) are defended. Marxist criminologists, such as Richard Quinney, have emphasized the degree to which the definition of crime carries a class bias. For example, predations committed by the wealthy classes are far less likely to be criminalized (for example, corporate malfeasance that causes injury, even physical injury and death) than those perpetrated by lower classes in the social order.

Carl Klockars made a significant criticism of Marxist criminology from a positivist perspective that charged radical criminologists with placing ideology above scientific objectivity. Conflict theorists themselves are divided between those who underscore the "scientific" status of their work and those who highlight their belief that criminal justice research should be "critical," that is to say, contributing to social change rather than simply reflecting social reality. Not all conflict theory is radical or Marxist; some, such as Georg Simmel's, portrays social action (including theory and research) as a complex interplay of subjective interests and cultural differences.

RECOMMENDED READING: William D. Bales, *Race and Class Effects on Criminal Justice Prosecution and Punishment Decisions: A Test of Some Conflict Theory Propositions*, Ph.D. thesis, (Florida state University, 1987); Carl Klockars, "The Contemporary Crisis of Marxist Criminology," *Criminology* 16 (Fall 1979): 477–515; Richard Quinney, *The Social Reality of Crime* (Boston: Little, Brown, and Co., 1970); George Vold, *Theoretical Criminology* (New York: Oxford University Press, 1958).

Daniel Skidmore-Hess

CONJUGAL VISITATION.   The word *conjugal*, in its most literal form, concerns the rights and activities associated with marriage or the activities that exist between a husband and a wife. In more recent times, however, the word has become associated with the sexual aspects of those activities that exist between married persons. Consequently, conjugal rights and conjugal visitation have become issues for those married persons who otherwise do not have the option of sexual contact available to them in their normal course of life. This implies that those most interested in conjugal visitation are those forced by circumstance to be separated, which makes it of central interest to those incarcerated within the correctional system.

Conjugal visitation is the practice whereby an inmate and his or her spouse spend private time together in housing located on prison grounds. While together, the inmate and spouse are not prohibited from engaging in sexual relations. While not uncommon in present correctional environments, conjugal visitations are far from typical. It is agreed that the informal process that established the practice of conjugal visits began around 1900 at the Mississippi State Prison at Parchman. The Parchman prison, which was built from the Parchman plantation, was originally divided into camps that housed 150–200 inmates. Each of these "camps" (with the exception of the maximum-security camp) contained a "red house" that was the space maintained for conjugal visits. Following this model, a few facilities in a few states, specifically California, Minnesota, New York, and South Carolina, created conjugal visitation programs. Other states and institutions (such as California) extended these visits to include social interaction between parents and children. These visits differed from the usual prison visit in that the time allowed was greater, the environment was more relaxed and casual, and the supervision was less restrictive. Nationally, however, the process never became mainstream, even though the advantages and successes were apparent from the experiences at Parchman, as well as in other institutions.

Operators and administrators of facilities have acknowledge that the inmates who receive conjugal visitation are happier and more relaxed. Given that the goal of the prison, be it rehabilitation, incarceration, retribution, or deterrence, is not significantly diminished by the use of these visits and in fact may be enhanced, it seems curious that the process has not achieved greater acceptance.

Those who support conjugal visitation base their beliefs on four main issues: (1) the idea that conjugal visitation decreases sexual tension among inmates and may reduce the incidence of homosexual rape; (2) the idea that conjugal visitation as a reward for good behavior enhances the administrative control over the inmate and improves the behavior of the inmate, making him more likely to take part in programs and ultimately benefit from the process of incarceration; (3) the fact that familial visits allow the inmate to maintain emotional bonds with spouse and family, which enhances the prospects for return to normal life on the outside and decreases the chances of further adult criminal activity, as well as decreasing the chances of delinquency for the children of the inmates; and (4) the idea that conjugal visits serve to maintain marital stability, which improves the quality of life for both the inmate and the spouse.

Those opposed to conjugal visitation cite practical reasons for this opposition, many of which are the result of attempting to provide disparate services while maintaining the security, economic viability, and efficiency of the institution. Opposition to these visits focuses on the interaction of the inmates, the public's perception of the duties of a prison, and the impact these visits could have on the inmates' spouses. Those opposed to conjugal visitation believe that the process could produce unfair practices, and inmates who were qualified for conjugal visits might not receive them due to the informal way these visits would be offered. This could result in a situation of inequality and possibly constitutional violations. In addition, those morally opposed to such practices see the potential for personal and institutional degradation, in that the prison would become a "whorehouse" that could corrupt both the inmate and the correctional officer and take a heavy toll on the human dignity of the inmate's spouse, who becomes viewed as a release for sexual energy rather than a person. Conjugal visitation is by its very nature a paradox. Allowing noninmates into an institution for the purposes of emotional or sexual gratification, while maintaining the security and integrity of the facility, is inherently problematic. Institutions consider inmates to be the property of the state; consequently, these institutions are less concerned about forcing upon inmates "indignities" for the security of the facility and the public. Spouses, however, are not the property of the state and are not as easily searched. Therefore, allowing persons into the institution for an extended period of time, in unsupervised surroundings, has the potential to present significant risks to institutional security. Society has been slow to support the idea of conjugal visitation, and with the continued financial strains created within these institutions by ever-burgeoning populations, finding the extra money to support these programs has become increasingly difficult.

Other societies, specifically those in Central and South America, have long allowed conjugal visitation, and it is an accepted and respected part of their correctional systems. Despite other less modern aspects of these societies, Central and South American prisons often have very progressive attitudes and operations. Nicaragua, for example, considers conjugal visitation a right and uses conjugal visits to encourage the social and educational aspects of incarceration. Visits by family and friends are the results of good behavior and the inmate adopting an attitude of reform. The incentive of conjugal visitation is unlike many of the other incentives utilized to encourage reform among the inmates, in that conjugal visits both motivate the inmate and provide something unavailable within the confines of the prison, as well as helping to maintain links to the outside society.

RECOMMENDED READING: Bonnie E. Carlson and Neil Cervera, "Inmates and Their Families: Criminal Justice, Family Contact, and Family Functioning," *Criminal Justice Behavior*, Vol. 18, no. 3 (1991): 318–331; Ramaswamy Sundararaman, *Conjugal Visitation Program of the California State Department of Corrections*, M. S. thesis (California State University, Long Beach, 1982).

Matthew C. Leone

CONTROLLED SUBSTANCE. A controlled substance is any substance that is subject to governmental regulation. Generally, the term *controlled substance* relates to illegal drugs. However, alcohol, prescription drugs, and gasoline are all controlled substances.

RECOMMENDED READING: Joseph R. Nolan and Jacqueline M. Nolan-Haley, *Black's Law Dictionary: Definitions of the Terms and Phrases of American and English Jurisprudence, Ancient and Modern*, 6th ed. (St. Paul, MN: West Publishing Co., 1991).

Glenn Zuern

CONTROLLED SUBSTANCES ACT. This 1970 act combined and refined most of the existing drug controls that were currently in place. It placed substances in one of five schedules and defined specific offenses and sanctions for illicit use of drugs within each of the five schedules. The Controlled Substances Act was amended by the Comprehensive Crime Control Act of 1984. The five schedules were modified, and sanctions were passed regarding the distribution of drugs and drug dealing in or near schools. The reform of the Controlled Substances Act was heavily influenced by the ongoing war on drugs.

Glenn Zuern

COOLIDGE v. NEW HAMPSHIRE, **403 U.S. 443 (1971).** An important Fourth Amendment case, in which the U.S. Supreme Court held that to be valid, a search warrant must be issued by a "neutral and detached magistrate." The individual who signed the warrant in this case, the state attorney general (who was directing the investigation of the case) acting in his capacity as justice of the peace, did not fit this characterization. Hence the search warrant he signed was not valid, and evidence gained via the search based on the warrant should have been excluded from the defendant's trial.

The case grew out of the murder of a fourteen-year-old girl in New Hampshire. After some time the investigation centered on Coolidge. At one point the results of the investigation were presented at a meeting between police officers working on the case and the state attorney general, who had personally taken charge of all police activities relating to the murder and was later to serve as chief prosecutor at the trial. At this meeting it was decided that there was enough evidence to justify the arrest of Coolidge on the murder charge and a search of his house and two cars. At the conclusion of the meeting a police officer made formal application for the arrest and search warrants. The warrants were then signed and issued by the attorney general himself, acting as justice of the peace.

Coolidge was arrested and the search was performed. Incriminating material found as a result of that search was entered as evidence into his trial over his objections. He was found guilty. The seriously divided court overturned the conviction, holding that the warrant for the search and seizure of some of the evidence did not satisfy the requirements of the Fourth Amendment as made applicable to the states because it was not issued by a neutral and detached magistrate.

David Jones

CORPUS DELICTI. Literally, "the body of the crime." This term does not refer to the victim of a homicide. Rather, *corpus delicti* is the presence of all elements needed to establish that a crime has been committed, which serves as the legal foundation for charging the accused.
RECOMMENDED READING: Joseph R. Nolan and Jacqueline M. Nolan-Haley, *Black's Law Dictionary: Definitions of the Terms and Phrases of American and English Jurisprudence, Ancient and Modern*, 6th ed. (St. Paul, MN: West Publishing Co., 1991).

Gordon M. Armstrong

CORRUPTION. Any material gain or monetary reward obtained through an individual's official position of employment. Corruption occurs in both the public and private sectors and is often based on one's status in the organizational structure.
RECOMMENDED READING: Joseph R. Nolan and Jacqueline M. Nolan-Haley, *Black's Law Dictionary: Definitions of the Terms and Phrases of American and English Jurisprudence, Ancient and Modern*, 6th ed. (St. Paul, MN: West Publishing Co., 1991).

Michael Palmiotto

COURTROOM WORKGROUP. The major actors in the trial court—the judge, the prosecuting attorney, and the defense attorney—who interact in an ongoing fashion to accomplish the work of that organization. Many observers have suggested that criminal courts can be studied from the perspective of organizational theory. A central concept in this perspective as applied to courts is the courtroom workgroup. These are the people who interact regularly in the courtroom in order to accomplish certain goals, which include the disposition of cases in an efficient manner and the reduction of uncertainty. These goals may be accomplished by such practices as the substitution of plea-bargaining agreements for trials.

In order to perform effectively, workgroups often establish norms, or expectations of behavior, by which members are expected to abide. For instance, one expectation may be that members do not pull surprises on each other. Individuals new to the workgroup (e.g., a new assistant district attorney) are often socialized into the norms of the group. That is, they learn these expectations. Those who do not follow the norms may be punished. For instance, a recalcitrant defense attorney may not receive the continuance s/he requests.

The existence of the workgroup may affect power relations within the courtroom. It may mean, for instance, that because s/he has access to a great deal of information about a case, the prosecutor may become more powerful than would be indicated from the formal definition of his/her role. The presence of the workgroup may also mean that formal processes (e.g., trials) and formal goals (e.g., "doing justice") may be modified in favor of other objectives (e.g., expeditious disposition of cases). In organizational theory this is known as "goal modification."

While courtroom workgroups exist in many criminal courts, their levels of cohesion may vary, and so may their operation. This may have an impact on such things as case disposition.

RECOMMENDED READING: Edward J. Clynch and David W. Neubauer, "Trial Courts as Organizations: A Critique and Synthesis," *Law and Policy Quarterly* 3 (1981): 69–94; James Eisenstein and Herbert Jacob, *Felony Justice: An Organizational Analysis of Criminal Courts* (Landham, MD: University Press of America, 1991).

David Jones

COY v. IOWA, 487 U.S. 1012 (1988). A leading case involving a defendant's rights under the confrontation clause of the Sixth Amendment, which gives a defendant the right "to be confronted with the witnesses against him." In this case the Court held that an Iowa law that allowed witnesses to testify from behind a screen violated the defendant's Sixth Amendment rights.

In this case the appellant was accused of sexually assaulting two thirteen-year-old girls. At the trial the court granted the state's motion, pursuant to a 1985 state statute intended to protect child victims of sexual abuse, to place a screen between the defendant and the girls during their testimony that allowed him to see them dimly and hear them. Appellant was convicted.

The Supreme Court held that the confrontation clause by its words provides a criminal defendant the right to confront face-to-face the witnesses giving evidence against him or her at trial. The core guarantee serves the general proposition that confrontation is essential to fairness, and helps ensure the integrity of the fact-finding process by making it more difficult for witnesses to lie.

The Court's ruling in *Coy* was modified in the subsequent case of *Maryland v. Craig (1990)*. In *Craig* the Court upheld a Maryland law requiring a pre-

liminary hearing on the issue of whether the potential child witness would suffer great trauma if face-to-face confrontations were required and making it possible for the trial court to order testimony via closed-circuit one-way television, whereby the child could not see the defendant.
RECOMMENDED READING: Lucy S. McGough, *Child Witnesses: Fragile Voices in the American Legal System* (New Haven: Yale University Press, 1994).

David Jones

CRACK. Crack is a form of refined cocaine. Cocaine is dissolved in water, mixed with baking soda, and then heated until the water is removed, leaving rock-like pieces of refined cocaine commonly called crack. Crack produces a short, intense high in users and is more psychologically addicting than cocaine. Crack-addicted women who conceive produce offspring who have a large number of health problems. These children are often referred to as crack babies.
RECOMMENDED READING: Drug Enforcement Administration, *Drugs of Abuse* (Washington, D.C.: U.S. Department of Justice, 1990); National Narcotics Intelligence Consumer's Committee, *The NNICC Report: The Supply of Illicit Drugs to the United States* (Washington, D.C.: NNICC, 1995).

Glenn Zuern

CRIME (COMMISSION OF). The arrest process begins with the police becoming aware of the commission of a criminal offense. This may occur in a number of different ways. The police may discover a crime in progress or happen upon a past crime; a victim or witness may call to report the commission of a crime; or police may receive information of suspicious activity that may upon investigation be determined to amount to criminal activity. The fact of the crime is recorded in official documents and becomes part of the criminal records of the locality and the state.
RECOMMENDED READING: Irving J. Klein, *Principles of the Law of Arrest, Search, Seizure, and Liability Issues* (South Miami, FL: Coral Gables Publishing Co., 1994).

Christopher J. Morse

CRIME CLOCK, FBI. This is the most aggregate representation of Uniform Crime Reports data and is designed to convey the annual reported crime experience by showing the relative frequency of occurrence of the crime-index offenses. In 1995 there was a crime-index offense every 2 seconds. These were broken down as follows: one violent crime every 18 seconds; one murder every 24 minutes; one forcible rape every 5 minutes; one robbery every 54 seconds; one aggravated assault every 29 seconds; one property crime every 3 seconds; one burglary every 12 seconds; one larceny-theft every 4 seconds; and one motor-vehicle theft every 21 seconds.

These are national aggregate figures and should not be thought of as applying to any given community, region, or state. Furthermore, the mode of display should not be taken to imply a regularity in the commission of the crime-index or Part I offenses; rather, it represents the annual ratio of crime to fixed time intervals.

RECOMMENDED READING: Federal Bureau of Investigation, *Uniform Crime Reports for the United States, 1995* (Washington, DC: U.S. Government Printing Office, 1996).

Ransom A. Whittle

CRIME CONTROL ACT OF 1984. Throughout the United States there have been wide ranges of sentencing disparity. One approach to this phenomenon is to reduce discretion among judges in sentencing decision-making. One of these approaches resulted in the Crime Control Act of 1984. This act pertained to the federal government only and set up the U.S. Sentencing Commission, an independent body in the judicial branch of government that has been charged with establishing sentencing policy for the federal government. The nine-member commission produced a set of guidelines that took effect on November 1, 1987. Among the major changes suggested by the commission was a significant decline in the number of "straight" probation sentences and the concomitant growth of "split sentences" that require as a condition of probation a period of confinement.

In addition, the guidelines increase the average time served for violent offenses and lower the average time served for nonviolent crimes such as property and immigration-law offenses. Among questions that remain about this act include the compliance rate of judges, the effect on the overcrowded prison system, whether the guidelines produce unanticipated and undesired sentencing disparity, and the effect of plea negotiations. It appears, according to Siegel (1995), that the rehabilitation-treatment goals of sentencing have been subordinated to goals of social control and public safety. As a result, the number of people behind bars has risen at a significant pace.

RECOMMENDED READING: Michael Block and Wilbur Rhodes, "The Impact of Federal Sentencing Guidelines," *National Institute of Justice Reports* 205, Sept/Oct. 1987 (Washington, DC: U.S. Government Printing Office, 1987); Larry J. Siegel, *Criminology*, 5th ed. (Minneapolis/St. Paul: West Publishing Co., 1995).

Ransom A. Whittle

CRIME-CONTROL MODEL OF JUSTICE. Underlying this model is the proposition that the repression of criminal conduct is the most important function of the criminal justice system. This model has its roots in classical theory. Fear of criminal sanctions is viewed as the primary deterrent to crime. Since people are rational and choose to commit crime, it is reasonable that their activities can be controlled if the costs of crime are too high. Swift, sure, and efficient justice is considered an essential element of an orderly society.

The criminal is someone who is responsible for his/her actions that has broken faith with society by choosing to violate the law for reasons of anger, greed, or revenge. Money spent in the criminal justice system should be directed not at making criminals more comfortable but at increasing the efficiency of police to arrest them and courts to effectively try them. To achieve liberty for all citizens to interact freely, the crime-control model requires that primary attention be paid to efficiency in screening suspects, determining guilt, and appropriately sanctioning the convicted.

Emphasis must be placed on speed and finality. There must be a high rate of arrest, sifting out the innocent, and conviction of offenders. This requires informality, uniformity, and the minimizing of occasions for challenge. Rather than stressing the adversarial elements of the courtroom, this model notes that bargaining between the state and the accused occurs frequently. Plea bargaining results in most charges, and most defendants plead guilty. For this reason Packer likened decision making under this model to an assembly-line process. According to Cole (1989), in some jurisdictions the filtering process works so well that, statistically, if a prosecutor says that a person is guilty, the person is guilty. From the standpoint of this model, the courts increasingly become tribunals of last resort after administrators of the system (police, prosecutors, and defense attorneys) have made their decisions. Even juvenile cases tend to be adjudicated in a style that conforms to the crime control model: most are settled in preliminary hearings by a plea agreement, and few go on to formal trial.

RECOMMENDED READING: George F. Cole, *The American System of Criminal Justice*, 7th ed. (Belmont, CA: Wadsworth Publishing Co., 1995); Larry J. Siegel, *Criminology*, 5th ed. (Minneapolis/St. Paul: West Publishing Co., 1995).

Ransom A. Whittle

CRIME INDEX (UCR). The crime index is composed of selected offenses used to gauge fluctuations in the overall volume and rate of crime reported to law enforcement. These selected offenses are known as Part I offenses in the Uniform Crime Reports (UCR). The offenses included are the violent crimes of murder and nonnegligent manslaughter, forcible rape, robbery, and aggravated assault and the property crimes of burglary, larceny-theft, motor-vehicle theft, and arson. In 1995 the crime-index total of reported offenses other than arson was 13,867,143, for a ratio per 100,000 inhabitants of 5,277.6. Arson totals reported by individual law enforcement agencies are displayed under its categorical entry (see **Arson**).

RECOMMENDED READING: Federal Bureau of Investigation, *Uniform Crime Reports for the United States, 1995* (Washington, DC: U.S. Government Printing Office, 1996).

Ransom A. Whittle

CRIME STATISTICS. In order to understand and evaluate criminal behavior statistics, a number of different data-collection techniques are used. The following are among the most often used by criminal justice scholars and practitioners:

Aggregate Data Sources. These sources consist of large databases gathered by government agencies as well as research foundations. U.S. Census Bureau data, Labor Department data, reports of state and federal correctional departments, and U.S. Department of Justice reports are all major examples of aggregate data sources. One of the most important of these sources is the Uniform Crime Reports (UCR) compiled by the Federal Bureau of Investigation. This is an annual report reflecting the number of crimes reported to law enforcement agencies by citizens and the number of arrests made. Another major source of aggregate data that differs from the UCR is the National Crime Survey, (NCS). This database measures the extent of criminal behavior by focusing on victims. The NCS is collected by the U.S. Bureau of Justice Statistics of the U.S. Department of Justice. The annual report is based on about 48,000 households containing about 110,000 persons. The persons sampled are asked (interviewed) about victimization suffered in the preceding six months, and the interviews take place twice a year.

Self-Report Surveys. The problems associated with official statistics have led to alternative sources of information to assess the true extent of crime patterns. One frequently employed alternative is the self-report survey. Most often, self-report surveys are administered to large groups through a mass distribution of questionnaires. They use people arrested by police, prison inmates, youths in school, and other populations. The basic assumption of these studies is that anonymity and confidentiality backed by academic credentials will encourage people to describe their illegal activities accurately.

It is almost universally accepted that all three sources— official crime statistics, victimization surveys, and self-report studies— seriously flawed in their respective abilities to present an accurate picture of crime in society.

One of the most useful sources is the *Sourcebook of Criminal Justice Statistics,* published yearly by the Bureau of Justice Statistics of the U.S. Department of Justice. The objective of this volume is to compile information from a variety of sources in order to make it available to a wide audience. Data included must meet two standards. First, the information must be national in scope or of national relevance. Second, the data must be methodologically sound with respect to sampling procedures, data-collection methods, estimation procedures, and reliability of information. The *Sourcebook* includes information from UCR, the National Crime Victimization Survey, self-report surveys, and other sources of the full spectrum of the criminal justice systems.

RECOMMENDED READING: Bureau of Justice Statistics, *National Crime Survey* (Washington, DC: The Bureau, 1995); Bureau of Justice Statistics, *Sourcebook of Criminal Justice Statistics* 1995; Federal Bureau of Investigation, *Uniform Crime Reports for the United States, 1995* (Washington, DC: U.S. Government Printing Office, 1996); Larry J. Siegel, *Criminology*, 5th ed. (Minneapolis/St. Paul: West Publishing Co., 1995).

Ransom A. Whittle

CRIMES AGAINST NATURE.   At common law, the term *crimes against nature* was both narrowly defined to include only those acts constituting the offense of sodomy and more broadly defined to include all unnatural copulation with humans or beasts. This has prompted modern courts to sustain allegations of vagueness and most states to replace this single general crime with specific offenses including sodomy, sexually assaulting an animal, indecent liberties with a child, and lewd and lascivious behavior, which includes publicly exposing and arousing one's own sexual organ.

RECOMMENDED READING: Joseph R. Nolan and Jacqueline M. Nolan-Haley, *Black's Law Dictionary: Definitions of the Terms and Phrases of American and English Jurisprudence, Ancient and Modern*, 6th ed. (St. Paul, MN: West Publishing Co., 1991).

Lee E. Parker

CRIMINAL BEHAVIOR.   Antisocial behavior that has been defined and prohibited by law and is usually enforced by punishment. Since the law of the state defines criminal behavior, "criminal behavior" by definition varies from one nation-state to another and is contingent upon time, place, and culture. Human behavior can be antisocial, but until law prohibits this behavior, it is not criminal behavior.

RECOMMENDED READING: Eric Goode, *Deviant Behavior*, 5th ed. (Upper Saddle River, NJ: Prentice Hall, 1997); John Hagan, *Modern Criminology: Crime, Criminal Behavior, and its Control* (New York: McGraw-Hill, 1987); Joseph R. Nolan and Jacqueline M. Nolan-Haley, *Black's Law Dictionary: Definitions of the Terms and Phrases of American and English Jurisprudence, Ancient and Modern*, 6th ed. (St. Paul, MN: West Publishing Co., 1991).

James R. Farris

CRIMINALISTICS.   The terms *forensic science* and *criminalistics* are often used interchangeably. Forensic science is that part of science applied to answering legal questions. It is the examination, evaluation, and explanation of physical evidence in law. Forensic science encompasses pathology, toxicology, physical anthropology, odontology, psychiatry, questioned documents, firearms, tool marks, serology, and molecular biology and genetics.

One branch of forensic science, criminalistics, deals with the study of physical evidence related to a crime. From such a study, a crime may be reconstructed. Criminalistics is interdisciplinary, drawing from mathematics, physics, chemistry, biology, and anthropology. Basically, the forensic sciences are criminalistics, pathology, and toxicology.

RECOMMENDED READING: Gino Arcaro, *Criminal Investigation: Forming Reasonable Grounds* (Toronto: McGraw-Hill Ryerson, 1997); James N. Gilbert, *Criminal Investigation*, 4th ed. (Upper Saddle River, NJ: Prentice-Hall, 1998).

James R. Farris

CRIPS. The Crips are believed to be the largest African-American street gang in the United States. The Crips were established in the late 1960s; however, black gangs have existed in California since the 1930s. In Los Angeles County, California, there are approximately 40,000 Crip gang members, while the total gang population is estimated at 150,000. Crips are comprised of numerous groups of gang members called sets. The sets are not peacefully united; they are often in competition with one another due to the competitive nature of drug sales. The sets range in size from a small number to 300 youths. These sets usually claim an area such as a block, apartment building, or housing project. The sets have little formal structure, but usually have an identifiable leader, known as the "shot caller." Within each set there is specialization concerning crimes of different natures. For a crime such as car theft there is one individual who is in charge of all car-theft operations. This type of leadership is the same for virtually every other crime committed within the set. The most common crimes committed by Crip members are robberies, burglaries, car thefts, homicides, assaults, and drug trafficking. It appears that the identity of today's Crip members is being developed through the dealing of drugs. The drug trafficking appears to be the reason for the perpetration of the other crimes previously mentioned. The sale of crack cocaine is widespread through the Crip sets because it is their major source of revenue, and this causes much of the tension between sets that ultimately results in violence. Approximately forty-five cities nationwide have reported that Los Angeles gang members, mostly Crips, are involved with the drug trafficking in their respective cities. The identification of the Crip member is becoming more difficult for authorities as well as the average citizen. The Crips have been predominately marked by wearing the color blue, but while they still wear blue, they are straying from that color in order to be less identifiable to the authorities and rival gang members.

RECOMMENDED READING: Bureau of Alcohol, Tobacco, and Firearms, *Crips and Bloods Street Gangs* (Washington, DC: The Bureau, 1989); Yusuf Jah and Shah'Keyah Jah, *Uprising: Crips and Bloods Tell the Story of America's Youth in the Crossfire* (New York: Simon & Schuster, 1997).

James R. Farris

CROFTON, SIR WALTER (1815–1897). Sir Walter Crofton was appointed director of the Irish prison system in 1854. A decade earlier Alexander Maconochie had been relieved of his duties as governor of the Norfolk Island penal colony near Australia. But Crofton was familiar with Maconochie's mark system and his process of graduated release from imprisonment, and he found these ideas to have much merit. His new position provided an opportunity to expand on the work Maconochie had started.

As with Maconochie's system, early release from the prison sentence was a central ingredient of Crofton's plan. Since each prisoner was an individual case, it was not reasonable to expect a judge, or anyone else, to anticipate how long it would take the prisoner to be ready for return to the community.

Instead, prisoners should be required to earn their release because of good behavior and diligence at work.

Crofton's version of graduated release comprised four stages. Prisoners began their confinement at the first stage, which required solitary confinement for eight to nine months. During the first three months the inmate lived on reduced rations and had no work assignment. Even the laziest of prisoners, Crofton reasoned, would crave work after three months of inactivity. During the remainder of this first stage the prisoner received full rations and was put to work. The second stage required transfer to another prison where the inmate worked with other prisoners. At this point Maconochie's mark system came into play, and the prisoners moved through four classes of liberty by earning marks for good behavior and hard work.

Crofton's most original contribution came at the third stage, which he called the intermediate stage. Prisoners began this stage with another transfer, this time to a completely open institution comprised of simple barracks with accommodations for a maximum of one hundred men (there were not enough women prisoners in Ireland to make as thorough a system practical for them). The first of these facilities was founded in 1856 at the town of Lusk (a few miles from Dublin). The institution was staffed by six people whom Crofton told must abide by two rules: (1) They were to convince the prisoners that they had faith in them and, with the continuing use of marks, should give them credit for the progress they achieved. (2) The staff should also convince the public that there was good reason to believe that a prisoner who was soon to be released was capable of handling a job.

During the fourth and final stage the prisoner was released to the community under a "ticket of leave." As a condition of that ticket the prisoner had to report to the local police, who provided supervision of the offender until the original sentence was fulfilled. In addition, if the person under ticket of leave misbehaved in the community, the ticket could be revoked as long as the time of the original sentence had not yet expired.

By the 1860s word of Crofton's plan was spreading to other countries. In the United States, where prison reformers were looking for alternatives to the Auburn and Pennsylvania models of prison administration, Crofton's ideas had an especially receptive audience. In 1870 the National Prison Association held its first conference at Cincinnati, Ohio, and Crofton was among those invited to make a presentation. The ideas and procedures of the Irish system, as Crofton's plan had come to be called, were seen by many to be a sound alternative to the current state of America's prisons. In 1876 the Elmira Reformatory opened in Elmira, New York, and provided the first opportunity in the United States to carry out the Irish system.

RECOMMENDED READING: T. Eriksson *The Reformers: An Historical Survey of Pioneer Experiments in the Treatment of Criminals*, translated by C. Djurklou (New York: Elsevier, 1976).

Philip Reichel

***CRUZ V. BETO*, 405 U.S. 319 (1972).** A case involving the rights of religious minorities held in state prisons. The Supreme Court held that if prison administration afforded certain rights to members of Christian and Jewish faiths, they could not keep them from an adherent to the Buddhist religion.

David Jones

CURFEW. Curfew regulations are thought to have been introduced into England by William the Conqueror (although during the reign of Alfred there was an ordinance that Oxford inhabitants should retire at the tolling of a curfew bell). The name is said to have come from the French words *couvre feu* (cover the fire). Originally the curfew was used to require, at a given signal or a given time, that the fires in homes be covered or protected for the night. William the Conqueror, however, used it to require the English to be off the streets or away from a given area at a prescribed time in order to prevent their gathering together.

In the United States, before the Civil War, there were curfew laws in southern towns to designate the times when slaves could be on the streets. Curfew legislation aimed at juveniles received its first substantial support in the latter part of the nineteenth century. By the turn of the century approximately three thousand municipalities and villages had adopted juvenile curfew ordinances. Subsequently, interest in such curfews waned until the Second World War. Then, with parents in the armed services or working in war plants, often at night, and with the influx of servicemen into urban areas, conditions again brought into vogue curfews aimed at preventing juveniles from roaming the streets or loitering in public places. (See **Loitering**.)
RECOMMENDED READING: Joseph R. Nolan and Jacqueline M. Nolan-Haley, *Black's Law Dictionary: Definitions of the Terms and Phrases of American and English Jurisprudence, Ancient and Modern*, 6th ed. (St. Paul, MN: West Publishing Co., 1991); *Thistlewood v. Trial Magistrate for Ocean City*, 236 Md. 548, 204 A.2d 688 (1964).

Lee E. Parker

D

DARROW, CLARENCE S. (1857–1938). Clarence Darrow was born on April 18, 1857, near Kinsman, Ohio. He attended Allegheny College, taught school, and then studied for a year at the University of Michigan Law School. He returned to Ohio, where he practiced for nine years. Then he moved to Chicago. Bringing in money was not enough for him. He campaigned for amnesty for the Haymarket Square bombing defendants. He rose to be chief corporation counsel for Chicago and then became counsel for the Chicago and North Western Railway, but quit to represent Eugene V. Debs and the American Railway Union after the Pullman strike.

Darrow went on to champion other labor leaders and unions. However, after he entered a guilty plea for the McNamara brothers in Los Angeles (they were accused of bombing the *Los Angeles Times* newspaper) and was himself charged with attempting to bribe jurors, he returned to Chicago and built a different kind of private practice. His clients included Nathan Leopold and Richard Loeb (teen murderers), John T. Scopes (for teaching evolution in Tennessee), the Sweet family (blacks who attempted to desegregate a community in Detroit and were in the midst of a riot), and the Scottsboro boys (young blacks charged with raping two white women in rural Alabama).

Darrow was a popular lecturer and debater, known for his iconoclasm. He died on March 13, 1938.

RECOMMENDED READING: Richard J. Jensen, *Clarence Darrow: The Creation of an American Myth* (New York: Greenwood Press, 1992); Daniel Kornstein, *Thinking Under Fire: Great Courtroom Lawyers and Their Impact on American History* (New York: Dodd, Mead, 1987); Iris Noble, *Clarence Darrow: Defense Attorney* (New York: Messner, 1958).

Martin Gruberg

DAVIS, LARRY (1967–   ). In 1986, twenty members of the New York Police Department (NYPD) went to the Davis home in the South Bronx to arrest nineteen-year-old Larry Davis for involvement in the deaths of several local drug dealers. Shots were exchanged, and Davis escaped from the apartment, leaving six police officers wounded. Despite a vigorous police search, he remained on the streets for six weeks, then negotiated a surrender.

Larry Davis was indicted for murder in the deaths of two drug dealers and for attempted murder of the six police officers. With the assistance of his lawyers, Lynn Stewart and William Kunstler, Davis was found not guilty of murder charges in three separate trials between 1987 and 1989. In 1991, in a fourth trial, with a new attorney, Davis was convicted of murdering a drug dealer in 1986 and was sentenced to twenty-five years to life in prison.

In his four trials Larry Davis told of having been recruited into drug dealing by members of the NYPD and of having been marked for revenge when he refused to continue these activities. The heavily publicized trials of Larry Davis in 1987 and 1988 foreshadowed the police corruption scandals that would astonish New Yorkers in the 1990s.

RECOMMENDED READING: John Epstein, "Can a Guy Who Shot Six Cops Get Justice?," *Village Voice*, Vol. 34, no. 50 (December 12, 1989): 10, 12.

Margaret Leland Smith

DAY-FINE SYSTEM. A system of punishment used in some jurisdictions in the United States, and more widely in Scandinavia and other parts of Europe. As the costs of incarceration increase, authorities are examining alternative forms of punishment. Day fines are one of these.

Fines are appropriate punishments for certain offenses. However, their use raises issues of fairness because individual wealth and income varies greatly. A fine of $100 might be a harsh penalty to a low-income person, but relatively insignificant to a wealthier person. Day fines are designed to deal with this problem by assigning "punishment unit" values to offenses for which fines are typically assessed. The dollar amount of the fine to be assessed against any one person is computed by multiplying that person's daily income by the number of punishment units assigned to that offense. This results in the same degree of financial burden being imposed on each offender for the same crime. If two offenders with different levels of wealth/income but similar criminal backgrounds are convicted of the same offense, the total dollar amount of the fine assessed the individual of greater means would be greater than the fine assessed the poorer offender. If either defaulted, the sanctions imposed, such as jail time, would be the same because they would be based on the number of punishment units for that offense.

Pilot projects utilizing day fines have been undertaken in this country. Initial results indicate that day-fine systems could be successfully adopted here.

RECOMMENDED READING: Sally T. Hillsman, Barry Mahoney, George F. Cole, and Bernard Auchter, *Fines as Criminal Sanctions* (Washington, DC: National Institute of Justice, 1987); Douglas C. McDonald, Judith Greene, and Charles Worzella, *Day Fines in American Courts* (Washington, DC: National Institute of Justice, 1992).

David Jones

DEADLOCKED JURY. A deadlocked jury is often referred to as a "hung jury." Because criminal trials are often time-consuming and are very expensive to conduct, a trial judge will normally encourage the jurors to continue their deliberations if a jury becomes deadlocked. If, after further deliberations, the jury is still unable to reach a verdict, the trial judge will declare a mistrial, and the case may be retried.

A second trial in these circumstances does not violate the Fifth Amendment's double-jeopardy clause because the accused remains in a state of "continuing jeopardy," which allows the prosecution to retry the defendant for the same offense. For example, in 1991 Byron de la Beckwith was brought to trial in the 1st Judicial District of Hinds County, Mississippi, for the 1969 murder of Medgar Evers, an early and important figure in the U.S. civil rights movement. Beckwith had previously been tried for the same crime in two separate trials, one in 1969 and one in 1970. Both trials resulted in deadlocked-jury mistrials. Following extensive delays for appeals, Beckwith was convicted in 1994 of murdering Evers and was sentenced to life in prison. Following a long-standing U.S. Supreme Court precedent (*U.S. v. Perez* [1824]), the Mississippi Supreme Court held that Beckwith's third trial following the two previous deadlocked-jury mistrials did not violate the double-jeopardy clause of the Fifth Amendment.

Several states have tried to address the problem of deadlocked juries by passing laws allowing less than unanimous verdicts in criminal cases. In *Apodaca v. Oregon* (1972) the U.S. Supreme Court upheld a conviction by ten votes of a twelve-member jury. Similarly, in *Johnson v. Louisiana* (1972) the Court sanctioned a guilty verdict by nine votes of a twelve-member jury. However, the Supreme Court has held that in cases involving capital crimes a unanimous verdict from a twelve-person jury is required. Moreover, a number of states have passed laws establishing six-member juries. In those states a six-person jury verdict must be unanimous. Similarly, defendants in all federal criminal trials are entitled to unanimous verdicts.

RECOMMENDED READING: J. Findlater, "Retrial After a Hung Jury: The Double Jeopardy Problem," *University of Pennsylvania Law Review*, Vol. 129, no. 3 (1981): 701–737.

Thomas J. Hickey

DEATH PENALTY. The legally sanctioned use of execution as a punishment for crimes. Although execution of criminals is practiced in more than half the countries of the world, all Western industrial societies except the United States have abolished the practice, most since the end of World War II.

Before World War II most capital cases in the United States were based on state statutes, and jurisdiction, including appeals, resided entirely at the state level. Federal courts, apart from a few cases that raised basic constitutional issues, were not involved in these cases. Despite a number of very controversial trials (the Scottsboro trial in Alabama, the trial and execution of Nicola Sacco and Bartolomeo Vanzetti in Massachusetts, the trial and execution of Bruno Hauptmann, convicted of the kidnap-murder of the Lindbergh baby), there was little challenge to the legal status of the death penalty itself.

Two highly publicized cases in the 1950s focused much national attention on the death penalty and raised questions regarding its fairness and effectiveness. In 1948 Caryl Chessman was convicted of the "red light bandit" crimes in California and sentenced to death. The evidence against Chessman was circumstantial, there were no homicides involved in the crimes, and he maintained his innocence until the end. Chessman pursued his case through every channel of appeal available, and the case dragged on for twelve years before Chessman, by then a national celebrity and a best-selling author of several books, was finally executed in 1960.

The case of Dr. Sam Sheppard in Ohio, accused of murdering his wife in the summer of 1954, ended differently. Sheppard was tried and convicted on circumstantial evidence in an atmosphere of public near hysteria, and prosecutors demanded the death penalty. Amid threats of lynching he was sentenced to life imprisonment. A few years later new evidence was discovered that proved his innocence, and in a new trial he was acquitted.

In the midst of these and other controversial cases that led to declining public support for the death penalty, the NAACP Legal Defense Fund launched its moratorium campaign against the death penalty, which involved appealing death sentences in the South to federal appeals courts. By the mid-1960s executions had stopped, and in 1972 the Supreme Court invalidated the Georgia death penalty law based on its potential for allowing arbitrary and capricious application of the death penalty (see *Furman v. Georgia*). The death penalty statutes of several other states were affected, and capital punishment was effectively suspended as a result. Yet within two years thirty-five states had passed new death-penalty laws incorporating mechanisms for overcoming the *Furman* objections and the Court specifically approved a two-step trial procedure for capital cases in 1976 (see *Gregg v. Georgia*).

Since its reinstatement the death penalty has become a major public issue. Proponents argue that it serves to deter violent crime. They regularly propose expanding its application to crimes other than homicide (drug trafficking, terrorist activities, and so on). Proponents also argue that the public should not have to support capital offenders for the rest of their lives in prison; that some warrant nothing less than death as a punishment; that victims and survivors of heinous crimes deserve finality in the punishment of those who have victimized them; and that opinion polls consistently indicate that a large majority of the public favors the death penalty.

Opponents argue that it is morally wrong for the state to kill and that the state does not have the right to decide who deserves to die. They also contend that the death penalty does not deter violent crime, and recent research indicates that executions might actually increase rather than decrease homicide rates. Opponents point out that because of the huge expense of capital trials it actually costs more to execute a person than to imprison her/him for life without parole. There is also recent research indicating that majority support for the death penalty in opinion polls occurs only when no specific alternatives are offered. When given a range of choices including a life sentence without parole, public support for the death penalty drops below a majority.

The most influential challenges to the death penalty have been based on research indicating that death sentencing is highly discriminatory against poor and minority defendants, and charges that safeguards against the execution of innocent defendants are inadequate. A large and growing body of research indicates that minority defendants accused of crimes against whites are much more likely to be sentenced to death than other defendants. In Georgia, for example, blacks accused of killing whites are more than twenty times as likely to receive a death sentence as blacks accused of killing other blacks and more than four times as likely to receive a death sentence as whites accused of killing other whites. This basic pattern of racial discrimination in death sentencing has been found in studies of at least a dozen death-penalty states.

Because most poor and minority defendants typically have grossly inadequate representation at trial, innocent defendants are sometimes convicted and sentenced to death. With state legislatures and state and federal appeals courts attempting to shorten the time between sentencing and execution, this problem seems likely to get worse in the future.

With growing conservative dominance of American politics and the high level of public support for the death penalty, it seems nearly certain that use of the death penalty will continue to increase in the near future. With continuing moral opposition by a persistent coalition of opponents and the growing evidence of discrimination and conviction of innocents, it seems just as certain that this issue will remain controversial.

RECOMMENDED READING: Enid Harlow, David Matas, and Jane Rocamora, *The Machinery of Death: A Shocking Indictment of Capital Punishment in the United States* (New York: Amnesty International U.S.A., 1995); Robert Johnson, *Death Work: A Study of the Modern Execution Process* (Pacific Grove, CA: Brooks/Cole Publishing Co., 1990); Franklin E. Zimring and Gordon Hawkins, *Capital Punishment and the American Agenda* (New York: Cambridge University Press, 1986).

Ernie Thomson

DEMAREST v. MANSPEAKER, 498 U.S. 184 (1991). A case involving issues of statutory construction of the U.S. Code as it applies to the rights of prisoners to receive compensation for testifying in a federal trial. A unanimous Supreme Court held that the U.S. Code requires such compensation.

In 1988 Richard Demarest, an inmate in a Colorado prison, was called to testify in a federal trial, which he did. After he had finished, Demarest sought fees as a "witness in attendance" pursuant to the U.S. Code. He requested that James Manspeaker, the clerk of the federal district court, certify that he, Demarest, was eligible to receive these fees. Manspeaker referred the request to the U.S. attorney for the relevant district, who denied it. Demarest sought a writ of mandamus in federal district court directing Manspeaker to certify his request for fees. The district court dismissed the petition, and the federal court of appeals confirmed the dismissal.

A unanimous Supreme Court overruled this decision. In the Court's view Congress in one section of the relevant act directed the payment of fees to individuals who testify in federal cases. In another section of the same act the law directs payment of subsistence fees for most witnesses, but provides an exception for prisoners. In still another section the act specifically provides that a certain class of incarcerated persons—detained aliens—would not receive fees for testifying. Consequently, held the Court, this should logically mean that Congress did intend that convicted state prisoners be compensated for testifying at a federal trial pursuant to a *habeas corpus ad testificandum*.

David Jones

DIRECT EVIDENCE. Evidence that proves a fact alleged directly, without the necessity of using an inference or a presumption. If accepted by the trier of fact, direct evidence establishes the truth of the fact alleged. Eyewitness testimony (as well as evidence gained by other senses) is a form of direct evidence. If a witness testifies that she saw A shoot B and the trier of fact believes her, it is established as a fact that A shot B.

RECOMMENDED READING: John C. Klotter, *Criminal Evidence*, 6th ed. (Cincinnati: Anderson Publishing Co., 1996); Christopher B. Mueller and Laird C. Kirkpatrick, *Evidence Under the Rules*, 3rd ed. (Boston: Little, Brown, and Co., 1996); Joseph R. Nolan and Jacqueline M. Nolan-Haley, *Black's Law Dictionary: Definitions of the Terms and Phrases of American and English Jurisprudence, Ancient and Modern*, 6th ed. (St. Paul, MN: West Publishing Co., 1991); Jon R. Waltz, *Introduction to Criminal Evidence*, 4th ed. (Chicago: Nelson Hall Publishers, 1997).

David Jones

DIRECT SUPERVISION. Direct supervision is a corrections management philosophy linked with architectural design innovations and implemented by staff trained in management principles and interpersonal communications. These elements combine to facilitate more effective management of inmates by reducing tension through an improved working environment for the staff and better living conditions for the inmates.

In the late 1970s the federal government built its metropolitan correctional centers in New York, Chicago, and San Diego and introduced the direct-supervision management philosophy. The philosophy gained momentum on the local level after Contra Costa County, California, built its direct-supervision jail in Martinez in early 1981. The awareness of the concept and its acceptance by local government have grown rapidly to the point that by late 1994 there were about ninety-four such facilities constructed and managed under this concept.

This philosophy emphasizes a more humanistic approach to inmate behavior management. Moreover, the predominant architectural feature is the absence of barriers between the staff and inmates and the use of noninstitutional decor and furnishings. There is little or no use of bars or other physical detention barriers. The staff interacts in direct contact with the inmates in the housing units. This mix of management philosophy and architectural innovation prompts positive behavior from the inmates toward the staff.

The management philosophy of direct supervision is based on the following eight basic principles: (1) The staff is in effective control of the inmates at all times; (2) the staff exercises effective supervision of the inmates by direct contact and personal interaction; (3) competent staff is hired, trained, and supervised in accordance with professional corrections standards; (4) safety of staff and inmates is ensured; (5) manageable and cost-effective operations are fostered; (6) effective communications between staff and inmates are established and maintained; (7) complete and accurate classification and orientation are used to "weed out" those who are not suitable for the direct-supervision management philosophy; and (8) public policy and federal case law dictate that inmates are afforded justice and fairness. There is strong evidence that direct-supervision jails are less costly to build, cheaper to operate, and generally can be staffed with less personnel than traditionally constructed and managed local detention facilities.

RECOMMENDED READING: Richard L. Swan, *Two Elements of a "Correctional Environment" for Podular Direct Supervision Jails*, M. S. thesis, University of Cincinnati, 1991.

Martin N. Nowak

DISCOVERY. A pretrial procedure that allows each party to inspect property in possession of the adverse party and that may be used as evidence in a criminal case. The prosecutor's discovery rights are limited by constitutional protections afforded the defendant. The process serves to eliminate surprise evidence and particularly affords the defendant an opportunity to prepare a defense to the charges. It also requires disclosure by the defendant of evidence relating to certain defenses available to him in order to give the people an opportunity to rebut such claim. Property that may be subject to discovery consists of any existing tangible property such as (but not limited to) records, reports, books, memos, photos, fingerprints, and weapons. Discovery gives the defendant, who usually has far fewer resources than the state, an enhanced opportunity for a fair trial through awareness of evidentiary material in possession of the prosecutor and increases his/her ability to defend against it if the prosecutor chooses to use it at trial. In some instances it also supplies a defendant with evidence favorable to his/her case that s/he might never have become aware of. Discovery may also be had on pretrial hearings and upon trial. In these instances it is limited, however, to criminal history information relative to either party's witnesses.

RECOMMENDED READING: J. Scott Harr and Karen M. Hess, *Constitutional Law for Criminal Justice Professionals* (Belmont, CA: Wadsworth Publishing, 1997); Irving J. Klein, *Constitutional Law for Criminal Justice*

Professionals, 3rd ed. (South Miami, FL: Coral Gables Publishing Co., 1992); Joseph R. Nolan and Jacqueline M. Nolan-Haley, *Black's Law Dictionary: Definitions of the Terms and Phrases of American and English Jurisprudence, Ancient and Modern*, 6th ed. (St. Paul, MN: West Publishing Co., 1991).

Christopher J. Morse

DISCRETION. For those who act in the name of the public, as criminal justice professionals do, discretion is the power, conferred upon them by law, to act officially based upon their own judgment, or discernment, of a situation. Discretion is the right for an official to choose an action that appears to be just and proper and that is not controlled by the judgment and conscience of others.

Discretion involves knowledge of that which is just and proper under the law, and of the ethical principles and guidelines of a professional organization. Police officers face questions of discretion about the decision to arrest an individual, about the use of force and deception in response to crime events, and about the nature of their conduct and communication with the members of a community.

Officers of the court choose the evidence and testimony that are presented at a hearing or trial, as well as the composition of a jury and relevant commentary upon the law itself. Those who guard imprisoned persons or keep track of probationers and parolees choose the point at which the skein of regulation surrounding the punishment process has been violated. Increasingly, organizations of criminal justice professionals have published their guidelines for wise conduct, or discretion, as codes of ethics.

RECOMMENDED READING: Lloyd E. Ohlin, "Surveying Discretion by Criminal Justice Decision Makers," and Frank J. Remington, "The Decision to Charge, the Decision to Convict on a Guilty Plea, and the Impact of Sentence Structure on Prosecution Practices," in *Discretion in Criminal Justice: The Tension Between Individualization and Uniformity*, ed. Lloyd E. Ohlin and Frank J. Remington (Albany: State University of New York, 1993).

Margaret Leland Smith

DISORDERLY CONDUCT. Disorderly conduct is a term of law that identifies behavior that disturbs the public peace or offends the public sense of morality. Drawn from the common-law "breach of peace" prohibitions, modern disorderly-conduct statutes are specific to the jurisdiction in which they apply.

Disorderly conduct statutes often include threatening or tumultuous behavior that does not reach the level of an assault; unreasonable noise; offensive or abusive language, gesture, or display; and behavior that creates a public hazard that serves no lawful purpose. Arrests for disorderly conduct are among the most common categories of arrest across local, city, and state jurisdictions.

Legislators and police have often used disorderly-conduct statutes to control the public social behavior of individuals and groups who are deemed to be "undesirable." Political dissidents and their supporters have been charged and convicted as disorderly persons. Public and private social gatherings of the poor, suppressed cultural or ethnic groups, and homosexuals have been labeled disorderly conduct. In the United States recent constitutional litigation has sharply limited the power of local authorities to use disorderly-conduct arrests to muffle dissent and enforce provincial standards of propriety.

RECOMMENDED READING: Joseph R. Nolan and Jacqueline M. Nolan-Haley, *Black's Law Dictionary: Definitions of the Terms and Phrases of American and English Jurisprudence, Ancient and Modern*, 6th ed. (St. Paul, MN: West Publishing Co., 1991).

Margaret Leland Smith

DISPOSITION HEARING (JUVENILE). After a child has been adjudicated delinquent in a juvenile court, the question becomes one of how to dispose of the case, and what action the court should take with the child. In juvenile court some states will immediately go into the disposition hearing when the child is adjudicated delinquent, but the disposition hearing is generally a separate hearing from the adjudication hearing and represents the second half of the two-part or bifurcated process. The reason that many states are separating the process is to address the rights of the child. A disposition hearing immediately after, or as part of, an adjudication hearing might introduce information about the child that is not related to the fact finding of what the child did, but might influence what the judge thinks about whether the child needs rehabilitation, and thus influence the adjudication hearing with nonlegal factors. To ensure that this does not happen, states with bifurcated hearings will hold the disposition hearing after a designated period of time and will offer the evidence for disposition only at that time.

The main question of a disposition hearing is what to do with the child, and as the child is already adjudicated delinquent, the procedure tends to be more informal. Evidence presented at the hearing covers the social history of the child and family, any psychological assessment, any previous contact with the court and the outcome of that contact, and any other information that can help the court to design the treatment plan for the child. Generally speaking, research indicates that there are many formal, legal factors that come into play when the judge determines the disposition of the case. Seemingly the most significant is the recommendation by the juvenile worker who puts together the social history and makes a dispositional recommendation to the Judge. Also significant are the seriousness of the offense, the previous court history of the child, and the resources available to the court.

With a juvenile offender, judges seem to have a greater flexibility and greater options in the disposition of a case than in adult court. The options vary widely from community to community and are dependent upon the resources of that community, the programs available to the judge, and the philosophy of the community and the juvenile court. Dispositions include dismissal of the case, fining, special court orders for special treatment such as alcohol or drug counseling, family involvement, or probation and supervision either in or out of the home. All these options retain the jurisdiction of the juvenile in the juvenile court and generally in the community. In the case where community treatment does not seem feasible, the juvenile can be committed to the state system of juvenile corrections, which in most states includes the juvenile correctional facilities. If that is the judicial option, the jurisdiction of the child moves to the state level and is taken out of the jurisdiction options of the local juvenile court. Today, as in adult courts, probation is the most widely used option in juvenile dispositional hearings.

RECOMMENDED READING: Clemens Bartollas and Stuart J. Miller, *Juvenile Justice in America* (Englewood Cliffs, NJ: Regents/Prentice Hall, 1994).

Frances P. Reddington

DNA PROFILING. A series of scientific tests used to determine whether blood, semen, or tissue came from a particular individual. Often called DNA fingerprinting, DNA profiling or testing began to appear in criminal cases in the late 1980s. Although DNA profiling was initially used primarily to convict defendants, since the early 1990s a number of those previously convicted have won appeals based on DNA technology indicating that they could not have been guilty of the crimes of which they were convicted. According to one attorney whose client in 1995 had his rape conviction overturned on the basis of DNA testing nearly eight years after the original conviction, approximately twenty-four defendants nationwide have been freed on the basis of DNA analysis. DNA evidence is based on the distinctive pattern of a person's deoxyribonucleic acid, a genetic material found in all living cells. Using this acid, scientists can examine blood, semen, or tissue at a crime scene or on a victim to determine with near certainty whether a particular person was at the scene of the crime and could have committed it. Other specimens that can be analyzed include saliva, vaginal secretions, hair roots, bones, teeth, muscle tissue, and fetal tissue. The federal government does not regulate DNA laboratories, although the American Society of Crime Laboratory Directors, a professional group, began accrediting labs in 1992. By late 1994, fifteen of the sixty-five labs that had applied as forensic DNA labs had been accredited. There are two basic types of DNA testing. RFLP (restriction fragment-length polymorphisms) is normally used to suggest a match between an evidence sample from a suspect or victim and a forensic sample from the same person. PCR (polymerase chain reaction) is a more general test used primarily to exclude a suspect from further consideration. Although less precise than RFLP, it is capable of excluding a suspect based on the information that the DNA retrieved from a crime scene could not match the suspect's. DNA profiling remains controversial due to the unlicensed nature of labs performing the testing and the awe in which many juries hold the results, attributing to it a scientific certainty that some maintain that it does not deserve.

RECOMMENDED READING: "DNA Testing Frees a Long-jailed Man," *New York Times*, October 22, 1994, 8; "DNA Tests Clear Man of Rape Nearly 8 Years after Conviction," *New York Times*, January 31, 1995, B5; Gina Kolata, "Two Chief Rivals in the Battle over DNA Evidence Now Agree on Its Use," *New York*

Times, October 27, 1994, B14; Barry Meier, "Simpson Team Taking Aim at DNA Laboratory," *New York Times*, September 7, 1994, B10; promotional material distributed by Cellmark Diagnostics, 1995.

Dorothy Moses Schulz

DOUBLE JEOPARDY. The Fifth Amendment's double-jeopardy clause guarantees that persons shall not "be subject for the same offense to be twice put in jeopardy of life or limb." This clause provides three independent protections for an accused. First, it does not permit a person to be retried for the same offense after a conviction. Second, it protects against reprosecution following an acquittal. Third, it protects against multiple punishments for the same offense.

The Supreme Court's double-jeopardy precedents have established several basic rules. Jeopardy attaches when the jury has taken its oath, or when the first witness is sworn in a nonjury trial. Moreover, a defendant waives double-jeopardy claims if he or she moves for a mistrial or successfully raises an appeal. The government may not appeal acquittals. However, it may appeal orders such as a ruling by a judge setting aside a guilty verdict.

At first glance double-jeopardy analysis seems straightforward. However, the law of double jeopardy is one of the more complex areas of U.S. criminal procedure. In *Albernaz v. United States* (1981) Justice William Rehnquist described U.S. Supreme Court cases interpreting the Fifth Amendment's double-jeopardy clause as "a veritable Sargasso Sea which could not fail to challenge the most intrepid judicial navigator." One of the central difficulties involves defining precisely what constitutes the "same offense" under the double-jeopardy clause.

The U.S. Supreme Court's long-standing test for determining if an accused is charged with the same offense for double-jeopardy purposes was developed in *Blockburger v. United States* (1932). The *Blockburger* test is sometimes termed a "same-evidence" double-jeopardy test, which focuses on the statutory elements of a charged offense. If a second charge requires the prosecution to prove different statutory elements of a crime than it was required to prove in the first trial, there is no violation of the double-jeopardy clause. For example, in *Brown v. Ohio* (1977) the defendant was first charged with "joy-riding" for taking another person's car. He pleaded guilty and was sentenced to thirty days in jail and received a $100 fine. After his release from jail, he was indicted for auto theft for the same incident that led to his joy-riding conviction. Brown was convicted and received a six-month jail sentence. On appeal, the U.S. Supreme Court reversed Brown's conviction because "joy-riding" and "auto theft" were not sufficiently distinguishable to satisfy the *Blockburger* test. In contrast, if a defendant is convicted of assaulting someone and is later charged with murder for the same conduct, the *Blockburger* test should permit the murder prosecution because the two crimes have different statutory elements.

Another significant double-jeopardy issue, raised in the recent Rodney King case, is successive state and federal prosecutions for the same criminal conduct. In *Bartkus v. Illinois* (1959) the Supreme Court held that successive state and federal prosecutions for the same criminal acts do not violate the double-jeopardy clause. Under the doctrine of "dual sovereignty" independent jurisdictions may try and punish those whose criminal offenses violate both sovereigns' laws.

RECOMMENDED READING: Michael A. Brazzell, *The Double Jeopardy Doctrine Under the United States Constitution: A Historical and Legal Perspective*, (Grambling, LA: Grambling State University, 1993); James Dickens and Thomas H. Thornburg, *Double Jeopardy and Civil Penalties: The Impact of United States v. Halper* (University of North Carolina at Chapel Hill, 1992); Victor Harvey Shernoff, *The Plea of Double Jeopardy*, M. A. thesis (Athens: University of Georgia, 1971).

Thomas J. Hickey

DOUGLAS, WILLIAM O. (1898–1980). William O. Douglas was born in Maine, Minnesota, on October 16, 1898. However, he spent most of his early years in the Far West. His father died in 1904, leaving the family in poverty. Douglas overcame not only these handicaps but also an attack of polio. He worked his way through Whitman College and Columbia Law School. He was one of Robert Hutchens's bright young men, a legal realist.

Leaving academe for public service, Douglas became chairman of the Securities and Exchange Commission in 1937. In 1939 President Franklin Roosevelt named him to the Supreme Court to succeed Louis Brandeis. Douglas was one of the youngest justices ever appointed to the Court, the youngest since Joseph Story. He served on the Court longer than any other justice, thirty-six and one-half years. (In 1944 he was suggested by Roosevelt for the vice presidential nomination.)

Douglas supported the use of governmental authority to regulate the economy. However, he opposed efforts by government to restrict individual liberties. He joined with Hugo Black to argue that the First Amendment gave absolute protection to thought and speech. He took a leading role in the Warren Court's strengthening the privilege against self-incrimination, extending the right to counsel, curbing coerced confessions, and prohibiting illegal searches and seizures. He argued that the Ninth Amendment includes a right to privacy.

Always a hard worker, Douglas urged the Court to consider more rather than fewer cases. Yet he was criticized for writing opinions that were too cryptic. He was a loner on the Court, not concerned with persuading his colleagues. He was content to let judges with whom he agreed do the theorizing. His opposition to the Vietnam War and his marriages to young women also aroused criticism. He traveled the globe and championed environmental causes. Health problems caused him to resign in 1975. Justice Douglas died in 1980.

RECOMMENDED READING: Howard Ball and Phillip J. Cooper, *Of Power and Right: Hugo Black, William O. Douglas, and America's Constitutional Revolution* (New York: Oxford University Press, 1992); William O. Douglas, *The Court Years, 1939–1975: The Autobiography of William O. Douglas* (New York: Vintage Books, 1980); James C. Duram, *Justice William O.*

Douglas (Boston: Twayne Publishers, 1981); James F. Simon, *Independent Journey: The Life of William O. Douglas* (New York: Penguin Books, 1980).

Martin Gruberg

DRIVING UNDER THE INFLUENCE. Driving under the influence is the operation of a motor vehicle while under the influence of a controlled substance. Alcohol is the drug most closely associated with driving under the influence. The legal standard as to the amount of alcohol that must be present in an individual's system for her/him to be considered guilty of driving under the influence of alcohol varies from state to state. Breath and blood tests are both used to measure the amount of alcohol present in the system of an individual suspected of driving under the influence by law enforcement officials. (See **Drunk Driving**.)

RECOMMENDED READING: Pennsylvania Bar Institute, *Driving Under the Influence* (Harrisburg, PA: The Institute, 1996).

Glenn Zuern

DRUG ABUSE. Drug abuse is the use of drugs in a manner that is harmful to the individual or society, on using drugs in a manner inconsistent with their design or purpose. Abuse can be the result of excessive use, inappropriate use, or use during specific tasks or time.

RECOMMENDED READING: Joseph R. Nolan and Jacqueline M. Nolan-Haley, *Black's Law Dictionary: Definitions of the Terms and Phrases of American and English Jurisprudence, Ancient and Modern*, 6th ed. (St. Paul, MN: West Publishing Co., 1991).

Glenn Zuern

DRUG-ABUSE PREVENTION PROGRAMS. In the mid- to late 1960s increased drug use stimulated public concern. Since then a broad range of preventive measures have been implemented in order to address this problem. Today, drug-abuse prevention programs continue to receive much attention in terms of funding, development, and implementation. Preventive strategies may be grouped into five major categories: public information and education, service measures, technologic measures, legislative and regulatory measures, and economic measures (McNeece and DiNitto 1994).

Public information and education have been used often as the primary means of prevention. Early programs throughout the 1970s relied on providing information and using "scare" tactics. The federal government's Special Office for Drug Abuse Prevention (SODAP) was so disillusioned with the effectiveness of these programs that it imposed a temporary ban on their funding (Wallack and Corbett 1990). More recently, local action-oriented groups such as Mothers against Drunk Driving (MADD) and Students against Drunk Driving (SADD) have had a significant impact on the prevention movement, especially in increasing public awareness.

Project DARE (Drug Abuse Resistance Education), one of the most popular prevention programs, was developed as a joint project of the Los Angeles Police Department and the Los Angeles Unified School District. DARE is conducted by trained local police officers in seventeen weekly sessions designed to help fifth- and sixth-grade students recognize and resist the peer pressure that often leads to experimentation with alcohol and drugs. Some studies have shown that students who received the full-semester DARE curriculum had significantly lower use of alcohol, cigarettes, and other drugs (DeJong 1987). The Research Triangle Institute (1994) conducted a more recent evaluation of Project DARE that concluded that DARE's core curriculum is largely ineffective in preventing drug use among participating groups and recommended shifting resources to longer-term interactive prevention programs (cited in Monroe 1994).

Service measures are aimed at ameliorating or reversing a condition resulting from alcohol or drug use or reducing the chances of the onset of drug use among members of high-risk populations. Some examples of service measures are detoxification, therapeutic communities, twenty-eight-day treatment programs, and Alcoholics Anonymous. The limited availability of some types of service measures, such as treatment programs, can limit their impact. Service measures are also more labor intensive and more expensive than other approaches. The debate over whether drug abuse is best addressed via treatment, incarceration, or a combination of both has not been resolved.

Technologic measures refer to altering the drug or the environment in which it is used in order to reduce the adverse effects of using the substance. These measures include, but are not limited to, air bags in automobiles, "tipsy taxi" services for drivers who have had too much to drink, and communities providing free needles and syringes to injection drug users to curb the spread of infectious diseases such as hepatitis and AIDS.

Legislative and regulatory measures can be used to control the location and hours of sale for alcoholic beverages, to limit the sale of drugs to minors, to impose incarceration as a consequence for illicit drug use, and to encourage bartenders or other servers to discontinue service to obviously intoxicated persons. Additionally, measures can restrict the advertising of alcohol, tobacco, and other drugs.

Economic measures have an impact on the volume of drugs sold, whether the increase or decrease in price is due to company policy or government order. Additional economic measures might include allocating tax revenues from the sale of drugs to prevention programs, or reducing insurance premiums for those who abstain from substance use.

No single prevention strategy has demonstrated a long-term impact on alcohol and drug abuse. Prevention efforts may prove to be more effective if they first seek to understand the root causes of alcohol and drug abuse.

RECOMMENDED READING: William DeJong, "A Short-Term Evaluation of Project D.A.R.E. (Drug Abuse Resistance Education): Preliminary Indications of Effectiveness," *Journal of Drug Education* 17, no. 4 (1987): 279– 294; C. A. McNeece and D. M. DiNitto, *Chemical Dependency: A Systems*

Approach (Englewood Cliffs, NJ: Prentice Hall 1994); S. Monroe, "D.A.R.E. Bedeviled," *Time*, October 17, 1994, 49; L. Wallack and K. Corbett, "Illicit Drug, Tobacco, and Alcohol Use among Youth: Trends and Promising Approaches in Prevention," in Hank Resnik, S. E. Gardner, R. P. Lorian, and C. E. Marcus, *Youth and Drugs: Society's Mixed Messages*, OSAP Prevention Monograph no. 6, Alcohol, Drug Abuse, and Mental Health Administration, Office for Substance Abuse Prevention (Rockville, MD: U.S. Department of Health and Human Services, Public Health Service, (1990).

C. Aaron McNeece

DRUG COURT. Drug courts represent a recent departure from traditional criminal case-processing practices in that they emphasize a combination of treatment and sanctions to reduce drug dependency and use while avoiding the stigmatization that frequently occurs with the processing of criminal offenders. Designed for defendants charged with drug use or possession and who have no history of violent crime, drug courts are intended to avoid the incarceration and circulation of such offenders through the criminal justice system by diverting them to a rigorous, court-monitored program of substance-abuse treatment backed up by a graduated range of criminal sanctions.

Typically, defendants who are invited and agree to participate in such programs are diverted from pretrial detention as well as from traditional prosecution. In the event that a defendant fails to comply with the treatment program, the court has the authority to apply sanctions ranging from more frequent contact with program staff to short jail stays. Serious infractions may result in transferring the case to a regular criminal court.

By using a graduated series of sanctions that increase in severity as a defendant's noncompliance increases, the drug court seeks to encourage compliance rather than ejecting a defendant from the program for a single infraction. Successful completion of the treatment program generally results in the criminal charges being dropped by the state; repeated or sufficiently serious failure to comply with the requirements imposed by the drug court results in the resumption of prosecution within the criminal court.

Drug courts refer clients to a wide range of treatment services, but generally maintain them in the community. A typical drug-court client may attend both group and individual counseling while also attending Alcoholics Anonymous (AA) or Narcotics Anonymous (NA) meetings. Weekly reports to a probation officer are normally required. Drug courts generally have the treatment components divided into three or more stages, with the client having to meet certain goals at each stage before moving on to the next. During the early part of the drug-court program, the client may have to provide three to five urine samples weekly, gradually decreasing to one every week or two during the later stages of the program, assuming no serious infractions of the rules. A majority of drug-court programs use acupuncture as a treatment component, some on a mandatory basis, others voluntarily.

RECOMMENDED READING: J. Goldkamp and D. Weiland, *Assessing the*

Impact of Dade County's Felony Drug Court (Washington, DC: U.S. Government Printing Office, 1993); T. Maugh and M. Anglin, "Court-Ordered Drug Treatment Does Work," *Judges' Journal* 33 (1994): 10–13, 38–40.

C. Aaron McNeece

DRUG CZAR. The drug czar is the leader of the war on drugs. Though not a cabinet-level position, the drug czar sits with the president's cabinet. The first drug czar was William J. Bennett. Under the Clinton administration the focus of the war on drugs has shifted toward treatment and the reduction of demand. The drug czar's staff was significantly reduced by the Clinton administration. (See **William J. Bennett**.)

Glenn Zuern

DRUG DEALERS. Drug dealers are people who sell drugs for economic gain outside the confines of legal transactions. Pharmaceutical companies deal in drugs, but are not considered drug dealers. Drug dealers profit from dealing in drugs in large part due to the criminal sanctions against the selling of drugs. These sanctions keep the price of drugs high and the profits of drug dealers high. Drug dealers range from street dealers who sell partial ounces of cocaine to cocaine cartels that smuggle tons of cocaine into the United States yearly. Profiles of various types of drug dealers have been developed by law enforcement agencies in their drug enforcement efforts.
RECOMMENDED READING: Richard H. Blum, *Drug Dealers: Taking Action* (San Francisco: Jossey-Bass, 1973).

Glenn Zuern

DRUG-LAW VIOLATION. Any act that violates laws regulating the sale, purchase, growing, producing, possession, storing, or transporting of drugs or attempts to commit any of these acts. Most drug-law violations are related to the sale and use of illegal drugs. Drug-law violations have had increasingly harsh penalties mandated as punishment for violations of these laws.

Glenn Zuern

DRUG TRAFFICKING. Drug trafficking is differentiated from drug dealing in several ways. (See **Drug Dealers**.) The amount of drugs and money and the movement of drugs are all variables that separate drug dealing from drug trafficking. Typically, drug traffickers sell larger amounts of drugs to drug dealers as opposed to drug users. They also acquire and move large amounts of money generated from their illegal trade in drugs. (See **Money Laundering**.) These dealers are also more likely to transport drugs across state and international borders. The penalties for drug trafficking have increased through the 1980s and 1990s in an effort to diminish the supply of drugs to users, but even harsher penalties have had little impact on stanching the flow.
RECOMMENDED READING: Jillian Powell, *Drug Trafficking* (London: Watts, 1996); U.S. Congress, *International Drug Trafficking and its Local*

Impact, Hearing before the Committee on Foreign Relations, July 29, 1996 (Washington, DC: U.S. Government Printing Office, 1996).

Glenn Zuern

DRUG TREATMENT FOR CRIMINAL OFFENDERS. Because criminal offenders frequently are addicted to or abuse or drugs or alcohol, it has become more common in recent years for law enforcement agencies or the courts to refer them for treatment. In 1990 drug offenses accounted for about one in three commitments to state prisons, and in 1991, 62 percent of all inmates reported being regular users of illicit drugs before their imprisonment. Incarceration rates for drug-related crimes almost certainly will continue to rise due to state and federal mandatory minimum sentencing laws.

One of the earliest federal initiatives was known as Treatment Alternatives to Street Crime (TASC). Beginning as a federally funded program in 1972, it was continued by most states with block grants. TASC was originally conceived as an assessment and case-management system. Suspected offenders are screened and referred to treatment, often as a diversionary measure. Both juvenile and adult TASC programs, sometimes known by other names, operate in every state.

The range of drug treatment programs for criminal offenders varies from in-jail counseling, sometimes by untrained volunteers and ministers, to intensive residential treatment. Methadone maintenance, boot camps, halfway houses, Narcotics Anonymous, and drug courts are other options. Frequently what is identified as treatment for offenders on pretrial release is little more than monitoring, primarily through the process of urinalysis and a mandatory check-in with a probation officer. Many of these programs were originally funded under the Anti–Drug Abuse Act of 1988. The available evidence seems to show that mandatory treatment for criminal offenders is just about as effective (or ineffective) as voluntary treatment for noncriminals. Methadone maintenance and the use of other antagonist drug therapies appear to be more effective than most other treatments, at least in the short run. Unfortunately, the recidivism rates for most groups of offenders are unacceptably high, with cocaine users running the greatest risk (over 80 percent) of relapse. The most successful treatment occurs when the offender is in treatment longer,   is employed in a legitimate job, and is part of an intact family.

Offenders maintained in the community are much more likely to obtain drug treatment than those who are incarcerated, and incarcerated women are less likely to get treatment than incarcerated men, even though a greater proportion of women inmates are diagnosed with a substance-abuse problem. The federal Bureau of Prisons has implemented a six-part drug treatment strategy in some of its facilities that includes screening, education, residential treatment, nonresidential treatment, transitional treatment, and evaluation.

RECOMMENDED READING: C. Daly and C. McNeece, "Treatment and Intervention with Chemically-Involved Adult Offenders," in *Policy and Practice in the Justice System*, ed. C. McNeece and A. Roberts (Chicago:

Nelson-Hall Publishers, 1997); James A. Inciardi, *Drug Treatment and Criminal Justice*, (Newbury Park, CA: Sage Publications, 1993); U.S. Department of Justice, *Drug Use Forecasting: 1995 Annual Report* (Washington, DC: U.S. Government Printing Office, 1996).

C. Aaron McNeece

DRUNK DRIVING. Drunk driving occurs when someone under the influence of alcohol drives a motor vehicle. Under pressure from interest groups, such as Mothers against Drunk Driving, states have passed laws mandating harsher penalties for individuals found guilty of drunk driving. The medical and social cost of drunk driving has been estimated to be in the billions of dollars. (See **Driving Under the Influence**.)

Glenn Zuern

DUE-PROCESS MODEL OF JUSTICE. Knowledge about crime, its causes, and its control has significantly affected perceptions of how criminal justice should be managed. Different philosophical viewpoints have arisen, and the due-process model is one of these important viewpoints. Herbert Packer in 1968 contrasted the crime-control model with the opposing view that he referred to as the due-process model. According to Packer, the due-process model combines elements of liberal positivist criminology with the legal concept of procedural fairness for the accused. This model adheres to principles of individualized justice treatment and rehabilitation of the offender. The civil rights of the accused should be protected at all possible costs.

This model tends to restrict the legal definition of criminal behavior by advocacy of removing certain offenses such as so-called victimless crimes (e.g., prostitution, gambling, and certain drug violations) from the criminal statutes. According to Larry J. Siegel (1995), proponents of this philosophy are usually members of the legal profession who see themselves as protectors of civil rights. Packer likened the crime-control model to an assembly line and the due-process model to an obstacle course and saw the models as the end points of a continuum.

The due-process model questions the reliability of fact finding. Persons should be termed criminal and deprived of their freedom only on the basis of reliable information. To minimize error, hurdles must be erected so that the power of the state can only be used when it has been proved beyond doubt that the defendant committed the crime. The best way to achieve this goal is to test the evidence through an adversarial proceeding. In the due-process model the possibility that a few who may be factually guilty will remain free outweighs the possibility in the crime-control model for governmental power to be abused and the innocent to be endangered. This model prefers full court proceedings to the large amount of administrative and discretionary decision making resulting in plea bargains.

RECOMMENDED READING: George F. Cole, *The American System of Criminal Justice*, 7th ed. (Belmont, CA: Wadsworth Publishing Co., 1995);

Larry J. Siegel, *Criminology*, 5th ed. (Minneapolis/St. Paul: West Publishing Co., 1995).

Ransom A. Whittle

DUI LEGISLATION, EFFECTS OF. American driving under the influence (DUI) legislation is generally based on the Scandinavian model, which includes six key elements. First, the codes are model "per se" laws that define the offense as driving with a specified concentration of alcohol in the blood. Second, chemical testing for blood alcohol is provided for in the codes. Third, refusal to provide appropriate samples (e.g., blood, urine, and breath) can be used as evidence in drinking-driving prosecution. Fourth, refusal may also result in a license suspension. Fifth, mandatory jail sentences are required for those found in violation of the codes. Sixth, the codes restrict the use of plea bargaining. The laws typically allow drunk-driving charges to be reduced but cause them to remain on record. In general, the laws are designed to deter the practice of driving while intoxicated and severely punish those caught in violation of the law.

The consequences of "tough" DUI legislation can be divided into two types: intended and unintended. Examples of evaluative case studies researching the intended effects can be drawn from across the United States and around the world. Early research on this topic presented a single overriding theme: Simply stated, DUI legislation does deter, but only in the short term. More recent research, however, has brought this conclusion into question. The decision to drink and drive is the result of a complex interplay between formal and informal sanctions, the physical and social environments, and the traditional model of marginal deterrence. The totality of this interplay must be evaluated before a conclusion about the effects of tough legislation may be made. It may be, for example, that the formal sanctions written into the law do not deter the individual in an immediate sense, but do work to change the social and self-perceptions of the drinking driver. These "changes" become informal sanctions (i.e., personal guilt and peer pressure) that do deter the behavior. The law change, therefore, has achieved its desired effect, only in a way that goes beyond the traditional model of marginal deterrence. Moreover, it has also been demonstrated that law changes that are coupled with increased publicity and enforcement can achieve long-term deterrent effects.

The most comprehensive study detailing the unintended effects that "tough" DUI legislation has had on the criminal justice system (Stewart and Laurence, 1987) identified three major adverse consequences. The first is an increase in court workloads. Jurisdictions have dealt with this in various ways: hiring additional judges, arranging for night and weekend arraignments, and opening up new facilities to handle additional DUI cases. The second unintended consequence has been an increase in the need for special programs and facilities to deal with the DUI offenders. These offenders are often allowed to serve their sentences under special guidelines or in areas or buildings apart from the mainstream jail populations. The third major adverse impact has been an increase in the numbers of DUI incarcerates and probationers. This often leads to jail overcrowding and a strained probation system. Two other effects that have been only anecdotally documented in relation to this type of law change are an increase in the need for county-provided defense and prosecuting attorneys and an increase in jail suicides.

The fact that major systemic consequences occur when DUI sentencing reform is adopted mandate policy development that allows for the consequences of such reform throughout the criminal justice system. An unplanned-for systemic adjustment is more costly than one that is preconceived and implemented. Indeed, the problems that emerge from radical DUI sentencing reform will often lead to a crisis in criminal justice administration.

RECOMMENDED READING: Kathryn Stewart and Susan Laurence, *Senate Concurrent Resolution No. 27 Report: A Review of the Implementation and Effectiveness of Drinking and Driving Legislation* (Walnut Creek, CA: Pacific Institute for Research and Evaluation, 1987; D. L. McMillen, S. Smith, and E. N. Wells-Parker, "The Effects of Alcohol, Expectancy, and Sensation Seeking on Driving Risk Taking," *Addictive Behaviors*, Vol. 14, (1989): 477–483.

Patrick Kinkade

DYING DECLARATION. A statement made by an individual concerning the cause and/or circumstances of his/her death when that individual understands that his/her death is imminent. It is used primarily (though not exclusively) in criminal cases, particularly homicides. The individual hearing the declaration, usually a law enforcement official, may repeat the declaration in testimony at trial under an exception to the hearsay rule.

Dying declarations are accepted in part because many feel that an individual knowing that his/her death is imminent will want to leave this life telling the truth. Thus, in order that such declarations may qualify as an exception to the hearsay rule, it must be shown that the "declarant" believed that his/her death was imminent.

Such declarations admissible as exceptions to the hearsay rule are confined to those factual statements (not opinions) concerning the cause and circumstances of the death. These may include the identification of the perpetrator and a description of circumstances surrounding the death. Their impact on the trier of fact is likely to be powerful.

RECOMMENDED READING: Joseph R. Nolan and Jacqueline M. Nolan-Haley, *Black's Law Dictionary: Definitions of the Terms and Phrases of American and English Jurisprudence, Ancient and Modern*, 6th ed. (St. Paul, MN: West Publishing Co., 1991).

David Jones

E

EARP, WYATT (1848–1929). This short-term sheriff has been described in some literature as a peace officer whose reputation was largely manufactured by himself and his biographer, Stuart N. Lake, and the television series of the 1950s. Others view Earp as a drifting opportunist, saloon-inhabiting card shark, and suspected outlaw. He was a policeman in Wichita, but was fired because he let his arrests degenerate into street brawls. He was hired as deputy sheriff of Tombstone, Arizona, in 1879. He was then hired after less than a year to be a deputy U.S. marshal at Tombstone. In this last capacity he participated in the gunfight at the OK Corral. He lived until age eighty, his last years relatively quiet in Los Angeles. He had hired the biographer, Lake, to ensure his fame. Earp's own wife repudiated the Lake biography.
RECOMMENDED READING: Glenn G. Boyer, *Wyatt Earp: Facts, Volume 3, Trailing an American Myth, and Those Marryin' Earp Boys* (Rodeo, NM: Historical Research Associates, 1997), Randall A. Morton, *Wyatt, the Man Called Earp* (Laguna Niguel, CA: RAMCO International, 1994); Casey Tefertiller, *Wyatt Earp: The Life Behind the Legend* (New York: J. Wiley, 1997).

David R. Struckhoff

EDMONSON v. LEESVILLE CONCRETE CO., INC., **500 U.S. 614 (1991).** In this case the U.S. Supreme Court held that the use of peremptory challenges in *voir dire* by a party in civil litigation to exclude jurors on the basis of their race is a violation of the equal-protection rights of those excluded jurors. Consequently, such use of peremptory challenges contravenes the U.S. Constitution.

Thaddeus Donald Edmonson, a black man, had been injured in an industrial accident and sued his employer, Leesville Concrete, in federal district court. During *voir dire* lawyers for the company exercised some of their peremptory challenges to exclude blacks from the jury. Edmonson's attorney asked the judge to require opposing counsel to articulate race-neutral reasons for the use of its peremptories, citing *Batson v. Kentucky* (1986), which disallowed the use of race-based peremptory challenges in criminal proceedings. The judge refused, holding that *Batson* did not apply to civil actions. This ruling was eventually upheld by the federal court of appeals.

The Supreme Court had to decide a number of issues. One of these was the question of whether the exercise of peremptory challenges on the part of Leesville's attorneys constituted "state action," since the conduct of private parties generally lies beyond the scope of the Constitution in most cases. Justice Anthony Kennedy, writing for the majority, argued that certain factors should be considered in determining whether a particular action is "governmental" in character. These were: Is the actor performing a traditionally governmental function? Does the actor rely on governmental assistance and benefits? Is the injury caused aggravated in a unique way by the incidents of governmental authority? On the basis of these criteria, argued Justice Kennedy, the use of peremptory challenges by a private party in *voir dire* constitutes "state action."

The Court also held that a private litigant may raise the equal-protection claim of a person whom opposing counsel has excluded from jury service on the basis of race since the factors allowing a defendant to do so in criminal proceedings also apply in civil proceedings. This case can be seen as the application of principles developed in *Batson v. Kentucky* (a criminal case) to civil proceedings.

David Jones

EMBEZZLEMENT. Embezzlement is the fraudulent appropriation of property by a person to whom it has been entrusted. The crime of embezzlement is consummated where the defendant, by virtue of his/her agency or other confidential relationship, has been entrusted with the property of another and wrongfully converts it to his/her own use. Embezzlement consists of four essential elements: 1- The defendant was the agent of the complainant; 2- Pursuant to the terms of his/her employment s/he was to receive property of the complainant; 3- S/he received such property in the course of his/her employment; and 4- Knowing that it was not his/hers, s/he either converted it to his/her own use or fraudulently misapplied it. Many states have consolidated the crime of embezzlement into the crime of theft.

RECOMMENDED READING: Robert Bryant Bates, *Property Crimes, Private Agendas, and the Criminal Justice System*, M. S. thesis (California State University, Fresno, 1992); Joseph R. Nolan and Jacqueline M. Nolan-Haley, *Black's Law Dictionary: Definitions of the Terms and Phrases of American and English Jurisprudence, Ancient and Modern*, 6th ed. (St. Paul, MN: West Publishing Co., 1991).

Lee E. Parker

ENTRAPMENT. An "affirmative defense," that is, a mechanism by which criminal behavior is waived because of some compelling reason asserted by the defendant. An entrapment defense is one in which the defendant alleges that s/he would not have committed the offense if the government had not taken certain actions to lure the defendant into the illegal endeavor. The defense is sometimes raised as a result of undercover actions undertaken by law enforcement personnel.

The issue of entrapment was first addressed by the U.S. Supreme Court in *Sorrells v. U.S.* (1932). In this case a federal Prohibition agent, posing as a civilian, visited Sorrells and asked several times if the defendant would sell him some liquor. Sorrells finally did so and was arrested and convicted. He argued that the agent had entrapped him, but the lower court would not allow this defense to be used. The Supreme Court reversed, holding that entrapment could have been used as a defense.

One of the more recent cases involving entrapment heard by the Court was *Jacobson v. United States* (1992). In this case agents for the federal government found Jacobson's name on an "adult" bookstore mailing list. They then sent material to him from fictitious organizations in order to explore his willingness to break child pornography laws. Many of these "organizations" represented that they were founded to protect sexual freedom and freedom of choice and that they promoted lobbying efforts through catalogue sales. After representations for two and one-half years Jacobson ordered a magazine depicting young boys engaging in sexual activities. He was arrested after a "controlled delivery" of a photocopy of the magazine. At his jury trial he pleaded entrapment, but was convicted.

The Supreme Court reversed, holding that the prosecution failed as a matter of law to adduce evidence to support the jury verdict that Jacobson was predisposed to violate the law. In the Court's view the government went too far in encouraging Jacobson to commit the illegal act.

In law there are two tests of entrapment. The one used in most jurisdictions, including the federal government, is the "subjective" test that focuses on the defendant's state of mind: Was the defendant predisposed to commit the act? If so, s/he cannot successfully plead entrapment. Some jurisdictions utilize the "objective" test, which focuses on the government's behavior: If law enforcement officers use methods (such as offers of inordinate gain) that create a substantial risk that an offense will be committed by persons other than those ready to commit it, then, by definition, entrapment has been used. While it has been attempted in a few high-profile cases, the entrapment defense has rarely been invoked successfully.

RECOMMENDED READING: Joseph R. Nolan and Jacqueline M. Nolan-Haley, *Black's Law Dictionary: Definitions of the Terms and Phrases of American and English Jurisprudence, Ancient and Modern*, 6th ed. (St. Paul, MN: West Publishing Co., 1991); Lawrence P. Tiffany, D. M. McIntyre, and Daniel L. Rotenberg, *Detection of Crime: Stopping and Questioning, Search and Seizure, Encouragement and Entrapment* (Boston: Little, Brown 1969).

David Jones

***ESCOE v. ZERBST, WARDEN*, 295 U.S. 490 (1935).** An early case involving the rights of individuals facing a sentence of probation. In this instance the U.S. Supreme Court held that under law a federal district court, acting on the request of a probation officer based on information received by him concerning a probationer's delinquency, is without power to revoke a suspension of sentence and commit the petitioner to prison to serve his sentence when the probationer was not "taken before the court" and afforded an opportunity to be heard in answer to the charges.

Petitioner Escoe was convicted of a crime in the U.S. District Court for the Eastern District of Texas. His sentence was suspended, and he was placed on probation. Conditions of probation included provisions that Escoe refrain from violation of state and federal laws and that he live a "clean, honest, and temperate life." Later, Escoe's probation officer received information that Escoe had violated his conditions of probation, and the officer conveyed this information to a court. Escoe was arrested and, rather than being brought before the judge, was sent directly to prison. Benjamin Cardozo, writing for a unanimous court, held that this action violated congressional mandates that probationers be taken before a court and be given an opportunity for a hearing. Petitioners' rights, the Court was careful to note in this case, were based on statute, not on a constitutional provision. The Court ordered that Escoe be discharged from confinement.

David Jones

***ESTELLE v. GAMBLE*, 429 U.S. 97 (1976).** *A* case involving the interpretation of the Eighth Amendment's prohibition against "cruel and unusual punishment" in the context of the medical needs of prisoners. In this case the U.S. Supreme Court held (at 104) that "deliberate indifference to serious medical needs of prisoners constitutes the 'unnecessary and wanton infliction of pain' proscribed by the Eighth Amendment." However, it was also the opinion of the Court that not every claim made by a prisoner that s/he has not received adequate medical treatment constitutes a violation of the Eighth Amendment. In this case the Court held that while it was possible that prison personnel made mistakes in the treatment of the prisoner, such mistakes — if they indeed did exist— did not constitute cruel and unusual punishment.

David Jones

ETHICS IN CRIMINAL JUSTICE. Ethics is the consideration of that which is good for persons, and of the conduct or duties that we owe to one another. Ethical principles may be derived from a religious source, a set of maxims, or an examination of utility. Ethical principles in criminal justice guide the decision making of individuals in the discretionary aspects of prosecution and defense, law enforcement, and punishment.

Actors in the criminal justice system must regularly make decisions that are not guided by law. The decision of a prosecutor to allocate resources for a specific investigation is such a decision, as is the decision that evidence is sufficient to prosecute an individual. The choices of a lawyer in crafting a defense for that individual will be constrained by ethical considerations.

Police face ethical choices in their investigative work as it involves deception and a population that includes disadvantaged members of the community. The work of police and corrections personnel mandates the use of force to restrain or subdue individuals. The evaluation of the amount of necessary force that is ethically permissible joins the potential abuse of authority for personal gain as the most pervasive ethical problems for workers in criminal justice. Many of the professional associations in the field of criminal justice have chosen to make their ethical principles explicit in a published code of ethics.

RECOMMENDED READING. Michael C. Braswell, Belinda R. McCarthy, and Bernard J. McCarthy, *Justice, Crime and Ethics*, 2nd ed. (Cincinnati: Anderson Publishing Co., 1996); Sam S. Souryal, *Ethics in Criminal Justice, In Search of the Truth* (Cincinnati: Anderson Publishing Co., 1992).

Margaret Leland Smith

EXCLUSIONARY RULE.   The exclusionary rule refers to the understanding, based upon U.S. Supreme Court precedent, that incriminating evidence must be seized according to constitutional specifications of due process, or it will not be allowed as evidence in criminal trials. Under the exclusionary rule, evidence illegally seized by the police cannot be used in a trial. The rule acts as a control over police behavior, and specifically focuses upon the failure of officers to obtain warrants authorizing them to either conduct searches or to effect arrests—especially where arrest may lead to the acquisition of incriminating statements or to the seizure of physical evidence.

Many legal scholars trace the origin of the exclusionary rule to the landmark U.S. Supreme Court case of *Weeks v. United States* (1914). In that case, the defendant, Freemont Weeks, was suspected of using the U.S. mail to sell lottery tickets, a federal crime. Weeks was arrested and federal agents went to his home to conduct a search. They had no search warrant, since at the time investigators did not routinely use warrants. They confiscated many incriminating items of evidence, as well as personal possessions of the defendant, including clothes, papers, books, and even candy.

Prior to the trial, Weeks' attorney asked that the personal items be returned, claiming that they had been illegally seized under Fourth Amendment guarantees. A judge agreed and ordered the materials returned. On the basis of the evidence that was retained, however, Weeks was convicted in federal court and sentenced to prison. He appealed his conviction through other courts, and eventually reached the U.S. Supreme Court. There his lawyer reasoned that if some of his client's belongings had been illegally seized, then the remainder was also taken improperly. The Supreme Court agreed, and overturned Weeks' earlier conviction.

It is important to recognize that the decision of the Supreme Court in the *Weeks* case was binding, at the time, only upon federal officers because it was federal agents who were involved in the illegal seizure. It was not until 1961 that the Court made the exclusionary rule applicable to criminal prosecutions

at the state level via its ruling in *Mapp v. Ohio*.
RECOMMENDED READING: Joseph R. Nolan and Jacqueline M. Nolan-Haley, *Black's Law Dictionary: Definitions of the Terms and Phrases of American and English Jurisprudence, Ancient and Modern*, 6th ed. (St. Paul, MN: West Publishing Co., 1991); *Mapp v. Ohio*, 367 U.S. 643 (1961); *Weeks v. United States*, 232 U.S. 383 (1914).

Frank Schmalleger

***EX POST FACTO* LAWS.**   Sections 9 and 10 of Article I of the U.S. Constitution prohibit *ex post facto* laws. Such laws punish criminal behavior in a retroactive manner. In *Collins v. Youngblood*, 497 U.S. 37 (1990), the U.S. Supreme Court defined an ex post facto law as one that "retroactively alter[s] the definition of crimes or increase[s] the punishment for criminal acts." For example, if a state's burglary statute provided that a person could be charged with burglary only if s/he committed the offense during the nighttime, s/he could not be charged with burglary if s/he committed an unlawful entry during the daytime, even if the statute was later changed to include unlawful entries committed during daylight hours. The constitutional protection against ex post facto laws would prohibit the burglary charge. Similarly, if on July 4, 1995, a state's criminal code did not prohibit the sale of fireworks, and a law was passed in 1996 prohibiting such sales, a person could not be charged with violating the law for sales that occurred in 1995.

The central reason for prohibiting ex post facto laws is based on the idea that the law must give people fair notice that their behavior is criminal. It is unfair to punish a person for an act that was not a crime at the time he or she committed it.
RECOMMENDED READING: Gerald Gunther, *Constitutional Law*, 13th ed. (Westbury, NY: Foundation Press, 1997).

Thomas J. Hickey

F

FEDERAL BUREAU OF PRISONS, HISTORY. Although Congress authorized the funds for the purchase of land for the first three federal penitentiaries in 1889, the history of federal corrections extends back to 1776. At this time the Continental Congress established that those individuals who committed federal crimes would be held in state and local facilities. Because the federal government placed relatively few inmates in these institutions and because the states enjoyed the benefit of being able to generate funds by contracting the labor of federal prisoners, this arrangement proved satisfactory for many years. However, when the federal government prohibited the practice of contract labor, the system began to collapse.

In 1895 the U.S. Department of Justice was given the charge of an old military prison in Leavenworth, Kansas, for the incarceration of federal prisoners. Because of the increase in the number of crimes that were being prosecuted in federal courts and because of the general increase in the American population, this facility soon became overcrowded. Congress then hastened to expand this facility and open others. The Leavenworth expansion began holding prisoners in 1906, and new prisons in Atlanta, Georgia, and McNeil Island, Washington, were opened in 1902 and 1903, respectively.

During the first part of this century (1900–1930) federal prisons were extremely punitive environments. Forced prison labor, harsh sanctions for even small rule violations, and inadequate resources due to overcrowding and lack of funds were the norm. Yet even under these rather bleak conditions several progressive reforms did make themselves apparent. In 1910 the federal government established a system of parole. In 1926 construction of the first federal reformatory was started, built in the hopes of segregating young offenders from general-population inmates. Finally, in 1927 the first federal women's institution opened.

The few progressive changes made during this time were, however, far overshadowed by the problems facing federal corrections. In 1929 the House of Representatives released a report that was very critical of the organization of and living conditions within federal prisons. The report also contained many ideas offered to improve the situation. Foremost among these was a suggestion that federal corrections become centralized and adopt uniform standards of operations. In 1930 President Herbert Hoover, reacting to the report and on a recommendation from Congress, created the federal Bureau of Prisons within the Department of Justice in an attempt to achieve these goals.

Immediately after its inception the bureau faced a number of problems. In the 1930s large amounts of anticrime legislation were passed, exacerbating the already-crowded federal institutions. Many new facilities were added to help with this influx of federal inmates, including the notorious Alcatraz. This institution held some of the most famous criminals in recent American history, including both Al Capone and "Machine Gun" Kelly. Ultimately, the costs of running the institution and the punishing nature of its regime led to its closure in 1963. At approximately this time one also saw a recommitment to the rehabilitative ideal in federal corrections. From the late 1950s to the 1970s classification systems in federal institutions were improved, leading to better vocational and therapeutic opportunities for the inmates. Moreover, efforts were made to better integrate the correctional institution and inmate with their surrounding community.

In the mid-1970s, however, the identification of rehabilitation as the sole goal of the federal correctional system began to be questioned by academics, practitioners, and civil libertarians. With the recognition that the system should work to other correctional ends came an upswing in the system's inmate population. Attempts to moderate this growth have been several, but have also been largely ineffective. The Sentencing Reform Act of 1984, which abolished parole after 1988 for federal prisoners, and the general "get-tough" attitude of most recent federal criminal justice legislation have minimized many anticipated positive outcomes with regard to inmate populations.

Through the 1980s the bureau worked with the American Correctional Association toward the accreditation of all its facilities to bring the system into compliance with all court-mandated standards for inmate living conditions. As of January 1, 1995, the federal correctional system had 95,034 convicts under institutional supervision. The largest number of these incarcerates were placed in the federal system for drug offenses.

RECOMMENDED READING: *Facts on the Federal Bureau of Prisons* (Washington, DC: The Bureau, 1992); Robert L. Trachtenberg, *The Federal Bureau of Prisons Proposed Organizational Changes to meet the Challenges of Growth* (Washington, DC: National Academy of Public Administration, 1993).

Patrick Kinkade

FEDERAL CORRECTIONAL SYSTEM, ORGANIZATION OF THE. Correctional activities at the federal level are organized under several different agencies, and although there is a great deal of coordination between these administrative agencies, they are not strictly centralized. The U.S. Department of Justice is primarily responsible for administering the federal Bureau of

Prisons; the U.S. Probation Service is organized within the U.S. Administrative Office of the Courts; and the U.S. Parole Commission is a semi-autonomous agency.

The federal Bureau of Prisons was operating eighty-two facilities by the fall of 1995, which included prisons, medical centers, classification facilities, prison camps, and juvenile institutions. In addition, the federal system is responsible for the administration of over three hundred halfway houses with which it has contracted for space. These facilities house over 70,000 prisoners, the vast majority (over 90 %) of which are male. Historically, because of the nature of federal criminal law, those offenders who were held in federal facilities tended to be more sophisticated than the inmates of state prisons. These trends have changed in recent years as more drug-related offenses have become appropriate for federal prosecution. The classification system used to organize the offenders within this system has moved away from the traditional minimum-, medium-, and maximum-security designations to a six-level system. In this system level 1 would suggest the least secure institution, and level six, the most secure.

Federal probation is much less centralized than federal corrections. Within federal probation officers are attached to a federal district court, and the chief probation officer of each district is accountable to that district's judge. In the 1990s federal probation populations have remained at approximately 60,000 individuals, with 33 % of that population turning over in any given year. Approximately 50 % of all federal offenders are given some sort of probation as part of their sentence.

Federal parole was abolished in 1988. Those prisoners who have been sentenced after the law change will be administered through designated mandatory release mechanisms. Those prisoners who were sentenced before the law change are still entitled to parole review by the U.S. Parole Commission, whose members make release decisions in accordance with guidelines in effect under the former parole system. Through the late 1980s and into the 1990s between five thousand and seven thousand inmates have been released on parole per year.

RECOMMENDED READING: Federal Bureau of Prisons, *The Federal Correctional System* (Washington, DC: U.S. Government Printing Office, 1996).

Patrick Kinkade

FEDERAL COURT SYSTEM. Article III, Section 1, of the U.S. Constitution states, "The judicial power of the United States, shall be vested in one Supreme Court, and in such inferior Courts as Congress may from time to time ordain and establish." Article III also provides for the life tenure of federal judges and for the jurisdiction of federal courts.

The federal court system is distinct from, and in many ways parallel to, the fifty state court systems. Federal court jurisdiction includes cases arising under the U.S. Constitution, from federal laws (both civil and criminal), and from controversies involving two or more states or citizens thereof.

The organization of the federal court system is provided for primarily by congressional statute, subject, of course, to relevant provisions of the U.S. Constitution. The U.S. Supreme Court sits at the apex of the system. In that position the Court, currently consisting of nine people (a chief justice and eight associate justices), makes ultimate determination of the meaning of the U.S. Constitution. It is arguably the most powerful court in the world. The U.S. Supreme Court has both original jurisdiction (provided for in the Constitution) and appellate jurisdiction as determined by Congress. Most cases heard by the Court reach it by a process known as "writ of *certiorari*."

Directly below the Supreme Court are the U.S. courts of appeals. Their jurisdiction is solely appellate. These courts are empowered to review decisions of federal district courts and to review and enforce orders of many federal administrative agencies. Decisions of these courts are final, subject only to discretionary review of the U.S. Supreme Court.

The United States is divided into twelve judicial circuits, and there is a court of appeals for each circuit. The number of judicial positions varies with the amount of judicial work in the circuit. In 1995 there were a total of 179 permanent circuit judges. Normally cases are heard by a panel of 3 judges. Each circuit also has a chief judge. In addition to the geographically established courts of appeals, there is the U.S. Court of Appeals for the Federal Circuit. Its jurisdiction, which is nationwide, deals with certain specialized types of cases (e.g., patent cases). This court, consisting of 12 circuit judges, sits in panels of 3 or more judges on each case.

The trial courts in the federal system are the U.S. district courts. There are eighty-nine district courts (at least one per state) plus one for the District of Columbia. The number of judgeships per district varies (from 2 to 28) with the amount of judicial business in each district. As trial courts, district courts deal with both civil and criminal litigation arising under the laws of the United States. Each district court contains at least one U.S. magistrate judge, a bankruptcy judge, a clerk, a U.S. attorney, and a U.S. marshal, together with probation officers, court reporters, and their staff. Cases from district courts may be appealed to the court of appeals in the circuit in which they lie.

It is important to note that all of the judges described here hold their positions for life or good behavior. It is extremely difficult to remove a sitting judge from his/her position. This fact contributes greatly to the independence of the federal judiciary, an important component of the American constitutional system.

In addition to these courts, the federal system is also served by territorial courts, the U.S. Court of International Trade (which deals with cases involving import transactions), the U.S. Court of Military Appeals (which deals with the appeals of courts martial), the U.S. Tax Court, and the U.S. Court of Veterans Appeals. Judges on most of these courts serve for specific terms.

RECOMMENDED READING: *The United States Government Manual* (Washington, DC: U.S. Government Printing Office, 1996).

David Jones

FEDERAL PROBATION SYSTEM. The federal probation system consists of a closely integrated network of 173 offices to serve the U.S. district courts in all fifty states, the District of Columbia, Guam, Puerto Rico, and the Virgin Islands. An act of Congress establishing a federal probation system was signed on March 5, 1925. In 1994 there were 3,660 probation officer positions authorized to the probation system. The minimum qualification for becoming a federal probation officer is the baccalaureate degree, preferably in the social sciences. First-time applicants for an officer position must be under the age of thirty-seven by the time of appointment. Salary is based on specialized experience as outlined in the Judiciary Salary Plan.

According to the Administrative Office of the United States Courts, the total federal population on supervision grew from 33,784 in 1983 to 48,722 in 1993. The system has jurisdiction over offenders charged with violating federal crimes such as interstate thefts, income-tax violations, frauds against the government and government-insured institutions, and counterfeiting. The system is admin-istered with considerable autonomy at the district level. Each probation office functions under the immediate direction of the district court, while the Administrative Office of the United States Courts, Division of Probation, located in Washington, D.C., formulates general policies and procedures. The basic duties of the probation officer, found in Title 18 of the United States Code; are as follows:

Investigation. Once an offender is found guilty, the probation officer investigates the details of the crime and the offender's background, calculates the relevant sentencing guideline score, and then prepares a presentence report to the court. The court uses the report to determine an appropriate sentence for the offender. The presentence report also presents relevant data for the super-vision of the offender if the offender is to be supervised in the community, as well as data for prison officials if the offender is to be incarcerated.

Supervision. Supervision involves the procedures for supervising offenders who were placed on probation, supervised release, or parole, to monitor their conduct to ensure progress under a supervision plan. Probation is a sentence that allows the offender to remain in the community if the probationer abides by specific conditions set by the court. Supervised release in the federal system is a new type of supervision for offenders who have been released after imprisonment. Supervised release replaces federal parole, which was abolished by the Sentencing Reform Act of 1984. Another program that the federal probation system has implemented for supervising federal offenders is the Enhanced Supervision Program. This program focuses on executing the sentence imposed by the court, controlling risk, and providing offenders with necessary correctional treatment. This new system differentiates between supervision activities designed to monitor offender behavior and activities designed to assist in changing the offender's behavior.

The federal probation system works closely with other federal agencies in the Departments of Justice and Treasury. For example, the probation system cooperates with the Bureau of Prisons in providing information about offenders within the custody of the attorney general or while on work release or furlough and in making prerelease arrangements for incarcerated offenders.

RECOMMENDED READING: Sanford Bates, "The Establishment and Early Years of the Federal Probation System," *Federal Probation* (June 1987): 4–9; Federal Judicial Center, *An Introduction to the Federal Probation System* (Washington, DC: The Center, 1976); National Advisory Commission on Criminal Justice Standards and Goals, *Task Force Report: Corrections* (Washington, DC: U.S. Government Printing Office, 1973).

Fred Allen

FELONY. One of the two general categories of crimes (see **Misdemeanor**), felonies is usually classified as a serious crime punishable by more than one year in prison. The federal government and some states require trial by indictment for felony charges. Although exact elements of felonies may differ among the states, common elements include use of a firearm or other weapon, level of danger or fear in which the victim is placed, degree of injury to the victim, or value of property stolen.

RECOMMENDED READING: Joseph R. Nolan and Jacqueline M. Nolan-Haley, *Black's Law Dictionary: Definitions of the Terms and Phrases of American and English Jurisprudence, Ancient and Modern*, 6th ed. (St. Paul, MN: West Publishing Co., 1991).

Christopher J. Morse

FINES. Fines are an ancient form of punishment predating the Code of Hammurabi and still used today as a criminal sanction. In the late 1980s estimates indicated that more than $1 billion in fines were being collected yearly in America's criminal courts. Nonetheless, fines are being underused in this country mostly because too little is known about how to administer them properly.

Proponents argue that fines are an effective punishment and alternative to incarceration for several reasons: Fines emphasize offender accountability, are inexpensive to enforce, can be modified to fit offenders' circumstances and the seriousness of their crimes, can be combined with other sanctions to meet sentencing goals, provide revenue to the criminal justice system, and relieve jail overcrowding. Critics, on the other hand, maintain that fines do not incapacitate offenders and therefore are inappropriate for individuals posing a public safety risk. In addition, they contend that fines are difficult to collect from poor offenders and may unfairly impact the indigent (e.g., imprisonment for defaulting on payments). The most effective use of fines involves an initial assessment of offenders' ability to pay and a strategy to ensure that monies are collected. In the words of Morris and Tonry (1990), for fines to become a critical component of sentencing practices in the United States, there must be "a principled means for adjusting the amount of the fine both to the offender's culpability and to his resources and, efficient and reliable systems of enforcement and collection to assure that fines imposed will in fact be paid" (123–124).

One method that addresses critics' concerns about monetary punishments is fines. Whereas fixed- or flat-fining systems base the amount to be paid on the seriousness of crimes, day-fine systems, which are common in Europe, adjust monetary penalties according to offenders' ability to pay. Specifically, for the same crimes, offenders who earn high incomes pay more than those who earn low incomes. Hence day fines are designed to eliminate the disparate impact that occurs when the same monetary penalties are levied against offenders with minimal and those with substantial financial resources: the effects on the former can be much more serious than on the latter in a flat-fining system.

A day-fine system was established with federal funds in Staten Island, New York. The Vera Institute in New York implemented the project. Its research staff found that judges under the day-fine system increased the amount of fines they imposed by 14 percent. Furthermore, fines were collected in full as frequently as they were under the flat-fining system even though day-fine penalties were significantly larger. (See **Day Fines**.)

RECOMMENDED READING: Sally T. Hillsman, Barry Mahoney, George F. Cole, and Bernard Auchter, *Fines as Criminal Sanctions* (Washington, DC: National Institute of Justice, 1987); Douglas C. McDonald, Judith Greene, and Charles Worzella, *Day Fines in American Courts* (Washington, DC: National Institute of Justice, 1992); N. Morris and M. Tonry, *Between Prison and Probation: Intermediate Punishments in a Rational Sentencing System* (New York: Oxford University Press, 1990); L. A. Winterfield and S. T. Hillsman, *The Staten Island Day-Fine Project* (Washington, DC: National Institute of Justice, 1993).

Arthur J. Lurigio

FINGERPRINTING. Fingerprinting is the art or science of taking and comparing fingerprints for identification. A fingerprint is an impression of the lines and whorls on the inner surface of the last joint of the finger used in the identification of a person. The imprint is an intricate design of skin ridges found on the palm side of a person's fingers. The ridges have little sweat pores through which perspiration is secreted. This perspiration and the coating of skin with other bodily oils are what make the impression of the ridge pattern on the finger stick whenever the finger touches a smooth surface. These impressions or prints are what are called latent prints.

There are three varieties of latent prints: plastic prints, visible prints, and invisible prints. The plastic print is a visible, long-lasting print impression made in candle wax, tar clay, grease, or putty. The visible print is an easily destroyable visible print made in dust, soot, blood, or powder. Finally, the invisible print is an easily destroyable invisible print resulting from the grease-sweat-dirt coating of the ridges of the skin. Fingerprints can be classified into three main pattern type groups. These are arches, loops, and whorls.

Inked prints are those taken by the police or other law enforcement agencies. When a person is arrested, his/her fingerprints are recorded on standard eight-by-eight-inch fingerprint cards. This is done in two ways, by a rolling motion in which the fingers are rolled one by one over an ink slab and then the paper, or by pressing down the fingers and thumbs without the rolling motion. Police keep records of fingerprints for those who have been arrested and forward the results to FBI Headquarters, which maintains a permanent record. (See **Automated Fingerprint Identification Systems**.)

RECOMMENDED READING: Andre A. Moenssens, Fred E. Inbau, and James R. Starrs, *Scientific Evidence in Criminal Cases,* 4th ed. (Westbury, NY: Foundation Press, 1995).

James R Farris

FIREARM.   An instrument used in the propulsion of shot, shell, or bullets by the notion of gunpowder exploded within it, or a weapon that acts by force of gunpowder. This word comprises all sorts of guns, such as fowling pieces, blunderbusses, pistols, rifles, and shotguns.

RECOMMENDED READING: Joseph R. Nolan and Jacqueline M. Nolan-Haley, *Black's Law Dictionary: Definitions of the Terms and Phrases of American and English Jurisprudence, Ancient and Modern,* 6th ed. (St. Paul, MN: West Publishing Co., 1991).

James R. Farris

FLORIDA v. BOSTICK, **501 U.S. 429 (1991).**   The Fourth Amendment to the U.S. Constitution prohibits unreasonable searches and seizures. The central issue in *Florida v. Bostick* involved the question of precisely when a person is "seized" for Fourth Amendment purposes. The police must have reasonable grounds to believe that someone is involved in criminal activity to justify his or her detention. If such grounds are not present, any evidence discovered will be excluded at trial.

Fort Lauderdale police officers developed a program designed to apprehend drug smugglers, which was called "working the buses." Without any specific suspicion that anyone on the bus was carrying unlawful drugs, officers routinely boarded the buses, questioned persons, and asked them for identification.

Two uniformed police officers boarded a bus in Fort Lauderdale that was traveling to Atlanta. The officers asked Terrance Bostick for identification and his bus ticket. They also asked to search his bag and informed him that he could refuse the search. Bostick agreed to permit the search, and the officers found a substantial amount of cocaine. At trial Bostick maintained that the cocaine was seized in violation of the Fourth Amendment and moved to suppress the evidence. The trial judge denied the motion, and Bostick pleaded guilty to trafficking in cocaine.

On appeal the central issue presented was whether Bostick was seized for Fourth Amendment purposes when the police officers approached him on the bus, questioned him, and asked to search his bag. Bostick maintained that the cocaine evidence should have been excluded from his trial because the police officers had seized him without any reasonable suspicion that he was involved in criminal activity. The Florida Supreme Court agreed that the evidence should have been places, question them, and request consent to search their belongings. The Court stated that the proper test to determine if a seizure has occurred is whether "taking into account all of the circumstances surrounding the encounter a reasonable passenger would feel free to decline the officers' requests or otherwise terminate the encounter." Because the Florida Supreme Court had apparently based its decision on a single fact—that the encounter between Bostick and the police occurred on a bus—the Supreme Court remanded the case to the trial court to use a "totality of circumstances" test to determine if Bostick was unlawfully seized.

Thomas J. Hickey

FORCIBLE ENTRY. Forcible entry is using, or procuring, encouraging, or assisting another to use, any force or violence in entering upon any lands or other possessions of another.
RECOMMENDED READING: Joseph R. Nolan and Jacqueline M. Nolan-Haley, *Black's Law Dictionary: Definitions of the Terms and Phrases of American and English Jurisprudence, Ancient and Modern*, 6th ed. (St. Paul, MN: West Publishing Co., 1991).

Lee E. Parker

FORCIBLE RAPE. Forcible rape is the act of penetrating the anus or vagina of a nonconsenting male or female by a finger, the male sex organ, or other object when the victim is overcome by force or fear caused by a threat, coupled with a present ability, to commit violence to the victim or another person. Any penetration, however slight, is sufficient to constitute rape. Forcible rape is distinguished from rape due to the victim's lack of capacity to consent due to being underage, under the influence of intoxicants, unconscious, or mentally deficient. (See **Rape**.)
RECOMMENDED READING: Joseph R. Nolan and Jacqueline M. Nolan-Haley, *Black's Law Dictionary: Definitions of the Terms and Phrases of American and English Jurisprudence, Ancient and Modern*, 6th ed. (St. Paul, MN. West Publishing Co., 1991).

Lee E. Parker

FORD v. GEORGIA, **498 U.S. 411 (1991).** A death-penalty case involving, among other things, the issue of when adequate and independent state grounds can be used to bar consideration of the constitutional issue raised by petitioner. In this case a unanimous Supreme Court held that independent state grounds could not be used to bar consideration of petitioner James A. Ford's claims because only a state practice that has been firmly established and regularly followed at the time at which it is to be applied may be invoked to prevent review by the Supreme Court of such a claim.

In this case James Ford, a black man, was indicted for the kidnap, rape, and murder of a white woman. The state informed the defendant that it was going to seek the death penalty. Prior to the trial defense counsel raised the issue of the state prosecutor's inappropriate use of race to exclude blacks from sitting as jurors. The motion raised was denied on the basis of *Swain v. Alabama* (1965), the ruling case at the time. At *voir dire* the prosecution used its peremptory challenges to exclude all but one black from the jury. Ford was convicted and sentenced to death. He appealed his conviction in part because, he alleged, blacks were impermissibly excluded from the jury.

While Ford's case was on appeal, the Supreme Court decided *Batson v. Kentucky* (1986), which changed the rules of proof in jury exclusion cases. The Court vacated Ford's conviction and asked that it be reconsidered in light of *Griffith v. Kentucky* (1987), which held that *Batson's* new evidentiary standard would apply retroactively in cases such as Ford's.

Upon remand, the Georgia Supreme Court held that Ford's counsel had not raised appropriate constitutional issues in a timely fashion under rules established by that court, and it refused to reconsider Ford's conviction. Moreover, the Georgia court held, on the basis of the doctrine of independent state grounds (see **Judicial Federalism**), that this rule barred federal judicial review of Ford's claim.

The U.S. Supreme Court, in a unanimous decision, overruled the Georgia Supreme Court, holding that ultimately the U.S. Supreme Court's standards for assessing the adequacy of independent state procedural bars to federal constitutional claims lay with the federal courts. These standards include the requirement that only a firmly established state practice may be used to prevent review by the U.S. Supreme Court of such claims. The rule invoked by the Georgia Supreme Court did not meet this standard. Thus the Georgia court's decision was reversed, and the case was remanded.

David Jones

FORENSIC ANTHROPOLOGY. This discipline focuses upon the identification of human remains in civil and criminal cases, a vital activity in civil and criminal cases such as mass disasters, suicides, and both natural and accidental deaths and homicides. The identification of human remains is done through analysis of skeletal remains and an examination of hard tissue such as teeth. The study of bones (human and animal) is called osteology. From this the sex, age, weight, height and race of the deceased can be determined. By analyzing the remains and its surroundings, ideas concerning the deceased and events before, during, and after the death can be made.

RECOMMENDED READING: *Handbook of Forensic Archaeology and Anthropology*, ed. Dan Morse, Jack Duncan, and James Stoutamire, (Tallahassee, FL: Florida State University Foundation, 1983).

James R. Farris

FORFEITURE.   Forfeiture is the fact of losing or becoming liable to deprivation of an estate, goods, life, or office in consequence of committing a crime, an offense, or a breach of management. For example, owners of "crack" houses may be forced to forfeit their houses if they are used for drug sales and distribution.   The owners give up their right to any property to the investigating law enforcement agency and, furthermore, give up any compensation or reimbursement the law enforcement agency might receive when it disposes of the property. In effect, the owners are being punished for allowing crimes to take place on and in their property. Forfeiture is a word that has throughout the English language has always meant giving up something of value unwillingly.

RECOMMENDED READING: Joseph R. Nolan and Jacqueline M. Nolan-Haley, *Black's Law Dictionary: Definitions of the Terms and Phrases of American and English Jurisprudence, Ancient and Modern*, 6th ed. (St. Paul, MN: West Publishing Co., 1991); Adam Starchild, *Protect Your Assets: How to Avoid Falling Victim to the Government's Forfeiture Laws* (Boulder, CO: Paladin Press, 1996).

James R. Farris

FRANKFURTER, FELIX (1882–1965). Felix Frankfurter was born in Vienna, Austria, on November 15, 1882. He came to the United States at age twelve but won honors attending the City College of New York and Harvard Law School. He taught law at Harvard from 1914 to 1939, with occasional leaves for public service. He advised the Wilson administration on industrial problems and at the Paris peace conference. He investigated the Tom Mooney and Sacco-Vanzetti cases. Frankfurter was a founder of the American Civil Liberties Union and the *New Republic* magazine. Many of his students and protégés, including Dean Acheson, James Landis, David Lilienthal, and Tom Corcoran, went into governmental service. Frankfurter corresponded with and collaborated with Justice Louis Brandeis. He advised President Franklin Roosevelt. In 1939 Frankfurter was named to the Supreme Court. In the tradition of James Bradley Thayer (his teacher at Harvard), Oliver Wendell Holmes, and Louis D. Brandeis, he argued that the courts should not declare laws unconstitutional where there was a reasonable basis for the legislation's enactment. He advocated strict observance of the constitutional criteria for allowing confessions or searches and seizures (especially where there was a shocking of the conscience, e.g., *Wolf v. Colorado* [1949] and *Rochin v. California* [1952]). Frankfurter was an eloquent defender of academic and political freedom.

Eventually he lost the majorities he had commanded in his earliest years on the Court to the intellectual leadership of Hugo Black. Frankfurter deplored both the conservative activism of the Hughes Court and the liberal activism of the Warren Court. His deference to the other branches of government sustained school flag-salute ceremonies, legislative apportionment, the Smith and McCarren acts, group libel statutes, and the investigations of the House Un-American Activities Committee. He insisted that free-speech claims involved a balance between competing interests and that reasonable governmental restraints were constitutional. There was a paradox in his jurisprudence: He was a literalist regarding the prohibition against an establishment of religion, yet he upheld mandatory flag salutes. He abhorred capital punishment, but would not bar a state from executing a person after a first attempt to do so had failed.

Frankfurter was known for writing lengthy scholarly opinions, often in concurrence. He was an intellectual gadfly, often interrupting attorneys during their oral arguments before the Court. He resigned from the Court in 1962 and died in 1965.

RECOMMENDED READING: Leonard Baker, *Brandeis and Frankfurter: A Dual Biography* (New York: Harper & Row, 1984); Liva Baker, *Felix Frankfurter* (New York: Coward-McCann, 1969); H. N. Hirsch, *The Enigma of Felix Frankfurter* (New York: Basic Books, 1981); Philip B. Kurland, *Mr. Justice Frankfurter and the Constitution* (Chicago: University of Chicago Press, 1971), *Felix Frankfurter*, ed. Wallace Mendelson (New York: Reynal, 1964); Bruce A. Murphy, *The Brandeis/Frankfurter Connection: The Secret Political Activities of Two Supreme Court Justices* (New York: Oxford University Press, 1982); Michael E. Parrish, *Felix Frankfurter and His Times: The Reform Years* (Free Press, 1982); Melvin I. Urofsky, *Felix Frankfurter: Judicial Restraint and Individual Liberties* (Boston: Twayne, 1991).

Martin Gruberg

FRATERNAL ORDER OF POLICE (FOP). Formed on May 14, 1915, by 23 Pittsburgh, Pennsylvania, police officers, not as a labor organization but as an organization for the "social welfare" of all police, by the early 1990s the FOP had approximately 250,000 members in more than 1,900 local lodges. Membership is open to all full-time law enforcement officers regardless of rank and regardless of type of police agency. Members are organized via local lodges, and although the FOP is not a labor group in the classic sense due to the crossing of ranks and jurisdictions, it lobbies generally to improve working conditions, wages, and benefits of police officers, primarily by monitoring and lobbying on behalf of legislation affecting law enforcement on the local, state, or national level. Supported by membership dues, the FOP maintains a national headquarters in Nashville, Tennessee, publishes the *FOP Journal*, and is run by a national board of directors elected by delegates attending a biennial conference held in odd-numbered years.

RECOMMENDED READING: Fraternal Order of Police: Building on a Proud Tradition (Nashville, TN: FOP, 1994): historical information from the FOP.

Dorothy Moses Schulz

FRAUD. Fraud is an untrue statement of material fact, known to be untrue by the party making it, made with either the intent to deceive or recklessly made with disregard for its truthfulness, where another party justifiably relies upon the statement and acts to its injury. Fraud requires proof that the defendant made a false representation or willful omission with respect to a material fact, with knowledge of its falsity, with intent to deceive the victim, and the victim acted in reliance on the false representation.

RECOMMENDED READING: Michael Levi, *The Investigation, Prosecution, and Trial of Serious Fraud*, (London, HMSO, 1993); Joseph R. Nolan and Jacqueline M. Nolan-Haley, *Black's Law Dictionary: Definitions of the Terms and Phrases of American and English Jurisprudence, Ancient and Modern*, 6th ed. (St. Paul, MN: West Publishing Co., 1991).

Lee E. Parker

***FURMAN v. GEORGIA*, 408 U.S. 238 (1972).** A leading death-penalty case in which the U.S. Supreme Court held in effect that all state death-penalty laws in existence at the time of the decision constituted "cruel and unusual punishment" and were thus prohibited by the Eighth Amendment.

The opinion was an unclear one. Five justices voted in favor of the basic decision, while four dissented from this holding. Moreover, each justice wrote an opinion explaining the reason for his vote. Two took the position that under evolving standards of decency, the death penalty was unconstitutional under all circumstances. Others disagreed.

The Supreme Court was seen to have held that existing laws were unconstitutional because they gave the sentencing authority (the judge or the jury) too much discretion. Because of this, the imposition of the death penalty under these laws was considered arbitrary, and hence cruel and unusual. Death-penalty statutes providing for "guided discretion" in the application of the death penalty were subsequently passed by a number of states. These were held to be constitutionally valid in *Gregg v. Georgia* (1976).

RECOMMENDED READING: Welsh S. White, *The Death Penalty in the Nineties: An Examination of the Modern System of Capital Punishment* (Ann Arbor: University of Michigan Press, 1991).

David Jones

G

GAMBLING. To play, or game, for money or other stake; hence to stake money or other thing of value on an uncertain event. Gambling involves not only chance, but a hope of gaining something beyond the amount played.

RECOMMENDED READING: *Legal, Economic and Humanistic Perspectives on Gambling*, ed. William R. Eadington (Reno: University of Nevada, Reno, 1982); National Criminal Justice Reference Service, *Gambling* (Rockville, MD: NCJRS, 1978); Joseph R. Nolan and Jacqueline M. Nolan-Haley, *Black's Law Dictionary: Definitions of the Terms and Phrases of American and English Jurisprudence, Ancient and Modern*, 6th ed. (St. Paul, MN: West Publishing Co., 1991).

James R. Farris

GARRETT, PATRICK FLOYD "PAT" (1850–1908). Pat Garrett killed Billy the Kid. Garrett was an Alabamian who moved west at age eighteen. During his work as a cowhand and restaurant manager, he made the fateful acquaintance of one William H. Bonney. Several years later Bonney, now known as "Billy the Kid," began to terrorize Lincoln County, New Mexico, with his outlawry (he bragged that he had already shot a man for every year of his age). It was a combination of Garrett's acquaintance with the Kid, his stature of six feet, four inches, and his shooting ability that enabled Garrett to be elected sheriff of Lincoln County in 1880.

Garrett put a posse together and actually caught the Kid and four accomplices. The posse laid siege to the gang, holed up in a stone hut near Stinking Spring, New Mexico. One outlaw was killed, and the others were starved into surrender. In April 1881 the Kid was convicted of murder and sentenced to be hanged in Lincoln on May 13th of that year.

Garrett incarcerated Bonney in a room on the second floor of the County Building because there was no adequate jail in Lincoln. Despite guards and shackles, Bonney managed to escape. He shot and killed his two guards.

After several weeks of intense pursuit, Garrett tracked Bonney to Fort Sumner. While Garrett was asking the Kid's whereabouts, the Kid inadvertently walked through the door of a resident's house in which Garrett was visiting. Garrett fired twice. Bonney was buried in the fort cemetery.

Garrett went on to serve as sheriff in Dona Ana County, New Mexico, and as a Theodore Roosevelt–appointed customs collector in El Paso, Texas. Ironically, he was shot to death as a consequence of a long-term dispute with a neighbor.

RECOMMENDED READING: Leon Claire Metz, *Pat Garrett: The Story of a Western Lawman* (Norman, OK: University of Oklahoma Press, 1974); Colin Rickards, *Sheriff Pat Garrett's Last Days* (Santa Fe, NM: Sunstone Press, 1986).

David R. Struckhoff

GIDEON v. WAINWRIGHT, 372 U.S. 335 (1963). In this case the U.S. Supreme Court extended the right to legal counsel to indigent defendants charged with a criminal offense. The reasoning of the Court is well summarized in this excerpt from the majority opinion written by Justice Black: "Governments, both state and federal, quite properly spend vast sums of money to establish machinery to try defendants accused of crime. Lawyers to prosecute are everywhere deemed essential to protect the public's interest in an orderly society. Similarly, there are few defendants charged with crime, few indeed, who fail to hire the best lawyers they can get to prepare and present their defenses. That government hires lawyers to prosecute and defendants who have the money hire lawyers to defend are the strongest indications of the widespread belief that lawyers in criminal courts are necessities, not luxuries. The right of one charged with crime to counsel may not be deemed fundamental and essential to fair trials in some countries, but it is in ours. From the very beginning, our state and national constitutions and laws have laid great emphasis on procedural and substantive safeguards designed to assure fair trials before impartial tribunals in which every defendant stands equal before the law. This noble ideal cannot be realized if the poor man charged with crime has to face his accusers without a lawyer to assist him."

Frank Schmalleger

GINSBURG, RUTH BADER (1933–   ). Ruth Bader Ginsburg was born March 15, 1933, in Brooklyn, New York. She attended Cornell University and Harvard Law School, transferring to Columbia Law School for her third year since her husband had obtained a job with a law firm in Manhattan. She tied for first place in her graduating class, but upon graduation she encountered the pattern of discrimination against women attorneys. Despite her scholastic laurels, she could get neither a job offer from a New York law firm nor a teaching post at an Ivy League school, and was rejected as a clerk by Supreme Court Justice Felix Frankfurter and Court of Appeals Judge Learned Hand. Instead she became a clerk for a U.S. district court judge.

Thereafter she taught at Rutgers University Law School and became the first tenured female faculty member at Columbia Law School. As a general counsel for the American Civil Liberties Union specializing in gender-discrimination cases, she was successful in five of the six cases she argued before the U.S. Supreme Court (including *Reed v. Reed* [1971], *Weinberger v. Wiesenfeld* [1975], and *Frontiero v. Richardson* [1973]).

In 1980 President Carter named her to the U.S. court of appeals. She gained a reputation for being conscientious and fair-minded. In 1993 she was nominated to the Supreme Court by President Clinton, thus becoming the first nominee by a Democratic president in twenty-six years.

RECOMMENDED READING: Christopher E. Henry, *Ruth Bader Ginsburg* (New York: F. Watts, 1994); Jack L. Roberts, *Ruth Bader Ginsburg: Supreme Court Justice* (Brookfield, CN: Millbrook Press, 1994).

Martin Gruberg

GOETZ, BERNHARD (1947–   ).   Known as the "subway vigilante," Bernhard Goetz (a white man) shot four black youths who approached him while he was riding a subway in New York City in 1984. One of the young men who was shot was paralyzed as a result of the shooting. After Goetz performed his deed, he left the city. He eventually turned himself in, and in 1986 his case went to trial. He was charged with a number of offenses, including the attempted murder of each of the four youths. The defense he used at trial was self-defense.

Goetz was found guilty only on one count of criminal possession of a weapon in the third degree (he did not possess a permit for the gun he was carrying). He was sentenced to six months in jail, a fine of approximately $5,000, and an additional four and one-half years on probation. Conditions of probation included community service and psychiatric counseling. The defendant's case raised important and controversial questions about the limits of self-defense in modern American urban society.

RECOMMENDED READING: George P. Fletcher, *A Crime of Self-Defense: Bernhard Goetz and the Law on Trial* (New York: Free Press, 1988).

David Jones

GRAND JURY.   A group of citizens brought together to consider whether the government has presented sufficient evidence to warrant the issuance of an indictment (a formal charge) against an individual. Like many other American legal, institutions the grand jury has its roots in English history. The antecedents of the grand jury predate the Magna Carta. According to its defenders, it is designed to protect citizens from frivolous and/or malicious prosecution, for if the grand jury refuses to issue an indictment, an individual may not be brought to trial for a serious crime. Grand juries are enshrined in the Fifth Amendment to the U.S. Constitution and are an integral part of the federal criminal law process. The right to grand-jury proceedings does not, however, apply under the U.S. Constitution to state proceedings. It is used, though, in a number of states.

The function and processes of the grand jury are different from those of a trial jury. The former does not determine guilt, but, instead, whether there is sufficient evidence to bring charges. The grand jury typically consists of twenty-three members. Assuming the existence of a quorum, a majority vote to indict will result in issuance of the indictment. Grand-jury proceedings are not trials. They take place in secret. Moreover, a witness called before a grand jury does not have the right to have an attorney present, though one may be nearby for consultation.

In current federal practice there are three types of grand juries. The most common is the "regular" grand jury, which is impaneled to deal with common and fairly simple federal crimes. Members typically meet several days per week for four to five weeks to consider evidence presented by federal prosecutors. "Additional" grand juries consider more complex offenses; they do not meet as often during a week, but consider evidence over a longer period of time (eighteen to twenty-four months). "Special" grand juries may be impaneled for as long as thirty-six months. They deal with charges brought against organized crime.

Although, in theory, grand juries can refuse to issue indictments requested by the government, this rarely happens. In fact, many of its critics argue that the grand jury is in actuality a rubber stamp for professional prosecutors. Moreover, if one grand jury refuses to indict an individual, the prosecution has the right to present evidence before a second grand jury involving the same charge in an attempt to secure a "true bill" there. Because of these factors many have suggested that the grand jury does not stand as a bulwark between the government and the individual, and that the United States should follow the example of Great Britain and abolish this institution.

RECOMMENDED READING: Blanche Davis Blank, *The Not So Grand Jury* (Lanham, MD: University Press of America, 1993); Marvin E. Frankel and Gary P. Naftalis, *The Grand Jury: An Institution on Trial* (New York: Hill and Wang, 1977).

David Jones

***GREGG V. GEORGIA*, 428 U.S. 153, 859–912 (1976).** In *Gregg v. Georgia* and companion cases the U.S. Supreme Court upheld the constitutionality of several new state capital-punishment statutes, thus essentially reversing an earlier decision in *Furman v. Georgia* (1972) that the death-penalty laws then in existence were unconstitutional. In *Furman* a five-justice majority of the Court had held that the death penalty was administered in an "arbitrary and capricious" and racially discriminatory manner and thus violated the "cruel and unusual punishment" and equal-protection provisions of the Eighth and Fourteenth amendments to the Constitution.

In the aftermath of *Furman* at least thirty-five states passed new death-penalty statutes, many of which tried to revise death-sentencing processes to meet the Court's *Furman* objections. The major features of the new statutes approved in *Gregg* included bifurcated trials (separate guilt/innocence and penalty phases), "guided discretion" for judges and juries in capital sentencing (consideration of aggravating and mitigating circumstances), and automatic review of death-penalty cases by state appeals courts.

Gregg appeared to most scholars to represent an unexpected reversal of the worldwide trend away from capital punishment in the post–World War II period, and several different explanations have been offered regarding why the Court's position changed in the four years between *Furman* and *Gregg*. One explanation emphasizes the (state) legislative response to *Furman* and the increase in public support for the death penalty as reflected in public opinion polls at the time. Another emphasizes changes in the composition of the Court. The four dissenters in *Furman* were all conservative Nixon appointees, and all were still on the Court four years later. One of the five *Furman* majority justices had retired by 1976 and had been replaced by yet another conservative justice. Thus by 1976 conservative appointees supportive of the death penalty constituted a solid Court majority.

Ernie Thomson

GUILTY BUT MENTALLY ILL. First adopted in Michigan in the 1980s, this is a finding allowed in some jurisdictions when an insanity defense is raised by a defendant. If the jury finds (either beyond a reasonable doubt or through a preponderance of evidence) that the defendant was guilty of the offense but was mentally ill at the time the offense was committed, and that the defendant was not legally insane at the time the offense was committed, the jury may return a verdict of guilty but mentally ill (GBMI). If this determination is made, the defendant may be sentenced to the punishment allowed for the crime committed. This may include probation with treatment as a condition of probation.

Several other states adopted this rule in the wake of the acquittal of John Hinckley (by reason of insanity) for his attempted assassination of President Reagan. GBMI has been criticized in part because many question the ability of the jury to distinguish between legal insanity and the state of mental illness. It was also intended to reduce findings of insanity while at the same time providing treatment for incarcerated criminals suffering from mental illness. Empirical studies have indicated that neither of these goals have been met in those jurisdictions that utilize it—verdicts of not guilty by reason of insanity have not gone down, nor have those found guilty but mentally ill been any more likely than other prisoners to receive treatment for mental disorders.

RECOMMENDED READING: John Klofas and Ralph Weisheit, "Guilty But Mentally Ill: Reform of the Insanity Defense in Illinois," *Justice Quarterly* 4 (March 1987): 39–50; Rita J. Simon and David E. Aaronson, *The Insanity Defense: A Critical Assessment of Law and Policy in the Post-Hinckley Era* (New York: Praeger, 1988).

David Jones

H

HABEAS CORPUS. See **Writ of** *Habeas Corpus.*

HAMMURABI, CODE OF. Hammurabi was a successful military leader and administrator who ruled Babylon for forty-three years in the eighteenth century B.C. In 1902 archaeologists discovered a seven-foot-high black carved stone monument and deciphered his "code" of 282 laws. It was not really a code (i.e., it was not comprehensive), but a sample-book of royal decisions rather than statutes. The text was still known and was based on earlier Sumerian law. The code had laws relating to personal property, real estate, trade, business relations, the family, labor, and personal injuries. It also covered false accusation, witchcraft, and military service. There were many harsh penalties. However, the code was progressive in having retribution exacted by the state rather than by the injured party. There were higher fines assessed for violations of personal property than for offenses against human life. Some marital and property rights were accorded to women. The main principle was that "the strong shall not injure the weak."
RECOMMENDED READING: Yousef Danesh-Khoshboo, *The Civilization of Law: A Commentary on the Laws of Hammurabi and Magna Carta* (Berrien Spring, RI: Vande Vere Publications, 1991); E. J. Urch, "The Law Code of Hammurabi," *American Bar Association Journal*, Vol. 15 (undated):437–441; Bill Yenne, *100 Men Who Shaped World History* (San Francisco: Bluewood Books, 1994).

Martin Gruberg

HAND, LEARNED (1872–1961). Judge Learned Hand was perhaps the greatest American judge in the twentieth century not to sit on the U.S. Supreme Court. Hand was appointed as a federal district judge in 1909. He served the U.S. Court of Appeals for the Second Circuit from 1924 through 1951, then was a reserve judge from then until his death in 1961. In these positions Hand wrote numerous opinions, many of which had a strong impact on the development of federal law. Hand was strongly considered for a position on the Supreme Court by both President Herbert Hoover and President Franklin Roosevelt.

Hand was one of the leading advocates of the position of "judicial deference" to the other branches of government. In this perspective the judges should not allow their own values to determine the constitutionality of government actions, but should leave a great deal of flexibility to the elective components of the government to make decisions. Courts should overturn legislation in only the most extreme circumstances. In Hand's view this position should apply not only to economic issues, but also to those involving civil rights and civil liberties. In holding this view, Hand was a philosophical ally of Justice Felix Frankfurter.

RECOMMENDED READING: Gerald Gunther, *Learned Hand* (New York: Alfred A. Knopf, 1994).

David Jones

HANDGUN. A handgun is a short firearm intended to be aimed and fired from one hand. Handguns are of three types; the automatic pistol, the revolver, and the derringer. The automatic pistol is a self-feeding handgun that fires, ejects an empty cartridge, reloads, and cocks itself each time the trigger is pulled. The term *semiautomatic* is more accurate, however, because the fully automatic weapon continues firing as long as the trigger is held back and the ammunition lasts. The derringer is very small in size and can be easily concealed. It may have one, two, or four barrels and fires a single bullet from each barrel. The revolver is perhaps the most common handgun made. It is a repeating handgun with a revolving cylinder chambered to hold the cartridges. The cylinder may contain as few as five chambers or as many as twelve, the most common number of cylinders being six. There are two types of revolvers: the single-action and the double-action. With the single-action revolver, the hammer must be cocked manually each time before the firing. The double-action revolver can also be cocked manually; however, when the trigger is pulled, it fires and cocks itself consecutively.

RECOMMENDED READING: Joseph R. Nolan and Jacqueline M. Nolan-Haley, *Black's Law Dictionary: Definitions of the Terms and Phrases of American and English Jurisprudence, Ancient and Modern,* 6th ed. (St. Paul, MN: West Publishing Co., 1991); Andre A. Moenssens, Fred E. Inbau, and James R. Starrs, *Scientific Evidence in Criminal Cases,* 4th ed, (Westbury, NY: Foundation Press, 1995).

James R. Farris

HASHISH. Hashish is a derivative of the marijuana plant. Marijuana is processed to produce a substance that has a much higher concentration of tetrahydrocannabinal (THC). THC is the chemical in marijuana that produces the drug's effects in users, and these effects are increased in users of hashish. Hashish can be smoked or chewed by users.

RECOMMENDED READING: Drug Enforcement Administration, *Drugs of Abuse* (Washington, D.C.: U.S. Department of Justice, 1990); National Narcotics Intelligence Consumer's Committee, *The NNICC Report: The Supply of Illicit Drugs to the United States* (Washington, D.C.: NNICC, 1995).

Glenn Zuern

HATE-CRIME STATUTES. "Penalty-enhancement" statutes passed by a number of states. This means that if an individual is convicted of a crime, his/her punishment can be increased up to a prescribed amount if the victim possesses certain attributes and it can be shown that s/he was victimized because of these attributes. For instance, the state of Wisconsin provides for penalty enhancements if it is shown that the actor selects his/her victim "in whole or in part because of the actor's belief or perception regarding the race, religion, color, disability, sexual orientation, national origin, or ancestry of that person" (*Wisconsin Statutes, 1994*, section 939.645[1][b]).

Hate-crime legislation is controversial. Opponents argue that such legislation is inappropriate because it punishes beliefs as well as action, may have a chilling effect on speech, treats certain groups in a paternalistic fashion, and is unlikely to achieve its purpose of reducing bigotry. Proponents have argued that the motive of the perpetrator is a proper factor in sentencing. Moreover, they argue, penalty enhancements can be justified on retributive grounds (a crime becomes more reprehensible because it is a hate crime) and/or because of the additional harm of such crimes to society.

At one point a number of people questioned the constitutionality of such legislation, primarily on the grounds that because it punishes speech, it violates the First Amendment. However, the U.S. Supreme Court upheld a Wisconsin hate-crime statute in the case of *Wisconsin v. Mitchell* (1993). In this case Todd Mitchell and some friends (all of whom were black) badly beat a young man (white) after Mitchell and his friends had been discussing a scene from the movie *Mississippi Burning* in which a young black is beaten by white racist thugs. Mitchell was found guilty of aggravated assault, and after the jury found that he intentionally selected his victim on the basis of the victim's race, Mitchell's sentence was enhanced. The Wisconsin Supreme Court ruled the state law unconstitutional because, in its view, the statute punished thought. The U.S. Supreme Court, in a unanimous decision, overruled the Wisconsin court and held that the law did not violate any provision of the U.S. Constitution. In the Supreme Court's view the Constitution does not erect a barrier to the admission of evidence of one's belief at sentencing simply because beliefs are protected by the First Amendment; such beliefs may be relevant to the consideration of the defendant's motive, and that is allowed. Therefore, sentencing-enhancement provisions in hate-crime laws do not violate the First Amendment. Thus they are not unconstitutional.

RECOMMENDED READING: Stanley Feingold, "Hate Crime Legislation Muzzles Free Speech," *National Law Journal,* Vol. 15, no. 45 (July 12, 1993): 15–16; Steven Freeman, "Hate Crime Laws: Punishment Which Fits the

Crime," *Annual Survey of American Law* 4 (1992): 581–585; Susan Gellman, "Hate Crime Laws are Thought Crime Laws," *Annual Survey of American Law* 4 (1992): 509–531; Valerie Jenness and Ryken Grattet, "The Criminalization of Hate: A Comparison of Structural and Polity Influences on the Passage of "Bias-Crime" Legislation in the United States," *Sociological Perspectives*, Vol. 39, no. 1 (Spring 1996): 129–154; James Weinstein, "First Amendment Challenges to Hate Crime Legislation: Where's the Speech?" *Criminal Justice Ethics* 11 (1992): 6–20; *Wisconsin v. Mitchell*, 508 U.S. 476 (1993).

David Jones

HEARSAY. Defined in Rule 801(c) of the 1994 *Federal Rules of Evidence* as a statement other than one made by the declarant while testifying to prove the truth of the matter asserted. In its simplest definition it is testimony by A that s/he heard B say something relevant to an issue being considered by the court.

The general rule of evidence is that hearsay is not admissible in court. The arguments for excluding hearsay are many. For one thing, the admittance of hearsay would arguably abrogate the defendant's Sixth Amendment right to confront his/her accuser. Moreover, admittance of hearsay could detract from the truth-finding function of a trial because it precludes cross-examination of the individual making the original statement as well as demeanor evidence. It also means that the person making the statement testified to has not been sworn to tell the truth.

While, in theory, hearsay is easily defined, it is sometimes difficult to identify in practice. What may be hearsay in one situation may not be hearsay in another. Moreover, although the rules of evidence state the principle that hearsay evidence will be excluded, there are many exceptions to this rule (approximately forty). Exclusions include "dying declarations" and "excited utterances." Previous sworn testimony, though technically hearsay, may be admissible if the witness is "unavailable" (e.g., dead or missing). There are many other exceptions. Some commentators have asserted that there has been a tendency to loosen hearsay rules in recent years, particularly in cases alleging child sexual abuse.

RECOMMENDED READING: Christopher B. Mueller and Laird C. Kirkpatrick, *Evidence under the Rules*, 3rd ed. (Boston: Little, Brown, and Co., 1996); Christopher B. Mueller and Laird C. Kirkpatrick, *1994 Federal Rules of Evidence* (Boston: Little, Brown, and Co., 1994); Dennis Murphy, "Hearsay: The Least Understood Exclusionary Rule," *Journal of Criminal Justice* 17 (1989): 265–275; Joseph R. Nolan and Jacqueline M. Nolan-Haley, *Black's Law Dictionary: Definitions of the Terms and Phrases of American and English Jurisprudence, Ancient and Modern*, 6th ed. (St. Paul, MN: West Publishing Co., 1991).

David Jones

HEROIN. Heroin is made by refining the gum from the opium poppy. First discovered by a scientist searching for a nonaddicting pain reliever to replace morphine, it usually is found in the form of a white crystalline powder. It is highly addictive and causes severe physical withdrawal symptoms in individuals trying to stop using it. Heroin is smuggled into the United States from both Europe and the Orient. Recently, a lower grade of heroin has increasingly been smuggled into the United States from Mexico. Heroin remains a popular drug and is the source of billions of dollars worth of drug trade.

RECOMMENDED READING: Drug Enforcement Administration, *Drugs of Abuse* (Washington, D.C.: U.S. Department of Justice, 1990); National Narcotics Intelligence Consumer's Committee, *The NNICC Report: The Supply of Illicit Drugs to the United States* (Washington, D.C.: NNICC, 1995).

Glenn Zuern

HICKOK, JAMES BUTLER "WILD BILL" (1837–1876). "Wild Bill" was a wagon master, and a courier, scout and spy for the North during the Civil War. He became a lawman later in his career. James Butler Hickok became sheriff of Hays City, Ellis County, Kansas, in August 1869. His killing of two men during his first three months in office gave him a fearsome reputation early in his law enforcement career, and he was subsequently able to keep the peace relatively easily.

Like many other sheriffs of his day, Hickok was closely connected with the saloons and gaming houses in his jurisdiction, and he did enjoy frequenting such places. The major event of his term was the shooting of an assassin trying to kill him. Hickok spotted the killer in a mirror in a saloon, turned, and put a bullet through the would-be assassin's head.

It is not well known that soon after that incident Hickok began having vision problems that became so severe that he eventually killed his own deputy marshal in Abilene by accident. He accepted the limits of his vision problem and tried acting but was dissatisfied with the actor's life.

After he had drifted to Deadwood in the Dakota Territory, the "Prince of Pistoleers" was shot in the back of the head by one Jack McCall at a casino while playing cards. McCall believed that Hickok had years earlier killed McCall's brother in Kansas. The hand Hickok held—including a pair of aces and a pair of eights—is still known as the "dead man's hand."

It should be noted that Hickok killed "only" seven men during his career, and some experts think that he was overrated as a gunfighter. Wild Bill certainly was a romantic figure, and there may well be solid foundation for his fame. He was a friend of General George Armstrong Custer and his wife Libby, who wrote that Hickok was "a delight to look upon." Many historians, though, attribute his fame not to the Custer association but to an account of Hickok's exploits published in the February 1867 issue of *Harper's New Monthly Magazine* by Colonel George W. Nichols.

RECOMMENDED READING: Mildred Fielder, *Wild Bill Hickok, Gunman* (Lead, SD: Bonanza Trails Publishers, 1974); Glenn Gabie, *Wild Bill Hickok (1837–1876)*, Kanata, Ontario: G. D. Gabie, 1994.

David R. Struckhoff

HIGHWAY ROBBERY. The term *highway robbery* is used in two very different ways, one constituting a criminal action and the other implying trickery and deceit. Depending on the intentions of the speaker, it can thus be employed both in a literal sense and as a figure of speech.

The phrase *highway robbery* can take on figurative meaning when one uses it to describe the action of someone gaining a particular advantage or reward in a situation that is not his/her due. It is often connected with shady business dealings in which one participant benefits at the expense of another. An example would be a new car buyer accusing a dealer of "highway robbery" when the dealer tries to sell him a car for much more money than it is worth. The literal definition of the term is the taking of property by force from someone on a public road. However, for the most part the term refers to being "ripped off" in an allegedly fraudulent business transaction.

RECOMMENDED READING: Joseph R. Nolan and Jacqueline M. Nolan-Haley, *Black's Law Dictionary: Definitions of the Terms and Phrases of American and English Jurisprudence, Ancient and Modern*, 6th ed. (St. Paul, MN: West Publishing Co., 1991).

James R. Farris

HIT-MAN COMPUTER CRIME (HCC). Hit-man computer crime refers to individuals who engage in computer "hacking" or other computer crimes for monetary or personal gain. The computer crimes can include destruction of data or programs, theft of information, illegal transfers of money, interception of data, and the altering of information. Such individuals take great pride in their ability to perform HCC and have an immense interest in computers.

RECOMMENDED READING: Frank Schmalleger, *Criminal Justice Today: An Introductory Text for the Twenty-First Century*, 4th ed. (Upper Saddle River, NJ: Prentice Hall, 1997): 651; William S. Sessions, "Criminal Justice Information Services: Gearing Up for the Future," *FBI Law Enforcement Bulletin* (February 1993): 2-4.

Troy D. Livingston

HIV SCREENING IN PRISONS. In mid-1989, fifteen state penal systems and the Federal Bureau of Prisons had implemented mass screening policies to test inmates for the presence of HIV antibodies, which the body produces as a result of infection with the virus that causes AIDS. Some jurisdictions test all inmates even if they have no symptoms of HIV infection; others only screen inmates at intake or release. A few states test inmates on the basis of whether they are known members of high-risk groups such as injection drug users, prostitutes, and homosexual or bisexual men. Most of the jurisdictions with mandatory HIV testing are in smaller states with few reported inmate AIDS cases; none of the five states with the highest cumulative AIDS incidences has mass screening policies.

Proponents of mass screening argue that testing is a basic strategy for identifying infected inmates in order to target them for HIV education and prevention programs. Its critics maintain that screening is unnecessary because HIV education and prevention efforts must be directed at all inmates, not just those in so-called high-risk groups. Furthermore, mass screening may encourage the segregation of HIV-infected inmates, a practice that may be viewed as unethical, inhumane, or unconstitutional.

A number of other crucial issues are associated with mandatory HIV testing, such as the accuracy and confidentiality of test results. One problem with mass screening is that in institutions with low HIV prevalence rates, blanket testing will yield a relatively high proportion of false positives (i.e., test results indicating that an inmate is HIV infected when he or she actually does not have the virus) In addition, despite prison policies to protect both the anonymity of inmates tested for HIV antibodies and the confidentiality of their test results, breaches of privacy appear to be rampant. According to Hammett and Moini: "It is apparent from lawsuits filed by inmates that news of a particular inmate's positive test results or seropositive status travels rapidly through an institution" (1990: 43). Expense is another disadvantage of mass testing, which led the National Commission on AIDS advocate reallocation of available resources to such preventive activities as education.   Many of the same arguments for and against HIV screening in institutions also apply to community corrections (i.e., probation and parole).

RECOMMENDED READING: M. Blumberg and D. Langston, "Mandatory HIV Testing in Criminal Justice Settings," *Crime and Delinquency* 37 (1991): 5–18; T. M. Hammett and S. Moini, *Update on AIDS in Prisons and Jails* (Washington, DC: National Institute of Justice, 1990); National Commission on AIDS, *HIV Disease in Correctional Facilities* (Washington, DC: The Commission, 1991).

Arthur J. Lurigio

HOLMES, OLIVER WENDELL (1841–1935). Oliver Wendell Holmes is widely regarded as one of the greatest U.S. Supreme Court justices. Holmes was the product of a privileged background. His father, Dr. Oliver Wendell Holmes, Sr., was a Harvard Medical School professor and influential writer. Following his graduation from Harvard Law School, the younger Oliver Wendell Holmes became a practicing attorney and a part-time lecturer at Harvard. For a brief time Holmes became a full-time professor at the Harvard Law School, but in 1882 his academic career was interrupted by his appointment to the Supreme Judicial Court of Massachusetts. He served on that court for approximately twenty years, until he was appointed to the U.S. Supreme Court in 1902. Holmes was a member of the U.S. Supreme Court for almost thirty years. During this time he made some of the most significant contributions to U.S. constitutional law since John Marshall.

In 1880 Holmes was invited to deliver a series of lectures, which became the basis of his most famous and influential work, *The Common Law*. This work is considered by many legal historians to be the single most significant and original work of legal scholarship by an American author. *The Common Law* emphasized that the law "cannot be dealt with as if it contained the axioms and corollaries of a book of mathematics." Rather, according to one of Holmes's most famous passages, "The life of the law has not been logic: it has been experience. The felt necessities of the time, the prevalent moral and political theories, intuitions of public policy, avowed or unconscious, even the prejudices which judges share with their fellow-men, have had a good deal more to do than the syllogism in determining the rules by which men should be governed." Holmes believed that the law should not be viewed as an abstract set of formalistic principles governed solely by pure logic; rather, practical considerations and "experience" should shape the legal rules that govern society. One of Holmes's most famous Supreme Court opinions was a dissenting opinion written in *Lochner v. New York* (1905). Lochner, a bakery owner, was convicted for violating a New York labor law that prohibited bakery workers from working more than ten hours each day, or sixty hours per week. The issue confronting the Supreme Court was whether a state had the power to pass such a law or whether it had violated due process. The Court held that the law was unconstitutional because "the freedom of master and employee to contract with each other in relation to their employment...cannot be prohibited or interfered with, without violating the Federal Constitution." Holmes's dissenting opinion argued that *Lochner* was decided "upon an economic theory which a large part of the country does not entertain." The laissez-faire economic theory to which Holmes referred maintained that all members of society were best served by a legal system based on the notion of Darwinism. Holmes, in contrast, believed that judges should not overturn laws passed by legislative bodies "unless it can be said that a rational and fair man necessarily would admit that the statute proposed would infringe fundamental principles as they have been understood by the traditions of our people." Holmes's view of the proper role of the judiciary is clear—judges should defer to the legislature's view of proper public policy unless it is clear that a law violates the Constitution. The relevance of Holmes's statements about the judiciary's proper role in the U.S. governmental system continues to the present day, as is evidenced by modern discussions of "judicial activism" versus "judicial restraint."

Oliver Wendell Holmes retired from the U.S. Supreme Court in 1932 and died in 1935. The significance of his contributions to U.S. constitutional law is difficult to overestimate. His legal scholarship and opinions have become virtual cornerstones of U.S. law.

RECOMMENDED READING: Liva Baker, *The Justice from Beacon Hill: The Life and Times of Oliver Wendell Holmes* (New York: HarperCollins, 1991); Mark De Wolfe Howe, *Justice Oliver Wendell Holmes* (Cambridge, MA: Belknap Press of Harvard University Press, 1957).

Thomas J. Hickey

HOSPICE OF ST. MICHAEL. Upon assuming the pontificate in 1700, Pope Clement XI expressed concern about the crimes committed by boys under age twenty as they drifted the streets of Rome. The pope, distressed that Rome's jails were unable to reform the youths, authorized the construction of a house of correction that would offer a better response to the young offenders. The building, which was next to the Hospice of St. Michael (Ospizio di San Michele), was opened in 1704. The pope ordered that all boys under age twenty who would otherwise be sent to the public prisons should be sent instead to the new house of correction at the Hospice of St. Michael. An area for women was added to the complex in 1735.

The Hospice of St. Michael provided the first example of three penal principles that would come to play an important role in the development of penitentiaries: isolation, work, and silence. The original building for boys had sixty small cells, distinct and separate from each other, clustered around a large hall. The boys slept alone in these rooms but worked together at workbenches, to which they were chained at one foot, in other large rooms. While the boys labored at such wool-industry activities as spinning and weaving, monks read aloud from religious texts. Profits from the boys' labor went to the hospice, but the youths' parents or guardians were also expected to compensate the hospice for food and other expenses related to their stay.

RECOMMENDED READING: T. Eriksson, *The Reformers: An Historical Survey of Pioneer Experiments in the Treatment of Criminals*, translated by C. Djurklou (New York: Elsevier, 1976).

Philip Reichel

I

INCAPACITATION. Incapacitation is a sentencing goal designed to deny convicted offenders the opportunity to commit additional offenses and further victimize society for the duration of their term of incarceration. The two types of incapacitation are collective and selective.

Collective Incapacitation. The term *collective incapacitation* is a term coined and used more in the psychology of crime than in other disciplines to refer to sentencing on instant offense and prior record only—generally what we usually understand sentencing to be but with an added requirement of mandated consistency in application for all convicts. It is believed by its proponents that, for example, a policy of a required five-year term for any felony conviction would reduce crime by about 15 percent, and a policy of a five-year term after repeated convictions would reduce it by about 5 percent. This notion has been criticized on several grounds. First, as repeaters become known to the police, they have more chances of arrest than beginners, so that the impact of subsequent penalties might overestimate the benefits of this strategy. Second, several studies have shown that between 60 and 80 percent of adults arrested for crime-index offenses have either no prior (adult) arrests or no prior convictions. (See **Crime Index.**) Thus only about one-quarter of crime-index crimes might have been prevented by imposing prison terms, of any length, on convicted offenders. Third, extensive use of collective incapacitation would likely raise prison populations to unacceptable levels because longer sentences mean a larger population, which increases inexorably until the first of those sentenced under a consistent policy are released.

Selective Incapacitation. The term *selective incapacitation* has been a viable concept in the discussion of criminal sanctions for decades. Selective incapacitation means sentencing offenders to terms of incarceration based on predictions of their expected future criminality. Thus a person considered to be a future serious risk would be assigned a more severe sentence than a future nonserious risk even for a similar instant crime. It has been argued that crime can be better deterred when there is a systematic policy of incapacitating high-rate offenders as opposed to all offenders collectively. The criticisms here are several. First, we do not know who is a high-rate offender until he or she is again convicted. Second, incapacitation based on the identification of future offenses involves ethical problems—if our system of justice punishes for past behavior (the instant offense), then to imprison for expected future behavior may be unethical. Third, the prediction of future offending is a risky business at best, involving a high rate of false positives (expected to commit crimes, but not committing them). Fourth, our prediction tools have not yet attained, given the complexities of human behavioral causation, any solid level of reliability.

RECOMMENDED READING: Lawrence A. Greenfeld, *Prison Sentences and Time Served for Violence* (Washington, DC: Bureau of Justice Statistics, April 1995); Tamasak Wicharaya, *Simple Theory, Hard Reality: The Impact of Sentencing Reforms on Courts, Prisons and Crime* (Albany: State University of New York Press, 1995).

Anna C. Hussey

INDETERMINATE SENTENCE. Criminal sentencing has always evoked great passion and controversy, and no other form of sentencing has been as heavily critiqued as the indeterminate sentence. On the one hand, there is the view that punishment of convicted criminals is its own justification; we call this retribution. On the other, there is the view that the only proper goal of criminal sanctions is the prevention of antisocial behavior; we call this deterrence. One assumption of deterrence is that crimes can be prevented by affixing a determinate sentence to them based upon their seriousness. That is, we can dissuade offenders from committing crime by making the sanction certain and severe. Furthermore, the concern over a judge's arbitrary discretion is removed since the sanction is mandated by legislative statute. Under this scheme the case and individual attributes of the convicted are not part of the decision-making process. Thus all like offenses are to be treated similarly despite mitigating or aggravating circumstances. Another element of deterrence considers whether the convicted defendant will learn from his/her mistake. That is, can the offender be rehabilitated? As early as 700 A. D., church books revealed a tension between establishing penance according to the sin or suiting it to individual offenders. In spite of this long-standing concern, reconciling the needs of offenders with the needs of society has become increasingly problematic. One attempt to bridge this gap is the indeterminate sentence.

The philosophy of the indeterminate sentence is to tailor the punishment to the offender and not the crime. This sentencing model allows a range of sanctions to be available to judges in order for them to take into account important attributes of the case or the offender. This sentence might be part fine, part incarceration, and part probation. In essence judges are allowed to judge and are not handcuffed by mandatory sentencing statutes, but rather are allocated some freedom of discretion. However, it is exactly this freedom upon which a watchful eye has been cast by an ever-fearful society that is critical of unchecked power, especially power that can be benevolent or harsh.

Controversy in colonial America arose when Governor John Winthrop of Massachusetts frequently tailored his penalties to an individual defendant's character and social conditions. The disparity and leniency in Winthrop's dispositions disturbed his detractors. Particularly offensive, they maintained, was the leniency he extended to serious wrongdoers. He felt that the poor should not have to pay as heavy a fine as the rich, that religious leaders should suffer harsher penalties for moral offenses, and that the powerful should be more severely sanctioned than the weak. The Massachusetts legislature did not agree and enacted a law prohibiting sentences to be fitted to individual offenders.

Nonetheless, the indeterminate sentence regained strength in 1870 when delegates to the first National Prison Association conference cited reformation as the key to penology. It decreed that sentencing should aim to reform criminals, not simply punish them. In 1878 New York State enacted the first truly indeterminate sentencing legislation. By the early 1920s all but four states had adopted some form of indeterminate sentencing statute. The idea was optimistic that individuals could be rehabilitated with the help of professionals. The offender would "serve" time and not just "pass" time. The rehabilitation model survived this time period despite a new push by scientists that human behavior was determined by individual biological or psychological drives or pathologies. Nonetheless, the indeterminate sanction remained the prevailing model until the 1970s when crime rates continued to burgeon, recidivism (repeat offending) was extreme, and media attention to early-release decisions gone awry took center stage. Prison riots of the 1960s, 1970s, and 1980s exacerbated public skepticism regarding rehabilitation. Prisons were seen as overcrowded warehouses incapable of reformation, and prisoners were seen as deeply dangerous and discontented.

Furthermore, research indicated that prisoners were likely to serve longer sentences rather than shorter ones under an indeterminate scheme, contributing to overcrowding problems. Charges that the poor and nonwhites were victims of sentencing disparity further damaged the rehabilitation experiment. In the late 1980s and early 1990s the shift to punishment focused on the crime and not the offender, hence leading to the decline of the indeterminate sentencing model. Perhaps the greatest influence toward mandatory sentencing statutes is the public's frustration with crime. Politicians run on platforms that assert that they will "get tough on crime." Presidential elections have been influenced by the anger over early release of rehabilitated offenders who have murdered again. Mandatory sentences allow politicians to dictate the will of the people. Judges have since operated under severe role constraints. Many judges felt that indeterminate sentencing allowed them to make some judicial decisions. The 1990s have seen an increase in plea bargains, jury decisions in matters decided in court, and limited judicial discretion. The role of the judge has been limited to one of a mediator during court proceedings and a sentencing clerk who punches in the charges and the jury decision to arrive at the legislated sanction. The emphasis in sentencing has shifted once again from a "due-process" model that sees the needs of the offender as the core of penal philosophy to a "crime-control" model that sees the needs of society as more dominant. The shift to mandatory and determinate sentencing is a return to "letting the punishment fit the crime, not the criminal."

RECOMMENDED READING: Albert W. Alschuler, "Sentencing Reform and Prosecutorial Power: A Critique of Recent Proposals for 'Fixed' and 'Presumptive' Sentencing," in *Criminology Review Yearbook*, ed. Sheldon L. Messinger and Egon Bittner, Vol. 1. (Beverly Hills, CA: Sage Publications, 1979): 416–445; Christopher T. Link and Neal Shover, "The Origins of Criminal Sentencing Reforms," *Justice Quarterly*, Vol. 3, no. 3 (September 1986): 329–342, National Council on Crime and Delinquency, *National Assessment of Structured Sentencing* (Washington, DC: Bureau of Justice Assistance, 1996).

Victor J. Larragoite

INDICTMENT (FILING OF AND PROCEDURES ON). An indictment by a grand jury must be filed in a superior court of the county since felonies must be tried in a superior court. The defendant will be required to appear in the superior court to be arraigned on this new accusatory instrument. At the arraignment the judge takes control of the case and determines the course of future events such as the next appearance, representation of counsel, and bail (procedures similar to those discussed at the arraignment on the original accusatory instrument in the lower criminal court). (See **Arraignment; Bail; Cash Bail Bond; Release on Recognizance.**)

RECOMMENDED READING: Irving J. Klein, *Constitutional Law for Criminal Justice Professionals*, 3rd ed. (South Miami, FL: Coral Gables Publishing Co., 1992); Joseph R. Nolan and Jacqueline M. Nolan-Haley, *Black's Law Dictionary: Definitions of the Terms and Phrases of American and English Jurisprudence, Ancient and Modern*, 6th ed. (St. Paul, MN: West Publishing Co., 1991).

Christopher J. Morse

INSANITY DEFENSE. One of a number of legal defenses available to the defendant. If the defendant can show that at the time the act was committed s/he was legally insane, s/he will not be held culpable for the act in question. Although the doctrine that one should not be held legally responsible if one is lacking in certain mental capabilities is an ancient one, the insanity defense remains controversial. The acquittal of John W. Hinckley, who attempted to assassinate President Reagan, on the basis of insanity led to many attempts to reformulate the doctrine and even to abolish it in many jurisdictions.

The controversies surrounding the defense are several. One concerns the standard for legal insanity (a legal, not a psychiatric, term). A number of standards have been proposed, and different standards are used by different jurisdictions. These include the M'Naghten (right-wrong) standard, the "irresistible impulse" test, and the "substantial capacity" test. Each rule defines the concept somewhat differently; some are very restrictive, others are less so.

A second controversy surrounds the use of expert witnesses: How should they be chosen and to what can they testify? In most jurisdictions each side, the state and the defendant, chooses its own set of experts (called forensic psychiatrists) to testify about the defendant's mental state at the time s/he committed the act in question. In a few instances the court is empowered to appoint the expert witnesses. In many jurisdictions experts can state an opinion concerning the defendant's mental state (i.e., was s/he or was s/he not legally insane); in others they cannot. Ultimately, it is up to the trier of fact to issue the verdict.

Burden of proof is also a source of controversy. In all jurisdictions the case begins with the presumption of sanity. However, in some states, once the accused produces a sufficient amount of evidence to allow the insanity defense to go forward, the burden of proof then shifts to the state. The prosecutor must show, either beyond a reasonable doubt or by a preponderance of evidence (a less heavy burden) that the defendant was sane. In other jurisdictions the burden of proof remains with the defense to prove insanity.

In most jurisdictions a verdict by reason of insanity (or by reason of mental disease or defect) does not free the defendant. Instead, commitment proceedings are instituted whereby the individual in question may be sent to a mental institution to stay until s/he is pronounced "cured."

Many in the United States seem to believe that the insanity defense is routinely invoked successfully by defendants as a means of avoiding punishment. However, empirical studies have shown that the defense is put forward in substantially less than 1 percent of all criminal cases and that it is unsuccessful in most cases in which it is invoked.

RECOMMENDED READING: Lincoln Caplan, *The Insanity Defense and the Trial of John W. Hinckley* (Boston: David R. Godine, 1984); Abraham S. Goldstein, *The Insanity Defense* (New Haven: Yale University Press, 1967); Rita J. Simon and David E. Aaronson, *The Insanity Defense: A Critical Assessment of Law and Policy in the Post-Hinckley Era* (New York: Praeger, 1988).

David Jones

INSANITY DEFENSE REFORM ACT. An act passed by Congress in 1984 in the wake of the acquittal of John W. Hinckley, Jr. of attempting to assassinate President Reagan on the basis of Hinckley's legal insanity. The law is the first federal codification of the insanity defense. It seeks to accomplish a number of goals.

One of these goals is to define the rule of legal insanity as it is to be used in federal courts. Under this definition the defendant must show that s/he was "unable to appreciate the wrongfulness" of his/her acts. This is a more restrictive definition than was previously used in most federal courts. The act also limits testimony of expert witnesses: they are not to express an opinion about the defendant's mental state, but are to leave that determination to the trier of fact. In addition, the act makes the insanity defense an "affirmative defense." That is, the burden is on the defendant to prove legal insanity at all stages of the trial. Finally, the act provides for the commitment to a mental institution of a defendant found to be legally insane. Under the law a hearing will be held to determine the individual's current mental state. If s/he is found to be a danger to himself/herself or others, s/he will be committed to a "suitable facility" until pronounced cured. The act is perceived as a means of restricting the effective use of the insanity defense in federal courts.

RECOMMENDED READING: Joseph R. Nolan and Jacqueline M. Nolan-Haley, *Black's Law Dictionary: Definitions of the Terms and Phrases of American and English Jurisprudence, Ancient and Modern*, 6ᵗʰ ed. (St. Paul, MN: West Publishing Co., 1991); Rita J. Simon and David E. Aaronson, *The Insanity Defense: A Critical Assessment of Law and Policy in the Post-Hinckley Era* (New York: Praeger, 1988).

David Jones

INTENSIVE PROBATION SUPERVISION. Intensive probation supervision (IPS), the most prevalent intermediate punishment, is widely regarded as the best hope for relieving prison overcrowding, lessening the financial burdens of building and maintaining prisons, and avoiding the harmful effects of imprisonment. IPS is also touted as a cost-effective, punitive, and safe alternative to regular probation for high-risk offenders. Hence it has received the enthusiastic endorsement of criminal justice practitioners, judges, public defenders, and the general public.

Although IPS is being hailed as a new and innovative correctional option, dozens of intensive probation programs were implemented in the mid-1960s and early 1970s. These original IPS projects were started with Law Enforcement Assistance Administration funds and were largely probation management tools.

Contemporary IPS programs have different objectives from their early counterparts. Whereas the first IPS efforts underscored offender assistance and reintegration into society, IPS now stresses surveillance and compliance with probation rules. The current emphasis on offender control is related to the fact that many IPS programs are designed to divert offenders from prison. The first attempts at IPS were directed toward offenders who normally would have received regular supervision. Since the 1980s, however, IPS candidates are usually offenders classified as too serious for regular probation, but whose conviction crimes and prior records are not so serious that they can only be controlled in prison.

The "newer," more control-oriented IPS programs emerged in the early 1980s and have been implemented across the country. At the beginning of 1990, forty states (and Washington, D.C.) had IPS programs. IPS programs monitor offenders under regulations significantly more harsh and restrictive than those of regular probation. Curfews, drug testing, daily contact with probation officers, and compulsory community service may all be part of an IPS program. The overall IPS goals of prison diversion and community surveillance are common to most programs, but there is considerable variation in how programs attempt to achieve those goals. Diversity in the basic features of IPS projects leads to the conclusion that no simple answer can be given to the question, "What does intensive supervision really mean?"

National surveys of IPS programs have found that no two are exactly alike. IPS programs use different supervision strategies and serve disparate target populations. The most broadly implemented and highly publicized IPS projects are in Georgia, New Jersey, and Massachusetts. They represent three basic program models, respectively: diverting offenders from prison, releasing offenders from prison early, and enhancing existing case-management strategies.

Joan Petersilia and her associates at the RAND Corporation conducted the most valid studies of IPS programs, utilizing experimental designs that randomly assigned offenders to IPS (treatment) and regular probation (control). After sentencing, the RAND researchers followed program offenders to determine how well they performed on IPS compared to those placed on regular probation. The researchers reported that program offenders did not differ from regular probationers on recidivism rates, but they did have more technical violations (i.e., rule breaking that does not involve a new arrest). In addition, while a relatively low percentage of IPS offenders received services, participation in treatment programs was associated with 10 to 20 percent reductions in recidivism.

Another important finding of the RAND experiment was that some offenders who were eligible for prison-diversion IPS programs opted instead to remain incarcerated (i.e., they preferred prison to the onerous conditions of IPS). Overall findings concerning IPS programs also suggest that the criminal justice system should begin to reexamine seriously the goals and impacts of intermediate punishments.

RECOMMENDED READING: J. M. Byrne, *Probation* (Washington, DC: National Institute of Justice, 1988); J. M. Byrne, A. J. Lurigio, and C. C. Baird, "The Effectiveness of the New Intensive Supervision Programs," *Research in Corrections* 5 (1989): 1–48; A. J. Lurigio and J. M. Petersilia, "The Emergence of Intensive Probation Supervision Programs in the United States" in *Smart Sentencing: The Emergence of Intermediate Sanctions*, ed. J. M. Byrne, A. J. Lurigio, and J. M. Petersilia, (Newbury Park, CA: Sage, (1992): 3–17; J. M. Petersilia, J. Peterson, and S. Turner, *Evaluating Intensive Supervision Probation/Parole (ISP): Results of a Nationwide Experiment* (Santa Monica, CA: RAND Corporation, 1992).

Arthur J. Lurigio

INTERDICTION. Interdiction is the drug-prevention strategy of interdicting drugs before they reach the streets of America. The idea is to stop drugs before they are distributed to local dealers. One gauge of successful interdiction programs is the street price of drugs. When interdiction is successful, the price goes up as the supply becomes limited. Interdiction also stresses the curtailment of drug-producing activities in other countries. In recent years Colombia and Peru have been the focus of this aspect of interdiction efforts.

RECOMMENDED READING: Barry D. Crane, A. Rex Rivolo, and Gary C.

Comfort, *An Empirical Examination of Counterdrug Interdiction Program Effectiveness* (Alexandria, VA: Institute for Defense Analyses, 1997); Mark Moore, *Drug Trafficking*, a National Institute of Justice Crime File Study Guide (Washington, DC: U.S. Government Printing Office, 1988): 3; Office of National Drug Control Policy, *National Drug Control Strategy*, (Washington, DC: U.S. Government Printing Office, April 1995).

Glenn Zuern

INTERNAL AFFAIRS DIVISION. The internal affairs division is the division of a law enforcement agency responsible for the investigation of crimes committed by personnel employed by that agency. In some agencies internal affairs units also conduct investigation of administrative irregularities committed by personnel within the agency. In other agencies supervisory personnel do this. Sometimes referred to as "head hunters," internal affairs units are responsible for "policing the police."
RECOMMENDED READING: Stephen J. Gaffigan and Phyllis P. McDonald, *Police Integrity: Public Service With Honor* (Washington, DC: National Institute of Justice, 1997); Mike McAlary, *Buddy Boys: When Good Cops Turn Bad* (New York: G. P. Putnam's Sons, 1987).

James R. Farris

INTERNATIONAL ASSOCIATION OF CHIEFS OF POLICE. Formed in 1893 by police chiefs who met in Chicago and founded the National Union of Chiefs of Police, the original association was created primarily to apprehend and return wanted persons who fled local jurisdiction. The initiator of the group was Webber S. Seavey, chief of police in Omaha, Nebraska, who in November 1892 sent out 385 invitations to the heads of the largest police departments in the United States, urging them to meet in Chicago in 1893 to visit the World's Columbian Exposition and to form a national police organization. Although only 51 of those he had invited showed up for the meeting, they spent the next three days creating the National Union of Chiefs of Police of the United States and Canada. In 1902 the name International Association of Chiefs of Police was adopted. As early as 1897 the group began to work toward national identification of criminals; in 1924 the IACP's criminal identification files became the basis of the FBI identification division, and in 1930 the files were turned over to the FBI to form the uniform crime records. The *Police Chief*, the IACP's journal that in 1993 reached 13,000 members in 84 different nations, was first published in 1935; a permanent headquarters was established in 1940 (in Washington, D.C., but since relocated to Alexandria, Virginia); and in 1955 a training division was established from the nucleus of what had for twenty years been the traffic safety division. Services to members increased after Quinn Tamm took over as executive director in 1962. The 1970s and 1980s were highlighted by establishment of international training programs, establishment of a police assessment center, development of a regional division in Europe, and extension of training for police executives into Europe and Asia. The annual conference, a five-day working seminar, is normally attended by more than 6,500 police executives and more than 400 manufacturers of police equipment, services, and technology.

RECOMMENDED READING: IACP, *The IACP Today: From 1893 to 1993, a Century of Serving Law Enforcement* (Alexandria, VA: IACP, 1994); James W. Sterling, "A History of the IACP Insignia," *The Police Chief*, October. 1994: 125–141.

Dorothy Moses Schulz

INTERPOL. The International Police Organization assists law enforcement agencies with investigative activities that transcend national boundaries. It was founded in 1923 through the efforts of the police chief of Vienna, Austria. The organization became dormant during World War II, but was reorganized at a conference in Brussels in 1946. There are currently 167 members. Each country has a designated liaison officer to maintain contact and coordination with the general secretariat in Lyons, France. INTERPOL has a headquarters staff of about 250 persons, 60 of whom are law enforcement officers from about 40 different countries. A large communications facility links 72 of the member countries into a radio network; other nations use telex or cable facilities. INTERPOL is under the day-to-day direction of a secretary general; it is a coordinating body and has no investigators or law enforcement agents of its own.

RECOMMENDED READING: Fenton S. Bresler, *INTERPOL*, (New York: Viking, 1992); Iris Noble, *INTERPOL: International Crime Fighter* (New York: Harcourt Brace Jovanovich, 1975).

James R. Farris

INTERROGATION. Any express questioning or its equivalent, including any words or actions on the part of the police (other than those normally attendant to arrests and custody) that the police should know are reasonably likely to elicit an incriminating response from the suspect.

RECOMMENDED READING: James N. Gilbert, *Criminal Investigation*, 4th ed. (Upper Saddle River, NJ: Prentice Hall, 1998); Joseph R. Nolan and Jacqueline M. Nolan-Haley, *Black's Law Dictionary: Definitions of the Terms and Phrases of American and English Jurisprudence, Ancient and Modern*, 6th ed. (St. Paul, MN: West Publishing Co., 1991).

James R. Farris

INTERVIEW. An interview is a formal, face-to-face meeting in a private conversational setting that involves two parties, an interviewer and an interviewee. The main purpose is to collect information and to ascertain the personal qualities of the interviewee. In criminal justice an interview can be conducted with witnesses, the accused, or anyone who might be remotely related to a crime.

RECOMMENDED READING: Joseph R. Nolan and Jacqueline M. Nolan-Haley, *Black's Law Dictionary: Definitions of the Terms and Phrases of*

American and English Jurisprudence, Ancient and Modern, 6th ed. (St. Paul, MN: West Publishing Co., 1991).

James R. Farris

INVESTIGATION. To investigate means "to observe or study closely; to inquire into something systematically, or to search for truthful information." The word *investigate* is derived from the Latin *vestigare*, meaning to track or trace. A criminal investigation is the systematic process of identifying, collecting, preserving, and evaluating information for the purpose of bringing a criminal offender to justice. Therefore, a criminal investigation seeks all facts associated with a crime to determine the truth—what happened and who is responsible.

The core elements of the investigative process are recognition, collection, preservation, and evaluation. Recognition is the perception of information relating to a crime that must be recognized as such by the investigator. Collection is the gathering of information and evidence relevant to the crime. For example, investigators might collect dried blood at the crime scene or interview a neighbor who witnessed the assault. Preservation of evidence is accomplished by properly collecting, documenting, and securing the evidence once discovered. Finally, evaluation is the investigator's analysis of the information to determine its worth and credibility, and whether the information will support arrest and prosecution of a particular suspect. An example of an investigator's evaluation could be that the blood collected at the scene of a crime was too common to identify a specific suspect, but does sufficiently eliminate other suspects.

The four main goals of all criminal investigations are (1) to determine whether a crime has been committed; (2) to legally obtain information and evidence to identify the person(s) responsible; (3) to arrest the suspect(s); and (4) to present the best possible case to the prosecutor.

RECOMMENDED READING: Wayne W. Bennett and Karen M. Hess, *Criminal Investigation*, 4th ed. (Minneapolis/St. Paul: West Publishing Co., 1994); Joseph R. Nolan and Jacqueline M. Nolan-Haley, *Black's Law Dictionary: Definitions of the Terms and Phrases of American and English Jurisprudence, Ancient and Modern*, 6th ed. (St. Paul, MN: West Publishing Co., 1991); James W. Osterburg and Richard H. Ward, *Criminal Investigation: A Method for Reconstructing the Past*, 2nd ed. (Cincinnati: Anderson Publishing Co., 1997).

James R. Farris

IRRESISTIBLE IMPULSE. One of the standards used to define legal insanity. Under this definition jurors are instructed to acquit the defendant by reason of insanity if they find that the defendant had a mental disease or defect that kept him/her from controlling his/her conduct, even if s/he knew that the act was wrong. It is one of the least restrictive definitions of legal insanity.

This standard was in some favor in the 1920s and at that time was seen as an improvement over the then-dominant M'Naghten rule. However, it has since fallen out of favor and is currently used in very few jurisdictions.

RECOMMENDED READING: Abraham S. Goldstein, *The Insanity Defense* (New Haven: Yale University Press, 1967); Joseph R. Nolan and Jacqueline M. Nolan-Haley, *Black's Law Dictionary: Definitions of the Terms and Phrases of American and English Jurisprudence, Ancient and Modern*, 6th ed. (St. Paul, MN: West Publishing Co., 1991); Rita J. Simon and David E. Aaronson, *The Insanity Defense: A Critical Assessment of Law and Policy in the Post-Hinckley Era* (New York: Praeger, 1988); Robert Tannenbaum, *Irresistible Impulse* (New York: Dutton, 1997).

David Jones

J

JAIL. Jails are confinement facilities used to hold suspects awaiting trial or convicted misdemeanants serving relatively short confinement sentences. More than a lockup in a police station, but less than a prison, jails are intended to be used for short-term incarceration. In the 1990s, however, jails are being increasingly used to house inmates from grossly overcrowded prisons. In a measure to increase use of jails in lieu of prisons, many states offer monetary incentives to local jurisdictions to incarcerate convicted offenders in local facilities. (See **Direct Supervision; Police Lockup; Prison.**)

RECOMMENDED READING: Joseph R. Nolan and Jacqueline M. Nolan-Haley, *Black's Law Dictionary: Definitions of the Terms and Phrases of American and English Jurisprudence, Ancient and Modern*, 6th ed. (St. Paul, MN: West Publishing Co., 1991); Frank Schmalleger, *Criminal Justice Today: An Introductory Text for the Twenty-First Century* (Upper Saddle River, NJ: Prentice Hall 1997); 465-472.

Gordon M. Armstrong

JAIL HISTORY AND CURRENT FUNCTIONS. Historically, jails have been the stepchild of the criminal justice system. The jail has been and still is today the dumping ground for the nation's criminals, homeless persons, public inebriates, mentally dysfunctional persons, and other social misfits. Thanks to the media, which frequently use the terms *jail* and *prison* interchangeably, many ordinary citizens cannot distinguish between jails and prisons. A newspaper headline that screams "Murderer Gets 100-Year Jail Sentence" illustrates the problem.

In the final decade before the twenty-first century, America's 3,272 jails process more than 20 million people a year in and out of the American jail system. The 1994 second edition of *Who's Who in Jail Management*, published by the American Jail Association, breaks the different jails down by the rated capacity of the jail. The following table indicates the number of jails at each rating level:

Rated Capacity	Number
1–50	1,739
51–250	1,108
251–500	199
501–1,000	151
1,001–3,000	67
More than 3,000	8

Roughly 45 percent of all jail inmates are housed in the 100 largest jails. If one were to count all jail prisoners on a particular day, the total would be around half a million. The majority of the 10 million plus booked into a jail either bond out in the first several hours or are released on their own recognizance. In the past decade the jail population has more than doubled, owing principally to mandatory DUI and drug sentences, crowded state prison systems forcing state inmates to remain in jail, abolition of parole in certain states, adoption of so-called "three-strikes-and-you're-out" legislation, mandatory minimum sentencing, and a hardened public attitude favoring more lengthy sentences.

American jails hold more mentally disturbed people than all the mental hospitals in the country, and the National Alliance for the Mentally Ill points to local mental health agencies as the main impediment for refusal to work with jails to provide training for the jail officers and programs to divert these people from jail. More than 50 percent of the people booked into jail are either illiterate or functionally illiterate; over 60 percent have substance-abuse problems. A recent survey of over 1,600 jails by the American Jail Association revealed that over 80 percent had no substance-abuse treatment programs at all. Other surveys show that jail administrators and sheriffs perceive the jails' most serious problems to be those of personnel, crowding, deficient physical plants, exercise space and programs, and budgets. More than 1,400 jails have been constructed since the 1970s, but many jails remain crowded. Over 130 jail systems still function under some kind of court order or consent decree arrangement.

The most significant trend in jail management is the increase in the numbers of direct-supervision jails, the first of which opened in Contra Costa County, California, in 1981. For the first time in jail history staff have a chance to control their jails, since officers now are physically situated inside the inmate living areas (called pods) twenty-four hours a day. The success of this new scheme, which emphasizes participatory management by the line officers, depends on the extent of the transition training and the officers' success in absorbing and acting upon the eight philosophical principles of direct supervision. There are now 147 jails housing over 70,000 inmates in the direct-supervision mode.

Another trend to watch is the slow regionalization of the small "mom-and-pop" jails that dot the American landscape. This foreshadows a continual decline of sheriff-run jails, which have dropped from around 90 percent in 1980 to 75 percent in 1994. Small counties find it an economic drain to operate and staff a jail twenty-four hours a day, seven days a week. States like West Virginia will have all their jails regionalized by the year 2000, and Virginia offers a 50 percent subsidy for local jurisdictions that combine to construct a regional facility; a single jurisdiction would receive only a 25 percent subsidy. Many jails in the Midwest are *de facto* regional jails where one county holds prisoners for several counties.

RECOMMENDED READING: Ron Carroll, "Jails and the Criminal Justice System in the 21st Century," in *American Jails*, March/April 1997: 26-31; Gary F. Cornelius, *Jails in America: An Overview of Issues*, 2nd ed. (Lanham, MD: American Correctional Association, 1996); Randall Guynes, *Nation's Jail Managers Assess Their Problems* (Washington, D.C.: National Institute of Justice, 1988); Christy Maganzini, *Almanac of Dungeons, Prisons, and Jails* (New York: Random House, 1997); Linda L. Zupan and Ben A. Menke, "The New Generation Jail: An Overview," in *American Jails: Public Policy Issues*, ed. Joel A. Thompson and G. Larry Mays (Chicago: Nelson-Hall Publishers, 1991): 180-182.

Ken Kerle

JOHN HOWARD ASSOCIATION. The John Howard Association (JHA) is a not-for-profit agency founded in 1901. JHA works for effective correctional programs and for the humane treatment of incarcerated persons. JHA has been in the forefront of systematic policy changes in Illinois through its advocacy, public education, and monitoring activities. It provides a vital link between the public and government on corrections issues.

The John Howard Association is named after a British man who served as high sheriff of Bedfordshire, England, in 1773. Almost twenty years earlier, on a tour of Portugal, he was taken prisoner by French pirates and imprisoned. He experienced severe abuse by soldiers and at times was deprived of light, food, clothing, and medical attention. This prison experience affected him so greatly that he spent the rest of his life working toward improving prison conditions. He visited over 500 institutions in England and Europe and laid the groundwork for modern prison architecture and management with a focus on humane physical conditions.

Illinois's John Howard Association began by providing services to ex-offenders, but later expanded its focus to public education, advocacy, and policy reform. In the 1970s the Illinois Prisons and Jails Program was formed, bringing citizen volunteers to assist JHA staff in visiting inmates and staff housed in Illinois's prisons and jails. Since that time volunteers have visited inside Cook County Jail nearly once a week and inside each adult prison and youth facility once a year. Their reports on the conditions of these facilities and on how the incarcerated are treated have resulted in change within these facilities.

Over the years JHA has earned the respect of public officials. JHA was invited to observe staff in the wake of riots and was appointed by the federal court to monitor federal consent decrees for the Stateville and Cook County correctional facilities. JHA was the first citizen group to be allowed to visit the "new Alcatraz," Marion Federal Prison, located in Illinois. JHA offers expert-witness and technical assistance to more than thirty-three states throughout the United States. JHA helped lead Illinois in the reform of its antiquated bail system; in the reduction in the number of juveniles held in adult jails; in an expansion of intermediate punishment programs for non-violent offenders; and in a change in Illinois's good-time laws, allowing inmates to earn days off their sentence for participation in basic literacy and vocational educational programs.

JHA's policy statements cover such diverse subjects as education and substance-abuse treatment opportunities inside prisons, privatization of corrections facilities, intermediate punishment programs for nonviolent offenders, crime prevention, and capital punishment. These statements promote reform and are the basis of JHA advocacy efforts in Springfield and throughout the state.

Michael Mahoney

JUDICIAL FEDERALISM. Also referred to as "adequate and independent state grounds," the concept of judicial federalism gained adherents beginning in the late 1970s as a means for expanding individual rights in the United States. It is based on the fact that in the American legal system a state supreme court is the final arbiter of the meaning of its state's constitution. Advocates of this movement, who include former U.S. Supreme Court Justice William Brennan, argue that while a state supreme court cannot interpret the basic documents of its state as providing fewer protections for individual rights than are required by the U.S. Supreme Court's interpretation of the U.S. Constitution, it may interpret its state's constitution so as to provide broader rights than those recognized in the U.S. Constitution. The concept has been validated by the U.S. Supreme Court, which held in *Michigan v. Long* (1983) that if a state's highest court explicitly states that it is basing a decision on adequate and independent state grounds, the U.S. Supreme Court will honor that interpretation.

Supporters of the concept note that many state constitutions provide guarantees (e.g., an explicit right to privacy) not provided for in the U.S. Constitution. Moreover, even if the language in state and federal constitutions is identical, state courts are not required to construe the meaning of the state provision in the same way the U.S. Supreme Court interprets the federal document. For instance, although there is identical language in the New Jersey state constitution and the U.S. Constitution concerning "unreasonable searches and seizures," New Jersey's highest court construed the provision in the state constitution as prohibiting the "good-faith exception" to the exclusionary rule, although such an exception is accepted under the current interpretation of the U.S. Constitution.

Proponents of judicial federalism see it as a means for expanding individual rights and liberties (at least in some states) as well as providing a means to allow greater flexibility to meet unique local needs. Opponents, however, have expressed fears that widespread use of the concept could lead to high levels of confusion in criminal procedure laws. Despite the theoretical arguments pro and con, there is not much evidence that it has been widely used in many states.

RECOMMENDED READING: Shirley S. Abrahamson, "Criminal Law and State Constitutions: The Emergence of State Constitutional Law," *Texas Law Review* 63 (1986): 1141–1192; William J. Brennan, "The Bill of Rights and the States: The Revival of State Constitutions as Guardians of Individual Rights," *New York University Law Review* 61 (1986): 535–553; William J. Brennan, "State Constitutions and the Protection of Individual Rights," *Harvard Law Review* 90 (1977): 489–505; Susan Fino, *The Role of State Supreme Courts in the New Judicial Federalism* (Westport, CT: Greenwood Press, 1987).

David Jones

JUDICIARY ACT OF 1925. Congressional legislation, still largely in effect today, that gave the U.S. Supreme Court a great amount of power to determine which cases it will decide. Prior to the passage of the act federal law provided that the Supreme Court was obliged to hear certain types of cases on appeal. As a result, the Supreme Court was faced with a large docket backlog. Since the passage of this law the court's backlog has declined significantly.

The act increased the Court's discretion by providing for greater use of the writ of *certiorari*, a discretionary writ, as a mechanism for determining which cases will be heard. Since the law was passed, *certiorari* has been the primary mechanism used by the Court for determining which cases it will decide. The Judiciary Act of 1925 has been called the "judges' bill." It was written in large part by a number of justices and was lobbied for energetically by several members of the Court, especially Chief Justice William Howard Taft.

RECOMMENDED READING: Alpheus T. Mason, *William Howard Taft: Chief Justice* (New York: Simon and Schuster, 1965); Walter Murphy, *Elements of Judicial Strategy* (Chicago: University of Chicago Press, 1964); Doris Marie Provine, *Case Selection in the United States Supreme Court* (Chicago: University of Chicago Press, 1980).

David Jones

JURY. Article III of the U.S. Constitution requires that "[t]he trial of all crimes ... shall be by jury," and the Sixth Amendment to the U.S. Constitution guarantees that, "In all criminal prosecutions the accused shall enjoy the right to a speedy and public trial, by an impartial jury ... ." States have the authority to determine the size of criminal trial juries. Most states use juries composed of twelve persons and 1 or 2 alternates designated to fill in for jurors who are unable to continue due to accident, illness, or personal emergency. Some states allow for juries with fewer than twelve members, and juries with as few as 6 members have survived U.S. Supreme Court scrutiny.

Jury duty is regarded as a responsibility of citizenship. Other than juveniles and certain job occupants such as police personnel, physicians, members of the armed services on active duty, and emergency service workers, persons called for jury duty must serve unless they can convince a judge that they should be excused for overriding reasons. Aliens, those convicted of a felony, and citizens who have served on a jury within the past two years are excluded from jury service in most jurisdictions. The names of prospective jurors are often gathered from the tax register, driver's license or motor-vehicle registration records, or voter registration rolls of a county or municipality. Minimum qualifications for jury service include adulthood, a basic command of spoken English, citizenship, "ordinary intelligence," and local residency. Jurors are also expected to possess their "natural faculties," meaning that they should be able to hear, speak, see, move, and so forth. Some jurisdictions have recently allowed handicapped persons to serve as jurors, although the nature of the evidence to be presented in a case may preclude persons with certain kinds of disabilities from serving.

Ideally the jury is to be a microcosm of society, reflecting the values, rationality, and common sense of the average person. The U.S. Supreme Court has held that criminal defendants have a right to have their cases heard before a jury of their peers. Ideally, peer juries are those composed of a representative cross section of the community in which the alleged crime has occurred and where the trial is to be held. The idea of a peer jury stems from the *Magna Carta's* original guarantee of jury trials for "freemen."

A related developing field is that of scientific jury selection, which uses correlational techniques from the social sciences to gauge the likelihood that potential jurors will vote for conviction or acquittal. It makes predictions based on the economic, ethnic, and other personal and social characteristics of each member of the juror pool. According to critics, however, the end result of the jury selection process may be to produce a jury composed of people who are uneducated, uninformed, and generally inexperienced at making any type of well-considered decision.

The jury system has received much criticism as an inefficient and out-moded method for determining guilt or innocence. Many experts feel jurors cannot be expected to understand modern legal complexities or appreciate all the nuances of trial court practice. They also believe that instructions to the jury are often poorly understood and rarely observed by even the best-meaning jurors and that, for many jurors, emotions are difficult to separate from fact.

Opponents of the jury system have argued that a panel of judges who would both render a verdict and impose sentence should replace it. Another suggestion for improving the jury trial process has been the call for professional jurors. Professional jurors would be paid by the government, as are judges, prosecutors, and public defenders. Their job would be to sit on any jury, and they would be expected to have the expertise to do so. Professional jurors would be trained to listen objectively and would be schooled with the kinds of decision-making skills necessary to function effectively within an adversarial context. They could be expected to hear one case after another, perhaps moving between jurisdictions in cases involving highly publicized crimes involving multi-jurisdictional conspiracies.

RECOMMENDED READING: J. Patrick Hazel and Jack Ratliff, *The Jury Trial—From Voir Dire to Final Argument* (Austin: University of Texas at Austin School of Law Continuing Legal Education, 1994); Joseph R. Nolan and Jacqueline M. Nolan-Haley, *Black's Law Dictionary: Definitions of the Terms and Phrases of American and English Jurisprudence, Ancient and Modern*, 6th ed. (St. Paul, MN: West Publishing Co., 1991); *Smith v. Texas*, 311 U.S. 128 (1940); *Williams v. Florida*, 399 U.S. 78 (1970).

Frank Schmalleger

JUSTICE, U.S. DEPARTMENT OF. Referred to in the *United States Government Manual (1996)* as "the largest law firm in the Nation" (366), the U.S. Department of Justice is one of the largest and oldest agencies in the federal government. Founded in 1870, it is headed by the attorney general, who is appointed by the president with the consent of the Senate and serves at the president's pleasure.

Working under the attorney general is the deputy attorney general, the associate attorney general, and several assistant attorneys general who are also appointed by and serve at the pleasure of the chief executive. Most of the rest of the department's several thousand employees are career officials who are protected by civil service regulations.

Much of the legal business conducted by the federal government is conducted through the Department of Justice. In order to deal with its multifaceted tasks, the department is compartmentalized in divisions staffed with agents especially trained for the functions of their unit. Some of the more important of these are the Tax, Civil Rights, Anti-Trust, and Civil divisions. There is also a Criminal Division in which the U.S. Attorneys work. These individuals represent the federal government in criminal (and certain civil) cases before the U.S. district courts located throughout the country. Although they nominally work for the attorney general, many U.S. attorneys have strong political ties with elected officials representing the state within which their particular district lies. Many U.S. Attorneys are considered political appointees, and soon after a new president takes office, he typically replaces existing U.S. attorneys with members of his own political party.

The U.S. Department of Justice also contains many, though not all, of the major federal investigative agencies. These include the Federal Bureau of Investigation, the Drug Enforcement Administration, the Immigration and Naturalization Service, and the U.S. Marshals Service. The Bureau of Prisons is also administratively housed in the Department of Justice.

Many research programs relating to criminal justice are also carried out under the aegis of the department through its Office of Justice Programs. This office was established to provide federal leadership and assistance needed to upgrade the country's criminal justice system.

RECOMMENDED READING: David Burnham, *Above the Law: Secret Deals, Political Fixes, and Other Misadventures of the U.S. Department of Justice* (New York: Scribner, 1996); *Department of Justice Budget Trend Data: From 1975 through the President's 1997 Request to the Congress* (Washington, DC: U.S. Department of Justice, 1996); James Eisenstein, *Counsel for the United States: U.S. Attorneys in the Political and Legal Systems* (Baltimore: Johns Hopkins University Press, 1978); *United States Department of Justice Legal Activities, 1995-1996: The Department of Justice—The Nation's Litigator* (Washington, DC: Office of Attorney Personnel Management, U.S. Department of Justice, 1996?); *The United States Government Manual* (Washington, DC: U.S. Government Printing Office, 1996); *The United States Statistical Abstract* (Washington, DC: U.S. Government Printing Office, 1995).

David Jones

K

KATZ v. UNITED STATES, **389 U.S. 347 (1967).** This case was one of the most important Warren Court decisions interpreting the Fourth Amendment to the U.S. Constitution. Prior to *Katz* there was a debate about the scope of Fourth Amendment rights. Clearly, individuals were protected from unreasonable searches and seizures occurring in their homes and in other private areas. *Katz*, however, raised the issue of whether its protections extended to public areas. The Supreme Court held that the Fourth Amendment's protections extend to any area in which a person has a reasonable expectation of privacy. In a now-famous passage the Court stated, "[T]he Fourth Amendment protects people, not places."

Katz was convicted of transmitting wagering information between states by telephone. At trial the government was allowed, over objection, to introduce evidence of Katz's telephone conversations that were recorded by Federal Bureau of Investigation (FBI) agents. Without a search warrant, agents had attached a recording device to the exterior of a public telephone booth. The U.S. court of appeals affirmed the conviction, holding that no Fourth Amendment violation occurred because the agents did not physically trespass into the telephone booth (the device was attached to the exterior). The U.S. Supreme Court held that the nature of the place to be searched and whether the defendant owned the premises did not determine if the government could lawfully search the area. Rather, Justice Potter Stewart asserted that the Fourth Amendment protects persons whenever they have a reasonable expectation of privacy in their activities. Because persons may reasonably expect that their conversations in public telephone booths will remain private, the FBI agents' failure to obtain "prior magisterial authorization" (a search warrant) required exclusion of the taped conversations.

Katz v. United States continues to be an important Fourth Amendment precedent. Associate Justice John Marshall Harlan's concurring opinion in *Katz* is still used by the Supreme Court to conduct Fourth Amendment analysis. Justice Harlan stated: "My understanding of the rule that has emerged from prior decisions is that there is a twofold requirement, first that a person has exhibited an actual (subjective) expectation of privacy and, second, that the expectation be one that society is prepared to recognize as reasonable."

Contrary to *Katz's* rights-expansive holding, the more conservative members of the Rehnquist and Burger Courts have used *Katz* to limit suspects' Fourth Amendment rights. In numerous cases throughout the 1980s and 1990s, especially those involving illegal drugs, the Court has consistently held that suspects have no reasonable expectation of privacy that society is prepared to recognize as reasonable.

Thomas J. Hickey

KENNEDY, ANTHONY M. (1936–   ). Anthony Kennedy was born on July 23, 1936, in Sacramento, California. He graduated from Stanford University and Harvard Law School. Kennedy took over his father's law-lobbying practice in Sacramento and taught constitutional law at McGeorge School of Law of the University of the Pacific in Sacramento. He was appointed to the U.S. court of appeals in 1975 by President Ford and served for twelve years. After President Reagan was unsuccessful in 1988 in his nominations to the Supreme Court of Robert Bork and Douglas Ginsburg, Kennedy (who was twice passed over for the honor) was appointed.

Kennedy, a moderate conservative, had a reputation for flexibility and pragmatism. With little known regarding his stands on abortion, affirmative action, and church-state relations, his nomination was noncontroversial. At first he was a pivotal voter like his predecessor, Lewis Powell. Then he was part of a swing center bloc with Sandra Day O'Connor and David Souter. In 1995 Kennedy was inclined along with O'Connor to join with the three conservatives (Antonin Scalia, William Rehnquist, and Clarence Thomas) to furnish the 5-4 majority, although sometimes he voted with the more liberal justices.

RECOMMENDED READING: Evelyn C. Ellison, *Middle Justice: Anthony Kennedy's Freedom of Expression Jurisprudence.* Paper presented at the 1996 Convention for the Association for Education in Journalism and Mass Communication, Law Division; Christopher E. Smith, "Supreme Court Surprise: Justice Anthony Kennedy's Move Toward Moderation," *Oklahoma Law Review,* Vol. 45, no. 3 (Fall 1992): 459–476.

Martin Gruberg

KING, RODNEY (1966–   ). On March 3, 1991, Los Angeles Police Department (LAPD) officers were videotaped beating a black man. The California Highway Patrol (CHP) began to pursue a vehicle wanted for speeding, but the driver failed to yield. The pursuit reached speeds of up to 115 miles per hour. After a fifteen-minute chase along the Foothill Freeway near San Fernando, California, CHP officers called for assistance from the LAPD. The pursuit ended at the Lake View Terrace area, where Rodney Glenn King, age twenty-five, apparently refused to comply with police orders completely and efficiently, resulting in the officers' use of force. Standing on his apartment balcony, George Holliday, age thirty-one, viewed the incident from across the street. He was able to videotape eighty-one seconds of the incident. The tape showed several officers kicking and repeatedly beating King over fifty times with night sticks as he lay on the ground. King was taken to the hospital and was treated for skull fractures, a broken leg, a shattered eye socket and cheekbone, and neurological damage. King at the time of the incident was an unemployed construction worker out on parole for a robbery conviction.

On March 4–5 1991, the videotape aired on national news programs, evoking anger and frustration among communities across the country. On March 14, four LAPD officers were indicted by a grand jury in connection with the beating. The four officers were Sgt. Stacey C. Koon, age forty; Theodore J. Briseno, thirty-eight, Laurence M. Powell, twenty-eight; and Timothy E. Wind, thirty. All of the officers were charged with one count of assault with a deadly weapon likely to cause great bodily injury and one count of unnecessary use of force by a police officer. Koon and Powell were also charged with filing a false police report.

On April 29, 1992, a California superior court jury in Simi Valley acquitted Koon, Wind, and Briseno of all charges and Powell of all but one charge. Hours after the verdict was announced, violence broke out in the south central area of Los Angeles. People were pulled from their vehicles and beaten. By nightfall people gathered in the streets, looting and burning down businesses and stealing food, alcohol, guns, stereos, and other electronic equipment. Mayor Tom Bradley declared a local state of emergency around 9:00 that night. A dusk-to-dawn curfew went into effect April 30. Local police were aided by the National Guard, the army, and marines. During the five-day riot 58 people were killed, 4,000 were injured, 11,900 arrests were made, and $1 billion in damage was done.

RECOMMENDED READING: Robert Deitz, *Willful Injustice: A Post-O. J. Look at Rodney King, American Justice, and Trial by Race* (Washington, DC: Regnery Publications, 1996); Greg Meyer, "Rodney King: The Lessons to be Learned," *Journal of California Law Enforcement*, Vol. 28, no. 1 (1994).

James R. Farris

KUNSTLER, WILLIAM (1919–1995). William Kunstler was born on July 7, 1919, in New York. He attended Yale University and Columbia Law School. Leaving representation of the more conventional clients to his law partner and brother, Kunstler, in the late 1950s, spent considerable time assisting those on the cutting edge of the civil rights movement, including Freedom Riders attempting to desegregate interstate bus transportation, and Martin Luther King. He was then a mainstream liberal, teaching at New York University Law School and popularizing legal issues in his radio programs. The Chicago Seven trial was a watershed period for him. After it he practiced "movement law," with the majority of his cases being *pro bono*. He was often jailed on contempt charges.

Kunstler represented the pariahs, both famous and unknown: Stokeley

Carmichael, H. Rap Brown, Jack Ruby, the Berrigan brothers, Lenny Bruce, Adam Clayton Powell, the Attica inmates, Marion Barry, the Black Panthers, John Gotti and other organized crime figures, Native Americans, flag burners, and Islamic militants. William Kunstler died suddenly in September 1995.

RECOMMENDED READING: William Kunstler, *My Life as a Radical Lawyer* (Secausus, NJ: Carol Publishing, 1994).

Martin Gruberg

L

LARCENY. Larceny is wrongfully taking, obtaining, or withholding another's property with the intent to deprive the other person of the same or to appropriate said property to the use of the perpetrator or a third person. At common law, larceny included the offenses of larceny by trespassory taking, larceny by trick, larceny by false promise, embezzlement, obtaining property by false pretenses, and knowingly possessing lost, mislaid, or stolen property. Currently some states still have the crime of larceny; however, many states have replaced larceny with theft statutes.

RECOMMENDED READING: Joseph R. Nolan and Jacqueline M. Nolan-Haley, *Black's Law Dictionary: Definitions of the Terms and Phrases of American and English Jurisprudence, Ancient and Modern,* 6th ed. (St. Paul, MN: West Publishing Co., 1991).

Lee E. Parker

LAW ENFORCEMENT CODES OF ETHICS. The ambiguous mandate of law enforcement personnel, whether peacekeepers or law enforcers, coupled with their position at points of civil disarray, presents particular ethical dilemmas. Their positions of authority and the potential for arrest or use of force make law enforcement professionals unusually vulnerable to corruption. Increasingly, law enforcement organizations have chosen to publish the principles that guide their discretionary activity in the form of law enforcement codes of ethics.

Codes of ethics in law enforcement generally take the form of an affirmation of duty, or public promise, that explicit standards will be observed in the provision of professional services. Whether the code is declaratory or promissory in form, law enforcement organizations usually provide both statements of principle and detailed explanations of conduct and may outline ideals of performance.

As law enforcement organizations seek to professionalize their occupations, the provision of an ethics code is an essential step to accreditation. Ethics codes set a performance standard for individuals, provide assurance to those who will interact with members of a profession, and place limits on organizational liability.

RECOMMENDED READING: Tom Barker, *Police Ethics: Crisis in Law Enforcement* (Springfield, IL: Charles C. Thomas Publisher, 1996; John Kleinig, *The Ethics of Policing* (New York: Cambridge University Press, 1996).

Margaret Leland Smith

LAWYER-CLIENT CONFIDENTIALITY. One of a number of testimonial privileges available to a defendant. This is the oldest of the privileges and can be traced back to Roman times. Under this privilege a client may refuse to disclose, and prohibit others from disclosing, confidential communications between himself/herself and his/her lawyer. The rationale for the privilege is that it encourages full communications between counsel and his/her client, which enables the lawyer to better represent the client in legal matters.

The privilege attaches to the client, not the lawyer, and applies only to confidential communications. If a third party other than an employee of the lawyer or a close friend or relative of the defendant is present and hears the conversation, the privilege is lost. However, this exception does not allow eavesdropping by an unknown party.

This privilege is not applicable if the services of the lawyer were sought or obtained as an aid to the planning or commission of a crime. This is the most important exception to the privilege in criminal proceedings. (See **Testimonial Privileges**.)

RECOMMENDED READING: Indiana Continuing Legal Education Forum, *Keeping Secrets in Litigation: Privilege and Confidentiality* (Indianapolis: The Forum, 1995; *Kansas Ethics Handbook*, ed. Mark F. Anderson, J. Nick Badgerow, and Charles R. Hay (Topeka, KS: Kansas Bar Association, 1996); Legal Action Center, *Confidentiality: A Guide to the Federal Law and Regulations* (New York: The Center, 1996).

David Jones

LEX TALIONIS. The law of equal retaliation. Found in the earliest book of the Bible (Exodus), this law states that the punishment a wrongdoer receives should be commensurate to the evil s/he perpetrates—an eye for an eye, a tooth for a tooth, a life for a life. Historically, this principle was established to prevent unrestrained blood vengeance.

RECOMMENDED READING: Franklin E. Zimring, "Making the Punishment Fit the Crime: A Consumer's Guide to Sentencing Reform," in *The Pursuit of Criminal Justice*, ed. Gordon Hawkins and F. E. Zimring (Chicago: University of Chicago Press, 1984), pp. 267–275.

David Jones

LIFERS. The term *lifers* in the criminal justice system refers to those individuals who have been sentenced to life in prison without parole. Life-without-parole statutes are divided into two categories: capital-offender statutes and career-criminal statutes. Although such laws eliminate parole, release is possible, albeit unlikely, through the commutation of a sentence by the proper state executive. Life-without-parole laws affect both the lifers who must serve the time and the institutions that are charged with their incarceration.

Numerous studies have been conducted regarding the effect of life in prison on the physical and psychological well-being of inmates. Gresham Sykes, for example, suggested that Lifers are deprived of many liberties to which they are accustomed, including, but not limited to, heterosexual contact and personal security. Conclusions are varied concerning the impacts of such an environment. Some researchers indicate that lifers experience complete debilitation, while others suggest that no such personal deterioration occurs. Those studies that support the argument that long-term incarceration is extremely injurious to inmates maintain that lifers are gravely debilitated and marked by an inability to relate to others, make decisions, or maintain mental health. Alternatively, researchers such as Paul Paulus and Mary Dzindolet indicate that whereas feelings of hostility toward the prison and its staff may increase over time while a person is incarcerated, physiological stress and related physical health problems may decline relative to the outside world because of the regimented routine and habitual nature of prison life.

Correctional institutions are also affected by the implementation of life-without-parole statutes. Internal prison security is difficult to maintain because lifers cannot accumulate "good time" in order to hasten their release. Consequently, lifers have little incentive to abide by prison rules and policies. Additionally, as young inmates sentenced to life grow older, the role of the correctional institution may significantly change in order to accommodate the incarceration of elderly individuals. Prisons are not currently equipped with adequate staff, health-care facilities, or financial resources to be converted into maximum-security convalescent homes.

Summarily, lifers is a term that refers to individuals sentenced to life without parole for either the commission of a capital offense or involvement in certain career-criminal activities. The experience of spending life in prison without the possibility of parole clearly affects the physical and psychological health of inmates. However, the extent and precise nature of the impact is still a matter of considerable debate. Correctional institutions are also presented with challenges as prison staff members and administration attempt to maintain internal security and provide for the long-term care of lifers.

RECOMMENDED READING: Jack Henry Abbott, *In the Belly of the Beast: Letters from Prison* (New York: Vintage Books, 1991); Paul B. Paulus and Mary T. Dzindolet, "Reactions of Male and Female Inmates to Prison Confinement: Further Evidence for a Two-Component Model," *Criminal Justice and Behavior*, Vol. 20, no. 2 (1993): 149–166; Paul B. Paulus, *Prison Crowding: A Psychological Perspective* (Secaucus, NJ: Springer-Verlag, 1988); Gresham M. Sykes, *The Society of Captives: A Study of a Maximum Security Prison* (Princeton, NJ: Princeton University Press, 1958).

R. Scott Phillips

LIMITED JURISDICTION, COURTS OF. Courts that are responsible for limited proceedings, usually of a less important nature. Sometimes referred to as "inferior courts," these exist in some form in all but six states in the United States. While there is a great deal of variation among the states in terms of jurisdiction, geographical area served, sources of financial support, and personnel selection procedures, some generalizations may be made about these courts. In general, they deal with traffic violations, misdemeanor, and small-claims cases. They may also have the power to hold preliminary hearings in felony cases, issue search and arrest warrants, and set bail.

In many jurisdictions, particularly in rural areas, the presiding judge may be a "lay judge" who does not possess a law degree. They often one who serve in a part-time capacity. This characteristic, together with the informality that often pervades the proceedings, has led some to question the quality of justice dispensed in these courts, though others would disagree with this position.

Often courts of limited jurisdiction are not "courts of record." That is, no formal transcript of the proceedings is kept. Individuals who appeal convictions from courts of limited jurisdiction will have a trial *de novo*, which is held in a court of general jurisdiction. (See **Trial *de Novo*.**)

RECOMMENDED READING: *State Court Organization, 1996* (Washington, DC: U.S. Department of Justice, 1997); Doris Marie Provine, *Judging Credentials* (Chicago: University of Chicago Press, 1986).

David Jones

LOITERING. Loitering is being aimlessly present in a public place, at a time or in a manner not usual for law-abiding individuals, under circumstances that warrant a justifiable, reasonable, and immediate concern for the safety of persons or property in the vicinity. Among the circumstances that may be considered in determining whether such concern is warranted is the fact that the person takes flight upon appearance of a law enforcement officer, refuses to identify himself, or endeavors to conceal himself or any object without a believable explanation as to his presence and conduct. (See **Curfew**.)

RECOMMENDED READING: Joseph R. Nolan and Jacqueline M. Nolan-Haley, *Black's Law Dictionary: Definitions of the Terms and Phrases of American and English Jurisprudence, Ancient and Modern*, 6th ed. (St. Paul, MN: West Publishing Co., 1991).

Lee E. Parker

LSD. LSD stands for the chemical lysergic acid diethylamide, a powerful hallucinogenic drug. Enough LSD can be placed on the back of a postage stamp to give hundreds of people hallucinogenic trips. A popular drug in the late 1960s and early 1970s, it declined in usage during the 1980s. Recently there has been an upward trend in the number of people using LSD.

RECOMMENDED READING: Drug Enforcement Administration, *Drugs of Abuse* (Washington, D.C.: U.S. Department of Justice, 1990); National Narcotics Intelligence Consumer's Committee, *The NNICC Report: The Supply of Illicit Drugs to the United States* (Washington, D.C.: NNICC, 1995).

Glenn Zuern

LYNCH LAW. Lynching is a practice in which one or more people are summarily executed, usually in a public ceremony and often preceded by brutal torture, on the pretext of retribution for an alleged wrongdoing, by a mob or agents representing the dominant group in the community. In the United States victims of lynching have included Tories during the Revolution; alleged "outlaws," along with Native Americans and Hispanics, in the western states; immigrants and political and labor activists in the northeastern and midwestern industrial states; and African Americans in the southern, midwestern, and border states from Reconstruction to the mid-1900s.

Lynching is typically accompanied by other forms of terrorism directed against the powerless group (random mob and individual violence that goes unpunished, arbitrary imprisonment and forced prison labor, and other actions) and is usually defended by public officials, prominent leaders of the dominant group, and local newspapers. Although lynching is often linked to crimes and criminal suspects (especially by local and state officials), many lynchings have no such links. Members of targeted groups have been lynched for not being deferential, for violating local mores (like Emmett Till, a fourteen-year-old black male lynched for whistling at a white woman in Mississippi), for trying to register to vote or helping others register to vote, and for other noncriminal activities.

Archivists at Tuskegee Institute have documented almost five thousand lynchings in the United States between 1882 and 1968. More than 80 percent of these occurred in southern and border states, and about 90 percent of those in the South involved African-American victims. There were many more lynchings at the time that have not been documented: as opposition to lynchings increased in the 1920s and 1930s, white racists in the South increasingly turned to quasi-secret unpublicized lynchings and to "legal lynchings," sham "trials" in which a guilty verdict was assured and execution immediately followed.

Following a brutal riot in Springfield, Illinois, in 1908 in which white racists lynched two African-American men and forced two thousand others to flee, a national conference on racist violence was held in New York City and the National Association for the Advancement of Colored People (NAACP) was founded. Both the group of conferees and the new membership of the NAACP began antilynching efforts focused on publicizing lynchings. They also sought to expose other racial injustices which entailed violence towards African-Americans. As hundreds of thousands of African-Americans migrated out of the South, and as racist violence escalated after World War I, the antilynching movement increasingly sought federal intervention.

Representative Leonidas Dyer of St. Louis introduced a bill into Congress in 1921 to establish federal jurisdiction over lynching. The Dyer bill and successors were repeatedly reintroduced into Congress over the next three decades, but were repeatedly blocked by southern congressmen. A federal antilynching bill was never passed by Congress. In 1951 William L. Patterson of the Civil Rights Congress published the antilynching pamphlet "We Charge Genocide: The Historic Petition to the United Nations for Relief from a Crime of the United States Government Against the Negro People," charging that in failing to protect its citizens against racist violence the U.S. government had become complicit in that violence.

While classic lynchings (public torture and executions of African Americans by white mobs) decreased after the 1920s, the practice has lingered in the anti–civil rights terrorism, assassinations, and church bombings of the 1950s and 1960s, and in the legal use of the death penalty (mostly in the South) up to the present, in which black men (the traditional victims of lynching) accused of crimes against whites are much more likely to be sentenced to death, and to be executed, than are other defendants accused of similar crimes.

RECOMMENDED READING: Stewart E. Tolnay and E. M. Beck, *A Festival of Violence*, (Urbana: University of Illinois Press, 1995); R. L. Zangrando, *The NAACP Crusade Against Lynching*, 1909–1950 (Philadelphia: Temple University Press, 1980).

Ernie Thomson

M

MACONOCHIE, ALEXANDER (1787–1860). Often called the "father of parole," Captain Alexander Maconochie earned this distinction because of his actions at British penal colonies near Australia from 1837 to 1844. Maconochie was born on February 11, 1787, in Edinburgh, Scotland. After serving in such capacities as a British naval captain, secretary of the Royal Geographical Society, and a professor of geography, he gave up his London activities in 1836 to accompany a friend to the British penal colony at Van Dieman's Land (now Tasmania). Maconochie immediately took an interest in the operation of the penal colony and showed the prisoners a level of humanitarianism unknown at most of the penal colonies of that time.

Because of his observations at the Van Dieman's Land penal colony and his reading of works by people like John Howard and Jeremy Bentham, Maconochie began formulating an idea for a penal system that emphasized reform over punishment. In 1840 he was appointed governor of the penal colony at Norfolk Island (one thousand miles off the eastern coast of Australia), where he was told that he could test his system.

The basic idea behind Maconochie's system was that criminal punishment should be linked to "tasks" rather than "time." That is, rather than prisoners receiving a specific sentence that would someday be completed no matter the prisoner's behavior or attempts to reform, Maconochie argued that sentences should require the completion of certain tasks. The sentence becomes "indeterminate" because it is not completed until the prisoner does those tasks. The tasks themselves became the key ingredient to another aspect of Maconochie's plan, a "mark system." If sentences were to be completed only after certain tasks were fulfilled, there had to be a way to decide when these tasks were finished. This was accomplished by tallying marks as prisoners did their assigned duties and by erasing, or not adding to begin with, marks when prisoners misbehaved or failed at their tasks.

The vehicles allowing Maconochie to carry out his indeterminate sentence and mark system were already in place. As early as 1790 penal-colony governors could grant conditional pardons to transportees. This "ticket of leave" was made a formal process in 1811 and was well in place by Maconochie's arrival at Norfolk Island. However, tickets of leave were being granted as a matter of course to well-behaving prisoners after they had served a certain number of years (similar in nature to the idea of "good-time credit"). Under Maconochie the ticket of leave had to be earned. In addition, simply being good was not enough; the prisoner must also complete tasks and earn marks.

Under the mark system it was possible to fulfill a seven-year sentence in one year by earning 6,000 marks. Upon earning 7,000 marks a prisoner could earn release from a ten-year sentence. Discharge from a life sentence would take about two and one-half years and 8,000 marks. While earning the marks, prisoners passed through levels of custody. The first stage was one of strict imprisonment where prisoners earned marks but were not allowed to use them as they wished. Upon movement to the second level, prisoners could work together in gangs and could use the marks to purchase extra privileges. At the next custody stage they had freedom of movement in certain areas of the island. When they reached the fourth stage, the prisoners received their ticket of leave, which eventually led to complete freedom.

The radical nature of Maconochie's ideas did not sit well with many colonists, and protests were sent home to England soon after word of Maconochie's system began spreading. His critics were successful in ending his experiment after only four years and Maconochie was called back to England in 1844. Officials were not, however, as successful at quashing his ideas as they were in ending his job. A decade later the new director of the Irish prison system, Sir Walter Crofton, would borrow and elaborate upon Maconochie's ideas. Two decades later both Maconochie's and Crofton's ideas would dramatically influence correctional practices in the United States.

Maconochie's system of penal discipline was not really original since he borrowed ideas from, and gave credit to, John Howard, Jeremy Bentham, Benjamin Rush, and others. However, making use of ideas first generated by others does not diminish his stature as a penal reformer. More important, where the others generated ideas, Maconochie put them into practice. Few would argue with calling him the "father of parole."

RECOMMENDED READING: H. E. Barnes and N. K. Teeters, *New Horizons in Criminology* (New York: Prentice-Hall, Inc., 1945); J. V. Barry, *Alexander Maconochie of Norfolk Island* (Melbourne, Australia: Oxford University Press, 1958); T. Eriksson, *The Reformers: An Historical Survey of Pioneer Experiments in the Treatment of Criminals,* translated by C. Djurklou, (New York: Elsevier, 1976); William R. Much and Thom Gehring, "The Correctional Education/Prison Reform Link: 1913–1940 and Conclusion," *Journal of Correctional Education,* Vol. 37, no. 1 (1986): 14–17; Robert G. Waite, "From Penitentiary to Reformatory: The Road to Prison Reform—

New South Wales, Ireland, and Elmira, New York, 1840–70," in *Criminal Justice History: An International Annual*, ed. Louis A. Knafla, Vol. 12–1991 (Westport, CT: Greenwood Press, 1993): 85–106; S. White, "Alexander Maconochie and the Development of Parole," *Journal of Criminal Law and Criminology* 67, no.1 (1976): 72–88.

Philip Reichel

MAGNA CARTA. *Magna Carta* (the great charter) is a symbol of limited government and the rule of law. Yet it was drafted to provide concrete remedies for specific abuses. A charter of liberties was demanded by barons rebelling against King John of England, an intelligent administrator but a capricious and untrustworthy sovereign. He twisted reasonable procedure to suit his own desired ends. He demanded excessive military service or exorbitant payments of money in lieu of it. He sold offices and imposed new and higher taxes. He had also alienated the Church. The rebels compelled John to agree to their terms in 1215 at Runnymede on the Thames River.

Magna Carta has 63 chapters, some dealing with bygone disputes, others of interest to posterity. It forbade arbitrary imprisonment and punishment without lawful trial. Chapter 12 expressed the principle of no taxation without representation, chapter 20 that punishment should fit the crime. Chapters 28–31 opposed requisitioning property without immediate compensation. Chapter 39 had the rudiments of due process of law, including trial by jury (although "judgment of his peers" did not expressly intend that in the thirteenth century) and the writ of *habeas corpus* (which awaited enactment in the seventeenth century). Chapter 40 promised that the courts should be open to rich and poor alike. Enforcement was to be supervised by twenty-five elected barons empowered to receive complaints against the king.

For the first time the king's vassals had forced him to agree that he was subject to the law. *Magna Carta* confirmed the legal developments of Henry II, the liberties of London and other towns, and the rights of the Church. John tried to renege on the charter, and the revolt resumed. On his death his minor son had to reaffirm allegiance to it. It was repeatedly reissued and modified under John's successors. Contravention of the charter was one of the charges against Henry III, Edward I, Edward II, and the Stuart kings.

Most of the provisions benefited the feudal nobility. However, the broad language later came to be more flexibly interpreted, especially by seventeenth century lawyers and historians in the bitter struggle with the Stuart monarchs. William Blackstone incorporated this interpretation in his *Commentaries*. This influenced American lawyers and statesmen. William Penn drew upon *Magna Carta* when drafting his Frame of Government for Pennsylvania. In 1687 he was responsible for the first publication of the charter in America.

RECOMMENDED READING: James C. Holt, *Magna Carta* (London: Longmans, Green & Co., 1965); A. E. Dick Howard, *The Road from Runny-*

mede: Magna Carta and Constitutionalism in America (Charlottesville: University of Virginia Press, 1968); Anne Pallister, *Magna Carta: The Heritage of Liberty* (Oxford: Clarendon Press, 1971); Louis B. Wright, *Magna Carta and the Tradition of Liberty* (Washington, DC: American Revolution Bicentennial Administration, 1976).

Martin Gruberg

MAPP V. OHIO, 367 U.S. 643 (1961). The exclusionary rule of evidence prevents the government from using unlawfully obtained evidence in a criminal trial to show that a defendant committed a crime. In *Weeks v. United States* (1914), the Supreme Court held that the exclusionary rule prohibited the use in a federal criminal trial of evidence unlawfully seized from a person's home by federal officers. In *Mapp*, the Court held that the exclusionary rule applies to state criminal proceedings through the due-process clause of the Fourteenth Amendment whenever police officers obtain evidence in violation of the Fourth Amendment.

In *Mapp v. Ohio* three Cleveland, Ohio, police officers went to Dolree Mapp's home to look for a suspect in a recent bombing case. They also had information that there was a large amount of unlawful gambling material in the residence. When police arrived , they knocked on the door and asked Mapp if they could search the house. After telephoning her attorney, Mapp refused to admit the police officers. Three hours later approximately seven police officers returned to Mapp's home and knocked on the door. When Mapp did not respond, the police gained entrance to the home by forcing the door open. Mapp demanded to see a search warrant. One of the police officers presented a paper that he claimed was a search warrant. Mapp immediately grabbed the "warrant" and placed it in her bosom. The police struggled with Mapp, retrieved the paper, and placed her in handcuffs because she was alleged to be "belligerent." Mapp was taken to her bedroom, where the officers searched a dresser, a chest of drawers, a closet, and some suitcases. They also examined Mapp's personal papers and photo albums. The search was later extended to the remainder of the house, including her child's bedroom, the living room, the kitchen, and the basement. While searching the basement, police officers found human-figure drawings that Mapp had completed as part of a college art class. Based on these sketchings, Mapp was convicted of knowingly possessing lewd and lascivious books, pictures, and photographs in violation of Ohio law.

In *Mapp* the Supreme Court applied the exclusionary rule of evidence to all state cases in which the police obtain evidence in violation of the Fourth Amendment. This case has generated substantial controversy in the U.S. legal system. Opponents of the exclusionary rule argue that this sanction distorts the truth and contravenes justice. Those who support the exclusionary rule believe that it ensures the integrity of the U.S. justice system and serves as a deterrent to unlawful police conduct. Since *Mapp v. Ohio* was decided, however, the U.S. Supreme Court has allowed the states to use evidence obtained in violation of the

Fourth Amendment in some circumstances. One such situation occurs when police officers conduct a search with a facilely valid search warrant that is later determined to be invalid. This is termed a "good-faith" exception to the exclusionary rule. Some scholars believe that in recent years a more conservative U.S. Supreme Court has tried to restrict the exclusionary rule's effect in order to promote governmental interests in prosecuting criminals.

Thomas J. Hickey

MARIJUANA TAX ACT. This 1939 act required anyone who imported, sold, or produced marijuana to register himself/herself and pay tax on earnings from marketing marijuana. Earlier, trading in narcotics had been made illegal, and marijuana was listed as a narcotic. Thus those who registered themselves for marijuana trade were subject to criminal sanctions.

Glenn Zuern

MARSHALL, THURGOOD (1908–1993). Associate justice of the U.S. Supreme Court from 1967 to 1991. Born in Baltimore, Maryland, on July 2, 1908, Marshall was the great-grandson of a slave and the son of a dining-car waiter and a schoolteacher. He received his bachelor's degree in 1930 from the all-black Lincoln University in Pennsylvania (where he waited on tables) and graduated first in his law class at Howard University (1933). Marshall worked first as special counsel for and then director of the NAACP Legal Defense Fund, winning twenty-nine of the thirty-two cases he argued before the U.S. Supreme Court (including *Smith v. Allwright* [1944], *Shelley v. Kraemer* [1948] and *Brown v. Board of Education of Topeka* [1954]). He then served for four years (1961–1965) on the U.S. Court of Appeals for the Second Circuit, where he wrote over 100 opinions. As a judge, Marshall was noted for his particular interest in cases involving civil rights and criminal law. In 1965 he was confirmed solicitor general of the United States for the administration of Lyndon Johnson, and in 1967 he became the first African-American justice of the U.S. Supreme Court. He replaced Associate Justice Tom Clark.

As an associate justice of the Supreme Court, Marshall was somewhat noted for his consistently high level of agreement with colleague William Brennan. Marshall wrote a number of significant decisions in a wide variety of fields, however, and continued to involve himself passionately in issues related to discrimination and criminal justice. One analysis noted, that Marshall wrote opinions in eighty-six major criminal cases during his first ten years on the Court. He provided an additional fifty-three dissents in that time period. Most notably, Marshall became an explicit opponent of the death penalty. In the longest of nine separate opinions in *Furman v. Georgia* (1972), Marshall voiced his opinion that "evolving standards of decency" render the death penalty "excessive and unnecessary punishment that violates the eighth amendment." Marshall further suggested that the consistent, widespread support for the death penalty in public opinion polls was the result of Americans knowing "almost nothing" about capital punishment.

On June 27, 1991, Marshall announced his intention to retire from the Court as soon as a successor was confirmed. He was eighty-three years old and in poor health, but had served remarkably for twenty-four years and one month. Marshall's replacement was the second African-American to serve on the Court, Clarence Thomas.

RECOMMENDED READING: Carl T. Rowan, *Dream Makers, Dream Breaker: The World of Justice Thurgood Marshall* (New York: Little Brown, 1994); Mark V. Tushnet, *Making Civil Rights Law: Thurgood Marshall and the Supreme Court, 1936-1961* (Oxford University Press, 1996).

Peter S. Ruckman, Jr.

MASS MURDER. There has been increasing public and criminological attention to perpetrators and situations of homicide with multiple victims. This form of homicide is called "multicide," and consists of two subtypes differentiated according to time, location, and number of victims. Serial murder refers to one offender killing several victims over a long period of time at several different locations, (usually) one by one. (See **Serial Murder**.) Mass murder refers to several people being killed by (usually) one offender at the same location. Some prominent examples of mass murderers include Charles Whitman, who in 1966 killed fourteen people from his perch on the top of a 307-foot-high tower at the University of Texas in Austin, Texas, and Pat Sherrill, who opened fire in a post office in Edmond, Oklahoma, and murdered fourteen people, mostly fellow postal employees, in 1986. Many of these cases involve family members or co-workers as victims. Mass murders result in immediate and sensational publicity, and the perpetrators are often easily apprehended. It should be pointed out that such cases are rather rare and constitute less than 1 percent of homicide victimizations. Probably the most sensational case of mass murder in the United States occurred under the direction of Charles Manson. His followers were found guilty of two such events collectively known as the Tate-LaBianca murders on August 8 and 9, 1969. Manson was a vagrant who after spending much of his early life in juvenile and adult institutions founded a commune near California's Death Valley. From there, apparently hoping to start a race war between blacks and whites, his followers were incited to attack the home of movie director Roman Polanski. They killed five people, including Polanski's wife, Sharon Tate, and Abigail Folger, heiress to the coffee fortune. The next night some of Manson's followers killed Leno and Rosemary LaBianca in the couple's house. Manson himself did not participate in any of the actual killings. Manson and his followers were convicted and sentenced to death, although due to changes in the death penalty-law between 1972 and 1978, their sentences were commuted to life imprisonment.

RECOMMENDED READING: Jack Levin and James Alan Fox, *Mass Murder:*

America's Growing Menace (New York: Plenum Press, 1985); Ed Sanders, *The Family; The Story of Charles Manson's Dune Buggy Attack Battalion* (New York: Avon, 1972).

N. Prabha Unnithan

MASTERSON, WILLIAM BARCLAY "BAT" (1853–1921). William Barclay Masterson was a Canadian whose somewhat nomadic family finally settled in Kansas. He took to the trail to hunt buffalo at age nineteen and as a young man participated in the battle of Adobe Walls, Texas, where about thirty-five hunters are reported to have held off about five hundred Indians.

Masterson's first and only killing in a gunfight was in 1876 in Sweetwater, Texas, where he shot an army sergeant over a Sweetwater girl, Molly Brown. Brown herself was said to have been killed, when she threw her body in front of Masterson to protect him from the sergeant's shot.

Elected sheriff of Ford County, Kansas, in 1877 at Dodge City, Masterson served less than two years until he was defeated in the next election. His reputation helped keep peace in Ford County. He went on to be the deputy marshal of Dodge under his brother, then managed a gambling house while serving simultaneously as marshal at Creede, Colorado. After a brief stint as a promoter of sporting events he became a sports writer and died at his desk.

RECOMMENDED READING: Robert K. DeArment, *Bat Masterson: The Man and the Legend* (Norman: University of Oklahoma Press, 1989).

David R. Struckhoff

MCKEIVER V. PENNSYLVANIA, **403 U.S. 528 (1971).** In 1968 a sixteen-year-old youth named Joseph McKeiver was accused of committing robbery, larceny, and receiving stolen goods, all acts of juvenile delinquency according to Pennsylvania statutes. McKeiver asked for a trial by jury, and that request being denied, he was adjudicated delinquent in a bench hearing held in juvenile court. The next year, in 1969, another youth named Edward Terry, age fifteen, was accused of assault and battery on an officer of the law and conspiracy. He also requested a trial by jury and, upon his request's denial, was adjudicated delinquent and committed to the Youth Development Center at Cornwalls Heights. The cases were both appealed to the Supreme Court of Pennsylvania, with the single question being posed to the court: "Do juveniles hold a constitutional right to trial by jury in juvenile court proceedings?"

The Pennsylvania Supreme Court, with only one dissenting vote, felt that juveniles did not enjoy a constitutional right to trial by jury. The case was appealed and to the U.S. Supreme Court in 1971, accepted by *certiorari.* The issue raised to the Supreme Court was again whether or not the Fourteenth Amendment affords the right to trial by jury during the adjudication hearing in juvenile court. The U.S. Supreme Court found that "trial by jury in the juvenile court's adjudicative stage is not a constitutional requirement." The Court held so for a number of reasons, including that the Court had previously not given juveniles blanket adult rights. The juvenile court, the Supreme Court stated, was not a fully adversary process as was the adult court, and the right to trial by jury for juveniles in juvenile court could well change the face of juvenile court into a full adversary process. An adversary juvenile court would lose the informal, intimate, and rehabilitative trappings specifically designed for juvenile court during its creation.

Furthermore, the Supreme Court cited that there was no evidence that a jury trial was necessary for a juvenile court hearing to be "fair and equitable." However, the Court noted that some states, through the state constitutions, did offer juveniles the right to trial by jury. That, the court clarified, was the "[S]tate's privilege and not its obligation." In sum, the Supreme Court issued a decision dealing with the very fundamental question, are juvenile and adult courts significantly different to hold different constitutional rights? The Court issued its opinion and hit at the core of the ongoing debate when it stated, "[I]f the formalities of the criminal adjudicative process are to be superimposed upon the juvenile court system, there is little need for its separate existence. Perhaps that ultimate disillusionment will come one day, but for the moment we are disinclined to give impetus to it."

Frances P. Reddington

McNABB v. UNITED STATES, 318 U.S. 332 (1943). In this case the U.S. Supreme Court, under its supervisory power over federal criminal proceedings, ruled that confessions obtained by federal law enforcement agents by holding the accused for extended periods of time before bringing them in front of a judicial officer were not admissible as evidence in trial proceedings. The facts here were that a federal officer was killed during a raid on an illegal still the McNabbs were allegedly operating. Several members of the McNabb family were arrested and held by officials for an extended period of time. They were not taken in front of a federal judicial officer for arraignment as provided for in the *Federal Rules of Criminal Procedure*. Eventually, admissions were extracted from some of them and were used to convict several members of the McNabb family. The Supreme Court overturned their conviction, ruling that the evidence, gained in contravention of rules of procedure prescribed by Congress, could not be used as evidence against them in their trial. The holding in McNabb, combined with the Court's decision in *Mallory v. United States,* (354 U.S. 449 [1957]), has led to the "McNabb-Mallory rule," applicable in federal proceedings, that when officials interrogate a suspect instead of taking him before a federal judicial officer without unnecessary delay, confessions obtained during the period of delay are not admissible in court.

David Jones

MEDIA AND CRIME, THE. Advances in communications technology have significantly impacted news distribution processes since the early 1980s. Television newscasts are beamed into America's livingrooms directly from active crime scenes and courtrooms, almost overwhelming viewers with an unprecedented flow of information. Viewers no longer learn of crime after the fact, but rather become voyeuristic participants in the crimes they are witnessing. Two significant elements of this news phenomenon are the crime reporting process itself and the increasing instances of imitative (i.e., "copy-cat") behavior of some news viewers.

Crime Reporting. Crime reporting involves the selection, packaging, and presentation of crimes by news agencies. Crime has been a popular news topic since the 1830s and the emergence of the first mass media newspapers, collectively called the "Penny Press." News about crime quickly became and has remained a staple of newspaper and (later) television news. Crime is valuable to news agencies because it is easy to collect, inexpensive to produce, and popular with the public. Between 5 percent and 30 percent of all reported news is news about crime. Crime news focuses heavily on the details of individual crimes and less often looks at crime as a social issue or criminal justice as a social policy. Most news of crime and justice is "front-end loaded" in that it concentrates on the discovery and investigation of crime and the arrest of criminals. Later steps in the judicial process are less frequently reported and issues in corrections are mostly ignored. In a few high-interest cases, however, court proceedings and periodic follow-up stories are reported. Coverage of these high interest cases sometimes assumes entertainment-style productions and, in turn, generates the harshest criticism of the news media.

Criticisms of crime news reporting most frequently include the intrusiveness of some reporters and the insensitivity of some coverage; the news' focus on heinous crimes; media disruption of law enforcement investigations and court proceedings; and media interference with defendants' rights to privacy, due process, and fair trials.

More general criticisms of crime reporting are related to the emphasis on crime in the news media. Negative social effects thought to result from an over-emphasis include unduly increasing the fear of crime among the general public; the polarization of society along racial, ethnic, and class lines; undue support for punitive criminal justice policies; the painting of a false picture of crime and violence in society; inappropriately creating social panics and anti-crime crusades; adversely influencing enforcement, prosecution, and sentencing policies; and eroding public confidence in the criminal justice system. In response to these criticisms, journalists point out that the news media are private, for-profit industries, competitively driven to maximize their audience size. Journalists argue that the news media's role is to inform the public of particular events, not to educate them about the workings of the justice system or about the nature of crime. The media's emphasis on noteworthy crimes and criminal cases is argued to be a more appropriate social task for the news media than an attempt at a general comprehensive educational review of crime and justice. Supporters also cite positive effects of crime news, arguing that it has a deterrent effect by showing crimes being solved and criminals being punished; that it educates the public about the criminal justice system and citizens' rights; and that it fulfills a pressing public interest in certain crimes and cases.

Another controversial aspect of crime reporting is its accuracy when compared with official crime statistics. The creation of crime news is a selection process in which a few crimes are picked from a large pool of crimes because of their newsworthiness and presented to the public as crime news. Beginning with crime victims, and continuing through the police, crime reporters, editors and producers, and ending with the public, the selection process involves gatekeepers. Each gatekeeper in the process discards some crimes and passes along others to the next gatekeeper. Crimes that become crime news tend to be uncommon crimes. Hence, although it is a rare criminal event, murder is the most frequently covered crime, while the more common crimes like burglary seldom become crime news. Some crimes have high newsworthiness and are selected because they involve famous persons; are particularly dramatic, violent, or heinous; provide good pictures. Sometimes crimes that would otherwise be ignored are selected as news because they fit in with other stories or ongoing news themes, such as "crimes with elderly victims," which a news agency might be currently highlighting. This selection process inevitably results in the creation of adverse public perceptions about crime rates that differ significantly from actual crime rates as reported in more precise measures such as the FBI's annual Uniform Crime Reports.

Establishing and maintaining standards for crime reporting has proven difficult. First, conflicts between the press and the justice system often involve constitutional issues and the Supreme Court is frequently involved in deciding disputes. The news media are protected under the first amendment and they are highly sensitive to restraints on the news-making process. The Supreme Court has tried to balance the rights of the press protected under the first amendment with the rights of defendants for fair trials protected under the sixth amendment. Conflicts between the press and the criminal justice system most often occur over pretrial publicity, access to official files and records, and closure of proceedings. The Supreme Court has not offered specific rules for resolving these conflicts but has issued broad guidelines while leaving individual case decisions to trial judges. Other conflicts occur when reporters are asked to divulge their sources of information or to testify in court. Legislative efforts in these areas have resulted in a number of states enacting shield laws to protect reporters from having to testify and sunshine laws to increase press access to government proceedings and records.

Disputes involving taste and responsibility in crime reporting are also common. Debate continues regarding what the media should report about how crimes are committed, about sex crimes and sex-crime victims, about confessions and prior criminal records, and about juvenile crimes. Charges of libel and invasion of privacy against reporters can result from inappropriate reporting. However, reporter practices vary greatly and attempts to set and enforce standards have not been well received or overly successful. Some jurisdictions have tried to create voluntary guidelines for press coverage but it has been difficult to get press and criminal justice personnel to agree on guidelines. Even when agreement is reached, there are few sanctions available when either the press or criminal justice personnel violate guidelines. Rarely used and applicable only to specific cases, the most powerful available sanction to control news coverage is a contempt of court finding against a reporter or news agency.

Copy Cat Crime. Copy cat crimes are crimes that are connected is some causative way by media coverage. A copy crime is a crime in which elements from an earlier, usually heavily publicized crime, are emulated by a new and different offender. A role model, criminal technique, or criminal motivation can be the copied element. Media coverage of the first crime is seen as a primary cause of the resultant copy cat crime. Without the media attention given the initial crime it is thought that the copy cat crime would not occur. News, entertainment, print, and visual media have all been indicated as capable of generating copy cat crimes. In 1912, Gabriel Tarde was the first criminologists to offer a theoretical discussion of copy cat crime, coining the term "suggesto-imitative assaults" to describe the phenomenon and stating that "Epidemics of crime follow the line of the telegraph."

Due to the requirement of a media connection between the crimes, it is difficult to study copy cat crimes empirically. Crimes that are actually independent but similar, follow each other in time, and receive media attention can be mistakenly identified as copy cat crimes. On the other hand, true copy cat crimes can go unrecognized. The problem of not recognizing true copy cat crimes becomes more likely as the mass media becomes more global and as the distance and time between the publicized crime and subsequent copy cat crimes increases. Because of these identification problems, copy cat crime has been predominately studied through anecdotal reports rather than empirical data.

Empirical research about copy cat crime remains sparse. Copy cat crime has been empirically studied through surveys of offenders and by applying research into other crime phenomena to copy cat crimes. Surveys of male correctional inmates find that between 20% and 40% of inmates report that they have copied crimes from the media. The inmates report that techniques to commit property crimes are more likely to be copied than aspects of violent crimes. Research on suicides also shows a relationship between the publicity of suicides and subsequent imitative suicides. The suicide research suggests that publicity can trigger fatal, imitative behavior and that the more publicity, the greater the level of imitation. Laboratory studies of media and aggression have also shown that some viewers of media violence will imitate that violence. Lastly, the study of terrorism has documented the copying of successful, innovative terrorist acts, labeled in the terrorism literature as a "contagion" effect.

Although property crimes appear to be more often copied, violent copy cat crimes are more likely to become the focus of intensive media attention. They therefore sometimes generate waves of copy cat crimes where the publicity given the first copy cat crime results in additional secondary copy cat crimes. Copy cat crime is theorized as resulting from characteristics of the initial crime and criminal, the media coverage, the social context of the crime and coverage, and the copy cat criminal interacting. However, the specific relationship between media attention and copy cat crime is not known. It is hypothesized that copy cat criminals are more likely to be career criminals involved in property offenses rather than first or violent offenders.

RECOMMENDED READINGS: Stanley Choen and Jock Young, *The Manufacture of News* (Newbury Park, CA: Sage, 1981); Ray Surette, *Media Crime and Criminal Justice: Images and Realities* (Pacific Grove, CA: Brooks/Cole, 1992); Alex Schmid and Janny de Graaf, *Violence as Communication* (Beverly Hills, CA: Sage, 1982); Gabriel Tarde, *Penal Philosophy* (Boston, MA: Little, Brown, 1912); Gabriel Weimann and Conrad Winn, *The Theater of Terror* (New York: Longman, 1994).

Ray Surette

MILKEN, MICHAEL R. (1946–   ). One of a number of Wall Street manipulators convicted of "insider trading," the illegal use of privileged corporate information not yet made available to the general public. Early in his career Michael Milken became famous for his pioneering use of "junk" (low-grade/high-risk) bonds in corporate takeover bids in the 1980s. While controversial, the use of these bonds was legal, and because of his efforts, Milken received compensation of over $1 billion during his tenure as a Wall Street trader.

In part perhaps because he refused to cooperate with government investigators, Milken received the harshest sentence of those convicted of insider trading at this time: a $600-million fine, ten years' imprisonment, and a lifetime ban from participation in the securities industry in the United States. The prosecution, conviction, and punishment of such individuals as Michael Milken and Ivan Boesky have raised questions about what is considered to be appropriate punishment of those convicted of "white collar crimes."

RECOMMENDED READING: Larry Schweikart, "Michael Milken," in *Encyclopedia of American Business History and Biography*, Vol. 7 (Facts on File, 1990): 291-301.

David Jones

MIRANDA v. ARIZONA, **384 U.S. 436 (1966).** In the area of suspect rights, no case is more famous than that of *Miranda v. Arizona,* which was decided in 1966. Many people regard *Miranda* as the centerpiece of U.S. Supreme Court due process rulings characteristic of the Warren Court era (1969-1986). The case involved Ernesto Miranda, who was arrested in Phoenix, Arizona, and accused of having kidnapped and raped a young woman. At police headquarters the victim identified him. After being interrogated for two hours, Miranda signed a confession that formed the basis of his later conviction on the charges. Upon appeal to the U.S. Supreme Court, the Court rendered what some regard as the most far-reaching opinion to have impacted criminal justice in the last few decades. The Court ruled that Miranda's conviction was unconstitutional because "The entire aura and atmosphere of police interrogation without notification of rights and an offer of assistance of counsel tends to subjugate the individual to the will of his examiner." The Court continued, saying that the defendant, "must be warned prior to any questioning that he has the right to remain silent, that anything he says can be used against him in a court of law, that he has the right to the presence of an attorney, and that if he cannot afford an attorney one will be appointed for him prior to any questioning if he so desires. Opportunity to exercise these rights must be afforded to him throughout the interrogation. After such warnings have been given, and such opportunity afforded him, the individual may knowingly and intelligently waive these rights and agree to answer the questions or make a statement. But unless and until such warnings and waiver are demonstrated by the prosecution at the trial, no evidence obtained as a result of interrogation can be used against him."

To ensure that proper advice is given to suspects at the time of their arrest, the now-famous *Miranda* warnings are read before any questioning begins. These include advisement that (1) the suspect has the right to remain silent, (2) anything the suspect does say can be used against him/her in a court of law, (3) the suspect has the right to talk to a lawyer and to have a lawyer present while s/he is being questioned, (4) if the suspect wants a lawyer before or during questioning but cannot afford to hire a lawyer, one will be appointed to represent him/her at no cost before any questioning, and (5) if the suspect begins to answer questions without a lawyer present, s/he still has the right to stop answering questions at any time.

After reading and explaining the rights of a person in custody, an officer must also ask for a waiver of those rights before any questioning. The officer must ascertain (1) that the suspect understands each of the rights that were explained, (2) whether the suspect, bearing these rights in mind, wishes to answer questions at that time, and (3) whether the suspect wishes to answer questions without a lawyer present. If the suspect is a juvenile aged 14 to 17, the officer must determine if s/he wishes to answer questions at that time without the suspect's parents, guardian(s), or custodian(s) present. These waiver questions must be answered affirmatively, either by express answer or by clear implication. Silence alone is not a waiver.

Once advised of his/her *Miranda* rights, the suspect is generally asked to sign a paper which lists each right, in order to confirm that s/he was advised of, and understood, each right. Questioning may then begin, but only if the suspect waives the right not to talk or to have a lawyer present during interrogation. A suspect in police custody may legally waive his/her *Miranda* rights through a voluntary "knowing and intelligent" waiver, which can only be made if the suspect has been advised of his/her rights and was in a condition to understand the advisement at the time it was given.

Frank Schmalleger

MISDEMEANOR. One of the two general categories of crimes (see **Felony**), a misdemeanor is usually classified as a less serious crime punishable by up to one year in jail. Although exact elements of misdemeanors may differ among the states, they usually include minor transgressions among persons and property, such as simple assault and petty larceny.

RECOMMENDED READING: Joseph R. Nolan and Jacqueline M. Nolan-Haley, *Black's Law Dictionary: Definitions of the Terms and Phrases of American and English Jurisprudence, Ancient and Modern*, 6th ed. (St. Paul, MN: West Publishing Co., 1991).

Christopher J. Morse

MITIGATING CIRCUMSTANCES. Circumstances surrounding a crime that may detract in some way from the seriousness of the offense. These might include a supporting statement from the victim, the age of the defendant, the defendant's impaired judgment, a recommendation from the district attorney, or (in death-penalty cases) such items as the age of the defendant at the time of the crime or the fact that the defendant's participation in the act was relatively minor. In many jurisdictions, when considering mitigating circumstances in death-penalty cases, juries are allowed to examine any other evidence of mitigation related to the character of the defendant or the case that it finds relevant.

If an individual is pronounced guilty and the existence of mitigating circumstances is found, s/he may receive a less harsh sentence than is typical. For instance, in some states (e.g., Wisconsin) that utilize "sentencing guidelines," a judge may give a less harsh sentence than is suggested by the guidelines if s/he finds mitigating circumstances to have been present.

The existence of mitigating circumstances is also very important in death-penalty cases. Under the laws of states using the death penalty, if a jury finds a defendant guilty, it must then consider whether mitigating circumstances were present. If the jury finds mitigating circumstances, or in some jurisdictions if it finds that mitigating circumstances outweigh aggravating circumstances, it is precluded from recommending the death penalty.

RECOMMENDED READING: Joseph R. Nolan and Jacqueline M. Nolan-Haley, *Black's Law Dictionary: Definitions of the Terms and Phrases of American and English Jurisprudence, Ancient and Modern*, 6th ed. (St. Paul, MN: West Publishing Co., 1991); Welsh S. White, *The Death Penalty in the*

Nineties: An Examination of the Modern System of Capital Punishment (Ann Arbor: University of Michigan Press, 1991).

David Jones

M'NAGHTEN RULE. One of the oldest and most restrictive rules for determining legal insanity. Under this definition a person cannot be convicted if, at the time the criminal act was committed, that person was laboring under such a defect of reason as not to know the nature and quality of the act s/he was committing, or if that person did know it, as not to know that the action was wrong. In most jurisdictions that use the rule (and many do), this means that a person must have a complete and total lack of capacity to distinguish right from wrong if s/he is to be found legally insane.

This standard was adopted in 1843 in England as the result of the trial of Daniel M'Naghten (often spelled McNaughten), a Scotsman. M'Naghten was convinced that he was being persecuted by, among others, Sir Robert Peel, then prime minister of Great Britain. Mistaking Edward Drummond, Peel's secretary, for the prime minister, M'Naghten shot and killed him. The Scotsman was found not guilty by reason of insanity and was committed to a mental institution where he spent the last twenty years of his life. This rule is still used in Great Britain and in many states in the United States.

RECOMMENDED READING: Abraham S. Goldstein, *The Insanity Defense* (New Haven: Yale University Press, 1967); Rita J. Simon and David E. Aaronson, *The Insanity Defense: A Critical Assessment of Law and Policy in the Post-Hinckley Era* (New York: Praeger, 1988).

David Jones

MONEY LAUNDERING. Significant logistical problems arise for law-breakers whose criminal enterprises bring in large amounts of cash. The root of the problem lies in the domestic cash transaction provisions of federal statutes which require that banks report any domestic transaction involving more than $10,000 in cash. Some criminals are hard pressed to conceal their ill-gotten gains because their stores of cash are huge and cannot be easily introduced into the legitimate money flow without detection. To circumvent the law, criminals may resort to "laundering" the money by various means.

Comparatively small-time crooks may simply open multiple accounts in multiple banks under various aliases and restrict each transaction to less than the $10,000 limit. Criminals may use two popular techniques to process the funds. The first is "smurfing," that is, buying bank checks in amounts less than $10,000 and sending them to accomplices around the country for deposit in existing accounts. The second, called "structuring," seeks to legitimize the money by making an initial deposit under $10,000, then diluting its traceability by redepositing it in small increments in numerous additional accounts.

Big-time operators, faced with millions in cash to be "cleaned," often cycle money through foreign banks where confidentiality is provided by the banking secrecy laws in the receiving country. A common technique is to smuggle the funds out of the country for deposit in a foreign bank. Funds can then be legitimately transferred back into U.S. banks via electronic transfer.

RECOMMENDED READING: Joseph R. Nolan and Jacqueline M. Nolan-Haley, *Black's Law Dictionary: Definitions of the Terms and Phrases of American and English Jurisprudence, Ancient and Modern*, 6th ed. (St. Paul, MN: West Publishing Co., 1991); Frank Schmalleger, *Criminal Justice Today: An Introductory Text for the Twenty-First Century* (Upper Saddle River, NJ: Prentice Hall, 1997): 592–593, 654–655.

Shelia C. Armstrong

MORPHINE. Morphine is made from opium. It can be used as a pain reliever or a sedative. Morphine is highly addictive, both physically and psychologically. Morphine was once commonly used as a pain killer and was used extensively during the Second World War for this purpose, but is now seldom used. Morphine-based compounds are now used instead. Many of the pain killers currently in use are morphine based.

RECOMMENDED READING: Drug Enforcement Administration, *Drugs of Abuse* (Washington, D.C.: U.S. Department of Justice, 1990); National Narcotics Intelligence Consumer's Committee, *The NNICC Report: The Supply of Illicit Drugs to the United States* (Washington, D.C.: NNICC, 1995).

Glenn Zuern

MORRISSEY v. BREWER , 408 U.S. 471 (1972). This case was one of the first to deal with the revocation of rights of offenders on parole and was an indicator of the due-process revolution of the time. Morrissey was convicted in 1967 of false drawing of checks and was sentenced to no more than seven years in the Iowa State Penitentiary. Morrissey received parole in June 1968 and, after serving seven months on parole, was arrested for parole violation and incarcerated in the jail of the county where he lived. His violations involved obtaining credit for an auto loan using a false identity, providing false insurance information following a minor auto accident, failing to obtain permission from his parole officer for the auto purchase, and failing to report his place of residence to his parole officer. Morrissey spent a week in the county jail, during which time the Iowa Board of Parole reviewed the report of the parole officer and decided to revoke his parole and return him to the Iowa State Penitentiary. Morrissey argued that his parole was revoked without the due-process protections afforded by a hearing. After failing at the U.S. district court, his case was consolidated with that of another petitioner (Booher) and brought to the U.S. court of appeals. At this level it also was defeated in a 4-3 decision due to the perception that parole is a privilege and not a right, and the subsequent removal of a privilege does not require due process, in that the person is still "in custody." The case was brought to the U.S.

Supreme Court, where it was granted *certiorari*. The decisions of the lower courts were reversed and remanded, with the opinion issued by Chief Justice Warren Burger, with Justice William O. Douglas dissenting.

Chief Justice Burger's opinion was that parole, while still punishment, represents a lower level of punishment than incarceration, and the increase in punishment that results from a revocation must not occur without the protections offered by the due-process clause of the Fourteenth Amendment. The question as to what constitutes due process in such a case is less easy to define.

The model proposed and adopted requires two stages, with several parts to each stage. The revocation process begins with the first stage, which seeks to determine if probable cause exists to revoke the offender's parole. This process begins with a formal notification of the hearing, followed by a written notice of the charges against the offender. The offender has the right to be present at the hearing, to present evidence and witnesses in defense of the charges, and to challenge and cross-examine the evidence used by the state. This part of the process must be conducted and decided by a neutral third party.

The second stage involves the actual decision to revoke or not revoke the parole. Again, the same rights as in the first stage apply, but the goal here is to determine if the actual contract for parole was breached by the offender. Initially, it was not clear whether counsel may be utilized at the first of these two stages (as was noted in the opinion of Supreme Court Justice William Brennan), but the current view is that counsel may be provided at either stage depending on the circumstances of the offender and the exigencies of the case. Following the *Morrissey* decision, the right to due-process protections for parole revocation was extended to probation revocation in *Gagnon v. Scarpelli* (1973).

Matthew C. Leone

MOTHERS AGAINST DRUNK DRIVING (MADD). An international organization and a social movement attempting to reduce the problem of drunk driving by working toward the implementation of "tough" legislation to deter driving drunk. As a movement it has been instrumental in the redefinition of the drunk driver as a major social problem.

In 1980 Cari Lightner was killed in an auto accident involving a drunk driver. Her mother, Candy Lightner, became outraged when she found that the driver who had killed her daughter had a history of drunk driving and yet had still been allowed back out on the road. Her upset over the situation increased when she found that the courts would not punish the driver to the fullest extent of the law. Because she felt that the criminal justice system's response to her situation was grossly inadequate, Lightner founded MADD and began an aggressive campaign designed to change judicial response to the crime of drunk-driving. Her efforts ultimately resulted in many states passing significantly tougher drunk-driving laws. Lightner's successes on the state level led her into a national forum. She began to lobby federally for drunk-driving reforms. In 1982 then President Ronald Reagan created, as a response to Lightner's lobbying effort, a Presidential Commission on Drunk Driving. Lightner was appointed to the panel. In 1984 national legislation was passed designating that all states establish a minimum drinking age of twenty-one or lose 5 percent of national highway funding. At the pinnacle of her organization's success, however, came Lightner's personal downfall. In 1985 Lightner was asked by the board of directors to step down from the executive directorship of MADD in favor of assuming a consultant's position. The reasons that were commonly cited for this request centered on Lightner's personal competencies. Although she was a charismatic grass-roots organizer, MADD's board of directors felt that she was ill prepared to manage a national organization. In October 1985 Lightner resigned under protest.

Despite the upheaval in top management during the mid-1980s, MADD's organizational growth and purpose continued unabated. As of 1993, it directed its social and political efforts into four major areas. The first was an attempt to increase "public awareness" of the dangers of drunk driving. It did this through the production of films, the printing of newsletters, and the use of a speakers' bureau. The second was the funding of victim services. This took the form of victim counseling, victim legal services, and written material designed to help others to assist victims. The third major direction the organization has taken involved the development of services for youth. It provides student education, ride services at graduation, and essay and poster contests for interested high schools. Its fourth and most important function involves the effort to influence the legal system and to create tough laws against the drunk driver. This occurred in three ways: (1) Court and legislative monitors were used to compile case histories on judges and politicians who were coming up for reelection. These were used to guide public voting behavior. (2) MADD also helped to sponsor legislation concerning the drunk driver on both state and federal levels. (3) MADD swayed public opinion through the use of the mass media. The correlative relationships between drinking and automobile accidents were used to garner public support for the creation of "stiff" penalties for drunk driving.

An understanding of MADD as a social movement is perhaps best achieved through consideration of the drunk-driving phenomenon. Joseph Gusfield proposed that the "killer drunk" is a creation of the media and the judiciary rather than an absolute reality. We, as a culture, see drunk driving as a problem because it is a part of the "agreed-upon" reality promoted by these institutions. We implement policy to deal with the problem that is directed at the individual because it is a social expectation to attribute responsibility only in these terms. Lightner, in other words, used the media to create a public understanding of the problem that was relative to her perceptions. The "drunk driver" of 1960 became the "killer drunk" of 1980 not because s/he posed a greater threat but because the public was led to perceive him/her differently.

MADD's developmental pattern has followed the traditional routes of most social movements. The movement, with the fall of Candy Lightner, became institutionalized. With the shift, an organizational structure has emerged led by administrators to replace the leadership of Lightner, the charismatic reformer.

Neil Smelser defined the conditions that will lead to the rise of a social movement, and these were all highly evident in the period of time preceding MADD's inception. A "strain" had appeared in the criminal justice system. American law in trying to achieve justice for the offender had lost sight of the rights of the victim. The cultural ideal that suggests that the sanction should "fit" the crime was not being met. The victim's suffering, in fact, was exacerbated by the courts' inability to mete out punishment equal to the offense. The willingness of the police to support Lightner's organization became a "facilitating process" for the movement and allowed for its expansion. Relating the movement to "motherhood" serves as an example of a "precipitating factor" that acts to exaggerate the condition of "strain." The reform that Lightner suggested was not simply to protect the victim but rather to defend the integrity of the mother/child relationship. A legal system that would allow for a violation of this relationship was clearly flawed, and any legislator who would not support its protection would be committing a serious political error. Using the media, Lightner spread this message and mobilized participants. An "esprit de corps" was quickly established. Much like Alcoholics Anonymous, members of MADD are encouraged to share their personal stories and tragedies at chapter meetings. This commonality of experience, shared and ritualized by the group, creates an intensification of commitment in its members. Perhaps of most importance to the understanding of MADD in terms of general social movement theory is Smelser's notion of "structural conductiveness." This refers to those social structures that encourage or inhibit the rise of any particular type of collective movement. MADD, as a movement, stresses two ideologies. The first can be conceptualized as the inherent responsibility of the individual to account and atone for his/her behavior. This idea is part of the Protestant ethic and is, as a result, deeply entrenched in American ideology. The second major philosophical stance taken by MADD concerns parity in justice. This again has roots deep in religious ideology. Demonstrated in early Christian doctrine as the concept of "an eye for an eye," the perspective has since been incorporated into the American cultural perspective. MADD, resting on both of these traditional themes, made use of yet another American cultural standard by presenting itself as a case of "the individual against the system." Lightner's personal tragedy became a symbol for the movement (the incident is still described regularly in MADD publications), and her need for justice became a rationale for the changes in law. Elaborating this theme into "motherhood" versus Gusfield's "killer drunk" made the development of a movement such as MADD in American culture almost inevitable.

RECOMMENDED READING: Mariette Hartley, *M.A.D.D.—Mothers Against Drunk Driving*, (Video Edition), MCA Bookservice, February 1988.

Patrick Kinkade

MOTOR-VEHICLE THEFT. Motor-vehicle theft is the felonious stealing or taking of any motor vehicle, as specified in the general theft statutes of a state or as defined in a specific motor-vehicle theft statute.

RECOMMENDED READING: Cal. Penal Code Sec. 487h (West 1992); 46 Fla. Stat. Ann. Sec. 812.014(2)(c)(4) (West 1992); Joseph R. Nolan and Jacqueline M. Nolan-Haley, *Black's Law Dictionary: Definitions of the Terms and Phrases of American and English Jurisprudence, Ancient and Modern*, 6th ed. (St. Paul, MN: West Publishing Co., 1991).

Lee E. Parker

MURDER. Traditionally, murder is defined as the unlawful killing of a human being or a fetus with malice aforethought. Such malice may be expressed or implied. It is expressed when there is a deliberate intention to unlawfully take away the life of a fellow creature. It is implied when the perpetrator is not provoked, or when the circumstances attending the killing show an abandoned and evil heart. Currently, states have adopted the broad category of homicide and have defined murder as a specific crime within the category. The more specific definition includes intentionally and knowingly causing the death of an individual; intending to cause serious bodily injury and committing an act clearly dangerous to human life that causes death to an individual; or committing or attempting to commit a felony other than manslaughter, and in doing so causing the death of an individual.

RECOMMENDED READING: Joseph R. Nolan and Jacqueline M. Nolan-Haley, *Black's Law Dictionary: Definitions of the Terms and Phrases of American and English Jurisprudence, Ancient and Modern*, 6th ed. (St. Paul, MN: West Publishing Co., 1991).

Lee E. Parker

N

NARCOTERRORISM. Narcoterrorism is a term used to describe the violent activity of drug cartels against governments seeking to disrupt their drug business. In the 1980s in Colombia, narcotics cartels waged a war of terrorism against the government to prevent members of the cartel from being prosecuted and convicted in the court system. Judges were assassinated and government buildings were bombed.

RECOMMENDED READING: James A. Inciardi, "Narcoterrorism: A Perspective and Commentary," in *International Narcotics,* ed. Robert O. Slater and Grant Wardlaw (London: Macmillan/St. Martins, 1989): 289-321.

Glenn Zuern

NARCOTICS CONTROL ACT. Congress passed the Narcotics Control Act in July 1956. It established minimum sentences for the sale of narcotics and prohibited probation as a sentencing option in these cases. The act also authorized the death penalty in some cases for narcotics offenders. The act also placed travel restrictions on drug addicts in an effort to reduce drug trafficking. It made heroin illegal and required all pharmacies to turn in any heroin currently in stock. The act also created a Division of Statistics and Records to develop and disseminate information on narcotics that would enhance law enforcement efforts in the area of narcotics.

RECOMMENDED READING: David Musto, *The American Disease: Origins of Narcotic Control* (New Haven, CT: Yale University Press, 1973).

Glenn Zuern

NATIONAL CENTER FOR THE ANALYSIS OF VIOLENT CRIME (NCAVC). The role of the National Center for the Analysis of Violent Crime (NCAVC) is to serve as a law enforcement clearinghouse and resource center for the most baffling and fearful of unsolved violent crimes. The NCAVC was created in June 1984 in response to the increases nationwide of violent crime.

The idea for the center was a joint effort by several federal and local agencies. It was believed that the FBI's Behavioral Science unit had the best chance of administering such a project. At first it was funded by the National Institute of Justice. Since then it has been supported within the FBI's budget. The NCAVC originally was broken into four parts: research and development; training; profiling and consultation; and the Violent Criminal Apprehension Program (VICAP). These four parts are now administered by the Behavioral Science Instruction and Research unit (BSIR) and the Behavioral Science Investigative Support unit (BSIS).

The main goal of NCAVC is to try to lower violent crime rates in America. It does this by concentrating on unsolved and particularly brutal crimes, such as homicide, forcible rape, child molestation/abduction, and arson. NCAVC's primary job is to gather information to help law enforcement agencies in identifying, locating, arresting, and convicting violent criminals. At the same time the NCAVC tries to create and implement new programs to prevent these types of crimes in the first place. Additionally, the NCAVC was and is an effort to help centralize information on violent crimes and criminals, because of increased movement of these types of criminals crossing state lines.

RECOMMENDED READING: Richard Ault, "NCAVC's Research and Development Program," *FBI Law Enforcement Bulletin*, Vol. 55, no. 12 (1986): 6–8; Roger L. Depue, "An American Response to an Era of Violence," *FBI Law Enforcement Bulletin* (Washington, DC: U.S. Government Printing Office, 1986); David J. Icove, "Automated Crime Profiling," *FBI Law Enforcement Bulletin*, Vol. 55, no. 12 (1986): 27–30.

James R. Farris

NATIONAL SHERIFFS' ASSOCIATION. The National Sheriffs' Association (NSA) has served the law enforcement/criminal justice professionals of the nation for fifty-six years. It is a nonprofit organization dedicated to raising the level of professionalism in the criminal justice field. Through the years NSA has been involved in numerous programs to enable sheriffs, their deputies, chiefs of police, and others in law enforcement to perform their jobs in the best possible manner and to better serve the people of their counties or jurisdictions.

NSA offers training, information, and recognition to sheriffs, deputies, and others throughout the nation and seeks to forge cooperative relationships with local, state, and federal law enforcement, as well as with citizens. NSA makes it possible for law enforcement professionals across the nation to network, sharing information about policies and programs.

NSA is the center of a vast network of information, filling requests for information and enabling law enforcement professionals locate the policies and programs they need. It seeks information from the membership, particularly the sheriffs and the state sheriffs' associations, in order to meet the members' needs and concerns. While working on the national level, NSA continues to seek grass-roots guidance in striving to work with and for its members.

Through the years NSA has assisted sheriffs' offices or departments and state sheriffs' associations in locating and preparing applications for state and federal grant funding. The NSA's record and reputation for integrity and dependability in the conduct of such programs among government agencies is well recognized and has led to continuing opportunities to apply for grants on the national, state, and local levels.

NSA publishes *Sheriff Magazine*, that covers subjects of broad general appeal to the diversified readership and provides up-to-date information on current issues and programs within the criminal justice community. *The Roll Call* is a newsletter that identifies and monitors proposed federal programs and activities, rule making, proposed federal legislation, and policies that relate to criminal justice.

A component of the NSA is the National Sheriffs' Institute (NSI). Established in 1972, the NSI provides management training for sheriffs and their command personnel, and is nationally recognized as a source of essential information for both sheriffs and chief deputies. NSI classes, usually held at the FBI Academy in Quantico, Virginia, provide sheriffs and their administrators with the opportunity to hear recognized experts in such diverse fields as jail administration, liability issues, crime prevention, budget preparation, and public relations. More than two thousand persons have graduated from NSI classes.

NSA also sponsors crime-prevention programs on a national level. These include Business Watch, Neighborhood Watch, Triad, and Operation Identification, taking the lead to support child fingerprinting and drug-abuse prevention. The National Neighborhood Watch Program disseminates community crime- prevention information to law enforcement agencies (police and sheriffs' offices equally) and citizens concerned about reducing home burglaries, vandalism, and other crimes in their homes and communities. Triad is a program to assist the nation's rapidly growing older population. NSA is working closely with the International Association of Chiefs of Police (IACP) and the American Association of Retired Persons (AARP) to create cooperative programs that reduce the criminal victimization of older persons, as well as their unwarranted fear of crime. Because three organizations are working together, the program has been dubbed the Triad. It is highly regarded.

A. N. Moser, Jr.

NATIONAL STOLEN PROPERTY ACT. As the regular movement of persons across state lines has constantly increased and has become an integral part of American life, federal involvement in the criminal justice system has increased. The assumption that acts committed in one state will have no effect on the citizens of another state is no longer true. Over time Congress has passed a number of laws with presumptive clauses that involve the crossing of state lines. All of this federal jurisdiction is based on the interstate-commerce clause of the U.S. Constitution. One of these laws is the National Stolen

Property Act of 1995, which authorizes the FBI to investigate thefts of over $5,000 in value under the presumption that the property is likely to have been taken across state lines. This situation may involve jurisdictional disputes because the offense is a violation of both state and federal laws. As a practical matter, the local district attorneys and U.S. attorneys make the decision as to which laws should apply and in which court, state or federal, the offender will face. It is rare that an offender is prosecuted in both courts even though double jeopardy is not involved.

Ransom A. Whittle

NATURAL LAW. Natural law may be defined as an inherent or transcendent code that includes both physical laws, (such as gravity) and universal moral standards. Natural law is frequently grounded in a metaphysical or theological belief that appeals to a "higher law" above that of civil governments or judicial systems. For instance, Thomas Jefferson's claim that all men are "endowed by their Creator with certain inalienable rights" is a claim of natural right (a corollary to natural law). In essence, Jefferson was claiming that rights were God given and thereby exist in nature (created by God) and are inherent in human nature, regardless of whether any government or civil or criminal legal system recognizes their existence. Jefferson was basing his claim in part upon the natural-law philosophy of John Locke, who argued that law and government rest upon a social contract that guarantees ordered liberty applied impartially to all citizens. Natural law and natural rights, it should also be noted, do not stop at any national boundary and place obligations to standards of right conduct upon all persons and governments alike.

Natural law can be traced back to Roman and Greek thought, especially the philosophy of Stoicism with its emphasis on the universal status of virtue and the good. Roman legal scholars, such as Gaius, developed the concept of "law of the peoples" *(ius gentium)*, which they associated with natural law *(ius naturale)*. The law of the peoples refers to the common legal and moral standards that appear in diverse societies, such as sanctions against killing other persons or the taking of what is not one's own. The law of the peoples was taken to be an observable indication of the reality of the natural law insofar as such standards were arrived at by different peoples independent of one another. The Roman jurists were concerned with these issues due to their need to develop a legal code for one of the world's first great multicultural political systems. Recently, the noted American criminologist James Q. Wilson has reemphasized the importance of the concept of a universal moral sense as a foundation for criminal justice.

RECOMMENDED READING: Gaius, *The Institutes*, translated by W. M. Gordon and O. F. Robinson (Ithaca, NY: Cornell University Press, 1988); Scott Douglas Gerber, *To Secure These Rights: The Declaration of Independence and Constitutional Interpretation* (New York: New York

University Press, 1995); John Locke, *Two Treatises of Government*, ed. Mark Goldie (London: Every-man, 1993); James Q. Wilson, *The Moral Sense* (New York: Free Press, 1993).

Daniel Skidmore-Hess

NEIGHBORHOOD WATCH PROGRAM. The neighborhood watch or block watch works toward making the community become more aware and knowledgeable of crime occurring in the neighborhood. The concept behind neighborhood watch is to reduce the fear of crime and reduce the opportunity for the commission of a criminal offense. The Neighborhood Watch Program has the purpose of creating a feeling of safety by allowing neighbors to participate willingly in the safety of one another. Neighborhood residents provide a constant surveillance for any unusual occurrence in their neighborhood. A strong neighborhood organization working in cooperation with a crime-prevention practitioner can do much to reduce crime in a neighborhood and provide a sense of security. The crime-prevention practitioner can teach neighborhood residents the techniques of crime prevention.

Another crime-prevention strategy that residents can become involved in is citizen patrols. Neighborhood residents provide surveillance of their community by actively engaging in patrolling. Citizen patrols only provide surveillance and notify the police when they observe a criminal offense. Patrol by neighborhood residents can be either foot patrol or mobile patrol. Almost any age group or sex could be involved in citizen patrols since they are to function as observers and not enforcers. It normally should be left up to the community as to the type and number of neighborhood patrols it wants to staff. Other types of patrol that have been implemented include using taxi drivers, truck drivers, and individuals with cellular telephones in their automobiles to notify the police when they observe something suspicious.

RECOMMENDED READING: Egon Bittner, "Community Relations," in *Police-Community Relations: Images, Roles, Realities*, ed. Alvin W. Cohn and Emilio C. Viano (Philadelphia: J. B. Lippincott, 1976), pp. 77–82; James Q. Wilson, *Varieties of Police Behavior: The Management of Law and Order in Eight Communities* (Cambridge, MA: Harvard University Press, 1968).

Michael Palmiotto

NEWGATE PRISON OF CONNECTICUT. America's first state prison is considered by many to have been also one of its most unusual. In 1773 the General Assembly of the colony of Connecticut authorized the conversion of an old copper mine to a prison for serious offenders. The copper mine at Simsbury, Connecticut, was named Newgate Prison (after the infamous Newgate Prison in London) and became the first facility in colonial America for long-term imprisonment. (See **Walnut Street Jail**.)

Explorers discovered a vein of copper in 1705. In 1707 mining operations were begun, and for nearly seventy years the mine was worked, but typically at greater cost than profit. By 1773, finding it harder to recruit laborers for the demanding work, the owners asked colonial officials about using the mine as a prison. A committee of the General Assembly visited the mine and agreed that it would be ideal for such purposes. In the act establishing Newgate, the assembly also identified the crimes that would result in imprisonment at the old mine. Sentence length, which ranged from less than ten years to a term of natural life, varied depending upon the offense and the criminal's prior record.

Newgate prisoners (of all ages and both sexes) worked at mining operations twelve hours a day, from 4:00 A.M. to 4:00 P.M. Some of that work was aboveground, but the sleeping quarters were in a cavern below. Using long ladders, the inmates descended a shaft 25 feet deep and 3.5 feet in diameter. At the bottom of the shaft was a cavern described as 21 feet long, 10 feet wide, and less than 7 feet high. Because space was at a premium, sleeping arrangements had the prisoners fitted dovetail onto straw-covered boards, with one inmate's feet resting on the straw pillow of his neighbor. But secure as these arrangements might sound, escapes (often through air shafts) were an all-too-frequent occurrence, the first being by the very first prisoner just eighteen days after his December 2, 1773, arrival.

As it became apparent that the mining operation would not be profitable, even with convict labor, inmates were instead put to work making nails, barrels, shoes, and wagons and doing other odd jobs. While at work, the prisoners were often chained to their workbench. Some more dangerous offenders were secured at the neck by a collar attached to an iron chain suspended from a beam in the ceiling.

During the American Revolution Newgate Prison held Tories, deserters, and prisoners of war, as well as the common felons. It is possible that some horrible conditions recounted at Newgate reflected the describer's politics more than the reality of general conditions, even so, there were few good things to say about Newgate. However, the prison was apparently relatively free from the insects and associated diseases found in aboveground jails, and the temperature in the caverns remained moderate even in the most severe seasons.

Newgate Prison finally closed in September 1827. Although it had not been in continuous operation as a prison over the preceding fifty-four years, Newgate had undergone several changes by the time of its closing. A fire in 1782 left it abandoned until 1790, when it was made the state prison. With its new status, Newgate got some new buildings aboveground, though prisoners were still confined below the ground. More additions were made in 1802 (a twelve-foot-high stone wall around the premises) and in 1824 (a four-story building that allowed the caverns to be used only for punishment rather than regular confinement). But within three years of the last major additions, cries for more humane policies, increasing operation costs, and word of the success of the new Auburn Prison brought an end to America's underground prison.

RECOMMENDED READING: H. E. Barnes and N. K. Teeters, *New Horizons in Criminology* (New York: Prentice-Hall, Inc., 1945); C. W. Dean, "The Story of New-Gate," *Federal Probation*, Vol. 43, no. 2 (1979): 8–14; A. M. Durham, III, "Social Control and Imprisonment during the American Revolution: Newgate of Connecticut," *Justice Quarterly*, 7, (1990): 293–323.

Philip Reichel

NOLO CONTENDERE. A plea of "no contest." A *nolo contendere* plea may be used when the defendant does not want to contest conviction, but also does not wish to admit guilt. Although such a defendant is typically found guilty of the criminal offense, no admission of guilt is recorded which could subsequently be used in a civil action brought by any party or parties injured in the criminal event which led to the conviction.

RECOMMENDED READING: Joseph R. Nolan and Jacqueline M. Nolan-Haley, *Black's Law Dictionary: Definitions of the Terms and Phrases of American and English Jurisprudence, Ancient and Modern*, 6th ed. (St. Paul, MN: West Publishing Co., 1991).

Shelia C. Armstrong

NULLIFICATION, JURY. Jury nullification is a controversial doctrine that argues that jurors have the right to refuse to find a defendant guilty because they believe in good conscience that s/he should be acquitted even if the evidence is strong that the defendant committed the crime alleged. It is a mechanism by which jurors can show opposition to a law or to its application in a particular case.

While the doctrine was quite widespread in the early nineteenth century, it is now more limited. At present, in only two states (Indiana and Maryland) are judges to apprise the jury of its right to disregard the law in favor of acquittal.

Opponents of the doctrine argue that in modern society it is the role of the judge to interpret the law; the jury's duty is to determine, on the basis of the facts presented, the guilt or innocence of the defendant, regardless of its views concerning the appropriateness of the law. To give more power to the jury, it is argued, would work against the equal application of the law and, indeed, lead to discrimination.

Proponents, on the other hand, take the position that nullification is a means by which the jury can inject the will of the community into the application of the law. It is a means by which the effects of the law can be mediated by the views of lay people.

Much of the argument between proponents and opponents of the doctrine is over the issue of whether judges should instruct jurors of their "rights" to nullify the law. In practice there is evidence that juries do at times engage in *de facto* nullification (i.e., nullification in fact) when they refuse to convict a defendant in spite of overwhelming evidence that s/he is guilty.

RECOMMENDED READING: Jeffrey Abramson, *We, the Jury* (New York: Basic Books, 1994); J. Patrick Hazel and Jack Ratliff, *The Jury Trial—From Voir Dire to Final Argument* (Austin: University of Texas at Austin School of Law Continuing Legal Education, 1994).

David Jones

O

O'CONNOR, SANDRA DAY (1930–   ). Sandra Day O'Connor was born on March 26, 1930, in El Paso, Texas. She received bachelor's and law degrees from Stanford University (graduating third in the law class where William Rehnquist was first). Despite her outstanding record, she found it difficult to locate a job as an attorney in 1952. After time off for raising a family with three sons, she resumed her legal career full-time in 1965. She served as an Arizona assistant attorney general for four years before being appointed to fill a vacancy in the Arizona Senate. She was elected and two years later was chosen Senate Republican majority leader, the first woman in the country to hold such a post.

In 1974 O'Connor was elected to the superior court. Five years later the Democratic governor, Bruce Babbitt, appointed her to the state court of appeals. In 1981 President Reagan selected her as his first nominee to the Supreme Court, the first woman ever to serve.

O'Connor is a mainstream pragmatist, opposed to judicial activism. She is for ordered liberty and the constitutional rights of the states. She believes that rights belong to individuals and not to the racial or gender groups of which they are members. She is a meticulous legal scholar.

RECOMMENDED READING: Judith Bentley, *Justice Sandra Day O'Connor* (Parsippany, NJ: Julian Messner, 1983); Suzanna Sherry, "Civic Virtue and the Feminine Voice in Constitutional Adjudication," *Virginia Law Review*, 1986: 543–616; Harold Woods and Geraldine Woods, *Equal Justice: A Biography of Sandra Day O'Connor* (Minneapolis, MN: Dillon Press, 1985).

Martin Gruberg

OPENING STATEMENT. The initial presentation by each side of the basic elements of its case to the jury. This is the next step in the trial process after the jury has been selected. In criminal cases the prosecutor presents his/her opening statement first. In many jurisdictions the defendant's attorney has the choice of presenting his/her opening statement immediately after the prosecutor presents his/hers or of waiting to do so until after the state has presented its case.

The opening statement of either side does not entail the presentation of evidence. Instead, counsel seeks to present an overview of its case to the jury. In an effective opening statement an attempt will be made to predispose the jurors to one's side. A good opening statement is generally fairly short and fairly succinct. Its purpose is to pique the interest of the jurors in the case. It is followed by the presentation of evidence.

RECOMMENDED READING: Jonathan D. Schiffman, *Fundamentals of the Criminal Justice Process*, 3rd ed. (Deerfield, IL: Clark Boardman Callaghan, 1994); Jon R. Waltz, *Introduction to Criminal Evidence*, 4th ed. (Chicago: Nelson Hall Publishers, 1997).

David Jones

OPIUM. Opium is the juice of the poppy flower. The juice is obtained by cutting the seed pod of the plant and scraping the residue from the pod. The resulting substance is gum-like and opaque. Both morphine and heroin are made from opium. The United States is involved in eradication programs with several countries trying to reduce the amount of opium produced in hopes of reducing the production of morphine, heroin, and other narcotics derived from opium. Currently, the use of heroin has begun to rise in the United States, with an increased percentage of the opium used to make it being grown in Mexico.

RECOMMENDED READING: Drug Enforcement Administration, *Drugs of Abuse* (Washington, DC: U.S. Department of Justice, 1990); National Narcotics Intelligence Consumer's Committee, *The NNICC Report: The Supply of Illicit Drugs to the United States* (Washington, DC: NNICC, 1995).

Glenn Zuern

P

PARDON. Article II, Section 2, of the Constitution provides that the president "shall have power to grant Reprieves and Pardons for Offenses against the United States, except in cases of impeachment." Although "pardon" is occasionally used interchangeably with "clemency," it is more accurately recognized as one of several forms of the clemency power. A pardon provides the most sweeping remission of consequences that normally attend the violation of the law. It "removes the penalties and disabilities, and restores [the offender] to all his civil rights; it makes him, as it were, a new man, and gives him new credit and capacity" (*Ex parte Garland*, 1866). Pardons may be granted before or after conviction, but are most commonly used to restore the reputation and civil rights of an individual (e.g., the rights to hold office, vote, and own property) who has completed a designated punishment and demonstrated rehabilitation by leading an exemplary life upon release. Pardons may also be "conditional," requiring an individual to perform (or refrain from) acts specified by the granting authority.
RECOMMENDED READING: Joseph R. Nolan and Jacqueline M. Nolan-Haley, *Black's Law Dictionary: Definitions of the Terms and Phrases of American and English Jurisprudence, Ancient and Modern*, 6th ed. (St. Paul, MN: West Publishing Co., 1991).

Peter S. Rukman, Jr.

PARENS PATRIAE. Literally, "parent of the country." This legal concept serves as the basis for state intervention when the state removes a delinquent from the home of his or her parents. Effectively, *parens patriae* is an assumption of responsibility by the state for the welfare of the delinquent child.
RECOMMENDED READING: Joseph R. Nolan and Jacqueline M. Nolan-Haley, *Black's Law Dictionary: Definitions of the Terms and Phrases of American and English Jurisprudence, Ancient and Modern*, 6th ed. (St. Paul, MN: West Publishing Co., 1991).

Gordon M. Armstrong

PAROLE. Parole is not a new concept, and its effectiveness has been debated for decades. The public tends to get probation and parole confused. Probation is a sentence prescribed by a judge in lieu of the probationer being sent directly to prison. Parole is supervision of a former inmate released from prison.

There are a number of reasons for having parole. The first is to send someone directly to prison for the crime(s) he or she has committed. The prison inmate would serve a part of his sentence, say one-third, then be paroled. For example, say a person was sentenced to five to ten years. Such sentences in a parole system are referred to as indeterminate sentences because the total length of incarceration is not determined prior to incarceration, but after the inmate has served a minimum statutory length of prison time. If s/he has been an inmate who has not caused trouble in prison, the parole board may grant his/her parole after a minimum of time. The inmate then becomes a parolee. If the inmate has been a lot of trouble in prison, then s/he will have to serve more than a minimum of time within the indeterminate period of his/her sentence. number of weekly contacts by the parole officer may increase from, say, one visit a week to three visits a week. Or the parole supervision may be reduced from three times a week to one time a week, two times a month, or one time a month.

In some states, like Illinois, the parole officers were to do home or work visits, but were still able to visit the parolee at his/her home. In Florida, on the other hand, parolees most often visit their parole officers at their office by appointment. The training for parole officers depends on what type of visitation a state requires of its parolees. In Illinois, California, and New York the parole officers are peace officers by state law. In Florida the parole officers' focus is more on the reintegration of the parolee into the public. The debate between a social work or law enforcement focus of parole still continues.

A parolee does not have to commit a new felony to be returned to prison. While under parole supervision, the parolee must not commit new crimes, either felony or misdemeanor. S/he also has to abide by the administrative regulations of parole in the state in which s/he is serving her/his parole. If s/he violates administrative regulations, if, for example, s/he absconds from parole without notifying her/his parole officer where s/he is going, a violation warrant may be requested from the state warrant officer after a specific period of time, say three to six weeks. This period of time gives the parole officer ample opportunity to attempt contact with the parolee.

When the parolee is returned to the county of her/his parole, s/he is given a Morrissey-Brewer administrative revocation hearing. The hearing judge may be another parole officer or a designee of the state's parole authority. The parolee may be released back to state parole supervision or returned to prison to serve the remainder of her/his sentence. If her/his parole is revoked, s/he is usually given credit for any jail time that s/he has served prior to the revocation.

Before being released from prison to parole, the inmate has to have her/his home and job verified. However, many states are happy to allow parolees to go to another state, and the out-of-state parolee has to abide by both the original and the visiting states' administrative rules and regulations. The Interstate Compact is the office that conducts the paperwork to sanction such a request. The Interstate Compact of the giving state contacts the Interstate Compact of the receiving state. When all paperwork is verified to the receiving state's satisfaction, then the parolee's move is officially permitted.

In some states parole is completed automatically after a specified time period. For example, a state's policy may be that all parolees are automatically off parole after two years (hypothetically) of parole supervision, with the parole officer's permission via official paperwork being submitted. Some parolees may have special parole board mandates from a particular agency to keep the parolee under extended parole supervision.

Parole is usually a state function, with parole officers having state jurisdiction. This is in contrast to many probation officers, who often have county jurisdiction. The trend is for states continuing with a parole system to have joint state probation and parole jurisdiction.

RECOMMENDED READING: Harry Allen, Chris Eskridge, Edward Latessa, and Gennaro Vito, *Probation and Parole in America* (New York: Free Press, 1985); Joan Petersilia, *Expanding Options for Criminal Sentencing* (Santa Monica, CA: The Rand Corporation, 1987).

John H. Lombardi

PAROLE BOARD. Parole boards function in states having indeterminate sentences (e.g., one to five years, two to ten years, one year to life) as compared to determinate sentences (e.g., eight years, ten years). The point at which an inmate is released to parole within the time frame of the indeterminate sentence depends on the rehabilitation of the inmate.

In this system the primary functions of a parole board are (1) to select out those prisoners to be placed on parole; (2) to set the conditions of parole; (3) to control the parolee in the community; (4) to discharge parolees upon completion of parole supervision; and (5) to revoke parole supervision. Only a few jurisdictions have statutory requirements for parole board members. Parole board members have a wide variety of experiences and skills such as police, business, or corrections, although few have had training in the law or related skills. In the recent decade there has been more emphasis on appointing parole board members who have career experience and graduate degrees in the social and behavioral sciences.

In considering parole eligibility, parole release is a privilege to be granted; it is not considered a right of every prison inmate. Second, an important factor in determining eligibility for parole is the state's statutes concerning "good time." Good time is earned by the inmate for good behavior, but may be forfeited by the inmate should s/he have poor behavioral performance in prison. Third, parole board hearings review an inmate's case. In its decision the board considers institutional reports from correctional officers, counselors, and others. The parole board also questions the inmate regarding his/her adjustment while in prison, his/her release plans, and the offense(s) that resulted in his/her incarceration. The inmate is also given the opportunity to make a statement in support of his/her parole request.

There are several models that exist for parole release. Some parole boards meet *en banc*. This means that the entire board meets in every case of parole release, although very few states operate in this manner. Other parole boards are divided into groups from the parole board and conduct simultaneous parole hearings in different parts of the state. The parole boards have wide discretion in the conduct of their hearings. Arguments have been made that parole release decisions are capricious. Most often, what parole boards share in common is the following of a vague policy that an inmate should only be paroled when his/her release is compatible with the welfare of the community.

In brief, parole boards make decisions based on (1) behavior that may or may not have happened prior to the parole release hearing or (2) the parole board's prediction of the inmate's potential criminal behavior in the future, after release from prison. The parole board may emphasize factors determining who should or should not be paroled. Some states have developed statistical prediction methods in an attempt to reduce arbitrary parole release decision making. Methods such as the Salient Factor Score Index/Objective Parole Guidelines may result in more consistency because of possible control of discretionary bias. But it is also highly possible that such attempts at offender fairness may handcuff prisoners to their criminal past when the statistical probability of release focuses on prior criminal history and the offense(s) committed that resulted in the inmate's current incarceration.

RECOMMENDED READING: George M. and Camille Graham Camp, *The Corrections Yearbook: Probation and Parole 1996* (South Salem, NY: Criminal Justice Institute, 1996)

John H. Lombardi

PAROLE OFFICER. The purpose parole is to allow supervision by a parole officer of a released prisoner for a length of time, for example, two or three years, sometimes much longer. During this time the parole officer assists the parolee in seeking employment or going through aptitude testing, vocational-school training, or even the pursuit of a general education diploma (G.E.D.) or college education. Depending on how the parolee is adjusting, the supervision may be reduced or increased. In other words, the number of weekly contacts by the parole officer may increase from, say, one visit a week to three visits a week. Or the parole supervision may be reduced from three times a week to one time a week, two times a month, or one time a month.

In some states, like Illinois, parole officers make home or work visits. In Florida, on the other hand, parolees most often visit their parole officers at their office by appointment. In some states parole officers carry weapons and have peace officer responsibilities, such as the arrest of parolees who violate parole supervision. While some parole officers may work in conjunction with sworn police officers to gather intelligence and information, they are usually considered unsworn peace officers, depending on the individual state's criminal code and statutes.

There is a difference between state and federal parole in that the federal parole officer reports directly to a federal judge. His/her jurisdiction, geographically, is usually larger than that of nonfederal parole officers. S/he often has to travel farther than other parole officers. Because of this, it is permissible for the federal parole officer to have long-distant parolees on his/her caseload mail in monthly postcards or letters and have only several visits a year by the parole officer to these parolees.

The qualifications for a parole officer usually include a four-year college degree. Good communication skills are required, as is a sense of fairness. Students are usually wise to take some criminal justice courses, as well as business management. Wanting to help people is a prerequisite, and the balance between wanting to help the parolee and wanting to help the public is a common and constant matter of debate.

RECOMMENDED READING: George M. and Camille Graham Camp, *The Corrections Yearbook: Probation and Parole 1996* (South Salem, NY: Criminal Justice Institute, 1996); Rolando V. del Carmen, *Potential Liabilities of Probation and Parole Officers* (Cincinnati, OH: Anderson, 1986)

John H. Lombardi

PCP. PCP (Phencyclidine, also called angel dust, killer weed, hog, lovely, and love boat) is a hallucinogen that can be taken orally, smoked, or injected.

RECOMMENDED READING: Drug Enforcement Administration, *Drugs of Abuse* (Washington, D.C.: U.S. Department of Justice, 1990); National Narcotics Intelligence Consumer's Committee, *The NNICC Report: The Supply of Illicit Drugs to the United States* (Washington, D.C.: NNICC, 1995).

Glenn Zuern

PENITENTIARY, HISTORY OF THE. The penitentiary is one of America's major contributions to criminal justice practices. The penitentiary is a correctional institution that houses offenders in cells rather than in congregate areas. The first penitentiary in America was opened in 1772 as an addition to Philadelphia's Walnut Street Jail.

The penitentiary is more than just a space to house convicted offenders, it is a concept. To understand the former, it is important to understand the latter. Although John Howard first used the word *penitentiary* in his report on prisons in 1777, the spirit of the penitentiary came from William Penn and the Quakers in both England and Pennsylvania. The Quakers reacted to the cruelties of corporal punishment and believed that long-term confinement would be a more humane alternative. In addition, they believed that confinement in an individual living space (i.e, a cell) would avoid the moral contamination encouraged by congregate prisons and would allow for reflection and penance.

Most indicative of the spirit of the penitentiary was the requirement of silence. The prevailing causal explanation of crime at the time was that criminals were morally depraved sinners. They were to use their period in confinement for solitary reflection, contemplation, and Bible reading in order to become reformed. Another idea, by no means novel, was that inmates were supposed to work while imprisoned. On the whole, the penitentiary had a certain monastic flavor that stressed penitence and meditation amid an all-pervasive silence.

Institutions that used cellular confinement existed in parts of Europe prior to 1772; however, cellular design and the Quaker ideas of confinement were first fully tested in America. Although the Walnut Street Jail was the first built, Eastern State Penitentiary in Pennsylvania exemplified the penitentiary in America. Eastern State Penitentiary was opened in Philadelphia in 1829. It was dedicated to the principles of solitary confinement and silence and was reported to be the largest and most expensive structure in America.

Eastern State was characterized by high, oppressive outside walls and a forbidding interior. Inmates were placed in large (8 by 10 by 12 feet) individual cells where they remained throughout their confinement. Cells were arranged in a series of blocks that radiated from a central point like spokes on a wheel. Inmates worked in their cells and were not allowed to communicate with one another. Exercise was permitted in a walled area outside of each cell. Also, inmates did not leave their cells, each of which had a toilet and a heating system. Such indoor plumbing and heating was architecturally innovative but very expensive. And, although it was located in a prison cell, it was viewed as somewhat of a luxury, which caused some consternation in the general public.

Because of its exercise areas and emphasis on strict solitary confinement, all but one of Eastern State's cellblocks were single story. Correctional administrators from all over the world visited Eastern State and hailed it as a true advance in corrections. However, Charles Dickens, the famous author, argued that the hopeless solitary confinement that this institution mandated was far more cruel than any corporal punishment.

RECOMMENDED READING: D. Fogel, *We Are the Living Proof*, 2nd ed. (Cincinnati, OH: Anderson, (1979); U.S. Bureau of Prisons, *Correctional Institution Design and Construction* (Washington, DC: U.S. Bureau of Prisons, 1949).

Arthur J. Lurigio

PENTOVILLE PENITENTIARY. In the early nineteenth century Eastern State Penitentiary in Pennsylvania implemented a correctional regime, known as the "separate system," that stressed solitary confinement and silence. This system was adopted in many parts of Europe, especially in England. The first separate-system penitentiary in England was built at Pentoville in 1842. As in Eastern State, the cells in Pentoville were large (13.5 by 7.5 by 9 feet) and contained a toilet, a copper wash basin, a three-legged stool, a table, and a hammock for sleeping. Pentoville Penitentiary was a multistory structure, but it did provide for exercising large groups of prisoners. To maintain solitude and silence in such groups, Pentoville required inmates to wear masks to prevent even the sight of other prisoners.

One result of solitary confinement at Eastern State was high rates of suicide and mental illness, which were also found at Pentoville. It has been reported that the insanity rate at Pentoville was 6.0 per 1,000 convicts, while it was 0.6 per 1,000 in prisons in the rest of England and Wales. Despite this finding, fifty-four Pentoville-like prisons were constructed in England from 1842 to 1848.

RECOMMENDED READING: H. Mayhew and J. Binny, *The Criminal Prisons of London and Scenes of Prison Life* (London: Frank Cass and Company, 1968); M. Wolff, *Prison: The Penal Institutions of Britain* (London: Eyre and Spottiswoode, 1967).

Arthur J. Lurigio

PEYOTE. Peyote is a cactus that produces a small crown that is dried and then eaten by individuals to produce visions. Peyote is used by Native Americans in some of their religious ceremonies. The active ingredient is mescaline. Peyote has been the focus of several court cases involving religious freedom. The U.S. Supreme Court has ruled that states may prohibit the use of peyote in religious rites. In response, a number of states have passed laws banning its use in religious ceremonies.

RECOMMENDED READING: Drug Enforcement Administration, *Drugs of Abuse* (Washington, D.C.: U.S. Department of Justice, 1990); National Narcotics Intelligence Consumer's Committee, *The NNICC Report: The Supply of Illicit Drugs to the United States* (Washington, D.C.: NNICC, 1995).

Glenn Zuern

PLEA BARGAIN. The process whereby a criminal defendant agrees to plead "guilty" with the expectation (either implicit or explicit) of receiving some favorable consideration from the state. The state's consideration, or "bargain," may relate to a reduction in the seriousness of the charge(s), a reduction in the number of charges pending, a reduction in recommended sentence, or combinations of these considerations. While the plea-bargaining process typically involves informal contacts between the defense attorney (in the absence of the defendant) and the prosecution, some judges take a very active role in the process, formalizing negotiations in pretrial conference.

As plea bargaining typically accounts for the disposition of 80 to 90 percent of criminal cases that are not dismissed, the decision-making process is of particular importance. It is generally assumed that the strength of the case, the seriousness of the crime, and the criminal record of the defendant (if any) provide important parameters for the bargaining process. The defense is likely to emphasize a client's redeeming characteristics and/or any circumstances that might reasonably mitigate his/her culpability. The members of a courtroom workgroup are likely to be attracted to the informal nature of plea bargaining, its cost-effectiveness, and the potential speed with which a bargain may be obtained. Judges want cases processed. Prosecutors want convictions.

While the U.S. Supreme Court has recognized plea bargaining as a fact and necessity of judicial life (*Santobello v. New York*, 1971), the practice remains the focus of considerable criticism. Opponents of plea bargaining generally emphasize (1) any evidence suggesting that plea bargaining is not necessary for the efficient processing of cases; (2) any evidence suggesting that the "quality" of individuals typically employed in the public defender office places the defendant at a disadvantage in the bargaining process; (3) the "cheapening" of justice and the adversary process that results from the typically private, secretive manner in which pleas are obtained; (4) the pressure that courtroom workgroups place upon truly innocent defendants to plead guilty; (5) the possibility that many defendants unwittingly discard critical constitutional protections by pleading "guilty," and (6) the belief that plea bargaining results in sentences that are disturbingly lenient.

Proponents of plea bargaining, such as they are, typically stress (1) any evidence indicating that plea bargaining contributes to the timely, efficient processing of cases; (2) the avoidance of the stress and possible humiliation of a public trial that plea bargains provide for victims of crime; (3) the necessity of some function to reward cooperative defendants; (4) the ability of the plea-bargaining process to individualize justice or "tailor" the criminal process to the specific circumstances of the crime and characteristics of the defendant; and (5) the fact that plea bargains do result in the conviction of individuals who might otherwise escape punishment via the technicalities of a trial.

The Supreme Court has also issued significant rulings with respect to the operation of the plea bargain. Defendants must provide judges with affirmative statements that pleas are made voluntarily (*Boykin v. Alabama*, 1969), and judges may accept such statements even if the defendant maintains innocence (*North Carolina v. Alford*, 1970). The terms of the bargain must also be respected by prosecutors (*Santobello v. New York*, 1971) and defendants (*Ricketts v. Adamson*, 1987).

RECOMMENDED READING: Barbara Boland, Wayne Logan, Ronald Sones, and William Martin, *The Prosecution of Felony Arrests* (Washington, DC: U.S. Government Printing Office, 1982); W. G. Bryant, *Disclosing Hidden Assets: Plea Bargaining and Use of the Polygraph* (Washington, DC: Bureau of Justice Assistance, 1992); H. L. Fink, *Rights of Passage: An Empirical Study of Judges' and Defendants' Ability to Communicate with Each Other During Guilty Plea Proceedings*, M. J. S. thesis (University of Nevada, Reno, 1994).

Peter S. Ruckman, Jr.

PLEAS. Pleas are the defendant's response to the state's charges in criminal proceedings. There are a number of pleas available to the defendant. One of these is the guilty plea. Often guilty pleas are the result of plea negotiations, in which the defendant agrees to plead guilty in exchange for some consideration from the state.

In many jurisdictions a plea available to the defendant is that of *nolo contendere*, or "no contest." In this plea the defendant does not admit guilt but chooses not to contest the charges. In criminal procedure the effect of a no-contest plea is the same as that of the guilty plea. However, a *nolo* plea cannot be used in civil proceedings as proof that the defendant committed a crime. This plea is most often a result of plea bargaining.

The defendant may also plead not guilty. By doing this, s/he challenges the state to prove guilt at trial. Another plea is that of "not guilty by reason of mental disease or defect," the insanity plea. If this plea is used by itself, the defendant admits that except for mental capacity s/he committed all of the essential elements of the crime charged. In that case, the trier of fact must determine whether or not the defendant was legally insane at the time the offense was committed, however legal insanity is defined in the jurisdiction in question. Because of this, defendants may "join" the plea of not guilty by reason of mental disease or defect with a plea of not guilty. If this is done, issues of both commitment of the offense and of mental state must be determined.

It is also possible that the defendant will stand mute or refuse to plead. If that happens, the judge will direct that a plea of not guilty be offered on the defendant's behalf. It is important to realize that because most defendants plead guilty or no contest, relatively few cases do go to trial.

RECOMMENDED READING: J. D. Schiffman, *Fundamentals of the Criminal Justice Process*, 3rd ed. (Deerfield, IL: Clark Boardman Callaghan, 1994).

David Jones

POLICE. The terms *police* or *law enforcement* are used to designate government officials who enforce the criminal laws of the states and the federal government. They have the specific responsibilities of preventing or deterring crime, the detection and investigation of criminal activities, and the recovery of stolen property and the apprehension and convictions of those individuals involved in a crime.

RECOMMENDED READING: National Advisory Commission on Criminal Justice Standards and Goals, *Report on the Police* (Washington, D.C.: U.S. Government Printing Office, 1973); Joseph R. Nolan and Jacqueline M. Nolan-Haley, *Black's Law Dictionary: Definitions of the Terms and Phrases of American and English Jurisprudence, Ancient and Modern*, 6th ed. (St. Paul, MN: West Publishing Co., 1991); President's Commission on Law Enforcement and Administration of Justice, *The Challenge of Crime in a Free Society* (Washington, D.C.: U.S. Government Printing Office, 1967).

Michael Palmiotto

POLICE ADMINISTRATION. Police administration requires that police supervisors perform specific duties and activities. The police administrator must perform administrative activities that support the police mission of preventing and controlling crime and apprehending offenders within U.S. constitutional restrictions. Police administration includes the traditional administrative activities required of all organizations. Generally, the administrative activities developed by Luther Gulick in 1937 are still appropriate for police administrators. The actions include planning, organization, staffing, directing, coordinating, reporting, and budgeting.

RECOMMENDED READING: *What Works in Policing?*, ed. David H. Bayley (New York: Oxford University Press, 1997); *Papers on the Science of Administration*, Luther Gulick and L. Urwick (New York: Garland, 1987 [originally published 1937]); Edward A. Thibault, Lawrence M. Lynch, and R. Bruce McBride, *Protective Police Management*, 4th ed. (Upper Saddle River, NJ: Prentice Hall, 1997).

Michael Palmiotto

POLICE-COMMUNITY RELATIONS. Unlike public relations, which is a one-way process, police-community relations is a two-way process. In public relations the organization only passes out information. Generally, this information will only be positive. Since the information only goes one way, the public relations officer constantly tells the public about the successes and accomplishments of the police department. Rarely does the public relations officer deal with the failures of the organization. In police-community relations, a two-way process, the police are getting feedback from citizens. This feedback can be negative and often deals with what the public considers to be wrong with the police department. Police-community relations when functioning effectively can assist the police in developing and maintaining rapport with the public they deal with. The police communicate with the people, and the citizens communicate with the police.

RECOMMENDED READING: Community Policing Consortium, *What Is Community Policing?* (Washington, DC: The Consortium, 1995); Louis A. Radelet, *The Police and the Community* (Encino, CA: Glencoe, 1980).

Michael Palmiotto

POLICE CORRUPTION. Police corruption exists when any police officer or employee, regardless of his/her rank, title, or position, obtains a material reward or monetary gain for service s/he is legally and organizationally required to provide, if s/he fails to perform a duty legally required, or if s/he provides information that s/he is prohibited to provide.

RECOMMENDED READING: Sarah Glazer, *Police Corruption: Can Brutality and Other Misconduct be Rooted Out?* (Washington, DC: Congressional Quarterly, Inc., 1995); Mike McAlary, *Buddy Boys: When Good Cops Turn Bad* (New York: G. P. Putnam's Sons, 1987); Joseph R. Nolan and Jacqueline M. Nolan-Haley, *Black's Law Dictionary*, 6th ed. (St. Paul: West Publishing Co., 1991); *Police Integrity: Public Service With Honor* (Washington, DC: National Institute of Justice, 1997).

Michael Palmiotto

POLICE LOCKUP. A police lockup is a secure facility located in a police building that is used for the custody and processing of persons who are being held for investigation pending the disposition of their cases by the judiciary or are awaiting transfer to another institution.

Persons are taken into custody for a wide variety of violations ranging from insignificant municipal ordinances to the most serious of criminal offenses. Regardless of the reason, whenever a person is placed in police custody, the authorities are responsible for the care, control, and security of such persons. Additionally, the police must be certain that the arrestee has not been deprived of his/her constitutional rights.

Specifically, these rights include, but are not limited to (1) the right to remain silent; (2) the right to be treated humanely and to be provided with proper food, shelter, and, if necessary, medical care; (3) the right and opportunity to communicate with his/her family; (4) the right and opportunity to confer with the attorney of his/her choice. Separate detention facilities must be maintained for male and female arrestees, and no minor under sixteen years of age may be confined to a cell.

An essential precaution of police custody incidents is that the period of police restraint must be of a short or temporary duration. Persons must be either released from custody or formally charged within a reasonable period. According to the Illinois Municipal Jail and Lockup Standards, the maximum period of detention should not normally exceed forty-eight hours.

During the period of police detention the arrestee will be subjected to a routine called booking. This procedure ensures an accurate identification of the arrestee and proper preparation of the necessary police forms and preliminary court documents. During the booking the prisoner is searched, his/her property is confiscated and inventoried, and s/he is be fingerprinted and photographed.

Once the booking has been completed, the arrestee is eligible for bond in nonfelonious charges. If s/he is unable to post bond or if the charge is a felony, s/he will be transported by police vehicle to the county jail to await a judicial bond hearing.

Rigid state standards and the complications and cost of maintaining a police lockup, as well as its limited use, have caused numerous small departments to delegate their lockup responsibilities to the local county jail.

RECOMMENDED READING: Joseph R. Nolan and Jacqueline M. Nolan-Haley, *Black's Law Dictionary: Definitions of the Terms and Phrases of American and English Jurisprudence, Ancient and Modern*, 6th ed. (St. Paul, MN: West Publishing Co., 1991).

Thomas M. Frost

POSSE COMITATUS. The roots of *posse comitatus* stem from the sheriff system in pre–eighth-century England. During the fifth and sixth centuries the Angles and the Saxons conquered British territory and brought with them seminal governmental organization. From this era sprang the notion of "king's peace," that is, an agreement between the king and his subjects that he would protect them, maintain the peace, and afford security to the nation in exchange for citizen cooperation and support of the king. The basic concept at that time, as populations grew and order was becoming problematic, was to involve all the people in an area in their own defense and protection.

By 890 King Alfred of England had established the office of "sciremen," or king's reeves, who may have performed several different specialized functions, such as tax collection or court supervision, that had formerly been done by aldermen. The *Books of Dooms*, prepared as census documents under Alfred's direction, prescribed relatively extensive responsibilities for these reeves in the areas of tax collection, law enforcement, and other services to the king. The same *Books of Dooms* gave the king's reeves the power of *posse comitatus*, enabling them to summon citizen assistance. These reeves were not necessarily the eventual shire reeves or sheriffs, but these functions are clearly precursors of the office of sheriff, which had many similar functions. The pattern of local law enforcement, even though it was by a king's man, has already been well established.

As the idea of *posse comitatus* for sheriffs emerged in England, similar ideas for citizen self-protection flowered elsewhere in Europe. The notions include the office of alguacil in Spain (which appeared in Mexico and the early American Southwest) and the French system of "frank-pledge" in which all citizens had a duty to keep the peace, much as in the modern sheriff system. Posses became ingrained in the American consciousness by virtue of the constant reference to such groups formed by sheriffs in the literature and drama of the Wild West. At present a group of individuals who seek to protest the U.S. tax structure have appropriated the name Posse Comitatus.

David R. Struckhoff

PRECEDENT. The use of a case, or set of cases, of a nature similar to that of the current case in reaching a decision on the present case. Under the doctrine of *stare decisis*, an important concept in Anglo-American law, precedent is generally supposed to guide the decision of a court in its present case. In theory, reasoning by precedent is a three-step process. First, similarity is seen between cases; second, the rule of law determined in the first case is announced; third, it is then applied to the next case. The process is designed to provide predictability and stability in the law. (See *Stare Decisis*.)

While precedents are generally binding, this does not mean that judges cannot play a creative role is interpreting the law. One of the issues in deciding which precedents to apply—to what cases is the current case similar? That is not always clear. Precedent may also be limited. For instance, at one point the U.S. Supreme Court forbade "taxpayers' suits" in an early case. However, the precedent-setting impact of that case was limited in subsequent decisions by excluding from it cases questioning the constitutionality of federal spending on establishment-of-religion grounds.

Moreover, precedent can be overruled. A court (often the U.S. Supreme Court) may announce that a previous decision was in error, and thus its impact as a precedent is no longer valid. This does not happen very often, but it does happen. Under norms of judicial decision making in the United States it is more likely to take place with respect to constitutional interpretation than in cases involving the "construction" (interpretation) of a statute.

RECOMMENDED READING: Edward H. Levi, *An Introduction to Legal Reasoning* (Chicago: University of Chicago Press, 1949); David W. Rohde and Harold J. Spaeth, *Supreme Court Decision Making* (San Francisco: W. H. Freeman and Company, 1976).

David Jones

PRELIMINARY INVESTIGATION. When police become aware of the commission of a criminal offense, a preliminary investigation is conducted in order to discover evidence needed to legally prove (1) the elements of the criminal offense and (2) who committed the offense. The investigation usually entails observations by the police, the questioning of the victim, witnesses, and suspects, visits to the crime scene, and searches for and seizures of evidence.

The law requires enough evidence to establish reasonable cause to believe that it is more likely than not that the criminal offense was committed and that the suspect did it. This is referred to as probable cause. The investigative process is prescribed by criminal procedure law. Failure to abide by the rules set forth in the law governing the investigative stage might result in a violation of a suspect's legal rights and could lead to prosecutorial difficulties.

RECOMMENDED READING: *Police Ethics: Hard Choices in Law Enforcement*, ed. William Heffernan and Timothy Stroup (New York: J. Jay Press, 1985); Irving J. Klein, *Constitutional Law for Criminal Justice Professionals*, 3rd ed. (South Miami, FL: Coral Gables Publishing Co., 1992).

Christopher J. Morse

PRESENTENCE REPORT. The presentence report has multiple functions and purposes in the criminal justice system. It provides background information with respect to a convicted offender and the offense prior to sentencing on a criminal matter so that judges have sufficient information to sentence the individual pursuant to statutory objectives. In the event the offender is sentenced to a period of probation, the report provides the supervising probation officer with historical information about the offender that will facilitate fashioning of a supervision plan ensuring the offender's compliance with the court order, community risk-control management, and appropriate correctional treatment. The presentence report assists correctional facilities in the designation, classification, programming, and release planning of inmates; provides information pertinent to parole consideration; and provides a source of information for research.

Jurisdictions vary in their requirements and use of presentence reports. In the federal judicial system Rule 32(c)(1) of the Federal Rules of Criminal Procedure and Title 18, United States Code, Section 3552, provide that the probation officer conduct an investigation, which report is to be submitted to the court at least ten days prior to the imposition of sentence. The court may waive the requirement for a presentence report if it finds that there is sufficient information in the record regarding the offense and the offender to take into consideration statutorily required sentencing objectives.

Rule 32(c)(2) of the Federal Rules of Criminal Procedure provides that the presentence report shall contain (1) information about the history and characteristics of the defendant, including prior criminal record, if any, financial condition, and any circumstances affecting the defendant's behavior that may be helpful in imposing sentencing or in the subsequent correctional treatment of the defendant; (2) classification of the offense and of the defendant under the categories established by the Sentencing Commission pursuant to Section 994(a) of Title 28 of the United States Code that the probation officer believes to be applicable to the defendant's case; the kinds of sentence and the sentencing range suggested for such a category of offense committed by such category of defendant as set forth in the guidelines issued by the Sentencing Commission pursuant to 28 U.S.C. Section 994(a)(1), and an explanation by the probation officer of any factors that may indicate that a sentence of a different kind or of a different length from one within the applicable guideline would be more appropriate under the circumstances; (3) any pertinent policy statement issued by the Sentencing Commission pursuant to 28 U.S.C. Section 994(a)(2); (4) verified information stated in a nonargumentative style containing an assessment of the financial, social, psychological, and medical impact upon, and cost to, any individual against whom the offense has been committed; (5) unless the court orders otherwise, information concerning the nature and extent of nonprison programs and resources available to the defendant; and (6) such other information as may be directed by the court.

The probation officer is ideally an impartial examiner of the information that has been verified in the presentence report, which includes interviews with the defendant, with attorney present if desired, and the defendant's family to corroborate social history background. Other information from the government and investigative law enforcement agencies is included. Third-party data such as employment, educational, psychological, medical, and financial information are added (within the provisions of federal and state privacy requirements). After the information is verified, corroborated, and carefully analyzed, conclusions and recommendations are made to the sentencing judge.

Jurisdictions vary regarding the composition and disclosure of a probation officer's recommendation. The probation officer's report expresses to the court his or her professional judgment based on reliable information.

The presentence report is generally not a matter of public record. In the federal judicial system it is disclosed only to the defendant, defense counsel, the U.S. attorney, and the Bureau of Prisons (unless by further order of the sentencing court). When protection of the community is an issue, the probation officer (as required by law or judicial directive) discloses certain information to those parties to whom the offender poses risk. Otherwise, disclosure is limited to reduce collateral disadvantage to the offender.

RECOMMENDED READING: Vincent O'Leary and D. Clear, *Directions for Community Corrections in the 1990s* (Boulder, CO: National Institute of Corrections, 1984); Frank Schmalleger, *Criminal Justice Today: An Introductory Text for the Twenty-First Century* 4th ed. (Upper Saddle River, NJ: Prentice Hall, 1997).

Gregory A. Prestipino

PRESIDENT'S COMMISSION ON LAW ENFORCEMENT AND ADMINISTRATION OF JUSTICE. In 1965 President Lyndon B. Johnson established a new advisory group, the President's Commission on Law Enforcement and Administration of Justice, and pledged the resources of the federal government to "banish crime from the United States of America." According to Skogan and Klecka (1977), during the next ten years the expenditures by all levels of government on the criminal justice system (police, courts, and jails) rose over 200 percent. In the same decade the FBI's crime index rose 160 percent for property crimes and 190 percent for violent crimes. The commission put out a number of reports concerning the status of law enforcement, prosecution, the courts, and correctional policies. The commission addressed numerous questions, including what social conditions tend to be experienced by those who commit street crime and those who are victimized by it. It also addressed the problems of white-collar crime and organized crime. These various reports and recommendations were published in 1967 under the title *The Challenge of Crime in a Free Society*.

RECOMMENDED READING: D. Stanley Eitzen and Doug A. Timmer,

Criminology (New York: MacMillan, 1985); President's Commission on Law Enforcement and Administration of Justice, *The Challenge of Crime in a Free Society* (Washington, DC: U.S. Government Printing Office, 1967); Wesley G. Skogan and William R. Klecka, *The Fear of Crime* (Washington, DC: American Political Science Association, 1977).

Ransom A. Whittle

PRETRIAL RELEASE. Historically, many criminal defendants who posed little or no risk to public safety and were unlikely to abscond were unnecessarily held jail while awaiting trial because they could not afford bond for bail, the most common condition of pretrial release. Besides inequitably confining less affluent defendants, major reliance upon monetary bail as a condition of pretrial release has contributed to overcrowding in jails and burdened local government finances. Pretrial services programs and agencies emerged in the mid-1960s as part of the bail-reform movement led by the federal government. They have since become recognized as critical to the ability of local governments and the courts to manage the size of local jail populations in a manner consistent with public safety needs and the limited funds available for jail construction and operation. These programs typically perform pretrial release investigations and inform the court concerning the risks associated with granting pretrial release to newly arrested individuals. Additional functions often include advising the court concerning the conditions of release necessary to assure public safety and future court appearances and may also include supervising released defendants, monitoring compliance with conditions of release, and informing them of upcoming court dates. Some programs may require periodic urine samples from the client, especially if drug charges are involved. Pretrial release programs are most commonly administered by either the circuit court, the sheriff, or jointly by both agencies. (See **Release on Recognizance**.)

RECOMMENDED READING: J. Goldcamp, "Judicial Responsibility for Pretrial Release Decisionmaking and the Information Role of Pretrial Services," *Federal Probation* 57 (1993): 28-35; B. Reaves, *Pretrial Release of Felony Defendants* (Washington, DC: U.S. Government Printing Office, 1992).

Joseph B. Byers

PRIVATE CORRECTIONS (HISTORY AND PHILOSOPHY). The concept of privatization is not historically new. Many an emperor in ancient history bestowed the responsibility of managing state agencies and resources upon some worthy follower. Whether the fortunate individual was successful in administering to the task better than the emperor or his staff will never be known. There is no indication that such individuals were also fortunate enough to have consultants ready to perform operational reviews and evaluations. The determining factor was whether the job was accomplished. To a great extent many current decisions are made on whether the job is simply accomplished, with an emphasis on simply. The final decision to go private is dependent on a multiplicity of determining factors, including administrative philosophy, goals and objectives, financial availability, public opinion, and political environment.

Administrative Philosophy. Correctional facilities and programs fall within a multitude of agencies and governmental levels. To a large extent there is a monitoring of facilities and programs by state oversight committees and private associations such as the American Correctional Association (ACA), but a good part of everyday operational direction comes from the facility administrator. How things are done on a daily basis is his/her decision, and there remains a great deal of discretion in the execution of standards. Who exerts this immediate authority and his/her particular philosophy are always important considerations.

Goals and Objectives. The newest technique to determine organizational continuum is through reengineering. Essentially, this is a reestablishment of goals and objectives resulting in the restructuring of the organization and its supporting infrastructures. Somewhere along the process someone or an advisory body must determine what it is that the correctional facility is supposed to do. If it is a jail, than what is the main responsibility and how will that responsibility be met? There is little use in determining that the jail will engage in behavioral modification if the majority of inmates stay in the system only thirty days. This would be an unrealistic goal. Once the goals are determined, the objectives become clearer and can be evaluated financially and operationally. The point here is that unless this process is approached in the formal manner, there will be no basis of evaluating financial alternatives.

Financial Availability. Administration by any type of body over a prolonged period of time leads to bureaucratic overspending. This is true of both private and public organizations. No organization is so fortunate as to never bow to fiscal restraints. The costs of meeting the goals and objectives are sometimes ameliorated by purchasing like services at lower rates through the competitive process. However, there must be some stability and continuity in order to meet objectives. This requires another balancing act.

Public Opinion. The public mandate can be a very strong one. In corrections the opinion of the public has ranged from total rehabilitation in the 1960s to "put them away" in the 1980s and 1990s. These swings in public sentiments are usually met at a premium cost. Future projections on attitudes and mores may have a major impact on contracting services.

Political Environment. Of course, much of the political attitude is dependent on public opinion, but the election of a public executive brings with it another level of philosophy and sentiment. The longevity of service contracts for capital facilities such as jails and prisons must by necessity extend beyond a political term in office. The way the facilities are utilized is more readily subject to revision and impacts the criteria used in the original evaluation of privatization.

There is no pat answer to the question of using privatization as an alternative in corrections. Any decision is dependent on the goals and objectives set in the analysis phase. Evaluation of the decision's alternatives could be an extremely complicated process, and the only way to resolve the question would be to reduce it to its simplest form: Where are you going and what will you spend to get there? This must be asked of each alternative, and then you make your decision.

RECOMMENDED READING: William C. Cunningham, John J. Strauchs, and Clifford W. Van Meter, *The Hallcrest Report II: Private Security Trends 1970–2000* (McLean, VA: Hallcrest Systems, 1990); National Institute of Justice, *Crime and Protection in America: A Study of Private Security and Law Enforcement Resources and Relationships*, Executive Summary (Washington, DC: U.S. Department of Justice, 1985).

Patrick J. Halperin

PROBATION. Probation is an alternative sentence of conditional release that is given by both federal and state courts. Although a probation sentence does not involve confinement, it imposes conditions on the probationer and allows modification of those conditions in the event of a violation by the probationer.

The creation of this sentence is credited to John Augustus, a Boston bootmaker, who believed that incarceration was not always conducive to rehabilitation. Augustus would instead post bail for nonserious offenders and provide them with friendship, support, and job-placement assistance. At the defendant's hearing Augustus would report the progress and activities of the person to the judge and ask that he or she only pay a small fine and court costs in lieu of a prison sentence.

Augustus and his methods influenced the first probation statute in Massachusetts in 1878. By the time the statute was passed, Augustus had bailed out almost two thousand defendants, effectively making him the first probation officer. By the year 1900, four other states had enacted similar legislation, thus making probation an established alternative to incarceration in the United States.

Today the term *probation* can refer to a status, a system, and a process. As a status, probation reflects the unique character of the probationer: he or she is neither a free citizen nor an inmate of a correctional center. As a system, probation is embodied in the agency in charge of it, which is also contained within the criminal justice system. As a process, probation refers to the set of functions, activities, and conditions of the sentence, which offenders must follow.

There are several forms of probation that are used today in the U.S. criminal justice system. Under the most frequently used form, the traditional form of probation, the offender is required to report regularly to a probation officer assigned to his or her caseload. The frequency of the visits is determined by a risk/needs assessment, which tells the amount of risk the offender is to the community and the needs of the probationer. The offender who is given standard probation is also required to follow any court-imposed conditions given.

When an offender is given the sentence of intense probation, he or she is supervised much more closely. This form of probation is being used more frequently now, due to the increase in prison populations and the growing number of convicted felons given this sentence. Many times, these probationers are rearrested and subsequently reconvicted of more serious crimes.

Antoinette M. Jackson

PROBLEM-ORIENTED POLICING. Problem-oriented policing is a concept developed by Herman Goldstein in 1979. Goldstein, along with other police scholars, believed that traditional policing functions primarily as incident-driven. This means that conventional policing works at solving individual incidents and not at attempting to solve group incidents or group problems. Basically, incident-driven policing reflects a reactive approach. Incident-driven policing can also be considered to be relying on limited information since the police goal has traditionally been to bring the incident into the criminal justice process. Finally, the police department uses aggregate statistics to judge its performance.

Problem-oriented policing offers an alternative to incident-driven policing. According to Goldstein, the reaction to a service call should be only the first step. The police should develop a solution for the call in the first place. A permanent resolution to a problem should be the goal of the police. The police need to recognize that underlying conditions often create problems. These conditions may generate numerous incidents that involve the police. Underlying conditions could include social interaction between individuals, the physical environment, or the social setting where people interact, for example, public housing, where there often have been deteriorated apartments, intimidation of youngsters not being allowed to use the playground, and the selling of crack cocaine by outsiders who do not reside in the public housing complex.

The problem-oriented policing concept, as developed by Goldstein, is embodied in a four-stage process with the acronym SARA: Scanning, or problem detection and identification; Analysis, or learning the problem's causes and consequences; Response, or designing and implementing a solution; and Assessment, or evaluating the effectiveness of the solution. A police officer under the problem-oriented policing concept is a problem solver. No longer will the police officer function in an incident-driven and reactive manner. If the officer receives a call about a domestic dispute, his/her objective will be to find a solution to the problem. Generally, the same individuals in domestic disputes routinely call the police. Therefore, the police officers know that there exist underlying causes to the domestic dispute. The officers' goal should be to find the underlying causes of the domestic problem and to develop possible solutions. By solving the problem, the officers will be free to perform other police activities.

RECOMMENDED READING: Herman Goldstein, "Improving Policing: A Problem-Oriented Approach," *Crime and Delinquency*, Vol. 25, no. 2 (1979): 236–258; Charles Hale, *Police Patrol: Operations and Management* (New York: John Wiley, 1981); Sam Souryal, *Police Administration and Management* (St. Paul: West, 1977); Paul D. Weston, *Police Organization and Management* (Pacific Palisades, CA: Goodyear, 1976).

Michael Palmiotto

PROGRESSIVES. During the 1920s the Progressives, a new group of social welfare activists from colleges, settlement houses, and medical schools, sought to revise the social response to deviant behavior. The Progressives set out to reform the institutions that had been built during the Jacksonian era to house delinquent youth, the mentally ill, and those incarcerated after being convicted of a crime.

The reformatories, asylums, and prisons had been designed to contain disorder and establish social control through a strict regimen of work and social isolation. The Progressives rejected this institutional mandate as misguided and condemned the often brutalizing conditions of the institutions. These social reformers understood themselves as both benevolent and optimistic—holding that people could be cured of crime, delinquency, and insanity through an individualized program of treatment. The Progressives were divided as to the primary cause of deviant behavior, whether environmental or psychological, but they established the direction that the control of deviance was to take for the next fifty years.

Primarily upper middle class and opposed to immigration, the Progressives sought to upgrade U.S. policing by strengthening the military model, divorcing police from local politics, and raising standards to attract a wider range of applicants. The Progressives strongly supported the entry of women into policing and the consequent policewomen's movement.

The most immediate and lasting effect of the program of the Progressives was to expand the power of the state and the discretionary capacity of those who staffed the institutions. Not until the 1970s would the "just-deserts" and mandatory sentencing movements challenge the methods of the Progressives.

RECOMMENDED READING: David J. Rothman, *Conscience and Convenience: The Asylum and its Alternatives in Progressive America* (Boston: Little Brown, 1980); J. Simon, *Poor Discipline: Parole and the Social Control of the Underclass, 1890-1990* (Chicago: University of Chicago Press, 1993).

Margaret Leland Smith

PROPERTY BONDS. A form of bail in which the defendant or a supporter obtains pretrial release by pledging a form of property as surety. If the defendant does not appear at trial, this property is forfeited to the court. This form of bail is not used very frequently, in part because courts generally require that the value of the property used as collateral be at least twice as much as the bail required.

David Jones

PROPERTY CRIME. Property crime is a broad category of crimes that concern real property, tangible or intangible personal property, including anything severed from land, and intellectual property and documents, including money, that represent or embody anything of value. Crimes under this category include such crimes as arson, criminal mischief, reckless damage or destruction of property, interference with railroad property, robbery, burglary, criminal trespass, theft, tampering with identification numbers, forgery, criminal simulation, credit-card and debt-card abuse, falsely obtaining property or credit, hindering secured creditors, fraudulent motor-vehicle transfer, bad checks, embezzlement, computer theft, and money laundering.
RECOMMENDED READING: Joseph R. Nolan and Jacqueline M. Nolan-Haley, *Black's Law Dictionary: Definitions of the Terms and Phrases of American and English Jurisprudence, Ancient and Modern*, 6th ed. (St. Paul, MN: West Publishing Co., 1991).

Lee E. Parker

PROSECUTING ATTORNEY. The attorney for the state in criminal cases. It is this individual's duty to present enough evidence to convict the defendant. This position is one of the most important and powerful ones in the criminal justice system. If the criminal case is a federal one, the role of prosecuting attorney is usually undertaken by the U.S. attorney for the district in which the crime allegedly occurred. However, for the most part, criminal law is state law, and the prosecuting attorney is therefore an official of a particular state.

There is variation among states in the method by which the position (often called district attorney or county attorney) is filled. However, in most states the District Attorney is elected for a limited term (usually two or four years) in a partisan election by the voters of the county. In many states the position is used by its incumbent as a stepping-stone to higher political office.

While the position of prosecuting attorney is formally similar throughout the country, in fact there are significant variations among practitioners. For one thing, the areas served vary significantly in total population and/or rate of population growth. For instance, Milwaukee County, Wisconsin, has approximately 1 million inhabitants, while other Wisconsin counties may have a population of less than 20,000, yet each is served by a district attorney. In larger jurisdictions the district attorney is supported by assistant district attorneys. In many jurisdictions they are selected via a "merit" process, while in others they are chosen primarily through a patronage process. In some states their position is a part-time one, and they may spend much of their week conducting their own private practice. In larger jurisdictions the primary role of the district attorney is administrative. S/he sees that appropriate people are chosen to serve as assistant district attorneys and that cases are prosecuted in an expeditious and consistent fashion. In smaller jurisdictions the district attorneys conduct most legal affairs themselves.

Prosecuting attorneys also vary in terms of personality. Some are very aggressive in the conduct of their office and in their relations with other members of the courtroom workgroup, while others are more accommodating.

The role of prosecuting attorney in the United States is not considered to be a lifelong career, at least in most jurisdictions. (It is in many European countries.) Individuals may serve in the office for a number of years and then move on to other positions, often in private practice. Many commentators have expressed concern that heavy turnover in this office may have an adverse impact on the quality of justice in the United States.

RECOMMENDED READING: Roy B. Flemming, Peter F. Nardulli, and James Eisenstein, *The Craft of Justice* (Philadelphia: University of Pennsylvania Press, 1992); Joan E. Jacoby, *The American Prosecutor: A Search for Identity* (Lexington, MA: Lexington Books, 1980); William F. McDonald, ed., *The Prosecutor* (Beverly Hills, CA: Sage Publications, 1979).

David Jones

PROSECUTORIAL DISCRETION. The ability of the prosecutor to have almost total control over charging decisions within his/her jurisdiction. The prosecutor's legal control over charging decisions is largely unfettered. For instance, the decision of whether or not to bring charges is largely controlled by the prosecutor. So, too, within broad limits, is the decision of what to charge; if, in theory, more than one charge could be entered against a defendant, it is up to the prosecutor to determine if all, or just some, of the charges will be brought. If the prosecutor decides to bring just one of the charges, it is up to him/her to determine which one. In death-penalty states it is up to the prosecutor to determine whether or not to ask for the death penalty.

The issue of whether to enter plea negotiations also lies with the prosecutor. If there is more than one defendant, the prosecutor may determine which defendant with whom to negotiate if s/he so desires. If an indictment is brought, courts in most jurisdictions are expected to honor a motion by the prosecutor to dismiss.

The exercise of prosecutorial discretion is affected by many factors. These may be associated with a prosecutor's personal priorities. Some individuals in prosecutorial positions may feel that certain types of cases (e.g., the possession of small amounts of controlled substances) are not "worth" prosecuting. Case "winnability"—is a guilty verdict likely?—may also affect the exercise of discretion. Another factor is the prosecutor's relations with other agencies in the criminal justice system. For instance, if the prosecution of certain types of cases enhances relations between the prosecutor's office and law enforcement agencies, the prosecutor is more likely to pursue such cases.

While great, the prosecutor's discretion is not unlimited. For instance, the U.S. Supreme Court has held in *Oyler v. Boles* (1962) that the decision to prosecute may not be based deliberately upon an unjustified standard such as race, religion, or the exercise of protected constitutional rights. Some states have sought to limit prosecutorial charging discretion in such areas as domestic abuse by writing statutes that encourage the prosecution of these types of offenses. Finally, in Colorado, by law, upon petition of a citizen, a prosecutor is required to explain the decision not to prosecute. The court has the right to order a prosecution if it finds the reasons given to be arbitrary and capricious.

The desirability of great prosecutorial discretion is hotly debated in certain legal circles. Some applaud it, while others would like to limit it significantly. Whatever its merits, in the American political and criminal justice system prosecutorial discretion is probably inevitable.

RECOMMENDED READING: James B. Haddad, James Zagel, Gary Starkman, and William Bauer, *Cases and Comments on Criminal Procedure*, 4th ed. (Mineola, NY: Foundation Press, 1992); Joan E. Jacoby, *The American Prosecutor: A Search for Identity* (Lexington, MA: Lexington Books, 1980); *Discretion, Justice, and Democracy* ed. Carl F. Pinkele and William C. Louthan, (Ames: Iowa State University Press, 1985).

David Jones

PSILOCYBIN. Psilocybin is obtained from a mushroom found in Mexico. It is not as potent as LSD but can produce hallucination along with distortion of time and space perceptions at higher doses. Like peyote, it has been used in religious services of Native Americans. Its use in these services may have begun in Central America.

RECOMMENDED READING: Drug Enforcement Administration, *Drugs of Abuse* (Washington, DC: U.S. Department of Justice, 1990); National Narcotics Intelligence Consumer's Committee, *The NNICC Report: The Supply of Illicit Drugs to the United States* (Washington, DC: NNICC, 1995); United States Pharmacopeial Convention, *United States Pharmacopeial Formulary* Vol. II, 11th ed. (Rockville, MD: USPC, 1991).

Glenn Zuern

PSYCHOLOGICAL THEORIES OF CRIME. In the past, psychology did not endeavor to formulate a specific psychological criminology, but rather was committed to explaining the origins and manifestations of the human mind and

202 PUNISHMENT, THEORIES OF

the interaction of mind and body. In this view crime was one of several possible behaviors that could be done by humans and identified as crime by society. This is not to say that psychology was not interested in criminality. Henry Maudsly, in his 1870 *Body and Mind*, wrote that crime is an outlet for pathological urges, contending that criminals would go mad if they did not use this outlet.

Psychology studies behavior in such contexts as IQ analysis, learning disabilities, personality measures, mental disorders, and human motivation. There are several macrolevel approaches to explaining behavior employing these contexts. These include psychoanalytic theory, moral development theory, social learning theory, and biologically rooted conditioning theory. The study of such phenomena as psychopathic (antisocial) behavior and interpersonal violence has been strong in recent criminological psychology.

Hans Toch discovered in the 1950s, when he started out to teach a course on the psychology of crime, that he was actually pioneering in his field. As he related, "There was then no civilized terrain charted by anyone as psychological criminology; worse, the field of 'criminal justice' had not yet been invented."

It has long been recognized that there is a strong relationship between mental illness and crime, though this is not to say that mental illness causes crime. Quite the contrary, mental illness may be an alternative to crime and vice versa. In one study of 1,072 encounters by police with 2,122 citizens, only 4 percent of the citizens showed signs of serious mental illness. Widely quoted in criminology texts, Seymour Halleck wrote in 1967 that "the stresses that lead to mental illness are often the same stresses that lead to crime...while both mental illness behaviors and criminal behaviors provide a certain degree of mastery over stress, the adaptations themselves often lead to some difficulty with the environment. Mental illness has always had a maladaptive quality, and criminality usually has a maladaptive quality."

RECOMMENDED READING: Curt R. Bartol, *Criminal Behavior: A Psychosocial Approach,* 3rd ed. (Englewood Cliffs, NJ: Prentice Hall, 1991); Seymour L. Halleck, *Psychiatry and the Dilemmas of Crime: A Study of Causes, Punishment and Treatment* (Berkeley: University of California Press, 1971); S. Giora Shoham and Mark C. Seis, *A Primer In The Psychology of Crime* (New York: Harrow and Heston, 1993); Hans Toch, *Violent Men: An Inquiry into the Psychology of Violence*, rev. ed. (Washington, DC: American Psychological Association, 1992).

David R. Struckhoff

PUNISHMENT, THEORIES OF. In attempting to explain personal or societal responses to criminal or deviant behavior, the following theories are commonly used. Theories often serve to guide decision-making processes within systems; therefore, they are valuable in both the understanding and the utilization of system practices.

Retribution Theory. Retribution has as its philosophical beginnings orientations of the earliest known societies. Both the Sumerian code (3100 B.C.) and the Code of Hammurabi (1750 B.C.) contained elements of law that could be considered today as retribution. Retribution as a goal is rather simple: the idea that a violation of the laws or norms of a society is unacceptable and demands the punishment of the offender to "balance the scales" for the society that was harmed by the actions. This perspective demands that the victim confer the right to punish the perpetrator onto the society. The theological explanation for retribution argues that the actions of the offender disrupt the morals of the society, and punishment serves to restore these damaged morals and make the society "whole" again. In contrast to this social perspective, the expiatory explanation for retribution argues that the offender must suffer to symbolically cleanse himself or herself for the acts against the group. By experiencing a painful punishment, the offender balances internally the pleasure that is believed to be the result of the criminal or deviant act. Finally, in the aesthetic view the act of the offender is believed to make the social group less "clean" or "pure," and the punishment of the offender serves to restore the harmony and perfection of this damaged group. This is similar to the expiatory view, but focuses on the condition of the group rather than the condition of the individual.

Incapacitation Theory. Incapacitation holds that the offender is unlikely to ever improve from the experience of the correctional process. Therefore, the only hope is to make the society safe by making it impossible or unlikely that the offender will be able to victimize the society for a set period of time. This is accomplished through the use of "disablement," which includes, but is in no way limited to, imprisonment. This is constructed on the idea that limitation of the offender's access to those things necessary to commit the crimes will make the crimes less likely to occur. By limiting the offender's access to the general public, the public will be safe from the criminal intentions of the offender. Those who share the prison with the offender may become victims, but the society at large will be safe, at least for a time. Similar to is perspective are the ideas of mutilation, castration, and transportation. These actions also limit the offender's actions by either destroying the physical elements (such as sexual or other organs, or limbs) necessary for the crimes, or by moving the offender to a location where s/he can victimize only those the society has no concern for or duty to protect. Related to this perspective is the idea of selective incapacitation, which involves moving into the prison environment those offenders who represent the greatest continuing danger to the society, while keeping in society those who are less consistently dangerous, irrespective of the crime committed.

Deterrence Theory. The philosophy of deterrence begins with the idea that humans are responsible for their actions and choose behaviors that produce maximum benefits and minimize risks or costs; or the idea that humans are pleasure seeking and pain avoiding—what is known as the hedonistic calculus. At the time this philosophy was being considered, the Church believed in a philosophy known as manifest destiny, which stated that the behaviors and actions of the world are preordained, and there is little society can do to affect behavior, in that it is already planned and is simply awaiting its completion. For the society to embrace deterrence, the Church had to relax its beliefs regarding manifest destiny. Once the Enlightenment philosophers had begun to change the social perception of humanity (including criminals), the goal became to utilize this new perspective to enhance the safety of society. In tandem with this belief system came the criminological perspective of utilitarianism, which sought to improve the quality of life for the entire society, not just the wealthy or noble. A major proponent of this perspective was Jeremy Bentham (1748–1832), who argued that in order to control crime, society only had to make the punishments for criminal behavior greater than the pleasures derived from the successful completion of the crime. Further, deterrence required three critical elements: certainty, severity, and swiftness. Certainty argued that there must exist a serious risk of apprehension and punishment for deterrence to be achieved. Severity required that the punishment for the crime be greater than the benefits for the crime, and to achieve deterrence the punishments need only exceed the benefits received. Finally, the goals of deterrence required swiftness of punishment, so the offender would be able to consciously link the criminal behavior with the punishment received. Later, criminologists realized that the experience of punishment was different for first-time offenders and repeat criminals. This required a modification of the ideals of deterrence to include the topics of general deterrence, which used standard amounts of punishment to deter a noncriminal populace, and specific deterrence, which used enhanced levels of punishment to further deter those who had already engaged in criminal behavior. With regard to those who committed crimes, it seemed obvious that the amount of punishment offered was insufficient to produce law-abiding behavior; therefore it became necessary to increase punishments to control the behaviors of these specific offenders.

This modification points out the two basic flaws of deterrence. The first is the idea that similar punishments can be used to deter dissimilarly motivated offenders. The idea of standardized punishments to control persons, some of whom are highly motivated to commit crimes, and some of whom are very unmotivated to commit crimes, indicates that some offenders will be receiving too much punishment, and some offenders will not be deterred by the punishment offered by the society. The second basic flaw with this theory is the idea that criminals are accurately balancing the costs and benefits of criminal activity prior to committing the crime. Statistics indicate that many crimes are committed while the offender is under the influence of some type of chemical, which it is assumed will change the accuracy of the decision-making process. Similarly, this perspective maintains that the offender has access to the documents and is knowledgeable about the punishments that may result from the commission of, apprehension for, and conviction for a specific criminal act.

Rehabilitation Theory. The punishment philosophy of rehabilitation believes that there is an underlying cause to most criminal behavior. The solution to crime in society, therefore, is to deal with the problems within the criminal, rather than the symptom of the problem, which is the criminal act. Rehabilitation is primarily based on the medical-model perception of crime and criminality, which proposes four basic elements: (1) there is something wrong with the criminal that has contributed to the problem of criminal behavior; (2) the system can test the person and determine what the problem is or what has created the problem; (3) the system can then treat the problem within the person to change those elements that were believed to cause the criminal behavior; and (4) the system can test the person prior to release in order to determine if the intervention has been successful and the person has changed and is no longer a threat or danger to the society. By performing these acts, it is believed that the person will improve in his or her ability to lawfully cope in society and will no longer pose a threat to the safety of the society. Historically, those who support the idea of rehabilitation have oversimplified the causal elements of criminality and have believed that rehabilitation would be effective for too broad a group of offenders. More recent beliefs argue that there may be a large core of the offender population whose members are able to be changed and are open to the goals of the therapeutic intervention, but this intervention may be unsuitable for those who are either unable or unwilling to change.

RECOMMENDED READING: Ralph D. Ellis and Carol S. Ellis, *Theories of Criminal Justice: A Critical Reappraisal* (Wolfeboro, NH: Longwood Academic, 1989); David Garland, *Punishment and Modern Society: A Study in Social Theory* (Chicago: University of Chicago Press, 1990); H. L. A. Hart, *Punishment and Responsibility: Essays in the Philosophy of Law* (Oxford: Clarendon Press, 1968); Colin Summer, *Censure, Politics and Criminal Justice* (Bristol, PA: Open University Press, 1990).

Matthew C. Leone

Q

QUAALUDES. Quaaludes are a nonbarbiturate synthetic sedative that come in a tablet form. They are taken orally. The drug causing the reaction in those that take Quaaludes is methaqualone. This drug is commonly used as a sedative and depresses an individual's central nervous system into a sleeplike condition. It is often the cause of drug-overdose deaths.

RECOMMENDED READING: Drug Enforcement Administration, *Drugs of Abuse* (Washington, D.C.: U.S. Department of Justice, 1990); National Narcotics Intelligence Consumer's Committee, *The NNICC Report: The Supply of Illicit Drugs to the United States* (Washington, D.C.: NNICC, 1995).

Glenn Zuern

R

RAPE. In most jurisdictions, rape has traditionally been defined as "unlawful sexual intercourse with a female, by force or without legal or factual consent." The FBI's Uniform Crime Reporting Program defines forcible rape as "sexual intercourse or attempted sexual intercourse with a female against her will, by force or threat of force."

In the past, statutory definitions of rape frequently made the crime of rape within marriage an impossibility, and assumed that a woman automatically gave her consent to sexual intercourse through the marriage contract. Within the past 20 years, however, a number of jurisdictions have modified their rape statutes to encompass marital rape, and homosexual (or "same-sex") rape.

Another form of rape, one that is commonly discussed in the literature but rarely distinguished statutorily, is date rape. Date rape is "unlawful forced sexual intercourse with a female against her will which occurs within the context of a dating relationship."

Statistical information on the crime of rape can be found in the FBI's annual publication, *Crime in the United States,* and in the Bureau of Justice Statistics's annual report entitled *Criminal Victimization.* Although many books and articles have been published on the topic of rape, A. Nicholas Groth's *Men Who Rape* remains one of the definitive works in the area.

While rape is one of the FBI's eight Part I offenses, and is considered a "violent crime" under the FBI's Uniform Crime Reporting Program, the crime of rape is generally excluded from the category of. "sex offenses" which, in current statistical usage, is the name given to a broad category of varying content, usually consisting of all offenses having a sexual element except forcible rape, prostitution, and commercial sex offenses. (See **Forcible Rape**.)
RECOMMENDED READING: Bureau of Justice Statistics, *Dictionary of Criminal Justice Data Terminology,* 2nd ed. (Washington, DC: U.S. Government Printing Office, 1982); Federal Bureau of Investigation, *Uniform Crime Reporting Handbook* (Washington, DC: U.S. Department of Justice, 1996); A.

Nicholas Groth, *Men Who Rape: The Psychology of the Offender* (New York, NY: Plenum Press, 1979).

Frank Schmalleger

REDIRECT EXAMINATION. The part of the trial process that takes place (if it takes place) following the cross-examination of a witness. After a witness has undergone cross-examination, the lawyer who called him/her as a witness in the first place may ask questions "on redirect." The purpose of these questions is to clarify issues raised in cross-examination. The questions asked in redirect examination are limited to issues raised in cross-examination. Opposing counsel then has the right to ask additional questions based on material brought out in the redirect examination. This process is known as "re–cross-examination."

RECOMMENDED READING: John C. Klotter, *Criminal Evidence*, 6th ed. (Cincinnati: Anderson Publishing, 1996); Jonathan D. Schiffman, *Fundamentals of the Criminal Justice Process*, 3rd ed. (Deerfield, IL: Clark Boardman Callaghan, 1994).

David Jones

REHNQUIST, WILLIAM (1924–   ). William Rehnquist was born in Milwaukee, Wisconsin, on October 1, 1924. He took a bachelor's, master's, and law degree from Stanford University as well as a master's in government from Harvard. Rehnquist served as law clerk to Supreme Court Justice Robert Jackson. In 1969 he was appointed assistant attorney general in charge of the Justice Department's Office of Legal Counsel (what Richard Nixon called "the President's lawyer's lawyer"). In 1971 President Nixon named Rehnquist to the Supreme Court. He was elevated to be chief justice in 1986 by President Reagan, the fourth associate to become chief. Rehnquist is one of the brightest judges ever to sit on the high court. He writes with style, force, and assurance and is agile in shaping a record and marshaling arguments to reach a conclusion. His opinions are short and lively. As associate he was dubbed "the lone ranger" because of his frequent dissents from the Court's majority. He dissented in *Roe v. Wade* (1973), argued that there is no constitutional barrier to school prayer, and sided with police and prosecutors on questions of criminal law. He opposed affirmative-action programs.

Rehnquist is an articulate pillar of the conservative bloc on the Court. He adheres to what he considers the original intent of the framers of the Constitution and believes in maintaining the role of the states as coordinate centers of power.

RECOMMENDED READING: Derek Davis, *Original Intent: Chief Justice Rehnquist and the Course of American Church/State Relations*, (Buffalo, NY: Prometheus Books, 1991); Sue Davis, *Justice Rehnquist and the Constitution* (Princeton, NJ: Princeton University Press, 1989); David G. Savage, *Turning*

Right: The Making of the Rehnquist Supreme Court (New York: Wiley, 1992).

Martin Gruberg

RELEASE ON RECOGNIZANCE (ROR). A form of pretrial release in which the defendant is allowed to go free based solely on his/her promise to appear in court as required by the judicial officer. If the defendant is granted ROR, s/he is not required to post monetary bond. The use of this form of pretrial release is based on the assumption that there are defendants with certain background characteristics and ties to the community who can be trusted to appear when required without having to post bail.

Under Section 3142(b) of the federal Bail Reform Act of 1984 the defendant must be released on personal recognizance or unsecured personal bail unless the judicial officer determines that such release "will not reasonably assure the appearance of the person as required or will endanger the safety of any other person or the community." Many states have comparable requirements. Studies of pretrial release procedures have shown that failure-to-appear rates of individuals released on their own recognizance are comparable to those released under other conditions. (See **Pretrial Release**.)

RECOMMENDED READING: Deirdre Golash, *The Bail Reform Act of 1984* (Washington, DC: Federal Judicial Center, 1987);   John S. Goldkamp and Michael R. Gottfredson, *Judicial Guidelines for Bail: The Philadelphia Experiment* (Washington, DC: National Institute of Justice, 1984);   Andy Hall, *Pretrial Release Program Options* (Washington, DC: National Institute of Justice, 1984).

David Jones

REPRIEVE. Occasionally referred to as a respite, a reprieve orders suspension of the execution of the sentence of a court and, as such, is probably the most limited of the several forms of clemency. A reprieve does not require or depend upon the consent of the recipient, but neither reduces a penalty nor changes its substance. After the termination of the period of the reprieve, the full purpose of the court (as expressed in the sentence) may be carried out. While limited in scope, a reprieve provides a critical function in the criminal justice system. In many instances this form of clemency is utilized in order to "stay" the execution of a prisoner while allegations of newly discovered evidence are considered. In other instances a reprieve provides additional time for the formal appeal of a conviction or the processing of a request for a more expansive grant of clemency (pardon or commutation).

RECOMMENDED READING: Joseph R. Nolan and Jacqueline M. Nolan-Haley, *Black's Law Dictionary: Definitions of the Terms and Phrases of American and English Jurisprudence, Ancient and Modern*, 6th ed. (St. Paul, MN: West Publishing Co., 1991)

Peter S. Ruckman, Jr.

RHODES V. CHAPMAN, 452 U.S. 337 (1981). The first case in which the Eighth Amendment's prohibition against "cruel and unusual punishment" was applied by the U.S. Supreme Court to the issue of conditions of confinement of inmates in state prisons. The Court held that while the prohibition does apply to conditions of confinement, in this case, it decided, the practice of "double-bunking" in the Ohio prison facility in question did not constitute cruel and unusual punishment.

The Court held that "conditions must not involve the wanton and unnecessary infliction of pain, nor may they be grossly disproportionate to the severity of the crime warranting imprisonment." Double-bunking under these circumstances did not meet these conditions. Moreover, the Court held that "the Constitution does not mandate comfortable prisons." Justice Lewis Powell, who wrote the majority opinion, also noted that federal courts should not assume that state authorities are insensitive to the needs of prisoners. Consequently, the Court overruled a district court ruling that conditions in the Ohio facility constituted cruel and unusual punishment.

David Jones

RICO (THE RACKETEER INFLUENCED AND CORRUPT ORGANI-ZATIONS ACT). The Racketeer Influenced and Corrupt Organizations Act (RICO) is considered by experts to be one of the most important pieces of legislation enacted to date against organized crime. Its crafter, Robert Blackey, was chief counsel to a Senate subcommittee on organized crime and a former member of the Justice Department's organized crime section. RICO was part of the Organized Crime Control Act of 1970, which created the federal witness protection program, expanded the use of immunity for witnesses, and instituted special Justice Department task forces to combat organized crime. The purpose of the Organized Crime Control Act was to "seek the eradication of organized crime in the United States by strengthening the legal tools in the evidence-gathering process, by establishing new penal prohibitions, and by providing enhanced sanctions and new remedies to deal with the unlawful activities of those involved in organized crime" (*Congressional Record*, 1970).

RICO permits prosecutors to pursue entire enterprises, which include businesses, labor unions, and other legal entities such as government units or offices. In *United States v. Turkette* (1981), the Supreme Court ruled that RICO could be applied specifically to criminal enterprises and broadened the term *enterprise* to encompass "individuals associated in fact [with illegal activities] although not a legal entity." In a similar case, *Russello v. United States* (1983), the Supreme Court affirmed that RICO's intent was a broad-based attack on organized crime's illicit activities and illegally obtained wealth. It stated that "the legislative history [of RICO] clearly demonstrates that...[RICO] was intended to provide new weapons of an unprecedented scope for an assault on organized crime and its economic roots."

Any two of several dozen crimes committed during a ten-year period are enough to convict a person of a "pattern of racketeering." Racketeering activities may consist of state felonies such as murder, kidnapping, arson, robbery, extortion, drug dealing, gambling, and bribery. The list also contains federal crimes such as drug violations, labor offenses, theft from interstate shipments, and mail fraud. Under RICO anyone planning or discussing crimes is as guilty as the actual perpetrators, and it is a separate crime to belong to a criminal enterprise (e.g., an organized crime family) even if the racketeering was committed by other members of the enterprise.

Prosecutors were initially reluctant to use RICO because it requires lengthy, painstaking investigations that may not lead to successful convictions. A pioneer in RICO prosecutions, Rudolph Giuliani, the current mayor of New York City and former U.S. attorney, used RICO to make significant inroads against New York's crime families by prosecuting their upper echelon for its diverse criminal activities.

The penalties for violating RICO are severe: imprisonment of up to twenty years to life and fines ranging from $25,000 to $500,000 or twice the gross profits or proceeds from specific offenses. In addition to criminal penalties, violators of RICO may be required to forfeit to the government any properties or businesses that they acquired in violation of RICO, and the government may freeze RICO defendants' assets before trial.

RECOMMENDED READING: Howard Abadinsky, *Organized* Crime, 5th ed. (Chicago: Nelson-Hall, 1997); *Congressional Record* 116th Cong., sess., 1970, 602; Michille Olk Hopp, *The Racketeer Influenced and Corrupt Organizations Act (RICO): A History of a Changing Law and its Relation to Organizational Crime*, M. A. thesis (Ypsilanti: Eastern Michigan University, 1994).

Arthur J. Lurigio

ROBBERY. Robbery is the taking of personal property in the possession of another, from his/her person or immediate presence, and against his/her will, accomplished by means of force or fear. Means of force or fear may include intentionally, knowingly, or recklessly causing bodily injury to another or threatening or placing another in fear of immediate bodily injury or death. In some states the perpetrator may have the intent to either permanently or temporarily deprive the owner of the property.

RECOMMENDED READING: Cal. Penal Code Sec. 221 (West 1992); 46 Fla. Stat. Ann. Sec. 812.13 (West 1992); Joseph R. Nolan and Jacqueline M. Nolan-Haley, *Black's Law Dictionary: Definitions of the Terms and Phrases of American and English Jurisprudence, Ancient and Modern*, 6th ed. (St. Paul, MN: West Publishing Co., 1991); Texas Penal Code Ann. Sec. 29.02 (Vernon's 1994).

Lee E. Parker

ROCHIN v. CALIFORNIA, **342 U.S. 165 (1952).** This case contributed significantly to the development of the exclusionary rule of evidence in Fourth Amendment cases. In *Wolf v. Colorado* (1949), the U.S. Supreme Court had held that although the Fourth Amendment applies to state criminal proceedings through the Fourteenth Amendment's due-process clause, the states were not required to exclude illegally obtained evidence from their criminal proceedings. The Court's rationale was that a vigilant press and the public would prevent police officers from abusing suspects' Fourth Amendment rights. Three years later, in *Rochin v. California,* the Supreme Court revisited the issue of whether the states are required to exclude unlawfully obtained evidence from their criminal trials.

In this case, police officers entered the defendant's home without probable cause or a search warrant to search for illegal drugs. During the search the police broke down the door to Rochin's bedroom and saw him swallow two capsules. The police immediately handcuffed Rochin and took him to a hospital where the capsules were retrieved by forcing him to swallow an emetic solution. Later analysis of the regurgitated capsules revealed that they contained morphine. Rochin was convicted of possession of morphine in state court and was sentenced to prison. On appeal, the U.S. Supreme Court ruled that the methods used by the police "were too close to the rack and screw to permit of constitutional differentiation" and were such that they "shock[ed] the conscience of a civilized society." The Court therefore held that the evidence could not be used to convict Rochin.

Rochin v. California is an important exclusionary-rule precedent. It established that the states are required to exclude evidence obtained in violation of a suspect's Fourth Amendment rights whenever police behavior "shocks the conscience." Later, in *Mapp v. Ohio*, 367 U.S. 643 (1961), the exclusionary rule was applied to all state cases in which the police obtained evidence in violation of the Fourth Amendment.

RECOMMENDED READING: Yale Kamisar, Wayne R. LaFave and Jerold Israel *Modern Criminal Procedure: Cases, Comments, and Questions*, 8th ed. (St. Paul, MN: West Publishing Co., 1994); Charles Whitebread and Christopher Slobogin, *Criminal Procedure: An Analysis of Cases and Concepts*, 3rd ed. (Westbury, NY: Foundation Press, 1993).

Thomas J. Hickey

S

SCALIA, ANTONIN (1936–   ). The son of an Italian immigrant, Antonin Scalia was born in Trenton, New Jersey, on March 11, 1936. He received his bachelor's degree from Georgetown University in 1957 and graduated Harvard Law School *magna cum laude* in 1960. After teaching at the law schools of the University of Virginia and the University of Chicago, Scalia was nominated by President Reagan in 1982 for the U.S. Court of Appeals for the District of Columbia. In 1986 Scalia became the second of three Reagan nominees to the U.S. Supreme Court. Confirmed by a vote of 98–0 by the U.S. Senate, Scalia replaced Justice William Rehnquist, who was elevated to chief justice.

Scalia is generally recognized as one of the Court's most articulate members. He engages in public appearances more frequently than other members of the Court and is frequently described as jovial in nature. Scalia's occasionally acerbic opinions have prompted some to wonder how much actual influence his views carry in the decision making of other justices. Despite the fact that he came to the Court with a slim record on criminal issues (as a circuit judge he wrote only five printed criminal procedure opinions, and sided with the prosecution in each), there is little doubt that Scalia has been a major player in the development and determination of critical issues of criminal justice.

In search and seizure cases Scalia has generally voted to loosen restrictions on law enforcement officers. His dissenting opinions in *Booth v. Maryland* (1987) and *South Carolina v. Gathers* (1989) provided the groundwork for the Court's 1991 decision (*Payne v. Tennessee*) endorsing the use of victim impact statements in death penalty trials. He also delivered the opinion of the Court in *Stanford v. Kentucky* (1989), ruling that it was not unconstitutional to execute persons for crimes committed at the ages of sixteen or seventeen. Scalia also authored the majority opinion in *Wilson v. Seiter* (1991) that radically revised the judicial standard of review for prisoners' civil rights cases. He has been a consistent supporter of decisions that limit opportunities for convicted offenders to file appeals and *habeas corpus* petitions.

An interesting 1992 study by Christopher E. Smith (*Kentucky Law Journal*) noted that although Scalia consistently joins other "conservative" justices as a dependable vote against assertions of rights by criminal defendants and prisoners, he is eager to assert his own viewpoints through concurring and dissenting opinions. Manifestly unwilling to "compromise," Scalia's views with respect to strict separation of powers, adherence to the text of the Constitution and statutes, and limits on the number of cases brought before the Supreme Court and other federal courts are prominently displayed in cases affecting the criminal justice system.

RECOMMENDED READING: Richard A. Brisbin, *Justice Antonin Scalia and the Conservative Revival* (Baltimore, MD: Johns Hopkins University Press, 1997); David A. Schultz and Christopher E. Smith, *The Jurisdential Vision of Justice Antonin Scalia* (Lanham, MD: Rowman & Littlefield Publishers, 1996).

Peter S. Ruckman, Jr.

SCHALL v. MARTIN, 467 U.S. 253 (1984). Fourteen-year-old Gregory Martin was taken into police custody in 1977, accused of first-degree robbery, second-degree assault, and criminal possession of a weapon. When taken into custody, Martin gave the police false information about where and with whom he lived and eventually was detained overnight. The next day, when Martin appeared in juvenile court for an "initial appearance," he was ordered detained pending further juvenile court action. Two weeks later Martin was adjudicated delinquent and given two years on juvenile probation. Before adjudication as delinquent, Martin, through his attorney, had filed a class-action writ of *habeas corpus* on behalf of himself and all others who were held in detention "preventively" per procedures in the New York Family Court Act. Section 320.5(3)(b) allowed preventive detention of a juvenile accused of committing a delinquent act if that juvenile "may before the return date commit an act which if committed by an adult would constitute a crime." The writ claimed that the preventive-detention clause violated the due-process and equal-protection clauses of the Fourteenth Amendment. The court of appeals agreed and found that preventive detention was more punitive than preventive, primarily because so many juveniles were released into nonsecure situations or had no court action taken after their release from detention. The case was appealed to the U.S. Supreme Court.

The Supreme Court looked at two issues: first, whether or not the preventive-detention clause in the New York statute served a legitimate state purpose, and second, whether or not the statute itself contained adequate safeguards to warrant its use with those juveniles at high risk of committing crimes if released. The Supreme Court found that juveniles could pose a unique dilemma to the juvenile courts, as courts were put into the position of "protecting" the child in a *parens patriae* capacity. Such protection included protecting the child from him/herself and any decisions that could bring him/her future harm, such as committing more delinquent acts. The Court also noted that all states, including the District of

Columbia used preventive detention in their juvenile courts. To both questions, the Supreme Court felt that the answers were yes.

Additionally, the Court stated that the New York statute did not seem to be designed to punish juveniles, as the statue stated that the need for preventive detention had to be determined for each child, and the length of the detention was restricted. Furthermore, the Court stated that the statistics and case studies relied upon by the appeals court that indicated that preventive detention must be more punitive than preventive were faulty and did not demonstrate that preventive detention was not warranted in cases that resulted in dismissals or less secure placements. In sum, the Supreme Court found that the statute in New York, which included possible preventive detention of juveniles charged with committing a delinquent act, was constitutional.

Frances P. Reddington

SCIENTIFIC JURY SELECTION. The use of social science methodology to aid in the selection of jurors likely to be predisposed to supporting one's side of a legal issue. There are a number of methodologies used in this area. The most typical of them is derived from social survey methodology. This entails the use of a telephone survey. Using scientific sampling techniques, a representative sample of potential jurors is chosen. Members of the sample are then subjected to a telephone survey comprised of three components. First, the respondents are questioned about their social background (e.g., their religion, their income); they are then asked a set of questions designed to measure beliefs and attitudes likely to be associated with a verdict at the trial (e.g., racial attitudes); finally, a brief description of the case is given, and the respondent is asked to vote as if s/he were a member of the jury. The consultant will then analyze data to determine what attitudes and background characteristics are associated with a tendency to vote in a particular direction concerning the issues at trial. In some cases telephone surveys are supplemented or supplanted by simulated trials in which mock jurors are asked to decide on a verdict after hearing a case similar to the one at trial. Backgrounds, attitudes, and decisional proclivities are analyzed in this instance also.

From this material scientific jury consultants seek to develop a profile of a juror who is likely to be predisposed to vote in a particular fashion. This profile is then used by counsel during *voir dire* to strike hostile jurors and keep sympathetic ones.

Scientific jury selection has been criticized on many grounds, such as: (1) it is relatively expensive and thus is not available to all; (2) its effectiveness is suspect; (3) while some defendants who have used scientific jury selection in some highly publicized cases (e.g., the Berrigan brothers in 1972) have not been convicted, it is hard to show that scientific jury selection contributed much to the trial's outcome; and (4) while it may be possible to link certain types of individual backgrounds with certain decisional tendencies within groups of people, social scientists cannot predict with much certainty how an individual juror will vote in a particular case. Most students of jury behavior would consider the nature and quality of the evidence presented at trial as the primary determinant of a juror's decision, not his/her background or attitudes.

In short, while it is popular in certain circles, scientific jury selection may be overrated as a strategy in criminal defenses.

RECOMMENDED READING: Jeffrey Abramson, *We, the Jury* (New York: Basic Books, 1994); *In the Jury Box: Controversies in the Courtroom, ed.* Lawrence S. Wrightsman, Saul M. Kassin, and Cynthia E. Willis (Newbury Park, CA: Sage Publications, 1987); Sharie Seidman Diamond, "Scientific Jury Selection: What Social Scientists Know and Do Not Know," *Judicature* 73 (1990); 178–183.

David Jones

SCOTTSBORO CASE. An infamous case involving the treatment of blacks in a southern state's criminal justice system in the spring of 1931. In this case nine young black men (aged twelve through nineteen at the time of the alleged offense) were accused of raping two white women while all were riding (illegally) on a freight train through northern Alabama near the small community of Scottsboro. Although the evidence against them was very flimsy, all were convicted at their first trial and sentenced to death. Convictions of the alleged perpetrators were overturned twice by the U.S. Supreme Court (the first time because of inadequate representation by counsel in a capital case, the second time because blacks had been systematically excluded from juries in Alabama). One of the defendants was tried four times on the charges and convicted each time. Ultimately, five of the youths were convicted and sentenced to long periods of incarceration. Charges against the rest were dropped by the state, although the evidence against them was the same. Those against whom charges were finally dropped had spent several years in prison while earlier convictions were appealed.

The case gained a great deal of notoriety throughout the country during the 1930s. It exemplified the mistreatment of blacks in the South. Eventually, all who had been convicted received early release from prison.

RECOMMENDED READING: Dan T. Carter, *Scottsboro: A Tragedy of the American South* (Baton Rouge: Louisiana State University Press, 1969).

David Jones

SEARCH INCIDENT TO AN ARREST. Upon making a lawful arrest, an officer is allowed to conduct a limited search of the arrestee, even without a valid search warrant. This is allowed in order to maintain the officer's safety and to prevent escape of the suspect or destruction of any evidence.

However, this search is limited. A search incident to a legal arrest is generally limited to the arrestee's person and the area within his/her immediate control, that is, the area within which s/he might be able to gain possession of a weapon or destroy evidence. Thus, if a person is arrested in his/her home, a search of the whole house by law enforcement officials (if they do not have a search warrant) is not allowed under the Fourth Amendment. However, if an officer has reason to believe that there are other suspects in the home, s/he has the right to look throughout the home in a "cursory safety check."

The search incident to the arrest does not have to take place immediately. It may even be conducted after the arrestee has been jailed. The search may be a thorough one; if suspicious items are found in a search incident to a legal arrest, these items may be closely inspected, at least under the provisions of the U.S. Constitution. Some state statutes limit more stringently what kind of searches may be conducted incident to a legal arrest.

If an officer makes a lawful custodial arrest of the occupant of a vehicle, the officer has the right to search the passenger compartment of the vehicle and examine the contents of any containers found therein. Thus searches incident to legal arrests are important, but limited, weapons in the arsenal of law enforcement.

RECOMMENDED READING: *Chimel v. California*, 395 U.S. 752 (1969); *Gustafson v. Florida*, 414 U.S. 260 (1973); *New York v. Belton*, 453 U.S. 454 (1981); *United States v. Edwards*, 415 U.S. 800 (1974); *United States v. Robinson*, 414 U. S. 218 (1973).

David Jones

SENSATIONAL MURDERS. Despite the existence and greater prevalence of several other forms of interpersonal violence (e.g., assault, robbery, sexual assault), research, the media, and public attention tend to be focused on homicides. Perhaps the finality of this crime results in intense public interest and better record keeping and investigation of the circumstances and perpetrators. Criminologists therefore make use of the better and larger amount of information on homicides for research purposes. Sustained media attention to murders is, however, highly selective and tends to focus either on the people involved (local or national celebrities) or on peculiar circumstances (e.g., "multicides," which may either be mass murders or serial murders) surrounding a given case.

In the mid-1990s the most sensational murders were those in which former football star and actor-celebrity O. J. Simpson was charged and tried for the killings of his ex-wife Nicole Simpson and her acquaintance Ronald Goldman in Los Angeles, California. Public fascination for details about this case can be viewed as an example of the focus on the people involved (i.e., murder among the rich and famous). This can also be the motivation for cases involving completed or attempted homicides on presidents and other heads of state.

Other cases of homicide become the focus of media sensationalism because of the circumstances involved. Robert Chambers, in the so-called preppie murder case of the late-1980s in New York City was charged in the killing of

Jennifer Levin, a woman who had gone out with him. In this case sensational stories in the media involved Chambers's focus on Levin's alleged prior sexual activity as a defense; his attempts to depict the death as a result of consensual "rough" sex; and his apparent lack of remorse. A plea bargain (which Levin's family could have vetoed but agreed to) was negotiated when it became clear after more than nine days of jury deliberations that a verdict could not be reached. Chambers pleaded guilty to first-degree manslaughter, expressed remorse, and was sentenced to from five to twenty-five years in prison. Similarly, the unusual circumstances surrounding the murders of the young children of Susan Smith in Union, South Carolina, were the focus of media attention in 1994. Smith first told the police that an African-American male had hijacked their car and kidnapped her children, leading to a nationwide search. A few days later she confessed to killing her children by drowning them after rolling their car off a bridge while the children were still buckled in their car seats.

Criminal justice scholars have identified both advantages and disadvantages to such sensational murder cases. Typically, such cases go through the entire gamut of the criminal justice process (including trial and the mounting of strong prosecution and defense efforts), thus helping to educate the public regarding the system. Unfortunately, these sensational cases also provide a false picture of the system in that the vast majority of cases are actually disposed of through negotiated plea bargains.

RECOMMENDED READING: Vincent Bugliosi, *Helter Skelter: The True Story of the Manson Murders* (New York: Bantam Books, 1994); Truman Capote, *In Cold Blood: A True Account of a Multiple Murder and its Consequences*, Modern Library ed. (New York: Modern Library, 1996); Linda Wolfe, *Wasted: The Preppie Murder* (New York: Simon and Schuster, 1989).

N. Prabha Unnithan

SENTENCING. During the time between a guilty verdict at trial and sentencing of the defendant, the probation department conducts a presentencing investigation and makes recommendations to the judge as to the sentence. The prosecutor and defense counsel also submit recommendations to the judge. The trial judge determines the sentence within the requirements of the law, taking into consideration the presentence report and recommendations of the prosecutor and defense counsel. Punishments may range from a fine, probation, or community service to a prison term of up to life imprisonment. The permissible punishment under the law is part of the substantive law of the state.

RECOMMENDED READING: Linda Drazga Maxfield, Willie Martin, and Christine Kitchens, *Just Punishment: Public Perceptions and the Federal Sentencing Guidelines* (Washington, DC: U.S. Sentencing Commission, 1996); U.S. Congress, House Committee on the Judiciary, *Mandatory*

Minimum Sentencing Reform Act of 1994 (Washington, DC: U.S. Government Printing Office, 1994).

Christopher J. Morse

SENTENCING PRACTICES. The philosophical perspective regarding the causes of criminality has long been reflected in the sentencing practices of any given society. When societies believed that criminal behavior was a choice that was made logically for the purposes of financial gain, the control of crime was believed to be accomplished through the use of longer and harsher sentences. Conversely, when crime was believed to be the result of a character flaw or problem, crime control would not be accomplished through punishment, but rather through treating the offender's problems that created the need to commit crime. Until recent years, however, societies have "officially" handled offenders using a singular perspective as to the causes of crime, not recognizing that for some offenders crime is a choice, while for others it is the result of circumstance. These differing beliefs have resulted in three distinct sentencing practices that each reflect different perspectives as to the causes of crime.

Determinate Sentences. Determinate sentences are those in which a set number of years is given to the offender for the crime(s) committed. Sentence length and the location of the sentence (minimum-, medium-, or maximum-security prison, or jail) are related to the severity of the crime and often to the past criminal history of the offender. These types of sentences are based on the idea of deterrence and the belief that offenders, as well as the general public, can be deterred from criminal behavior through the use of certain, swift, and severe sentences. The determinate sentence philosophy carries along with it the idea of limiting sentence reduction due to statutory or work good time, because it is believed that these reductions weaken the certainty and severity aspects of punishment, which are critical to the goal of deterrence. This philosophy, while logical if one assumes that criminal behavior is based on a rational and informed decision process, is nonetheless flawed by three significant problems. First is the lack of motivation to change for the offender. The time spent in the prison setting is independent of the behavior of the inmate, in that the sentence is set by the court, and the prison is only responsible for the holding of the inmate for the dura-tion of the sentence. Inmates are not motivated to change because change would in no way affect the amount of time s/he is required to serve. Consequently, the system could release back into society persons who are no better, or in many cases much worse, than when they were brought in. A second flaw with this type of sentence practice is that the judge's hands are tied by legislation, and often the offender deserves a more or less serious sentence than the law supports, but the judge is duty bound to provide the sentence mandated by the law of the state. The change to determinate sentences decreases the authority and status of the judge. Judges go from being persons who hear and see all of the evidence of the case and use that information to decide the sentence if the court has found the person guilty to being arbiters of evidence and enforcers of due-process rights—certainly an important role, but one that carries with it less authority and creates less impact on the overall society. Last, this type of sentence creates the potential for the waste of resources. It has not been uncommon that some offenders have been sentenced by law to an amount of time that was in excess of the amount necessary for the control of future criminal behavior. Consequently, the system is expending resources further incarcerating persons who have already achieved the maximum deterrent effect of incarceration. This not only represents the potential for unnecessary suffering, but is inefficient as well.

Indeterminate Sentences. Indeterminate sentences are those where a range of time is given, rather than a set number of years. As with determinate sentences, sentence length and location are related to the severity of the crime and often to the criminal history of the offender. Unlike determinate sentences, however, the judge (who often is responsible for the actual sentence) is expected to assess the offender's potential for rehabilitation and sentence accordingly. These types of sentences are based on the philosophy of rehabilitation and the belief that each offender will take a different amount of time to reform, and the criminal justice system needs the authority to keep each offender as long as necessary to assure that the person who returns to society presents only a minimal risk of reoffending. An obvious problem with this perspective is that judges are not psychologists or psychiatrists and may be unable to predict the length of time an offender will take to reform in prison or jail. Consequently, a common sentence given when this sentencing philosophy was popular was "one year to life." This allowed the institution to hold the inmate until the party in charge of release deemed it appropriate to deliver the offender back into society. The inability to predict the amount of time each inmate would require to reform, shortages of the programs necessary for reform to occur, recalcitrant inmates, and parole boards who were unwilling to release inmates who had not successfully completed these programs eventually led to a backing-up of inmates in prison environments and to crowded conditions of confinement. This philosophy assumes that institutions will be able to assess the problems of an inmate, repair these problems, and determine that these repairs have been successful.

Presumptive Sentences. Presumptive sentences are essentially a hybrid between the determinate and indeterminate policies wherein the state imposes minimum and maximum sentences for a specific crime, and the judge is able to sentence within that range based primarily on the facts of the case, rather than the ability of the offender to reform in the time allotted. Philosophically, presumptive sentences are closer to deterrence than to rehabilitation, in that the range of sentence time is designed to encourage offenders to commit the least damaging crime and receive a lesser sentence. An example would be burglary which might receive a standard sentence of four years in prison, but could realistically receive as little as two and as many as six, based on the facts of the case. Burglars, knowing that carrying a deadly weapon during the commission of a burglary carries a two-year enhancement over the standard sentence, would assumedly choose not to carry a deadly weapon. This would decrease their potential sentence and would doubtless enhance the safety of the public. Two problems exist with the process used in the presumptive sentencing model. The first is that these enhancements are often used as plea-bargain mechanisms and may be more related to coercion than to deterrence. Second, with the advent of habitual-offender and "three-strikes" laws, the crime and the enhancement are less important than the conviction, and therefore these laws may encourage offenders to either fight or flee, or to commit the most serious crime, because any conviction, irrespective of the crime, may result in a life sentence.

RECOMMENDED READING: Andrew R. Klein, *Alternative Sentencing, Intermediate Sanctions, and Probation*, 2nd ed. (Cincinnati: Anderson Publishing Co., 1997); Molly Treadway and Scott A. Gilbert, *The U.S. Sentencing Guidelines: Results of the Federal Judicial Center's 1996 Survey: Report to the Committee on Criminal Law of the Judicial Conference of the United States* (Washington, DC: Federal Judicial Center, 1997).

Matthew C. Leone

SERIAL MURDER. Recently, homicides with multiple victims have drawn increasing attention. Collectively called "multicides," they consist of two subtypes based on time, location, and number of victims. Mass murder refers to several people being killed by (usually) one offender at the same location. (See **Mass Murder**.) Serial murder refers to one offender killing several victims over a long period of time at several different locations, (usually) one by one. These cases are somewhat difficult for law enforcement authorities to deal with because testimony or clues that suggest that a single perpetrator may be operating in widespread geographical locations and/or at various times are elusive and easily missed. Some well-known serial killers are Albert DeSalvo (the Boston Strangler), who in the early 1960s raped and killed thirteen young females, leaving bows around their necks, and Theodore "Ted" Bundy, who admitted to murdering (by strangulation) twenty-eight young women in nine states, raping them before and after they died. Attempts to identify common biological and psychological characteristics of serial killers have been largely unsuccessful. Ronald Holmes and James De Burger identified four main types of serial killers. "Visionary killers" are out of touch with reality and murder at the direction of some inner voice. "Mission-oriented killers" wish to rid the world of some category of undesirables, for example, prostitutes. "Hedonistic killers" receive excitement and pleasure from their acts of murder. "Power/control-oriented killers" are motivated by the complete control they exercise over their victims, whom they can kill at will. Law enforcement officials have suggested that many murders in which the identity of the perpetrator is unknown may actually be the work of serial murderers. It should be mentioned that such cases are rather rare and constitute less than 1 percent of homicide victimizations.

Jeffrey Dahmer was the most prominent serial killer of the early 1990s. He preyed on young gay males in Milwaukee, Wisconsin. After befriending and seducing his victims, Dahmer tortured and killed them. He then carved up their body parts, stored them in his apartment, and sometimes consumed them. One of his seventeen victims was a fifteen-year-old boy, Konerak Sinthasomphone, who was found wandering the streets disoriented, naked, and bleeding. Police officers responding to a citizen's complaint returned Sinthasomphone to Dahmer after the latter convinced them that the boy was his adult homosexual lover. Dahmer was ultimately caught in 1991. Following a sensational trial, he was convicted and was sentenced to sixteen consecutive terms of life imprisonment. He was killed by a fellow inmate in 1994.

RECOMMENDED READING: Steven A. Egger, *The Killers Among Us: Examination of Serial Murder and its Investigation* (Upper Saddle River, NJ: Prentice Hall, 1998); Ronald M. Holmes and James De Burger, *Serial Murder* (Newbury Park, CA: Sage Publications, 1988).

N. Prabha Unnitha

SHERIFF. The office of sheriff arose in old England and predates the invasion of William the Conqueror in 1066. The original sheriffs were "shire reeves" or attendants to earls and kings in the shires (counties). The office was transplanted to the United States, and today the sheriff operates in various capacities in forty-nine states.

In general, sheriffs serve multiple functions as elected officers of the county. These roles are (1) conservator of the peace, (2) jailer, (3) court bailiff, (4) server of civil and criminal process, and (5) collector. These official functions/roles are typically regulated by state constitutions.

According to the National Sheriffs' Association's last survey, there are 3,134 county and independent city sheriffs and county police departments in the United States. The vast majority of these officers are elected, with exceptions in select jurisdictions. The most recent (1993) Law Enforcement Management and Administrative Statistics (LEMAS) show sheriffs employing 226,000 persons, with annual aggregate expenditures of $11.2 billion. About 69 percent of employees are sworn. In forty-three states the sheriff is the primary county law enforcer; in forty-seven states s/he controls county jails; in forty-six states s/he provides court services; and in all states except Alaska s/he is in charge of process service. In three states s/he is still the tax collector.

Popular election is the selection mechanism of choice in all states excepting Hawaii, Rhode Island, and Alaska—which has no sheriffs. Some local jurisdictions within states are also exceptions. This adds an element that is simply not present in other law enforcement and court offices. In the past, the political partisanship of the sheriff was viewed as a liability by many liberal academics, but recently citizens have welcomed the greater accountability and immediate responsiveness they generate in electing the sheriff directly.

In reality, sheriffs have become generally more professional and more law enforcement oriented recently. This improvement is due to the increasing sophistication and availability of communications, transportation, incarceration, and other technologies for sheriffs. Also, in those instances where counties have tampered with consolidation of law enforcement, the sheriff's office has become the central coordination agency. Moreover, the sheriffs have become very well organized and are expanding training and communications at the state and national level.

RECOMMENDED READING: Jason Bollen, *Common-Sense Jail Reform: An Examination of the Jail Policies of Sheriff Joseph Arpaio of Marcopa County, Arizona* (Virginia Beach, VA: Regents University, 1996); David R. Struckhoff, *The American Sheriff* (Chicago: The Justice Research Institute, 1994).

David R. Struckhoff

SILVERTHORNE LUMBER CO., INC. v. UNITED STATES, 251 U.S. 385 (1920). An early extension of the exclusionary rule as applied to the practices of federal law enforcement officials. In this case the Supreme Court held that knowledge gained by the government's wrongful search and seizure of objects may not be used to develop a basis for a legal warrant. Further, the Court held that the Fourth Amendment rights extended to individuals in *Weeks v. United States* (1914) also applied to corporations.

In this case federal officials unlawfully seized records of the Silverthorne Lumber Company. Copies were made of these documents. This material was then used to subpoena the original documents, which were incriminating to the company. The U.S. Supreme Court, speaking through Justice Oliver Wendell Holmes, held that this was not allowable. "The essence of a provision forbidding the acquisition of evidence in a certain way is that not merely evidence so acquired shall not be used before the Court but that it shall not be used at all."

David Jones

SIMPSON, ORENTHAL JAMES "O.J." (1947-   ). Former football star (played for the Buffalo Bills and San Francisco 49ers during the 1970s and 1980s; inducted into the Professional Football Hall of Fame in 1985) and television and movie actor charged with the 1994 murders of ex-wife Nicole Brown Simpson and actor Ronald Goldman. Simpson was acquitted of murder charges during a lengthy and highly publicized 1995 California trial. Simpson was defended by a stable of attorneys referred to by the media as "the dream team," including F. Lee Bailey, Robert Shapiro, and Johnnie Cochran. Prosecuting attorneys included Los Angeles County District Attorney Gil Garcetti and staff members Marcia Clark and Christopher Darden.

The Simpson trial has been referred to as the "trial of the century," and takes it place in the annals of other judicial proceedings with a huge public following, including those involving Nicola Sacco, Bartolomeo Vanzetti,

Bruno Hauptmann, Patty Hearst, and Julius and Ethel Rosenberg. The Simpson trial may well have been the best documented criminal proceeding in the history of the United States (the trial produced more than 40,000 pages of transcribed materials, and countless other pages of commentary and analysis, along with videotaped testimony were associated with the event).

The trial was noteworthy not only for the media coverage it received, but also for the fact that it provided an intense and informative look into the psyche of American society—highlighting divergent attitudes between racial and ethnic groups, the depths of which few had previously suspected.

In 1996 Simpson was found responsible for the deaths of Nicole Brown Simpson and Ronald Goldman in a California civil suit brought by surviving relatives of the deceased. The plaintiffs were awarded $33.5 million in damages, forcing Simpson to the verge of bankruptcy.

RECOMMENDED READING: Frank Schmalleger, *Trial of the Century: People of the State of California vs. Orenthal James Simpson* (Upper Saddle River, NJ: Prentice Hall 1996).

Frank Schmalleger

SLAVE PATROLS. Slave patrols were premodern versions of policing in which laws were enforced in a specific rather than general manner (toward slaves rather than the general public). The patrols were established primarily to prevent slaves from running away or engaging in riots or other uprisings. Rural areas were more likely than urban ones to use patrols to control slaves, but patrols have been documented in nearly all the southern colonies and states from 1704 to the mid-1860s. It has been proposed that the patrols provided a transition between informal and modern policing in much the same manner that citizen watches served to move northern cities from the constable/sheriff standard to adoption of modern uniformed police departments.

Slave patrols generally had the power and authority to enter any plantation and break open slave quarters or other places where slaves might keep weapons; to punish runaways; to whip slaves who caused the patrollers problems as they tried to carry out their duties; and to take to the nearest magistrate any slaves suspected of committing a crime. Administration of the patrols fell to a variety of government authorities ranging from county court justices (North Carolina) and parish judges (Louisiana) to town commissioners (Tennessee) and county boards of supervisors (Mississippi). Several of these entities would eventually supervise formal police organizations that developed in these jurisdictions as enforcement moved from a specific population (slaves) to the general enforcement identified with modern policing.

In 1704 the colony of Carolina (the northern two-thirds of which was divided, in 1712, into North Carolina and South Carolina) enacted the South's first Slave Patrol Act. Militia captains selected ten men to form patrols that would ride from plantation to plantation making sure that slaves were on the plantation to which they belonged and punishing as runaways those slaves who could not prove that they were authorized to be away from their owner's plantation. The South Carolina patrols operated as an alternative to militia duty from 1704 to 1721, then were merged with militia duty from 1721 to 1734. In 1734 separate slave patrols were again authorized, with one patrol established for each of the colony's thirty-three districts. The patrols had elaborate search and seizure powers and could administer up to twenty lashes to slaves they identified as having violated a slave code. Revisions to the 1734 act increased the number of patrollers to fifteen, required patrols to make weekly rounds, and included women plantation owners as obligated to fulfill patrol duty. Few women actually served as patrollers since both male and female owners could hire any white person between age sixteen and sixty to ride patrol for them.

Although they are distasteful reminders of unpleasant history, southern slave patrols are a part of the historical development of policing in the United States. In the slave patrols we see the beginning of such modern police criteria as focused duty (policing alone, rather than with fire watch and/or tax collection), accountability to a government authority, and efforts to prevent, rather than simply control, crime.

RECOMMENDED READING: P. L. Reichel, "Southern Slave Patrols as a Transitional Police Type," *American Journal of Police* 7 (1988): 51–57.

Philip Reichel

SOCIOLOGICAL THEORIES OF CRIME. As social science developed in Europe and the Americas, sociology, a system of thought for explaining collective behaviors and the mutual influence of social factors and variables of individuals emerged as a dominant viewpoint for attempting to explain crime and delinquency. The main schools of sociological inquiry have focused on anomie, learning, strain, social control, and conflict as variables affecting behavior that is deemed criminal. These schools have been developed and argued by many notable scholars; most are mentioned here.

Anomie (normlessness), conceptualized by Emile Durkheim to explain suicide, was taken over by Robert Merton to explain the state of normlessness experienced by people who are unable to employ appropriate means to the espoused goals of the culture. It was also the underlying principle of the eco-logical and Chicago schools, which focused on disorganization. From Merton on, this line of inquiry has evolved into strain theory and been continued by Albert Cohen, Richard Cloward and Lloyd E. Ohlin, and Alden Miller. The object of inquiry is the amount and types of social and cultural pressures that are prevalent in select milieus and their effects upon individuals in society.

Learning theory was introduced by Edwin Sutherland and has come to be known as differential association. Donald Cressey collaborated with Sutherland. Marvin Wolfgang and Franco Ferracutti, Daniel Glaser, and Ron Akers continued this line of inquiry.

Social control theory, originated by Albert Reiss, is the other side of the strain coin, with emphasis on the personal and social control mechanisms that allow individuals to tolerate strains in the culture and society. Walter C. Reckless, Gresham Sykes and David Matza, and Travis Hirschi have continued to elaborate on this trend, and today social control thinking is a dominant theme in criminology.

Conflict is more a perspective than a theory. This view argues that social phenomena may be better understood by assuming that individuals and groups are in varying intensities of conflict rather than in constant agreement or consensus. Thorstin Sellin, George B. Vold, Richard Quinney and Ian Taylor, Paul Walton and Jock Young in England have argued these views forcefully. Conflict thinking has been done in terms of group conflict, on more radical (activist) themes, and from Marxist economic perspectives.

There are a number of emerging perspectives or combinations and permutations of sociological thinking about crime, including feminist views, sociobiology, and synthetic theories that attempt to mesh the varying sociological perspectives and to successfully incorporate the scientific evidence being presented by economics, biology, neurology, psychology, psychiatry, and other fields of scientific analysis of human behavior.

RECOMMENDED READING: Ronald L. Akers, *Social Learning and Social Structure: A General Theory of Crime and Deviance* (Boston: Northeastern University Press, 1997); Stephen E. Brown, Finn-Aage Esbensen and Gilbert Geis, *Criminology: Explaining Crime and its Context*, 2nd ed. (Cincinnati, Ohio: Anderson, 1996); Frank Schmalleger, *Criminology Today* (Upper Saddle River, NJ: Prentice Hall, 1996).

David R. Struckhoff

SOLICITOR GENERAL. One of the top-ranking officials in the Department of Justice, the solicitor general represents the U.S. government before the U.S. Supreme Court. S/he or his/her staff argue most of the federal government's cases before the Supreme Court.

It is the function of the Solicitor General's Office to decide which of the cases in which it is involved the federal government should ask the Supreme Court to review. The office also determines the legal position the government will take in cases that go before the Court. In carrying out the former role, the Solicitor General's Office screens cases carefully. It does not seek *certiorari* in all cases that government agencies want taken before the Supreme Court. In part because of the office's careful screening procedures, when the government submits a case for review, it is far more successful in getting its case accepted than are most types of petitioners (see **Writ of** *Certiorari*).

The position of solicitor general is filled via the process of presidential nomination and senatorial confirmation. Because of the importance of the office, it has been able to attract extremely competent attorneys. Several solicitors general (including Thurgood Marshall, Robert Jackson, and William Howard Taft) have gone on to serve as justices of the U.S. Supreme Court. The solicitor general oversees a relatively small staff of assistant and deputy solicitors general. All of these are career civil servants who are carefully selected for their ability and expertise.

While the solicitor general is appointed by the president (and serves at his pleasure), s/he is also seen as an officer of the Supreme Court. Because of this dual allegiance, the office has some independence from both branches. However, there are tensions in such positions also—how far should the solicitor general go in representing the policy views of the incumbent president before the Supreme Court? Some have argued that the office has become more politicized in recent years. Others disagree with that assessment.

While there are disagreements about the appropriate role of the solicitor general in the American criminal justice system, all serious commentators agree that it is an extremely important one.

RECOMMENDED READING: Lincoln Caplan, *The Tenth Justice* (New York: Random House, 1987); R. M. Salokar, *The Solicitor General: The Politics of Law* (Philadelphia: Temple University Press, 1992).

David Jones

SOUTER, DAVID H. (1939–   ). David Souter was born on September 17, 1939, in Melrose, Massachusetts. He attended Harvard College, Oxford University (as a Rhodes Scholar), and Harvard Law School. Souter rose from assistant attorney general of New Hampshire to deputy attorney general to attorney general. In 1978 he was nominated to the New Hampshire Superior Court. He was elevated to the New Hampshire Supreme Court in 1983.

President Bush nominated Souter to the U.S. court of appeals in 1990 and to the Supreme Court three months later. (Souter had good support from White House Chief of Staff and former New Hampshire governor John Sununu and New Hampshire senator Warren Rudman.) He was called a "stealth candidate "because he had a limited public record on controversial social and constitutional issues.

Souter is a centrist on the Court. He lacks a personal agenda, has respect for precedents, and does case-by-case balancing. He favors prosecutors and resists reversal of criminal convictions. He does the hard work of original historical research.

RECOMMENDED READING: John F. Brigdon, "Justice Souter's Import on the Supreme Court's Criminal Procedure Jurisprudence," *American Criminal Law Review*, Vol. 29, no. 1 (Fall 1991): 133–168; Paul Deegan, *David Souter* (Minneapolis, MN: Abdo and Daughters, 1992); William S. Jordan, "Justice David Souter and Statutory Interpretation," *The University of Toledo Law Review*, Vol. 23, no. 3 (Spring 1992): 491–530; David K. Koehler, "Justice Souter's 'Keep-What-You-Want-and-Throw-Away-the-Rest' Interpretation of

Stare Decisis," *Buffalo Law Review*, Vol. 42, no. 1 (Winter 1994): 859–892.

Martin Gruberg

SPEEDY TRIAL, RIGHT TO. The belief that the speedy disposition of criminal cases is fundamental to justice predates the Magna Carta. The right to a speedy trial is one of the guarantees found in the Sixth Amendment to the U.S. Constitution. This right is supplemented (at least in theory) by the Speedy Trial Act of 1974, which provides that a federal trial must begin no more than seventy days after the filing of an information or indictment or from the date the defendant appears before an officer of the court in which the charge is pending, whichever is later.

Among the reasons for this right are the avoidance of lengthy pretrial incarceration, avoidance of anxiety associated with a public accusation, and avoidance of delay that may increase the difficulty for the defendant of mounting a strong defense. The Sixth Amendment right to a speedy trial was first applied to state action in the case of *Klopfer v. North Carolina*, 386 U.S. 213 (1967).

Like many other constitutional rights, the Sixth Amendment right to a speedy trial has raised many specific issues for final determination by the Supreme Court. One of these concerns timing—when does the right begin to take effect? The Court has held that the right will come into play only after a formal accusation has been lodged against the defendant. Therefore, if a potential defendant is under suspicion for having committed a crime, even for many years, s/he cannot invoke the Sixth Amendment if the trial proceeds soon after a formal accusation is lodged.

The Supreme Court has developed criteria for determining whether a defendant's right to a speedy trial has been violated in a particular case. It has established a four-pronged test: (1) the length of the delay (the Court has set no specific time limit); (2) the reasons for the delay (to what degree was the defendant responsible for the delay);   (3) whether the defendant promptly asserted his/her right to a speedy trial; and (4) the amount of prejudice suffered by the defendant because of the delay. The Court has refused to give specific weight to any of these factors, but has held that they must be examined together to determine whether excessive delay has occurred. The Court has held that if a determination is made that the defendant's rights to a speedy trial have been violated, the defendant's remedy is that charges will be dismissed.

Under the provisions of the Speedy Trial Act, if the government does not meet the statutory time limits, a trial judge may dismiss the charges either "with prejudice" (in which case charges may not be reinstituted) or "without prejudice" (which allows charges to be reinstated). It appears that in most cases where charges have been dismissed under the act, they have been dismissed without prejudice. Moreover, the act also provides for many exceptions to the time limit imposed. For instance, if the defendant asks for a delay, that delay is not considered part of the seventy days included in the limitation. Commentators have suggested that because of these provisions, the act does not appear to have met its goal of speeding up the trial process.

RECOMMENDED READING: Alfredo Garcia, *The Sixth Amendment in Modern American Jurisprudence: A Critical Perspective* (New York: Greenwood Press, 1992); *Klopfer v. North Carolina*, 386 U. S. 213 (1967); Steven M. Wernikoff, "Sixth Amendment—Extending Sixth Amendment Speedy Trial Protection to Defendants Unaware of Their Indictments," *Journal of Criminal Law and Criminology* 83 (1993): 804–835.

David Jones

STANDING MUTE. A defendant facing criminal prosecution may refuse to enter a plea, an action which is referred to as "standing mute." A defendant who stands mute will find that the presiding judicial officer (usually a judge or magistrate) will enter a plea of "not guilty" on his or her behalf. (See **Pleas**.)

RECOMMENDED READING: Joseph R. Nolan and Jacqueline M. Nolan-Haley, *Black's Law Dictionary: Definitions of the Terms and Phrases of American and English Jurisprudence, Ancient and Modern*, 6th ed. (St. Paul, MN: West Publishing Co., 1991).

STARE DECISIS. A Latin term meaning "let the decision stand." It is the doctrine, generally followed in Anglo-American law, that courts are expected to follow precedent when deciding cases. (See **Precedent**.)

RECOMMENDED READING: Joseph R. Nolan and Jacqueline M. Nolan-Haley, *Black's Law Dictionary: Definitions of the Terms and Phrases of American and English Jurisprudence, Ancient and Modern*, 6th ed. (St. Paul, MN: West Publishing Co., 1991).

David Jones

STATE COURT SYSTEMS. Under the American system of federalism each state has its own system of courts. The jurisdiction of these courts is determined by the laws (civil and criminal) and constitution of each individual state. Because most criminal law in the United States is state law, most criminal cases in this country are processed by state courts.

In part because of the diversity inherent in federalism, there is a significant amount of variation among state court systems. One source of variation is in the organization and finance of the different court systems. A few sparsely populated states have a system of trial courts of general jurisdiction and a court of last resort (usually, but not always, called the state supreme court). A growing number of state systems include trial courts of general jurisdiction, intermediate appellate courts, and a court of last resort. Many, though not all, states also contain specialized courts. Montana, for instance, provides for a Water Court, while Tennessee contains a Chancery Court. Texas has two courts of last resort, one criminal and one civil. States also vary in how they finance their court systems. In some states the court system is totally funded by the state; in others, counties and municipalities fund court functions.

State court systems also vary in the procedures by which judges are chosen. In most states (unlike the federal system) the voters play an important formal role in the selection of judges. Most state judges have to face the electorate at some point in their career. However, the type of electoral system used varies. In some states judges are selected through partisan elections; candidates run as Republicans or Democrats. In others the elections are nonpartisan.

A growing trend among states is toward adoption of a merit selection, or "Missouri plan," system. In this system, when a vacancy occurs, a nominating commission (usually selected by the state's governor) chooses three nominees; the governor will then select one of these; the individual thus selected will serve for a period of time. After the term is completed, the sitting judge will run in an election in which the voters are asked to respond yes or no to the question "should judge X continue in office?" If the voters respond affirmatively (which happens most of the time), the judge continues for another term. If the voters respond negatively, a vacancy is declared and the process starts again. Other states use other variations of selection procedures. There is a substantial amount of controversy concerning the relative desirability of the different selection procedures.

State systems also vary in levels of "judicial activism." In some states the general norm is that the courts should defer to the other branches of state government and should adhere closely to precedent, that is, that courts should follow norms of "judicial restraint." In other states (e.g., California and New Jersey) there is a stronger tradition of judicial activism and innovation. In these states the courts (particularly the state supreme courts) are more likely to declare state laws unconstitutional and to overrule precedent. In a related fashion, some state supreme courts have higher levels of prestige than others. Courts in other states often cite their decisions.

In addition to variations among state court systems, there are also important similarities. All state court systems are, of course, constrained by relevant portions of the U.S. Constitution. Moreover, all states (with the possible exception of Louisiana) rely on basic traditions found in Anglo-American law. Finally, all court systems play a significant role in the policy-making arena in their respective states. They are important components of each state's criminal justice and political system.

RECOMMENDED READING: *State Court Organization, 1996* (Washington, DC: United States Department of Justice, 1997); Harry P. Stumpf and John H. Culver, *The Politics of State Courts* (New York: Longman Publishing Group, 1992); G. Alan Tarr and Mary Cornelia Aldis Porter, *State Supreme Courts in State and Nation* (New Haven: Yale University Press, 1988).

David Jones

STATUS OFFENSE. An offense that is defined as such because of the status of the individual who commits that offense; for example, in the case of a legal child, his/her age may make him/her an offender. Offenses that are considered inappropriate for children, but a matter of judgment for adults, are typically considered to be status offenses. Historically, status offenses have included smoking, truancy, drinking, running away from home, cussing, being sexually active, disobeying parents, being incorrigible, and being ungovernable.

Since the juvenile court was created, status offenses committed by children have been a main concern of the court. In many states status offenses were part of or quickly added to the list of offenses falling under the juvenile court jurisdiction. Just two years after the Juvenile Court Act of 1899 created the first juvenile court in Illinois, the act of May 11, 1901 added incorrigibility and "growing up in idleness or crime" to the list of behaviors falling under the jurisdiction of the juvenile court, and six years later the act of June 4, 1907 added running away from home, loitering, and using profane language. The court, having been created in a *parens patriae* capacity and acting as a surrogate parent to the troubled child, had no hesitancy in considering these behaviors by children as worthy of court attention and intervention. Thus status offenses and those children who committed them—status offenders—were considered under juvenile court jurisdiction and handled through the juvenile court well into the 1960s.

During the 1960s and 1970s the juvenile justice system came under much scrutiny. There was concern about the power that the system held over juveniles, and whether or not the initial rehabilitative goals of serving in the best interests of the child were being fulfilled. One area of concern was the treatment of status offenders, nonserious youth who were treated in the system, in many instances, as delinquent youth. Juvenile court practices and conditions of confinement were two major areas of review. During this time frame there were reforms designed to deal specifically with the issues of status offenders and juvenile court jurisdiction. The major reform act, the Juvenile Justice and Delinquency Prevention Act of 1974 (JJDPA), specifically targeted juvenile status offenders in one of its three main mandates. First, the act called for the treatment of status offenders to become that of children requiring special help by the juvenile court, much as dependent and neglected children would, and for them no longer to be treated as a delinquent child might be by the juvenile court. The second mandate was the removal of juveniles (including status offenders) from adult jails; and the third was the creation of community–based treatment programs to lessen the use of juvenile facilities such as detention centers and state training schools (including their use for status offenders).

Thus began an argument that still rages today: Should juvenile status-offender jurisdiction be eliminated from the jurisdiction of the juvenile court altogether and delegated to a more social service agency? Many states are unable or unwilling to do so, but other states have changed the distinction of the status offender by changing the legal terminology. In many states juvenile status offenders now are found in need of supervision (not as an adjudicated delinquent) and are labeled CHINS or CINS (child in need of supervision), MINS (minor in need of supervision), or JINS (juvenile in need of supervision). Legally, this places status offenders in a different category from juvenile delinquents and prevents the institutionalization of status offenders with delinquents in juvenile correctional facilities. What a state does with status offenders depends greatly on that state's individual resources and juvenile justice philosophy. For example, in Washington State, the juvenile court was redesigned in 1977 to resemble a miniature adult court. Jurisdiction over status offenders was removed from the juvenile court totally and redirected. Maine also has complete decriminalization of status offenders by statute. Most states, however, have redefined the status offender, have retained the status offender in juvenile court, and continue to support noninstitutionalization of status offenders with delinquent youth.

In addition, many states have had to redefine status offenses in the eyes of their juvenile or family code. Many states try to limit the vague areas of "incorrigibility" and "ungovernability" and stick with definable offenses such as running away from home and being absent from school. In sum, this is a controversial area and one of current debate in the juvenile justice system. There are many seemingly good arguments both in favor of keeping juvenile status offenders under the juvenile court and in decriminalization of status offenders and removal from juvenile court jurisdiction. As more states move toward tougher juvenile laws to deal with violent and serious juvenile offenders, the question of what to do with status offenders will continue to be asked, and the answers will continue to be debated.

RECOMMENDED READING: Barbara Flicker, "A Short History of Jurisdiction over Juvenile and Family Matters" in *From Children to Citizens*, Vol. 2: *The Role of the Juvenile Court*, ed. Francis X. Hartman (New York: Springer-Verlag, 1987).

Frances P. Reddington

STEVENS, JOHN PAUL (1920–   ). Associate Justice of the U.S. Supreme Court, born in Chicago, Illinois, on April 20, 1920. He married Maryan Mulholland Simon and has four children: John Joseph, Kathryn Stevens Jedlicka, Elizabeth Jane Sesemann, and Susan Roberta Mullen.

Justice Stevens received an A.B. from the University of Chicago in 1941 and a J. D. from Northwestern University School of Law in 1947. He served in the United States Navy from 1942 to 1945, and was a law clerk to Justice Wiley Rutledge of the U.S. Supreme Court during the 1947–1948 Term. He was admitted to law practice in Illinois in 1949.

Justice Stevens was Associate Counsel to the Subcommittee on the Study of Monopoly Power of the Judiciary Committee of the United States House of Representatives (1951–1952, and a member of the U.S. Attorney General's

National Committee to Study Anti-trust Law (1953–1955). From 1970 to 1975 he served as a judge of the United States Court of Appeals for the Seventh Circuit. Following nomination by President Ford, he took his seat as an Associate Justice of the U.S. Supreme Court on December 19, 1975.

Frank Schmalleger

SUBSTANTIAL CAPACITY TEST. One of the standards used to define legal insanity. Under this standard a person is held not to be legally responsible for his/her act if s/he lacked "substantial capacity" to appreciate (i.e., know intellectually or effectively) the wrongfulness of his/her conduct or to conform the conduct to the requirements of law. The American Law Institute first proposed this standard in 1953 as part of its proposed Model Legal Code.

This test can be seen as a combination of the M'Naghten rule and the "irresistible impulse" test. As such, it is one of the least restrictive tests used in the United States. It is also widely used, having been adopted by more than half the states. It was also used by the federal government prior to the passage of the Insanity Defense Reform Act of 1984.

RECOMMENDED READING: Lincoln Caplan, *The Insanity Defense and the Trial of John W. Hinckley, Jr.* (Boston: David R. Godine, 1984); Rita J. Simon and David E. Aaronson, *The Insanity Defense: A Critical Assessment of Law and Policy in the Post-Hinckley Era* (New York: Praeger, 1988).

David Jones

SUPERIOR COURTS. These are also called courts of general trial jurisdiction. Superior courts are courts that hear, in the first instance, virtually all types of cases (both criminal and civil) regardless of the importance of the case, the parties involved, or the type of case. Superior courts may also hear an appeal from courts of limited jurisdiction (sometimes called inferior courts) in the form of "trial *de novo*." (see **Trial** *DE Novo*.)

RECOMMENDED READING: *State Court Organization, 1996* (Washington, DC: U. S. Department of Justice, 1997); N. Gary Holten and Lawson L. Lamar, *The Criminal Courts: Structures, Personnel, and Processes* (New York: McGraw-Hill, 1991).

David Jones

T

TESTIMONIAL PRIVILEGE. Privileges that allow an individual to refuse to disclose, or to prevent another from disclosing, certain types of information at trial. These are considered privileges, not rights, and are based on society's decision that some relationships are very important, and that assured confidentiality strengthens them. Their importance in society's eyes is such that their preservation takes precedence over the truth-finding function of a trial.

Some privileges are grounded in common law, while others are based on statute. Jurisdictions vary in terms of which privileges they grant and how they define these privileges. One of the most common privileges is the marital privilege. In some states (and in the federal rules of procedure) the privilege attaches to the witness-spouse, while in others it attaches to the defendant-spouse. In some jurisdictions it may stay in force only as long as the marriage does. That is, in some states divorced people cannot invoke the privilege even if it relates to communications that took place while the marriage was in force.

Other common privileges involve confidential communications between attorney and client (which attach to the client), physician-patient relationships (which have many exceptions), certain clergy-penitent communications, and those between a reporter and his/her sources. Further, in many situations (i.e., when an informant was only used to gain information sufficient to establish probable cause) the name of a government informant need not be revealed.

As in the assertion of certain rights (e.g., against self-incrimination), a prosecutor cannot comment on the invocation of privileges. Like rights, the party to whom the privilege attaches may voluntarily waive privileges. Because the invocation of a privilege can mean that important information may not be brought into trial, privileges are usually construed narrowly by the courts.

RECOMMENDED READING: John C. Klotter, *Criminal Evidence*, 6th ed. (Cincinnati: Anderson Publishing, 1996); Jon R. Waltz, *Introduction to Criminal Evidence*, 4th ed. (Chicago: Nelson Hall Publishers, 1997).

David Jones

THEFT. Theft is stealing, taking, carrying, leading, or driving away the personal property of another without right or permission, or fraudulently appropriating property that has been entrusted to the perpetrator. It includes defrauding, by any false or fraudulent representation or pretense, any other person of money, labor, real property, or personal property. It also includes obtaining credit, money, property, or the labor or services of another by causing or procuring others to falsely report the perpetrator's wealth or financial character.

RECOMMENDED READING: Joseph R. Nolan and Jacqueline M. Nolan-Haley, *Black's Law Dictionary: Definitions of the Terms and Phrases of American and English Jurisprudence, Ancient and Modern*, 6th ed. (St. Paul, MN: West Publishing Co., 1991).

Lee E. Parker

THOMAS, CLARENCE (1948–   ). Clarence Thomas was born on June 23, 1948, in Pin Point, Georgia. He attended Holy Cross College and Yale Law School, then served as a Missouri assistant attorney general under John Danforth. When Danforth became a U.S. senator, Thomas joined his staff. In 1981–1982 he was an assistant secretary in the Department of Education. From 1982 to 1989 he headed the Equal Employment Opportunity Commission. President Bush nominated Thomas to the court of appeals, then nominated him to succeed Thurgood Marshall on the Supreme Court in 1991.

The nomination became controversial. Thomas was a natural-law conservative who opposed affirmative action. Some blacks supported his appointment so as not to lose their slot on the Supreme Court. Others opposed him because of his ideology. When Anita Hill accused Thomas of sexual harassment, the Senate and the country divided regarding whom to believe. Despite the opposition, he was narrowly confirmed.

Thomas is the most conservative member of the Court. He votes with Rehnquist and Scalia. When these three are joined by Kennedy and O'Connor to make a majority, the two centrists often write separate opinions to distance themselves from the other three justices' reasoning.

RECOMMENDED READING: Norman L. Macht, *Clarence Thomas* (New York: Chelsea House Publishers, 1995); Paul Simon, *Advice and Consent: Clarence Thomas, Robert Bork, and the Intriguing History of the Supreme Court's Nomination Battles* (Washington, DC: National Press Books, 1992).

Martin Gruberg

TRANSPORTATION. One technique of social control is to give someone else your troublemakers. The first example of this "out of sight, out of mind" philosophy was the practice of banishment, in which villagers expelled wrongdoers from the community. Similarly, transportation served to remove criminals to a place where they could do no harm. But while banishment had little economic benefit for the sending village, other than being a cheap method of social control, transportation had definite economic advantages.

Over the centuries many countries have transported their criminals to faraway places. France (to French Guiana), Russia (to Siberia), Italy (to islands off the Tuscan coast), and Chile and Ecuador (to islands in the Pacific) each has a history of transportation. But the country attracting the most attention when transportation is discussed has been England.

England began using transportation of criminals in 1598 when officials decided to ship some offenders off to the American colonies where labor was lacking. Transportation to the American colonies continued in an informal manner until the late seventeenth and early eighteenth centuries when acts of Parliament began making it an official aspect of England's punishment system. Especially important was the Transportation Act of 1718, which had as its stated purpose to deter criminals and supply the colonies with labor. The second purpose was more clearly accomplished than the first. The ships' captains charged with transporting the criminals from England were allowed to contract for the rights to the convicts' labor. The captains, who could transfer that right to another person, auctioned prisoners off to the highest bidder after the ships arrived in the colonies. The transportees became indentured servants, and the British government gave up all responsibility for them. Historians estimate that some 50,000 prisoners were transported to the American colonies before 1775. Almost all the American colonies except those in New England received some convicts at some time. Most, however, went to Maryland and Virginia, where agriculture was more labor intensive.

Not surprisingly, some American colonists were unhappy with the transportation policy. Maryland tried unsuccessfully to banish it in 1676, but in 1722 Pennsylvania prohibited the receiving of transported criminals. A year later Virginia did the same. Finally, in 1775 the American Revolution brought a halt to England's dumping of its convicts on American shores. But the British, undaunted and patient, did not have to wait long to find another grouping of colonies in need of labor.

Transportation of criminals to the British colonies in Australia occurred over a shorter time than it did to the American colonies, but it involved considerably more criminals. The first convict ship from England landed in 1788 at Sydney Cove in Australia. By 1868, when the last ship dropped off the final transportee, about 160,000 convicts had been transported to Australia.

Most criminals transported to Australia were habitual offenders, with the most common convictions being for crimes against property. Crimes for which transportation was a possible punishment, although it could also substitute for a death sentence, included grand larceny, buying or receiving stolen goods, stealing letters, stealing fish from a pond, and assault with intent to rob. Both men and women were among the transportees, at least until 1851, when the transportation of women ended. During the entire transportation period about

15 percent of the transportees were women, typically in their teens and early twenties, but there was considerable variation over the years. The percentage of women was especially high during the first decade of the 1800s, when more than 80 percent of all convicts transported were women (50 percent from Ireland and another 30 percent from Great Britain), but fell to less than 20 percent of all transportees in the 1820s.

Unlike the convicts transported to the American colonies, those sent to Australia remained prisoners rather than becoming indentured servants. However, the penal colony governors in Australia could "assign" a convict to a free settler who would put the prisoner to work (essentially forced prostitution for many female convicts) and accepted the responsibility of providing for the laborer's food and shelter.

Following the history of their American counterparts, the Australian colonists expressed increased displeasure with the system of transportation. Transportation to the eastern colonies (the ones most populated) was abolished in 1852, and the new arrivals were sent instead to Western Australia. In 1868 the last of the British convict transportees was dropped off in Australia, and the British government began relying on other methods of social control.

RECOMMENDED READING: "Convicts in Australia," in *Australians: A Historical Atlas*, ed. J. C. R. Camm and J. McQuilton, (Broadway, New South Wales, Australia: Fairfax, Syme & Weldon Associates, 1987): 200–201; R. Hughes, *The Fatal Shore* (New York: Alfred A. Knopf, 1987); E. O'Brien, *The Foundation of Australia* (1786–1800) (Westport, CT: Greenwood Press, 1970); original work published in 1937); A. G. L. Shaw, *Convicts and the Colonies* (London: Faber and Faber, 1966).

Philip Reichel

TREASON. Treason occurs when anyone owing allegiance to the United States levies war against the United States or adheres to enemies thereof, or gives said enemies aid or comfort within the United States or elsewhere. Treason is usually prosecuted under federal law. However, states also have similar treason statutes.

RECOMMENDED READING: Nathan Aaseng, *Treacherous Traitors* (Minneapolis, MN: Oliver Press, 1997); Joseph R. Nolan and Jacqueline M. Nolan-Haley, *Black's Law Dictionary: Definitions of the Terms and Phrases of American and English Jurisprudence, Ancient and Modern*, 6th ed. (St. Paul, MN: West Publishing Co., 1991).

Lee E. Parker

TRIAL. Once preliminary legal issues in a case have been decided by the judge, the search for an answer to the fact question takes place in the form of the trial. A defendant has a right under the federal and state constitutions to a trial by jury, but the defendant may waive such right. If s/he does, the trial judge will also be the trier of fact in what is termed a bench trial as opposed to a jury trial. The jury trial commences with the selection and swearing in of the jurors. After instructions to the jury by the judge, opening statements are made and the prosecutor presents his/her case. Each witness presented is subject to cross-examination by defense counsel. The defendant may then put on his/her case. His/her witnesses are subject to cross-examination by the prosecutor. Each party may then give a summation to the jury. The judge then instructs the jurors as to their deliberations. The jury then retires to the jury room to consider the evidence presented at trial in order to attempt to reach a verdict. The verdict is presented in open court and consists of some finding of guilt or innocence on the various charges against the defendant. If the jurors cannot agree upon a verdict, they so inform the judge, who declares a mistrial. (Some jurisdictions require a unanimous verdict in criminal cases, while others only require the majority of jurors to agree upon a verdict. See **Deadlocked Jury; Verdict**.) The defendant possesses the constitutional right to remain silent and is under no obligation to do anything or present any evidence at trial. The burden of proof of guilt always remains with the prosecutor.

Two different systems of justice are found in the world. The adversarial system of justice is followed in the United States and Canada, as opposed to the inquisitorial system found in other nations. Significant differences between the two lead to fundamental differences in the protection afforded individual rights.

The adversarial system gives each side a strong incentive to expose the other's shortcomings. It pits the state against the accused in a contest to see which of them can convince a neutral fact-finder that their version of events is the truth. Under the adversarial system the accused is presumed innocent until proven guilty beyond a reasonable doubt. The burden of proof always resides with the government. The accused may not be compelled to be a witness against him/herself, and no inference of guilt may be made from the fact that the accused did not testify in his/her own defense.

In the inquisitorial system there is no presumption of innocence. The accused bears the burden of proving his/her innocence and may be compelled to give testimony. The protection afforded individual rights under the two systems is clearly different.

In order to convict a defendant of a criminal offense at trial, the government prosecutor must prove two facts beyond a reasonable doubt: (1) that a violation of the criminal (substantive) law of the state occurred; and (2) that the defendant (accused) is the one who committed the violation. Evidence of these facts constitutes the prosecutor's case in chief. These are the two ultimate facts that the trier of fact (the jury in a jury trial) must determine. The criminal trial, the most visible part of the criminal justice process, is just that: only a part of the process involved in criminal actions and proceedings.

If the defendant is found not guilty, charges are dismissed and the defendant is free to go. If the jurors cannot agree on a verdict, they will be discharged from duty and the defendant may be remanded to custody or released on bail or recognizance to await a new trial. If the verdict is guilty, the judge will set an adjourned date for sentencing.

RECOMMENDED READING: Irving J. Klein, *Principles of the Law of Arrest, Search, Seizure, and Liability Issues* (South Miami, FL: Coral Gables Publishing Co., 1994); Joseph R. Nolan and Jacqueline M. Nolan-Haley, *Black's Law Dictionary: Definitions of the Terms and Phrases of American and English Jurisprudence, Ancient and Modern*, 6th ed. (St. Paul, MN. West Publishing Co., 1991).

Christopher J. Morse

TRIAL *DE NOVO.* A new trial that takes place when a defendant who has been tried in a court of limited jurisdiction seeks to appeal his/her case to acourt of general jurisdiction. Generally, courts of limited jurisdiction are not "courts of record." That is, transcripts are not made of proceedings held in these courts. Therefore, when a case is appealed to a court of general jurisdiction, the trial must be conducted all over again, with witnesses being called and the entire trial process being followed. Some commentators see this process as a wasteful one.

RECOMMENDED READING: Joseph R. Nolan and Jacqueline M. Nolan-Haley, *Black's Law Dictionary: Definitions of the Terms and Phrases of American and English Jurisprudence, Ancient and Modern*, 6th ed. (St. Paul, MN: West Publishing Co., 1991).

David Jones

TRIAL MOTIONS. A motion is an application for a court order, typically made by an attorney before a judge, requesting that the judge make a favorable ruling on a legal issue in the case. It is expected that the motion be in writing, that it state the grounds (or basis) for the requested action, and that it specify the relief sought. A motion can be submitted at any time during the legal processing of a defendant, that is before, during, or after the actual trial.

Pretrial motions are usually made at, or shortly after, the arraignment. They may be used by the defendant to request that the judge dismiss the charge on various legal grounds, suppress evidence believed to have been illegally seized, change the trial venue (the location in which the trial is conducted), or to order a separate trial. The motion must be made in writing within specified time limits and must be decided by the court on the basis of information in the request and the prosecutor's response to the request. If the judge cannot decide on the basis of this information, s/he will order a hearing held on the motion.

The hearing will usually be done by a hearing officer. The rules of evidence must be followed and a record made of witnesses and testimony offered at the hearing. This information and the hearing officer's recommendation are placed in a report to the judge. The judge must then decide the motion.

Posttrial motions may be made by the defendant's attorney following criminal trials wherein a verdict of guilty is announced. Potential posttrial motions include a "motion in arrest of judgment" to set aside the verdict. In this motion the judge is asked to overrule the jury's verdict and dismiss the charges. Grounds for such a motion may include the allegation that the court lacks jurisdiction in the case at hand, that the evidence presented was not sufficient to convict, or on a claim of double jeopardy. Another is a "motion for new trial," in which counsel asks that his/her client be retried either because of legal errors committed prior to or at trial, or because of "after-discovered" evidence, that is, important evidence that became available to the defendant only after completion of the trial that could not have been expected to have been discovered prior to the trial.

The use of motions allows the defense attorney to raise legal issues that may serve as a basis for the appeal of the finding of guilt. In many jurisdictions the filing of post-verdict motions is a necessary prerequisite to any appellate court review. Decisions on motions resolve questions of law and serve to structure the trial. In criminal actions there are two types of questions that must be resolved: questions of law and questions of fact. Legal questions are answered by the judge and fact questions by the trier of fact, (the jury in a jury trial; the judge in a bench trial). The ultimate fact question to be decided is the guilt or innocence of the defendant.

A defendant not filing an appeal may, if s/he is sentenced to imprisonment or ordered to pay a fine, within appropriate time limits move that the court modify the sentence or the amount of the fine.

RECOMMENDED READING: David F. Herr, Roger S. Haydock, and Jeffrey W. Stempel, *Motion Practice* (Boston: Little, Brown and Co., 1985); Minnesota Institute of Legal Education, *Effective and Efficient Motion Practice* (Minneapolis: The Institute, 1996); Jonathan D. Schiffman, *Fundamentals of the Criminal Justice Process*, 3rd ed. (Deerfield, IL: Clark Boardman Callaghan, 1994); Jon R. Waltz, *Introduction to Criminal Evidence*, 4th ed. (Chicago: Nelson Hall Publishers, 1997).

David Jones

U

UNITED STATES v. KARO, **468 U.S. 705 (1984).** A case involving the relationship between the Fourth Amendment prohibition against "unreasonable searches and seizures" and electronic surveillance. In this case a divided U.S. Supreme Court held that the monitoring of a beeper in a private residence, a location not open to visual surveillance, violates the Fourth Amendment rights of those who have a justifiable interest in the privacy of the residence.

An informant, working with federal drug agents, installed an electronic beeper on a can of ether sold to defendants. The ether was to be used to extract cocaine from clothing, after which the cocaine was to be sold on the streets. Because the beeper had been installed and because it was being monitored, agents were able to follow it as it was moved from place to place. Eventually it was taken to defendant's house. Agents then got a search warrant, entered the house, and seized the cocaine. Defendants were charged and convicted.

The Court held that the installation of the beeper violated no one's Fourth Amendment rights, but that monitoring it did. If the monitoring was critical to establishing probable cause for the issuance of the warrant, the warrant would be tainted and hence invalid. But, since there was other untainted evidence presented to establish probable cause, the warrant was valid. Consequently, the Court held, the evidence seized in the house should not have been suppressed.

David Jones

UNITED STATES v. MONTOYA DE HERNANDEZ, **473 U.S. 531 (1985).** A case involving the standards for detaining a traveler beyond routine customs searches at the border who is suspected of smuggling contraband (usually drugs) in his/her alimentary canal. In this case a divided U.S. Supreme Court ruled that such a detention is justified if customs agents, considering all relevant facts, reasonably suspect that the traveler is smuggling contraband in his/her alimentary canal.

The facts of the case before the Court were that Montoya de Hernandez was detained at the Los Angeles International Airport on a flight from Colombia by customs officials who suspected her of being a "balloon swallower," a person who tries to smuggle narcotics into the United States in his/her alimentary canal. Montoya de Hernandez was detained without being allowed to speak to a lawyer or anybody else for about sixteen hours. During this time she was given the option of returning to Colombia, agreeing to an X-ray, or remaining in detention until she produced a monitored bowel movement. While she agreed to the first option, it turned out that this was not available. She resisted the X-ray because she maintained that she was pregnant, and she refused to use the toilet facilities. After sixteen hours a customs agent obtained a court order for a pregnancy test (which proved negative) and a rectal examination that resulted in the obtaining of eighty-eight cocaine-filled balloons that had been smuggled in the defendant's alimentary canal.

Montoya de Hernandez moved for suppression of the contraband as evidence, but the district court admitted it. The court of appeals reversed, holding that the detention violated respondent's Fourth Amendment rights. A majority of the Supreme Court, over the spirited dissent of Justices William Brennan and Thurgood Marshall, disagreed. The Court's majority ruled that under the circumstances the customs agents had reasonable suspicion to detain Montoya de Hernandez. Moreover, it decided, while respondent's detention was long, uncomfortable, and humiliating, it was not unreasonably long. This was true in large part because both the length of respondent's detention and its discomfort resulted solely from the method she chose to smuggle illegal drugs into the United States.

David Jones

U.S. v. RABINOWITZ, 339 U.S. 56 (1950). A federal case in which the Supreme Court held that a search incident to a legal arrest of a place of business consisting of a one-room office without a search warrant was not unreasonable under the Fourth Amendment. The probability that the officers had time to procure a search warrant in this case did not mandate that they do so.

In this case federal agents, possessing a valid arrest warrant but no search warrant, arrested Rabinowitz in his place of business, a one-room office, and searched the desk, safe, and filing cabinets in the office, where they found incriminating materials. Evidence gained from this search was used as evidence in Rabinowitz's conviction. Rabinowitz appealed, arguing that the search of his office was unreasonable under the Fourth Amendment.

A majority of the Court disagreed, holding, in this case, that the search and seizure were reasonable because they were incident to a valid arrest; the place of the search was a business room, to which the public was invited; the room was small and under the immediate and complete control of the defendant; the search did not extend beyond the room used for unlawful purposes; and the possession of the materials seized was a crime. The Court's holding in *United States v. Rabinowitz*, as it related to the scope of a search incident to a legal arrest, was severely restricted in the subsequent case of *Chimel v. California* (1969). (See *Chimel v. California*).

David Jones

UNITED STATES v. SOKOLOW, 490 U.S. 1 (1989). A refinement of the concept of "reasonable suspicion" first articulated by the U.S. Supreme Court in the case of *Terry v. Ohio* (1968). The Court held in *Sokolow* that a "totality of circumstances" test, rather than more specific tests, should be used to determine if "reasonable suspicion" does exist to detain a defendant.

In this case defendant, Andrew Sokolow, using an assumed name and paying cash (in twenty-dollar bills) bought round-trip tickets between Hawaii and Florida and stayed in Florida for only two days before returning to Hawaii. He was stopped on his return by Drug Enforcement Administration (DEA) agents, who, while defendant was trying to hail a cab, grabbed him by the arm. His luggage was examined by a narcotics detector dog, and, based on the dog's reaction, a warrant was obtained. In their search agents found 1,063 grams of cocaine in the defendant's luggage.

Sokolow contended that he should not have been stopped because DEA agents did not have a reasonable suspicion to detain him. The circuit court denied Sokolow's motion, but was overruled by the court of appeals, which, applying its version of reasonable suspicion, held that it did not exist. Hence the detention was illegal.

The Supreme Court overruled the court of appeals in a 7-2 decision, arguing that the determination of whether reasonable suspicion applies should be based on a "totality of circumstances" test. Under this test, the Court held, the agents had a reasonable suspicion that Sokolow was transporting illegal drugs. Hence their detention of the defendant and other actions following that detention were legal.

David Jones

UNITED STATES v. VILLAMONTE-MARQUEZ, 462 U.S. 579 (1983). A search and seizure case involving vessels in U.S. waters. In this case the U.S. Supreme Court held that the boarding of a vessel in such waters by law enforcement officials, even though they do not have reasonable suspicion of a law violation, does not violate search and seizure provisions of the Fourth Amendment. Therefore, contraband seized as the result of such a boarding need not be excluded as evidence in a case against the defendant.

U.S. law authorizes customs officers to board any vessel at any time and at any place in the United States to examine the vessel's manifest and other documents. Customs officers, while patrolling a shipping lane near Louisiana, sighted an anchored sailboat. The wake of a passing vessel caused the boat to rock violently, and when one of the respondents aboard the vessel shrugged his shoulders in an unresponsive manner when asked if the vessel and crew were all right, one of the customs officers boarded the sailboat and asked to see the vessel's documentation. While examining the document, the official discovered marijuana in the hold of the boat. Respondents were then arrested and given their *Miranda* warnings, and a subsequent search revealed more marijuana in the vessel. Respondents were tried and convicted of various drug offenses in federal district court, but the court of appeals overturned the conviction, holding that the officers' boarding of the sailboat violated the Fourth Amendment because the boarding occurred in the absence of "reasonable suspicion of a law violation."

Justice William Rehnquist, writing in a 6–3 opinion, reversed the court of appeals' decision. His reasoning was that Congress, even before it promulgated the Fourth Amendment, passed legislation authorizing the suspicionless boarding of vessels by government officials. This reflected its views that such boardings are not contrary to the Fourth Amendment. Moreover, waterborne commerce in waters providing ready access to the open sea is sufficiently different from the nature of vehicular traffic on highways to warrant the type of intrusion undertaken in this case.

David Jones

V

VAGRANCY. Vagrancy was first criminalized by statute in England in 1349. Over time, vagrancy evolved into the broad offense of being able to work but having no property to live on while wandering or strolling about in idleness; leading an idle or immoral life; living in idleness upon the wages or earnings of a mother, wife, or children under the age of eighteen years old; or having a fixed abode but living by stealing or buying stolen property. Vagrancy also included professional gamblers living in idleness and keepers of places where illegal sexual intercourse is habitually carried on. After the Second World War vagrancy laws were successfully challenged in the courts as being too broad and vague. Vagrancy was subsequently replaced with specific crimes including loitering, gambling, and prostitution.

RECOMMENDED READING: Joseph R. Nolan and Jacqueline M. Nolan-Haley, *Black's Law Dictionary: Definitions of the Terms and Phrases of American and English Jurisprudence, Ancient and Modern*, 6th ed. (St. Paul, MN: West Publishing Co., 1991).

Lee E. Parker

VANDALISM. Vandalism is damaging, destroying, or maliciously defacing by scratching, writing on, or by spraying with paint or any other liquid any real or personal property not owned by the perpetrator.

RECOMMENDED READING: Joseph R. Nolan and Jacqueline M. Nolan-Haley, *Black's Law Dictionary: Definitions of the Terms and Phrases of American and English Jurisprudence, Ancient and Modern*, 6th ed. (St. Paul, MN: West Publishing Co., 1991).

Lee E. Parker

VEHICLE SEARCH. The Fourth Amendment states, "The right of the people to be secure in their persons, houses, papers, and effects, against unreasonable searches and seizures, shall not be violated, and no Warrants shall issue, but upon probable cause, supported by Oath or affirmation, and particularly describing the place to be searched, and the persons or things to be seized." The Fourteenth Amendment made the Fourth Amendment applicable to the states. Generally, a police officer must obtain a search warrant to search a vehicle. However, the owner or driver of the vehicle has the authority to allow a police officer to search his vehicle. The owner must voluntarily give the approval to the officer. Usually the driver signs a document stating his approval for the search. Often the officer has a video camera that videotapes the interaction between the driver and the police officer.

A police officer may search vehicles incidental to arrest. The Chimel rule applies to vehicles. In 1981 the U.S. Supreme Court in *New York v. Belton* established the *Belton rule*. The Belton rule allows the police to search the passenger compartments of a vehicle as an incident to an arrest and to examine the contents of any container found in the passenger compartment, whether it is closed or opened. However, the rule does not justify that the trunk of an automobile be searched incident to an arrest.

The U.S. Supreme Court in 1970 established a "moving vehicle doctrine" in the case of *Chambers v. Maroney*. In this case the Supreme Court affirmed the right of police officers to search a vehicle that may be about to leave the jurisdiction, provided that the police officers have probable cause to believe that the vehicle contains contraband that the officers have the right to seize. The justification for the police officers' action is that the police officers have little or no time to obtain a search warrant.

RECOMMENDED READING: Irving J. Klein, *Principles of the Law of Arrest, Search, Seizure, and Liability Issues* (South Miami, FL: Coral Gables Publishing Co., 1994).

Michael Palmiotto

VERDICT. In criminal cases, the decision by the trier of fact (judge or jury) concerning the guilt or innocence of the defendant on the counts for which s/he has been charged. In states utilizing the death penalty the jury is also expected to make a pronouncement concerning punishment.

Jury deliberations leading to a verdict are undertaken in secret. In criminal cases, before a verdict of guilty can be reached, jurors must conclude that the defendant is guilty beyond a reasonable doubt. After the verdict is reached, it is announced in open court before the judge, the defendant, counsel, and others. The jury leader either announces the verdict or hands a written notice to the proper authority (the judge or the clerk), who announces it and reads it into the record. Typically, the judge will make appropriate inquiries to ensure that jurors agree with the verdict announced.

While it is not mandated by the U.S. Supreme Court's current interpretation of the U.S. Constitution, most states require unanimity among the jurors before a verdict of guilty can be announced. Occasionally jurors are unable to agree upon a verdict. They then become members of a "hung jury." If this happens, a "mistrial" is declared, and the state has the option of reinstating criminal proceedings against the defendant.

RECOMMENDED READING: Irving J. Klein, *Principles of the Law of Arrest, Search, Seizure, and Liability Issues* (South Miami, FL: Coral Gables Publishing Co., 1994); Christopher B. Mueller and Laird C. Kirkpatrick, *Evidence Under the Rules*, 3rd ed. (Boston: Little, Brown, and Co., 1996); Joseph R. Nolan and Jacqueline M. Nolan-Haley, *Black's Law Dictionary: Definitions of the Terms and Phrases of American and English Jurisprudence, Ancient and Modern*, 6th ed. (St. Paul, MN: West Publishing Co., 1991); Jonathan D. Schiffman, *Fundamentals of the Criminal Justice Process*, 3rd ed. (Deerfield, IL: Clark Boardman Callaghan, 1994).

David Jones

VICTIM AND WITNESS PROTECTION ACT. This 1982 federal legislation was the result of public concern over violent crime in the early 1980s and the work of the President's Task Force on Victims of Crime. It required judicial consideration of victim impact statements during sentencing hearings in federal criminal cases; improved protection for victims of and witnesses to crimes to prevent their harassment; tougher bail standards; and increased use of victim restitution. The restitution provisions were controversial and subject to conflicting interpretations about how sentencing judges were supposed to calculate them. Was restitution to be confined to damages suffered by the victim of the crime for which an offender was convicted, or should it include losses suffered by victims of other crimes that were part of the offender's pattern of criminal activity? In a 1990 revision the U.S. Congress opted for the broader interpretation. Overall, this act resulted in the development of guidelines for the participation in and fairer treatment of crime victims and witnesses by the federal criminal justice system.

RECOMMENDED READING: National Organization for Victim Assistance, *Victim Rights and Services: A Legislative Directory 1985* (Washington, DC: The Organization, 1986).

N. Prabha Unnithan

VICTIMLESS CRIMES. Criminologists have traditionally paid attention to offenses that are predatory in nature (e.g., homicide, rape, robbery), where harm could be relatively easily assessed and the roles of perpetrator and victim or complainant were easily identifiable. Many behaviors that are found in the penal codes of various states and the federal system pose a variety of problems (both for criminologists and criminal justice personnel) in that they do not share these characteristics. What if some act that was forbidden by criminal law was carried out with the knowledge and participation of two parties in such a way that it was impossible to say who was harmed how and by whom?

A number of behaviors mainly related to the expression of sexuality and the consumption of particular substances are committed in this manner and are identified as victimless crimes. These generally include prostitution, homosexuality (and other forms of "sodomy"), pornography, drug use, and alcohol use (by minors). Others would add gambling and abortion, both of which have been illegal at various times and in various states, to this list. Partly as a result of these definitional and other uncertainties, criminologists do not even agree on what these offenses should be called. The term *victimless crime* (or crimes without victims) is objected to by some because they claim that "victims" of some of these offenses (e.g., drug abuse) are identifiable. The term *public order crime* (offenses that interfere with the smooth functioning of society and the orderly flow of social life) is sometimes used. Finally, others use the term *crimes without complainants* to indicate the atypical nature of these crimes in comparison to the more "regular" offenses mentioned at the beginning.

Prostitution is illegal in most states and localities. This does not mean that it will not occur and when it does occur that the prostitute or the customer is going to report their consensual sexual behavior to the police. In the first place, should such private behavior be defined as criminal? Even if we agree that prostitution may be harmful to public morality, why should our view of morality prevail over others who do not agree? Next, who is the victim and what is the nature of the harm done to him or her? How would the police enforce the law against prostitution in the absence of complainants without resorting to extraordinary (and often unethical) methods? Given the demand for such illegal services, is it not likely that criminal organizations would rush in to provide them? Who is to be punished for the offense and how are sentences to be assessed when we are unable to tell what the harm was? Finally, what should the objective of any sentence be? As can be seen, victimless crimes raise fundamental questions about the definition of behaviors considered criminal and the interaction between law, society, and public/private morality, as well as the operation of the criminal justice system in enforcing, adjudicating, and correcting such offenses.

Joseph Gusfield has argued that victimless crimes exist because certain behaviors are defined as illegal to highlight the "superior" morality of some groups in society. The use and sale of alcohol was prohibited nationally in the United States between 1919 and 1933. Gusfield suggested that this happened to underscore the felt moral superiority of rural, Protestant groups who had migrated earlier and for whom alcohol and drunkenness were symbols of urban, Catholic groups who had come to the United States later. The role of "moral entrepreneurs" (those who take it upon themselves to lead and crusade against certain behaviors they find offensive and immoral) in encoding victimless offenses into criminal law is thus crucial. Others have suggested that such behaviors are criminalized because criminal law has an educational function to perform indicating to members behaviors that society stands against, even if the harm in these behaviors is difficult to assess.

RECOMMENDED READING: Joseph R. Gusfield, *Symbolic Crusade: Status Politics and the American Temperance Movement*, 2nd ed. (Urbana: University of Illinois Press, 1986).

N. Prabha Unnithan

VICTIMS. Criminologists have traditionally paid attention to the perpetrators of crime rather than to their victims. However, beginning in the 1960s, a number of researchers uncovered the important roles victims often play in criminal events. For example, Marvin Wolfgang coined the term "victim-precipitated homicide" to describe cases in which the victim was the first to use physical force against the person who would ultimately kill him or her. Subsequent studies of a variety of criminal events have shown that prior victim-offender relationships and particular victim lifestyles that place individuals in "high-risk" crime locations such as bars and crack houses are important factors in victimization. In an important 1979 article Lawrence Cohen and Marcus Felson attempted to integrate these and other findings into what has come to be called the "routine activities theory" of crime victimization. They argued that given some people in every society who are willing to break the law for a variety of reasons, three factors affect the amount of violent crime and direct property crime. These are the availability of "motivated offenders" (e.g., illegal drug users or alcoholics who wish to support their habit); "suitable targets" (e.g., liquor stores or convenience stores open during the night); and "capable guardians" (e.g., the number of workers, managers, and customers and the nature of security monitoring in each store).

Data available beginning in 1972 from the National Crime Victimization Survey (NCVS, formerly the National Crime Survey) have allowed victimologists to assess victimization risks and patterns in greater detail. The NCVS is a national survey of 48,000 American households selected through a complex multistage sampling process. Residents of these households are interviewed twice a year about their victimization experiences in the immediate past six months. (Each household stays in the sample for three years and is then replaced.) Studies based on these data suggest that central-city public areas are usually the locations where victimization most often takes place. Men are more likely to be victims of most crimes, with the exception of rape. African Americans are victimized by crime proportionately more often than other racial groups. The age group twelve to twenty-four has the highest rate of victimization, a risk that steadily declines after age twenty-five. Those who belong to the lower socioeconomic status groups (family income below $7,500) face the greatest risk of victimization. Finally, the NCVS data show that many characteristics of victims coincide with those of their assailants (e.g., similarities in age, race, or socioeconomic status).

Public concern about the victims of crime resulted in the constitution of the President's Task Force on Victims of Crime by President Ronald Reagan in the early 1980s and passage by the U.S. Congress of the Victim and Witness Protection Act of 1982. (See **Victims' Task Force; Victim and Witness Protection Act**.) A number of tangible results can be attributed to these and other efforts in the various states (e.g., California, which passed a Victims Bill of Rights in 1982 through a referendum) to focus attention on victims and to include them in the criminal justice process. These include the creation of victim and witness protection and assistance (crisis intervention, counseling on judicial procedures) programs, increased utilization of victim impact statements and victim restitution and compensation during sentencing, and greater sensitivity on the part of criminal justice personnel to the needs and concerns of victims.

RECOMMENDED READING: William G. Doerner and Steven P. Lab, *Victimology*, (Cincinnati: Anderson Publishing Co., 1995); Andrew Karmen, *Crime Victims: An Introduction to Victimology*, Belmont: Wadsworth Publishing Co., 1996); *Victimology*, ed. Paul Rock (Brookfield, VT: Dartmouth, 1994).

N. Prabha Unnithan

VICTIMS' TASK FORCE (PRESIDENT'S TASK FORCE ON VICTIMS OF CRIME, [1982]). In response to public concern about victims of crime, President Ronald Reagan constituted the President's Task Force on Victims of Crime in the early 1980s. The task force sought to develop proposals for how victims could be assisted. The most tangible result of this task force's work was its final report and its impact on the passage by the U.S. Congress of the Victim and Witness Protection Act of 1982. The task force emphasized the importance of balancing the needs and concerns of the victim with those of the accused in criminal justice. It urged that victims should be kept informed of the status of their cases through all stages of the criminal justice process, including delays and postponements; their views regarding bail, plea bargains, and restitution should be taken into account; they should be protected against intimidation; convicted offenders should be required to pay restitution; and that government victim compensation programs should be expanded. Perhaps the most notable suggestion was that the following statement be added to the Sixth Amendment to the U.S. Constitution: "In every criminal prosecution, the victim shall have the right to be present and to be heard at all critical stages of the judicial proceedings."

RECOMMENDED READING: U.S. Department of Justice, *Final Report of the President's Task Force on Victims of Crime, 1982* (Washington, DC: U.S. Government Printing Office, 1983).

N. Prabha Unnithan

VIDEOTECHNOLOGY IN THE CRIMINAL COURTS. Modern videotechnology systems are occasionally used to present evidence in criminal trials, but their major uses are in arraignments or "first appearances" of defendants. Prior to the development of video links, criminal offenders had to be physically transported from a jail or detention facility in order to appear before the court. Common practice was to awaken inmates to be transported at a very early hour, feed them, handcuff and shackle them, load them on a van or bus, and take them to court. There all prisoners would remain until all had been processed, and then they were returned to jail or detention.

In courts with closed-circuit video links, prisoners are awoken at a normal hour, fed, shown a tape explaining the court procedure, and then led to a video room in the same building. There they face a television camera and a monitor display of one to three images of the courtroom. Typically the monitor will display the judge and both the prosecuting and defense attorneys' tables or benches. The judge and other court officials go through the same procedures that they would if the prisoner were physically present in the courtroom. The judge will ordinarily read the charge, set bail where appropriate, ask the defendant whether he or she has obtained counsel (or would like the court to assign counsel), and ask for a plea. In some cases a defendant may have an attorney present in the video room, but it is more likely at arraignments that the defendant will have no attorney, or that a public defender will be available in the courtroom. If the plea is guilty or *nolo contendere*, the judge may proceed to immediate sentencing. For such defendants, their entire exposure to the court will have been through a television monitor, and this worries many who are concerned with issues of due process. Inmates not eligible for immediate release are escorted back to their cells by officers.

The great majority of offenders who have gone through both the video arraignment and physical appearances in the courtroom prefer using the video system. Most believe that their due- process rights are no less protected under the video system, and they appreciate sleeping longer and not having to go through the humiliation of shackling and transportation. The process takes about four to six hours less for most defendants. The advantage to courts/corrections comes not only from the convenience, but in the cost savings that result from not having to physically transport prisoners over long distances. The benefit/cost ratio for installing a video link is favorable for most urban areas with a population of 150,000 or more. In addition to the cost savings, there are intangible improvements to public safety, since the use of video appearances forestalls the possibility of escape. Corrections officials also report a dramatic decrease in contraband coming into the jail or detention facility where video systems have been installed.

Many courts have found other uses for their videotechnology systems. With as many as five cameras positioned in the courtroom, some courts are now using videotaped proceedings as official transcripts of court proceedings, frequently over the strong objections of court reporters (Hewitt 1992). Other courts are using the video links to allow conferences between in-custody clients and their attorneys.

Transmission of the video signal can be through a microwave system or a cable (usually fibre-optic) network. Fibre-optic transmission is generally considered to be the optimal technology, but it is seldom used for extended distances because the cost becomes prohibitive. Microwave equipment is less expensive to acquire and install, but is subject to more maintenance problems and greater maintenance costs.   In a statewide evaluation of court video systems, fibre-optic systems were judged to be of significantly higher quality and had fewer episodes of equipment failure and downtime than microwave systems (McNeece 1993).

RECOMMENDED READING: W. Hewitt, "Video Court Reporting: A Primer for Trial and Appellate Judges," *Judges' Journal* 31 (1992): 2–6.

C. Aaron McNeece

VIOLENT CRIME. Although violent crimes constitute a minor proportion of the total number of crimes committed in the United States, they generate the most amount of public concern. Perhaps as a result, criminologists have researched these crimes (particularly homicides) more, and criminal justice personnel pay greater attention to them in comparison to others, such as victimless crimes, white-collar crimes or political crimes. Public concern about these offenses, for example, homicide, rape, aggravated assault, and robbery (which has elements of property crime involved as well), is probably due to the personal nature of the threats embodied by these offenses.

Individuals can be hurt physically and may even die as a consequence of the commission of these crimes. The fear of violent crime motivates individuals to alter their lifestyles (installing extra locks and alarm systems to fortify their homes) and interaction patterns (venturing out less often, refusing to help strangers) in an effort to remain safe and secure.

Violent crime is defined as any criminal act resulting from the use or threat of force on a victim. Along with property crime, these offenses against persons are a basic category of English Common law (from which American criminal justice is derived) and most other traditional classifications. This shows that societies have historically attempted to control, and if possible, prevent violent crime among their members.

The seriousness and long history of concern about violent crime are also reflected in the Federal Bureau of Investigation's Uniform Crime Reports (which are based on crimes known to police and are the most influential sources of information regarding crime in the United States). Part I offenses of the Uniform Crime Reports are known as index crimes; they are relatively more serious violent and property offenses used to construct crime rates at the national, state, and local levels that are often utilized in media reports. The following violent offenses are index crimes: (1) murder and nonnegligent manslaughter, (2) forcible rape, (3) robbery, and (4) aggravated assault. (Simple assaults, those in which no weapon was used and those that did not result in serious bodily injury to the victim, are included in Uniform Crime Reports Part II offenses.) (See **Crime Index; Crime Statistics**.)

While overall rates of index crime in the United States increased 11 percent between 1986 and 1995, shorter trends showed that the 1995 rate of violent crime was 4 percent lower than in 1994 and 10 percent below the 1991 rate. Although it may be too early to tell, it appears that a continuing decrease in the rate of violent crime is now occurring.

If societies have always attempted to control and prevent violent crimes, why do individuals commit them? A number of scholarly disciplines and schools of thought within them have attempted to answer this age-old question. Some biologists have suggested that aggression is an evolutionary mechanism that allows particular individuals to survive and propagate and may thus be used in confrontational situations, while others have attempted to identify violence-prone individuals based on physical, genetic, neurological, or physiological characteristics. Some psychologists have focused on personality (cognitive, emotional, behavioral) characteristics that they believe are influential in determining whether individuals will turn violent, while others have used Freudian notions regarding   problems in the psychosexual development of individuals as explanatory factors.

Sociologists typically explained violent crime in terms of the social environment in which individuals are embedded structurally (e.g., poverty, unemployment, lack of opportunity, discrimination) and the cultural or socialization processes that affect them (e.g., growing up in a violent family, associating with violent peers, subcultures advocating violence for conflict resolution).

RECOMMENDED READING: Federal Bureau of Investigation, *Uniform Crime Reports for the United States, 1995* (Washington, DC: U.S. Government Printing Office, 1996); N. Prabha Unnithan, Lin Huff-Corzine, Jay Corzine, and Hugh P. Whitt, *The Currents of Lethal Violence* (Albany, NY: State University of New York, 1994).

James R. Farris

VOICEPRINT IDENTIFICATION. The term *voiceprint identification* was coined by Lawrence G. Kersta, who worked for the Bell Telephone Laboratory, in which he used a sound spectrograph to identify individuals by their speech. The basic idea was that each individual has his/her own unique vocal characteristics. Our body cavities, vocal chords, and articulars are so unique to our voice that when spectrographically printed they can be identified.

The sound spectrograph is a device that produces a visual graph of speech as a function of time, frequency, and voice energy or intensity. In order for a voice to be identified correctly, three things are required: (1) a recording of the voice in question; (2) a recording of known origin for comparison; and (3) a sound spectrograph instrument adapted for voiceprint studies. An example of how voice identification works is as follows: A suspect has been arrested and charged with making a bomb threat to the police on 911 that was recorded. Under court order the suspect is required to give a sample of his or her voice. A voice sample is taken of the suspect, saying the same thing and in the same manner as what was said on the 911 call. The sample is spectrographically printed and compared to the spectrographic prints of the recorded 911 caller. If everything matches up, the identification can usually be made.

There has been some disagreement within the forensic community regarding whether this method works and should be used. Most law enforcement agencies do not rely solely on voiceprint evidence, and the FBI uses the method for investigative purposes only. In the early days courts had a split decision on voice identification. Some courts said that it was admissible, while others said it was not. Today, voiceprint evidence is not admissible in court because the technique is not reliable and the research is biased.

RECOMMENDED READING: Criminal Justice Section, American Bar Association, *Voiceprint Identification* (Washington, DC: The Section, 1976); *Selected Materials on Legal and Technical Aspects of "Voiceprint" Identification* (Houston: National College of Criminal Defense Lawyers and Public Defenders, 1976).

James R. Farris

VOIR DIRE. During pretrial courtroom activities, the prosecutor and defense attorney have the opportunity to question potential jurors during an open examination termed *voir dire*. Its purpose is to determine each juror's suitability for service on the jury panel at trial. Should either attorney so choose, s/he may seek dismissal of a prospective juror during *voir dire* by voicing a challenge of that juror's suitability to the judge.

RECOMMENDED READING: Joseph R. Nolan and Jacqueline M. Nolan-Haley, *Black's Law Dictionary: Definitions of the Terms and Phrases of American and English Jurisprudence, Ancient and Modern*, 6th ed. (St. Paul, MN: West Publishing Co., 1991).

Shelia C. Armstrong

VOLSTEAD ACT. Also referred to as the National Prohibition Act, the Volstead Act of 1919 aimed to "prohibit intoxicating beverages, and to regulate the manufacture, production, use, and sale of high-proof spirits for other than beverage purposes, and to ensure an ample supply of alcohol and promote its use in scientific research and in the development of fuel, dye, and other lawful industries." The act was principally drafted by legal counsel to the Anti-Saloon League and was initially vetoed by President Wilson. Congress overrode the President's veto by a two-thirds vote, however, leaving Wilson with but one option: pardoning many of those convicted under the act. The Volstead Act allowed for convictions resulting in fines up to $1,000 and imprisonment for up to six months for those convicted of first offenses. Property used to violate the law could be seized and sold to pay fines.

RECOMMENDED READING: *Prohibition: The 18th Amendment, the Volstead Act, the 21st Amendment* (Washington, DC: National Archives and Records Administration, 1986).

Martin Gruberg

VON **OBERMAIER, GEORG MICHAEL (1789–1885).** Although often lost to history, and occasionally misspelled even when remembered, Georg Michael von Obermaier helped set the stage for reformatory ideas, humane treatment of offenders, good-time procedures, and indeterminate sentencing. In 1830 von Obermaier became governor of the prison in Kaiserslautern in Bavaria. He immediately began experimenting with a humanitarian approach to the treatment of criminals by reorganizing the state prison according to reformatory ideas. His successes at Kaiserslautern led the government to introduce von Obermaier's methods in all Bavarian prisons and earned him a transfer in 1842 to the prison in Munich. Under his direction the Munich prison became a model facility and brought von Obermaier positive public reviews, but the acclaim did not last. Political struggles, growing negative public opinion, and legislative changes eventually forced von Obermaier to resign in 1862. Nevertheless, his pioneering efforts earned him a place among prison reformers before prisons had even really caught on.

When von Obermaier became governor of the Munich prison, the three most severe classes of punishment in Bavaria were (1) chain punishment, (2) penal servitude, and (3) sentence to the workhouse. Chain punishment, which replaced the death penalty, was for life. The punishment involved chaining the prisoner at both feet by a long chain carrying a heavy iron ball. Penal servitude was for either an indefinite time, with a pardon possible for nonrecidivists who had served sixteen years and had at least ten years of good behavior, or for a fixed period between eight and twenty years, with a pardon possible for nonrecidivists after serving at least three-fourths of that term. Prisoners under penal servitude generally carried a lighter chain attached to their feet. Prisoners sentenced to the workhouse were generally not shackled. They served a fixed term between one and eight years from which they could be pardoned after completing three-fourths of the sentence.

Von Obermaier had to carry out his rehabilitative philosophy under procedures geared toward deterrence. He did this by following that part of the law favoring his ideas and by evading, and even ignoring, the parts that did not. For example, upon his arrival at the Munich prison von Obermaier found the six hundred to seven hundred prisoners chained and under the guard of about one hundred soldiers joined in their duty at night by twenty or thirty large bloodhounds. Either in violation of the law, or by obtaining special pardons, he freed the prisoners from their chains by essentially abolishing the distinction among the three types of punishment. He then replaced most of the soldiers with more considerate guards, stopped the use of bloodhounds, and abolished brutal discipline methods in favor of more refined methods in which good behavior could bring the prisoner daily rewards (like buying extra food or weak beer) and the ultimate reward of early release. Through such efforts he succeeded in shifting the accent of punishment from deterrence to reformation.

In 1858 disciplinary problems at the Munich prison turned public opinion against him, but the real end to his efforts came in 1861 when a new Bavarian criminal code abolished the indeterminate sentence and the use of good behavior to shorten fixed terms. Since these procedures were key ingredients in von Obermaier's discipline approach, his methods became impractical, and he resigned a year later. However, the idea of a more humane system of prison discipline through good time and indeterminate sentencing was becoming increasingly popular in other parts of the world even as Bavaria was rejecting such procedures.

RECOMMENDED READING: F. Hoefer, "Georg Michael von Obermaier, a Pioneer in Reformatory Procedures," *Journal of Criminal Law and Criminology* 28 (1937): 13–51.

Philip Reichel

W

WALNUT STREET JAIL. Before the American Revolutionary War a building called the Walnut Street Jail opened in Philadelphia, Pennsylvania, in 1772 to house pretrial detainees and people awaiting sentencing. In 1790 the Quakers in Philadelphia persuaded the Pennsylvania legislature to designate a section of the Walnut Street Jail as a penitentiary to incarcerate all convicted felons except those sentenced to death.

The idea of this Pennsylvania system, as it came to be called, focused on the correction of the individual. Cells housed only one person. This solitary confinement allowed the individual to read his Bible in peace and contemplate his evil ways. Each cell came attached with a small exercise yard that permitted one to enjoy the fresh air without the possible contamination from other prisoners. Unfortunately, the Quakers knew little about the impact a lack of human contact had on the mental stability of an inmate, and the original idea of the Pennsylvania system—solitary confinement without work—only succeeded in precipitating suicides and mental disorders. Organized work programs seemed more humane.

The harsh treatment needed modification. Largely instrumental in bringing about this change was a group of reform-minded citizens known as the Philadelphia Society for Alleviating the Miseries of Public Prisons.

This group insisted that male prisoners should be housed separately from females, that people imprisoned for debt should be segregated from criminals, that the sale of alcohol and food to inmates should be abolished, and that prisoners should be furnished food and clothing even though they had no means to pay for it. Religious services were held on the Sabbath, and attendance was compulsory. Inmates worked at prison industries and received compensation for their work, although maintenance and living expenses were deducted. (This last provision was in direct opposition to the original notion held by the Quakers that the inmates should spend their time in contemplative solitary confinement so as to come to a realization of the errors of their ways.)

Inmate work programs were developed that focused on industry and included weaving, tailoring, beating hemp, sawing and polishing marble, and shoemaking. A member of the Philadelphia society, Caleb Lownes, worked as a prison industry supervisor, but by the early part of the nineteenth century an influx of new prisoners began to disrupt the work program, and Lownes resigned. In 1816 Walnut Street Jail's bad conditions caused by crowding and idle prisoners triggered a fire that destroyed the industry shops.

Despite the breakdown of the Walnut Street program, many considered this new approach a breakthrough, and the Walnut Street Jail approach to managing prisoners achieved popularity. Many foreign countries and several states copied this Quaker approach to corrections. Though the Pennsylvania system did not survive in the United States, it made an impression on the public's reaction to the nature of crime and the ways society's citizens would deal with it. (See **Newgate Prison of Connecticut.**)

RECOMMENDED READING: Negley King Teeters, *The Cradle of the Penitentiary: The Walnut Street Jail at Philadelphia* (Philadelphia, PA: Sponsored by the Philadelphia Prison Society, 1955); Douglas R. Yost, *An Early American Prison: The Walnut Street Jail—Its History and Its Message*, M. A. project (Ashland Theological Seminary, 1989).

Ken Kerle

WARREN, EARL (1891–1974). Earl Warren was born in Los Angeles, California, on March 19, 1891. Like William O. Douglas, he had to overcome poverty and personal tragedy. His father was murdered. Warren studied at the University of California, earning a bachelor's and a law degree. From 1925 to 1938 he was a district attorney. He was attorney general of California for the next four years and was then elected governor for three terms. A liberal Republican, he had bipartisan support. In 1948 he was Republican candidate for vice president and in 1952 sought his party's presidential nomination. Thus, before his elevation to be chief justice, he had never served as a judge.

Warren was nominated to be chief justice of the Supreme Court by President Eisenhower in 1953, inheriting (and helping to unify the Court on) the *Brown v. Board of Education of Topeka* (1954) school desegregation case. Warren was not a legal scholar. He brought to the Court his liberal social values. He was preoccupied with fairness, individual rights, and justice. He expressed himself in simple language.

After the assassination of President Kennedy, Warren headed a commission to investigate. He wished to retire in 1968 in time to prevent his California foe, Richard Nixon, from selecting his successor. The effort miscarried, and Warren retired in 1969. He died in 1974.

RECOMMENDED READING: Bernard Schwartz, *Super Chief: Earl Warren and His Supreme Court: A Judicial Biography* (New York: New York University Press, 1983); Bill Severn, *Mr. Chief Justice: Earl Warren* (New York:

D. McKay Co., 1968); Robert J. Steamer, *Chief Justice: Leadership and the Supreme Court* (Columbia: University of South Carolina Press, 1986); Mark Tushnet, *The Warren Court in Historical and Political Perspective* (Charlottesville: University Press of Virginia, 1993); John D. Weaver, *Warren: The Man, The Court, The Era* (London: Gollancz, 1968); G. Edward White, *Earl Warren: A Public Life* (New York: Oxford University Press, 1982).

Martin Gruberg

WARREN COURT. Refers to the U.S. Supreme Court while under the leadership of its fourteenth chief justice, Earl Warren (September 30, 1953, through June 8, 1969. "Revolution" and "activism" are words typically used in passages discussing the Warren Court. In 23 separate cases it held acts of Congress unconstitutional in whole or in part. In 185 cases state constitutional and statutory provisions and municipal ordinances were ruled unconstitutional on their face or as administered. The Warren Court even overruled 53 of the Supreme Court's own previous decisions in whole or in part. The total number of petitions on the Court's yearly docket had remained between 1,000 and 1,700 for almost twenty-five years, but during the Warren Court the total number of petitions quickly increased from 1,453 (in 1953) to 4,172 (in 1969).

While the Warren Court issued watershed opinions on issues of segregation (*Brown v. Board of Education of Topeka*, 1954), obscenity (*Roth v. United States*, 1957), reapportionment (*Baker v. Carr*, 1962, and *Reynolds v. Sims*, 1964), libel (*New York Times Co. v. Sullivan*, 1964), school prayer (*Engel v. Vitale*, 1962) and the "right to privacy" (*Griswold v. Connecticut*, 1965), its controversial opinions with respect to criminal justice issues may have provoked the most widespread and sustained attack, both outside and within the judicial system. In *Mapp v. Ohio* (1961) the Court ruled that the Fourth Amendment imposes the exclusionary rule on state court proceedings. *Gideon v. Wainwright* (1963) required the provision of representation for indigent criminal defendants, and *Miranda v. Arizona* (1966) required the clear application of specific procedural safeguards (such as "Miranda warnings") once custodial interrogation becomes a factor in a case.

RECOMMENDED READING: Lee Epstein, Jeffrey A. Segal, Harold J. Spaeth, and Thomas Walker, *The Supreme Court Compendium*, 2nd ed. (Washington, DC: Congressional Quarterly, 1996); *The Warren Court: A Retrospective*, ed. Bernard Schwartz (Cary, NC: Oxford University Press, 1996).

Peter S. Ruckman, Jr.

WEEKS V. UNITED STATES, 232 U.S. 383 (1913). A very important federal case in which the exclusionary rule was applied for the first time to evidence gained by law enforcement officials in violation of the defendant's Fourth Amendment rights. A federal law enforcement official went into the home of Fremont Weeks without a search warrant and seized a number of items, including illegal lottery material. Weeks asked for all of it back, but received only some of it. Some was held as evidence and was used against him in trial. He was convicted.

Justice William Day, speaking for the Court, held that the material used against Weeks in court was taken in violation of the defendant's rights. He held further, "[I]f letters and private documents can thus be seized and held and used in evidence against a citizen accused of an offense, the protection of the 4th Amendment...is of no value, and, so far as those thus placed are concerned, might as well be stricken. The efforts of the courts and their officials to bring the guilty to punishment...are not to be aided by the sacrifice of those great principles established by years of endeavor and suffering which have resulted in their embodiment in the fundamental law of the land." In short, stated the Court, evidence seized in this manner without a warrant violated Weeks's Fourth Amendment rights and   hence should have been excluded as evidence against him in his trial.

David Jones

WHITE, BYRON RAYMOND (1917–   ). An associate justice of the U.S. Supreme Court from 1962 to 1993, Justice White was born in Fort Collins, Colorado in 1917. A 1946 graduate of the Yale Law School, Justice White served as U.S. deputy attorney general from 1961 until his appointment to the Supreme Court in 1962 by President John F. Kennedy. During his 31 years of service on the Supreme Court, White established a reputation as one of the court's keenest legal thinkers. He was known as a centrist whom his colleagues respected. At the time of White's retirement in 1993, Justice Harry A. Blackmun said, "His presence was always a steady and influential one, characterized by a firmness of purpose and of belief." Justice Sandra Day O'Connor described having served with White as "a great privilege" and praised his "strong intellect and good common sense."

RECOMMENDED READING: John A. Haddad, *Justices Byron R. White and Arthur J. Goldberg: A Study in Judicial Values*, M. A. thesis (Texas Technological College, 1967); Allan Ides, *The Jurisprudence of Justice Byron White* (New Haven, CT: Yale Law Journal Co., 1993): 419–461.

Frank Schmalleger

WITNESSES. Individuals who give testimony as evidence at trial. A substantial amount of the evidence entered into trial proceedings comes via the process of direct and cross-examination of witnesses.

There are basically two types of witnesses. The most common is the "lay witness," an individual who has observed something relevant to trial proceedings. At times, "expert witnesses," individuals who have specialized knowledge relevant to trial proceedings, may also be called. An example of an expert witness might be a psychiatrist called to give an opinion on the mental state of the defendant.

To be allowed to testify, a witness must be competent. This means that s/he must understand the duty to tell the truth and be able to answer questions about the issues at trial. This is almost invariably based on personal knowledge of the events being testified to. The general presumption is that a witness is competent unless shown to be otherwise. The issue of witness competency may be more likely to arise when children are involved as potential witnesses.

Witnesses give testimony through the process of examination by counsel. In direct examination an attorney will elicit information by asking questions, the form and content of which are regulated; for instance, counsel is not supposed to ask "leading questions" (those that invite a particular answer).

The credibility of a witness may be attacked in cross-examination or, in some circumstances, by the introduction of evidence not directly related to witness's testimony. This is called witness impeachment. In this process questions might be raised about the witness's ability to have observed that to which s/he testified (e.g., sensory deficiencies). It is also possible to attack the witness's character, his/her psychological condition, and/or his/her objectivity. Previous inconsistent statements, as well as prior convictions for serious crimes, may also be used to impeach the credibility of a witness.

RECOMMENDED READING: David W. Neubauer, *America's Courts and the Criminal Justice System*, 5th ed. (Belmont, CA: Wadsworth Publishing Company, 1996); Jon R. Waltz, *Introduction to Criminal Evidence*, 4th ed. (Chicago: Nelson-Hall Publishers, 1997).

David Jones

WOMEN AND CRIME. Women have long been both victims and initiators of criminal acts, but they have only recently been involved in shaping the definition of crime and the professions of crime control. The status of a woman in the law of a particular society has framed both the understanding of her actions and that society's response. For much of ancient and early modern history, a crime against a woman was prosecuted, if it was prosecuted at all, as a property injury to her husband or father. If the agent of the violent act was her husband, often there was no crime. The crimes of women that were selected for prosecution frequently involved violence to children and adultery.

The definition of crime reflects the goals of social control, and in modern Western history the list of crimes of women lengthened with the effort to control sexuality. Prostitution and disorderly conduct became frequent causes of arrest for women. However, U.S. crime statistics regularly show theft to be the most common crime for which women are arrested.

In contemporary Western society, as women approach legal and social equality with men, arrests of women have stabilized at a ratio of one to five, women to men. The participation of women in criminal justice professions has grown in number and character. In the last twenty years sexual harassment and stalking of women have been established as criminal acts.

RECOMMENDED READING: Clarice Feinman, *Women in the Criminal Justice System*, 3rd ed. (Westport, CT: Praeger, 1994); Nicole Rafter, *Partial Justice: Women, Prisons and Social Control*, 2nd ed. (New Brunswick, U.S.A., Transaction Publishers, 1990).

Margaret Leland Smith

WOMEN, CRIMINALITY OF. The analysis of the disposition to criminal behavior, or criminality, of women has identified various structural gender-linked differences as key determinants. The explanations vary as to the substance of their claims, but not in the significance of gender.

During the Middle Ages and in early modern Europe, criminality in woman was seen as a feature of their imperfect control by men, either husbands or fathers. The majority of women prosecuted for witchcraft in New England were single mothers, widows, or spinsters.

In the heyday of positivist criminology Cesare Lombroso declared women less evolved as humans and more disposed by their nature to crime than men. Since the 1960s criminal behavior by women has been described as a response to specific and general gender-linked social oppression. Although arguments have been advanced that the patterns and amount of crime by women have been influenced by the feminist movement, research has not shown this to be the case.

There has not been thoroughgoing examination of the criminal behavior of women sufficient to allow such summary judgments to be made. When crimes by women are examined, the results show a complex matrix of disposition, opportunity and social context. The discussion of the criminality of women continues to be limited by instability in the definitions of crime.

RECOMMENDED READING: John Demos, *Entertaining Satan: Witchcraft and the Culture of Early New England* (New York: Oxford University Press, 1982); Professor Ceasare Lombroso and William Ferrero, *The Female Offender* (New York: Specially published for the Brunswick Subscription Co. by D. Appleton & Co., 1915); Anne Worrall, *Offending Women: Female Lawbreakers and the Criminal Justice System* (New York: Routledge, 1990).

Margaret Leland Smith

WRIT OF *CERTIORARI.* A writ that originated in early English law meaning an order to a lower court from a higher court ordering that the records of a case be sent up to it. In the United States it is a wholly discretionary decision on the part of the U.S. Supreme Court whether or not to hear a case. If the Court grants *certiorari*, that means that it has decided that it will hear the case. Most of the controversies that come before the Court at this time come via the process of *certiorari*.

A petitioner who seeks a writ must apply and must meet certain criteria (e.g., timeliness, length of petition) before the petition is considered. These petitions are first screened by the justices' law clerks (who are recent top graduates of prestigious law schools), who prepare "*cert* memos" for the justices to consider. The decision to grant or deny *certiorari* is made by the Court sitting as a collegial body. The operative rule for granting *certiorari* is the "rule of 4": if four of the justices vote to hear a case, it will be heard. Most applications for a writ of *certiorari* are denied. In fact, while the Court receives more than 4,000 applications for the writ per term, it agrees to hear only about 200 cases.

When the Court denies an application, it does not indicate the reason for its action. Denial of a petition for the writ is not a legal precedent. Lower courts are not supposed to rely upon a denial as an indication of the position of the Court concerning the legal issues involved in a case.

The criteria used by the justices for their decisions on *certiorari* are vague. They may include, but are not limited to, whether the cases in question indicate a division among appellate courts concerning important issues of law, involve decisions by appellate courts (including state supreme courts) about important constitutional issues on which the Court has not yet ruled, or involve decisions of appellate courts in important cases that are likely to be at variance with case law as it has been developed by the Court. Petitions involving capital punishment tend to receive heightened scrutiny from the justices. Studies have also shown that applications in which the United States is a party tend to be more favorably received than are most others. This is probably due to the solicitor general's familiarity with the Court's informal criteria and his ability to tailor applications to meet these. In fact, since many of the Court's decision criteria are informal, "repeat players" (those who bring many cases before the Court) tend to be advantaged in this process. Whatever the pros and cons of this situation, the discretion inherent in the use of the writ of *certiorari* allows the U.S. Supreme Court to have a great deal of control over which cases it chooses to decide.

RECOMMENDED READING: H. W. Perry, Jr., *Deciding to Decide: Agenda Setting in the United States Supreme Court* (Cambridge: Harvard University Press, 1991); Doris Marie Provine, *Case Selection in the United States Supreme Court* (Chicago: University of Chicago Press, 1980).

David Jones

WRIT OF *HABEAS CORPUS*. Literally, "you have the body," this is a written judicial order commanding a person who is holding a prisoner to appear before a judicial officer with that prisoner. The purpose of the appearance is to present facts to the judicial officer that will enable him or her to determine the lawfulness of the imprisonment.

Shelia C. Armstrong

Z

ZENGER, JOHN PETER (1697–1746). John Peter Zenger was born in 1697. He migrated to America from Germany at age thirteen. By 1733 he was editor of the *New York Weekly Journal,* an organ of the opposition party of lawyers, merchants, and others. (All contributions were anonymous). Governor William Cosby had removed the Supreme Court chief justice, Lewis Morris, after the latter had ruled against the governor's petition to receive part of the compensation of the acting governor. Zenger's paper publicized the removal. A grand jury refused to indict Zenger, but the governor succeeded in 1734 in having him charged with seditious libel.

After his two New York lawyers had been disbarred for questioning the right of the Cosby-appointed chief justice and associate to preside over the case, Zenger's allies had to import attorney Andrew Hamilton, the most distinguished lawyer in the colonies, from Pennsylvania. Though the judge stated that an alleged libel existed regardless of truth, Hamilton asked the jury to take truth into consideration. It did, and Zenger was acquitted. (Truth as a defense against criminal libel was not generally guaranteed in the United States and the United Kingdom before the nineteenth century.) The case has been credited with establishing a new rule of law as well as establishing an important precedent for freedom of the press. Jury nullification is still a touchy subject. William Kunstler wished to use part of Andrew Hamilton's summation in the Catonsville Nine case (the defendants had destroyed draft-board records during the Vietnam War) but was threatened by the judge with contempt.

Zenger was made public printer for the colony of New York in 1737 and of New Jersey in 1738. He died in 1746.

RECOMMENDED READING: Livingston Rutherfurd, *John Peter Zenger; His Press, His Trial, and a Bibliography of Zenger Imprints* (New York: Arno, 1904); *The Trial of Peter Zenger,* ed. Vincent Buranelli (New York University Press, 1957).

Martin Gruberg

TABLE of CASES

BIBLIOGRAPHICAL ESSAY

This essay is intended to serve as a guide for further investigation into the many diverse aspects of American criminal justice, violence, and crime-control policy. This reference differs from many of the more traditional sources that it cites and builds upon by virtue of the fact that it emphasizes contemporary terminology, issues, trends, and institutions, while the contents of the large majority of existing sources are primarily historical in orientation. Typical of the contemporary approach is this volume's inclusion of terminology covering DNA fingerprinting, AIDS in law enforcement and correctional contexts, and crime and the media (including coverage of the recent double murder trial of O. J. Simpson). Moreover, the present work contains a futuristic perspective lacking in any other published encyclopedia, dictionary, or bibliographic source presently available in the area of crime, violence, and the American system of criminal justice. Nonetheless, this volume builds firmly upon the work of earlier authors and editors who, through the compilation of reference works on American criminal justice, have contributed much to the field. Due to its special emphasis, however, this concise encyclopedia might aptly be called a sourcebook of contemporary terminology, law, and issues in criminal justice, crime, and violence.

HISTORICAL INTRODUCTIONS TO AMERICAN CRIMINAL JUSTICE

Today's criminal justice field is vast and dynamic. Constant change categorizes the area as political initiatives, statutory modifications, and court rulings routinely modify the subject matter that any bibliographic compilation seeks to describe. Nonetheless, a number of works have attempted to capture the essence of the criminal justice field—many of them focusing on the history of police, courts, and corrections. Primary among such volumes are historical approaches to the subject matter and encyclopedias of crime and justice.

Historical volumes of this type include Lawrence M. Friedman, *Crime and Punishment in American History* (New York: Basic Books, 1993); Nancy E. Marion, *A History of Federal Crime Control Initiatives, 1960–1993* (Westport, CT: Praeger, 1994); Piers Beirne, *The Origins and Growth of Criminology: Essays in Intellectual History, 1760–1945* (Aldershot, UK: Dartmouth, 1994); and Christopher Hibbert, *The Roots of Evil: A Social History of Crime and Punishment* (New York: Funk and Wagnall, 1967).

Friedman's *Crime and Punishment in American History* provides a social history of crime, punishment, and corrections in the United States and chronicles the development of the American system of criminal justice. Friedman's theme is that value-laden judgments about crime and punishment reflect the social norms of specific times and places and thereby determine the nature and structure of the criminal justice system during that particular historical epoch. Nancy Marion's *A History of Federal Crime Control Initiatives* follows Friedman's general thesis, but focuses on U.S. federal crime-control policies that were in place from 1960 to 1993. Marion maintains that the social phenomenon of crime became entrenched as a federal issue demanding an effective policy response during the Kennedy administration and suggests that each succeeding president has had his own particular brand of crime-control policy. Piers Beirne's *The Origins and Growth of Criminology* documents the rise of positivist (or scientific) criminology and the growth of the criminological enterprise in the United States.

HISTORICAL ANTHOLOGIES

Some historical works are more comprehensive than others. These larger "anthologies" include the eleven-volume series edited by Eric H. Monkkonen entitled *Crime and Justice in American History: Historical Articles on the Origins and Evolution of American Criminal Justice* (Munich and London: K. G. Saur, 1992); Herbert A. Johnson, *History of Criminal Justice* (Cincinnati, OH: Anderson, 1988); Paul W. Keve, *Prisons and the American Conscience: A History of U.S. Federal Corrections* (Carbondale: Southern Illinois University Press, 1991); Clive Emsley and Louis A. Knafla, *Crime History and Histories of Crime: Studies in the Historiography of Crime and Criminal Justice in Modern History* (Westport, CT: Greenwood Press, 1996); and *Criminal Justice History: An International Annual*, ed. Louis A. Knafla (Westport, CT: Greenwood Press, 1993).

Monkkonen's eleven-volume edited work includes reprints of historical articles on the courts, juvenile delinquency, policing, prisons and jails, organized crime, violence and theft, and theory and methods prevalent throughout American criminal justice history. Keve's study traces the history of U.S. federal imprisonment from its establishment by the Continental

Congress through the late 1980s, while Johnson's book surveys the history of criminal justice from ancient times through medieval and early modern Europe and throughout American history. Emsley and Knafla provide a wide-ranging work that examines aspects of crime and criminal justice from medieval Western Europe to modern-day Canada, while Knafla's *Criminal Justice History* focuses on the general history of crime, criminal courts, policing, and corrections in all parts of the world, from ancient to modern times.

ENCYCLOPEDIAS OF CRIME AND CRIMINAL JUSTICE

A number of encyclopedias on various aspects of crime, violence, and criminal justice currently exist. Among them are Carl Sifakis, *The Encyclopedia of American Crime* (New York: Facts on File, 1982); Jay Robert Nash, *Bloodletters and Badmen: A Narrative Encyclopedia of American Criminals from the Pilgrims to the Present* (New York: M. Evans, 1973); and the more tangentially related *The Encyclopedia of Violence: Origins, Attitudes, and Consequences* (New York: Facts on File, 1993) by Margaret DiCanio.

The volume by Sifakis includes more than 1,500 entries consisting of historical biographies of people involved with crime or criminal justice, detailed descriptions of various types of crimes, histories of American law enforcement agencies, descriptions of famous weapons used in the commission of crime and by enforcement agents, definitions of underworld and police slang, and stories of famous crimes, trials, and hoaxes. The volume by Nash details the lives of famous past American criminals, including "outlaws, thieves, brothel keepers, syndicate gangsters, arsonists, rapists, kidnappers, murderers, forgers, embezzlers, bombers, assassins, bank-robbers, and hijackers." Dicanio's work consists of a comprehensive, alphabetically arranged description of topics and issues related to crime and violence, including statistical data, theories of the sociocultural and psychological roots of crime and violence, and descriptions of historical responses undertaken by agencies of prevention, enforcement, and control within the criminal justice system.

A number of currently available quasi-encyclopedic textbooks also cover the field of American criminal justice in considerable detail. Most of these contain quite a bit of historical information as well as contemporary analysis. Among them are Frank Schmalleger, *Criminal Justice Today: An Introductory Text for the Twenty-First Century*, 4th ed. (Upper Saddle River, NJ: Prentice Hall, 1997); Joel Samaha, *Criminal Justice*, 3rd ed. (St. Paul, MN: West, 1994); Freda Adler, Gerhard O. W. Mueller, and William S. Laufer, *Criminal Justice* (New York: McGraw-Hill, 1994); George C. Cole, *The American System of Criminal Justice*, 7th ed. (Belmont, CA: Wadsworth,

1995); and George Senna and Larry Siegel, *Introduction to Criminal Justice*, 7th ed. (St. Paul, MN: West, 1996).

AREA-SPECIFIC RESOURCES

Other published resources tend to be area-specific, describing various aspects of one of the three major component areas of criminal justice: police, courts, or corrections. Of these, most are police oriented, including works such as *The Encyclopedia of Police Science*, 2nd ed., ed. William G. Bailey (New York: Garland Publishing, 1995); George Thomas Kurian, *World Encyclopedia of Police Forces and Penal Systems* (New York: Facts on File, 1989); John J. Fay, *The Police Dictionary and Encyclopedia* (Springfield, IL: Charles C. Thomas, 1988); Cyril D. Robinson and Richard Scaglion, *Police in Contradiction: The Evolution of the Police Function in Society* (Westport, CT: Greenwood Press, 1994); and H. Kenneth Bechtel, *State Police in the United States: A Socio-Historical Analysis* (Westport, CT: Greenwood Press, 1995).

Bailey's encyclopedia contains approximately 150 contributed essays on diverse topics in American policing, including organization, operations, technology, administration, support systems, culture, values, intergovernmental and community relations, history, and historical biographies of leaders. The encyclopedic work by Kurian provides descriptions of the national law enforcement and corrections systems of 183 countries with details on the history, background, organizational structure, and recruitment, education, and training of each. Fay's combined encyclopedia/dictionary is a lengthy reference work that defines more than 4,900 terms, phrases, and concepts characteristic of the law enforcement field. Robinson and Scaglion, on the other hand, assume a historical orientation in order to formulate a theory of the origin and evolution of the police function. They explain incremental changes in the police function associated with macrohistorical events, such as the transition from kinship-based to class-dominated societies, and they examine the implications of these changes for modern police-community relations. Bechtel's *State Police in the United States: A Socio-Historical Analysis* focuses specifically on state police agencies and provides an account of historical legislation establishing such agencies.

CRIMINAL JUSTICE DICTIONARIES—GENERAL AND AREA-SPECIFIC

Less detailed than encyclopedias or encyclopedic textbooks, but nonetheless useful for the wealth of information they provide, are general and area-specific dictionaries of crime and justice. Among such works are the definitive and widely respected *Black's Law Dictionary* (St. Paul, MN: West, 1991) edited by Henry Campbell Black, now in its sixth edition; Virginia Benmaman, Norma C. Connolly, and Scott Robert Loos, *Bilingual Dictionary of Criminal Justice Term (English/Spanish)*, 2nd ed. (Binghamton, NY: Gould Publications, 1991); George E. Rush, *Dictionary of Criminal Justice* 4th ed. (Guilford, CT: Dushkin Publishing Group, 1994); George C. Kohn, *Dictionary of Culprits and Criminals* (Metuchen, NJ: Scarecrow Press, 1986); Ralph De Sola, *Crime Dictionary*, revised edition (New York: Facts on File, 1988); Search Group, *Dictionary of Criminal Justice Data Terminology*, 2nd ed. (Washington, DC: U.S. Justice Department, Bureau of Justice Statistics, 1981); Julian A. Martin and Nicholas A. Astone, *Criminal Justice Vocabulary* (Springfield, IL: Charles C. Thomas, 1980); Conference of State Court Administrators, *State Court Model Statistical Dictionary, 1989* (Williamsburg, VA: National Center for State Courts, 1989); and Erik Beckman, *The Criminal Justice Dictionary*, 2nd ed. revised (Ann Arbor, MI: Pierian Press, 1983).

Although called a "dictionary," Vergil L. Williams's *Dictionary of American Penology*, a revised and expanded edition (Westport, CT: Greenwood Press, 1996) is not in the same genre as other works cited in this brief section, consisting as it does of relatively detailed descriptions of a wide variety of topics related to corrections and biographical sketches of important figures in corrections and criminal justice reform. Similarly, Kohn's *Dictionary of Culprits and Criminals* consists of a listing of infamous offenders, including what Kohn calls "known and proven assassins, murderers, spies, traitors, terrorists, kidnappers, poisoners, rapists, gangsters, racketeers, prostitutes, procurers, con artists, swindlers, imposters, forgers, counterfeiters, pirates, smugglers, thieves, burglars, robbers, gunfighters, western outlaws, conspirators, highwaymen, megalomaniacs, war criminals, and others." For inclusion in this published typology, says Kohn, "an individual must have committed or been accused of committing an offense or crime that society at the time was prepared to punish by law." Although the book covers the last six centuries, Kohn chose to include only those offenders "who have achieved, in one way or another, a notoriety or significance."

MISCELLANEOUS AND SPECIALIZED RESOURCES

A number of specialized resources are available that deal with contemporary issues of concern to modern-day students of criminal justice. Issues included here are those such as crime causation and prevention, the social basis of the law, drugs and drug courts, prisoners' rights, victims' interests, and the like, which can be found in volumes as diverse as the following: National District Attorneys Association, *Victim Witness Coordination Program: Bibliography on Victims in the Criminal Justice*

System—A Sourcebook (Alexandria, VA: NDAA, 1986); *Prisoners' Rights Sourcebook* (New York: Clark Boardman, 1980); Carroll R. Hormachea, *Sourcebook in Criminalistics* (Reston, VA: Reston Publishing Company, 1974); United Nations, *Compendium of United Nations Standards and Norms in Crime Prevention and Criminal Justice* (New York: United Nations, 1992); Ila J. Sensenich, *Compendium of the Law on Prisoners' Rights* (Washington, DC: Federal Judicial Center, 1979); Jeffrey S. Tauber, *A Judicial Primer on Drug Courts and Court-ordered Drug Treatment* (Dana Point, CA: California Continuing Judicial Studies Program, 1993); S. Giora Shoham and John Hoffman, *A Primer in the Sociology of Crime* (Albany, NY: Harrow and Heston, 1991); and Dragan Milovanovic, *A Primer in the Sociology of Law* (New York: Harrow and Heston, 1988).

As its name implies, the bibliography provided by the National District Attorneys Association focuses on a wide range of topics relating to victims of crime. Included are documents on victim and witness programs, victims' rights legislation, elderly victims, rape, domestic violence, compensation and restitution, witness intimidation, and homicide. Milovanovic's book, in contrast, attempts to "introduce readers to some of the dominant thoughts in Western Society on the subject of the sociology of law" and covers topics such as sociological jurisprudence, legal realism, the critical legal studies movement, the structural approach to law, and a critical-semiotic understanding of the law. Jeffrey S. Tauber provides one of many special reports on drugs in American society, but an especially useful one that explores the historical development of drug courts and the associated movement toward court-ordered drug rehabilitation programs. Sensenich's focus is the prisoners' rights movement of the 1960s and 1970s, although her compendium is aimed at assisting the federal judiciary to effectively handle prisoners' rights cases and to help prisoners, prison officials, and defense attorneys understand the extent and limits of the basic rights guaranteed to prisoners under the U.S. Constitution. Similarly, Robbins's work provides original articles and reprints of recent articles concerning legal developments in the area of prisoners' rights. Hormachea's work, on the other hand, is specially designed to introduce students of criminal justice to criminalistics, but also provides a philosophical basis for the scientific investigation of crime prevention and describes the application of technological advances to crime prevention.

INDEX

NOTE: The page numbers in **boldface type** indicate the principal reference to a main entry subject.

EDITORS and CONTRIBUTORS

EDITORS

Frank Schmalleger, Ph.D., Editor-in-Chief

Dr. Schmalleger is Executive Director of The Justice Research Association, a private consulting firm and "think-tank" focusing on issues of crime and justice. He has authored numerous articles and many books, including the renowned and widely used introductory texts *Criminal Justice Today* (Prentice Hall, 1997) and *Criminology Today* (Prentice Hall, 1996).

Gordon M. Armstrong, Senior Editor

Mr. Armstrong is Assistant Professor of Justice Studies at Georgia Southern University, Associate Director of The Justice Research Association, and co-author (with his wife, Shelia) of the supplements to the Schmalleger texts.

ASSOCIATE EDITORS

David Jones, Ph.D.
Associate Editor–Courts

University of Wisconsin, Oshkosh
Oshkosh, WI

Michael Palmiotto, Ph.D.
Co-Associate Editor–Police

Wichita State University
Wichita, KS

Dorothy Moses Schulz, Ph.D.
Co-Associate Editor–Police

John Jay College of Criminal Justice
New York, NY

David R. Struckhoff, Ph.D.
Associate Editor–Corrections

Loyola University of Chicago
Chicago, IL

CONTRIBUTORS

Fred Allen, Ph.D.
Central Michigan University
Mount Pleasant, MI

Gordon M. Armstrong
Georgia Southern University
Statesboro, GA

Shelia C. Armstrong
Georgia Southern University
Statesboro, GA

Joseph B. Byers, Ph.D.
Florida State University
Tallahassee, FL

James R. Farris, Ph.D.
California State University, Fullerton
Fullerton, CA

Thomas M. Frost
Retired from Loyola University of
Chicago, Chicago, IL

Martin Gruberg, Ph.D.
University of Wisconsin, Oshkosh
Oshkosh, WI

Patrick J. Halperin, Ph.D.
The Justice Research Institute
Joliet, IL

Thomas J. Hickey, Ph.D.
Roger Williams University
Bristol, RI

Anna C. Hussey
The Justice Research Institute
Joliet, IL

Antoinette M. Jackson
The Justice Research Institute
Joliet, IL

David Jones, Ph.D.
University of Wisconsin, Oshkosh
Oshkosh, WI

Ken Kerle, Ph.D.
The American Jail Association
Hagerstown, MD

Patrick Kinkade, Ph.D.
Texas Christian University
Fort Worth, TX

Victor J. Larragoite

Texas Christian University
Fort Worth, TX

Matthew C. Leone, Ph.D.

University of Nevada, Reno
Reno, NV

Troy D. Livingston

Wichita State University
Wichita, KS

John H. Lombardi, Ph.D.

Troy State University
Troy, AL

Arthur J. Lurigio, Ph.D.

Loyola University of Chicago
Chicago, IL

Michael Mahoney

John Howard Association of Chicago
Chicago, IL

C. Aaron McNeece, Ph.D.

Florida State University
Tallahassee, FL

Christopher J. Morse, J.D.

John Jay College of Criminal Justice
New York, NY

A. N. Moser, Jr., J.D.

The National Sheriff's Association
Alexandria, VA

Martin N. Nowak

Will County Sheriff's Department
Joliet, IL

Philip R. Orawiec

Governors State University
University Park, IL

Michael Palmiotto, Ph.D.

Wichita State University
Wichita, KS

Lee E. Parker, J.D.

Wichita State University
Wichita, KS

R. Scott Phillips

Texas Christian University
Fort Worth, TX

Gregory A. Prestipino

U.S. Probation Office
Chicago, IL

Frances P. Reddington, Ph.D.

Central Missouri State University
Warrensburg, MO

Philip Reichel, Ph.D.

University of Northern Colorado
Greeley, CO

Peter S. Ruckman, Jr., Ph.D.

Northern Illinois University
De Kalb, IL

Frank Schmalleger, Ph.D.

The Justice Research Association
Hilton Head Island, SC

Dorothy Moses Schulz, Ph.D.

John Jay College of Criminal Justice
New York, NY

Magnus Seng, Ph.D.

Loyola University of Chicago
Chicago, IL

Harvey Siegel

Phillips Swager Associates
Peoria, IL

Daniel Skidmore-Hess, Ph.D.

Armstrong Atlantic State University
Savannah, GA

Margaret Leland Smith

John Jay College of Criminal Justice
New York, NY

David R. Struckhoff, Ph.D.

Loyola University of Chicago
Chicago, IL

Ray Surette, Ph.D.

University of Central Florida
Orlando, FL

Ernie Thomson, Ph.D.

Arizona State University West
Phoenix, AZ

N. Prabha Unnithan

Colorado State University
Fort Collins, CO

| Ransom A. Whittle | Federal Bureau of Investigation
Retired |
| Glenn Zuern, Ph.D. | Albany State University
Albany, GA |

ISBN 0-313-29409-7

90000>

EAN

9 780313 294099

HARDCOVER BAR CODE